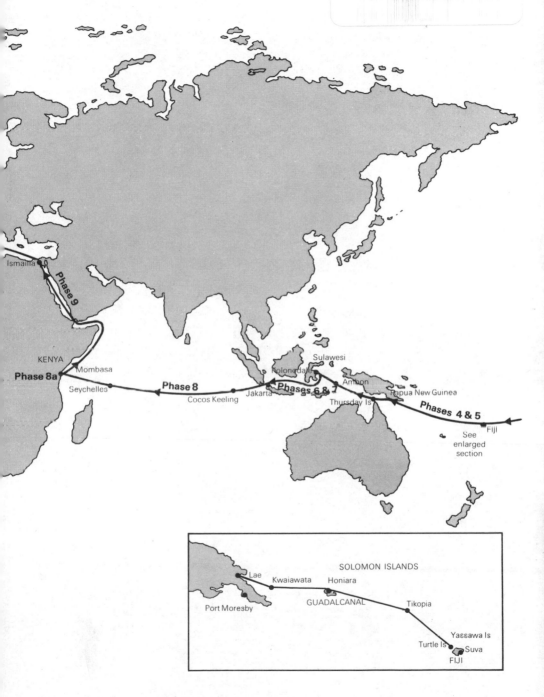

Ismailia

Phase 9

KENYA

Phase 8a   Mombasa

Seychelles   Phase 8

Cocos Keeling   Jakarta

Sulawesi

Polongdale

Phases 6 & 7

Ambon

Thursday Is   Papua New Guinea

Phases 4 & 5

Fiji

See
enlarged
section

SOLOMON ISLANDS

Lae   Kwaiawata   Honiara

Port Moresby   GUADALCANAL   Tikopia

Yassawa Is

Turtle Is   Suva

FIJI

OPERATION DRAKE

OPERATION DRAKE

John Blashford-Snell
with
Michael Cable

W. H. ALLEN · LONDON
A Howard & Wyndham Company
1981

This book or parts thereof may not be reproduced in any form whatsoever without permission in writing

Typeset by Computacomp (UK) Ltd,
Fort William, Scotland
Printed and bound in Great Britain by
Mackays of Chatham Ltd, Kent
for the Publishers, W. H. Allen & Co. Ltd,
44 Hill Street, London W1X 8LB

ISBN 0 491 02965 9

Dedication

This book is dedicated to the memory of Richard Hopkins of Great Britain and Andrew Maara of Kenya, Young Explorers who were greatly admired by their friends and sadly died in motor accidents in Kenya.

Contents

List of maps

Acknowledgements

I am deeply grateful to all the members of Operation Drake who have kindly allowed their personal diaries and photographs to be used in this book. My old friend Christopher Sainsbury, in addition to being the Chief Photographer, kept a full and amusing log for my use whilst he was aboard *Eye of the Wind*, and this has been of the greatest value. We have also used material from many of our supporters and committees throughout the world. I am also deeply grateful to my long-suffering PAs Sara Everett and Cathryn Barker (alias Margot) who lovingly gathered material for this book and helped type it.

It is no easy task to write one book about, what was in effect, ten expeditions in twelve countries, involving almost 2,000 people. However, this has been done by the dogged determination of Michael Cable, who apart from helping me in the search for the giant lizard in Papua New Guinea, has gathered and sifted hundreds of diaries, logs and reports. And Jill, his wife, who did much of the typing and kept us going with suitable beverages, also deserves a special thank you. Mike spent hours interviewing many of the team to produce the bulk of this work, which I had simply to edit. If any credit is due, I believe it belongs to him.

To cover all the aspects of Operation Drake in one book is quite impossible, and whilst this volume concentrates on the general story, Andrew Mitchell, Scientific Co-ordinator on the expedition, has written a highly illustrated book, entitled *Operation Drake: Voyage of Discovery*, which gives a detailed account of the many scientific and community projects undertaken.

Operation Drake was an enormous effort, by a very big team and it was only possible because of the generosity of thousands of sponsors. We have tried hard to mention as many people and organisations as possible, but inevitably there will be some who are left out. May I, in advance, ask them to forgive us. However, to everyone who helped, I must, on behalf of all those who took part in the expedition, say how very grateful we are for your generous support.

John Blashford-Snell, April 1981

PREFACE

In an age when it all seems to have been done before and one can book a package holiday to those faraway places in the back of beyond that were once inaccessible to all but the most intrepid explorers, true pioneering adventure is hard to find.

Real challenges are becoming scarce in a shrinking world where all the frontiers have been pushed back as far as they will go, where all the rivers have been crossed, all the mountains climbed and all the trails blazed.

Maybe, in centuries to come, the outer limits of the galaxy will offer space explorers the chance to venture out into the complete unknown as Francis Drake did four hundred years ago.

In the meantime, however, there is a growing need to satisfy the questing spirit of a restless younger generation that is increasingly frustrated by missing out on the action.

It was with this very much in mind that Operation Drake was conceived.

Some of the more remote corners of the Earth were picked out as the locations for various ambitious and worthwhile projects that were carefully designed to provide tough imaginative and exciting outlets for the energies of youngsters, anxious for opportunities to prove themselves in genuinely demanding situations.

I am delighted to have been so closely associated with a venture which succeeded in bringing out the best in so many young people, while at the same time promoting international understanding by encouraging the kind of teamwork that breaks down all barriers of race, creed and country.

Charles.

HRH The Prince of Wales

Patron of Operation Drake

[11]

Introduction

Dateline: Plymouth, 13 December 1577

On a raw winter's morning a small flotilla of five ships under the command of Francis Drake slipped quietly out of Sutton Pool, eased along the Sound, and then headed into the open sea to begin what was destined to become one of the greatest epic voyages of all time. There was no great ceremony to mark the departure of the most heroic of Queen Elizabeth I's swashbuckling sea captains on this new venture. The big send-off had been a month earlier, but a violent storm off the Cornish coast had severely damaged Drake's hundred-ton flagship, the *Pelican*, forcing her to limp back home for repairs, together with the eighty-ton *Elizabeth*, the fifty-ton *Swan*, the thirty-ton *Marygold* and the tiny *Benedict*. The result was that now there was an air of slight anti-climax.

This suited Drake well, for, although he could not conceal the fact that the enterprise was on a far larger scale than anything previously attempted, he had been doing his best to play down the full dramatic extent of his plans. The crews of the five ships had signed on only for a voyage to Alexandria and it was not until they were well on their way that Drake revealed his true aim – to plunder the Spanish Main in search of the wealth so desperately needed by Elizabeth to solve her nation's financial crisis, and then to push on into the unknown in the hope of opening up new trade routes. This was a secret that, up until that moment, he had shared only with his Queen, for the very good reasons that many of the 164 men who set sail with him would probably never have done so had they known what they were really letting themselves in for, while at the same time he had to be wary of spies, even among his fellow officers, who might betray his intentions to the Spaniards.

Not even Drake himself knew exactly what lay ahead of him – that after nearly three years of high adventure aboard the *Pelican*, renamed the *Golden Hind* during the voyage, he would return to Plymouth in triumph as the first sea captain and the first Englishman ever to have sailed right round the world. The treasures he brought back – enough

[13]

to make the country solvent again, as well as providing his backers with a 4,000 per cent profit and himself with a £10,000 fortune – assured him of a hero's welcome. Furthermore, Drake's voyage had proved an inspiration to his nation. Queen Elizabeth was so delighted with his efforts that she went in state to Deptford, where, cocking a snook at the King of Spain, she ordered the French Ambassador to knight her loyal subject on the quarterdeck of his ship. It was a famous moment in British history.

Four centuries later, when we started to plan the most ambitious round-the-world expedition of modern times and were looking for a name that would conjure up exactly the right spirit of adventure, discovery and challenge, we selected Operation Drake as an obvious choice. Our venture coincided very closely with the four hundredth anniversary of his round-the-world trip and, although we would not be following his exact route, we would certainly be following his example.

Chapter One

Dateline: London, 13 December 1977

Four hundred years to the day after Francis Drake set sail from Plymouth, Operation Drake was formally launched by its Royal Patron, Prince Charles, at a private reception held at Buckingham Palace, and later the world's press crowded excitedly into the Athenaeum Hotel in Piccadilly to hear an outline of our plans. Unlike Drake, we were only too happy to announce exactly where we were going and what we intended to do.

We could claim without fear of contradiction that it was the most ambitious, imaginative and wide-ranging expedition of its kind ever mounted. It was to be focused on the round-the-world voyage of the 150-ton British brigantine *Eye of the Wind*, which would act as our flagship and support vessel linking four main theatres of land operations in Panama, Papua New Guinea, Sulawesi and Africa. The whole venture was to be spread over a period of two years and would be divided into nine separate phases – later extended to ten – each lasting for between ten and twelve weeks. For every phase there would be a changeover of Young Explorers (YEs) – youngsters aged from seventeen to twenty-four who were carefully selected from countries all over the world to work alongside seasoned explorers, scientists and other experts on a varied programme of activities aimed at combining the thrill of adventure with the worthwhile achievement of serious scientific exploration, research and community projects.

Operation Drake was to begin with the voyage of *Eye of the Wind* across the Atlantic via the island of St Vincent, where tests were to be carried out in the crater of the volcano La Soufrière, after which the first land phase would be based at Caledonia Bay. In this desolate but historically fascinating spot on a remote stretch of the Caribbean coast of Panama, the main projects would include the archaeological excavation of the site of a seventeenth-century Scots settlement in an effort to find out more about the tragedy which overwhelmed the doomed colonists of Fort St Andrew, and also an attempt to pinpoint the site of the famed Lost City of Acla. A special aerial walkway was to be constructed in the jungle to give scientists an invaluable close-up view of wildlife in the normally inaccessible forest canopy 120 feet above the ground; while divers were to probe beneath the shark-infested waters of the Bay for sunken wrecks. Hardier souls in search of real physical challenge would be able to pit their powers of stamina and endurance against the jungle on a series of hard-slogging patrols.

From Panama, *Eye of the Wind* was to embark on what promised to be a romantic South Sea odyssey to Costa Rica and thence across the Pacific to Papua New Guinea, stopping off on the way at many islands, including the Galapagos, Tahiti and Fiji. Plenty of research and community aid projects were planned to ensure it did not develop into a pure pleasure cruise!

Papua New Guinea (PNG) is the second largest island in the world after Greenland, and yet it truly remains the 'Last Unknown' – an adventurer's paradise where large areas are still unmapped and relatively unexplored. Here, once again, the construction of an aerial walkway high up in the treetops for the benefit of biologists, entymologists, botanists and ornithologists would be one of the main features of our programme. Elsewhere teams were to tackle a variety of projects including a daring first-ever attempt to run the ferocious white-water rapids and explore the gorges of the Upper Strickland River. A medical survey was to be made among the primitive peoples of the interior, some of whom had possibly never seen white people before. The search for Second World War aircraft wrecks and old wartime trails long since swallowed up by the dense jungle would provide some testing treks, while night-time crocodile counts on behalf of the United Nations Development Programme could be guaranteed to keep people alert.

After PNG would come the immense problem of moving stores, equipment and personnel to the isolated location in Sulawesi, Indonesia, where the third major land phase was to be based. For those going aboard *Eye of the Wind* it would be relatively straightforward, but for everybody else just getting there was likely to prove a challenge.

Once there, all efforts would be directed towards gathering the information needed for the preparation of a Management Plan for a proposed Nature Reserve to be created in this area by the Indonesian government. This would involve our sending out patrols to survey a 2,500-square-mile region which includes some of the toughest terrain to be found anywhere on Earth and for which no detailed maps exist. In addition, a third aerial walkway was to be erected, and results and observations obtained by the scientists would eventually be matched with those from PNG and Panama to produce a unique comparative study.

[16]

When Operation Drake started, the last land phase, following the crossing of the Indian Ocean, was to have taken place in the Sudan, but later this had to be cancelled owing to local political complications, and the expedition was hurriedly switched to Kenya. Despite the need for some frantic reorganisation, a full programme of activities was set up and an extra phase, the tenth, was added, allowing us to include yet more YEs. The prospect of investigating an unexplored 'Lost World' plateau in the middle of the crater of the extinct Susua volcano caught everybody's imagination and the archaeologists were delighted with the chance to undertake the first really extensive excavation on the twelve-acre medieval coastal site at Shanga. A 180-mile camel trek along the route taken by the eighteenth-century explorer Count Teleki von Szek would provide a stern physical test, and game counts in the Masai Mara Reserve would enable YEs to render a valuable service and at the same time enjoy the thrill of getting closer to the animals than they could ever hope to do as an average tourist on safari.

The final stage of the expedition would take *Eye of the Wind* back to Plymouth by way of the Mediterranean, where she was to carry out a special pollution survey in conjunction with the Goodyear airship.

This was only a summary of the main highlights of a schedule which had taken four years to plan, and involved over 100,000 miles of land, sea and air travel by reconnaissance teams, and yet no one was left in any doubt about the sheer scope of the enterprise. A great many sceptics shook their heads and said, 'J.B.-S. has bitten off more than he can chew this time.' I was determined that a dedicated team and motivated young people would prove them wrong.

What even we did not appreciate at that stage was just how much bigger and better the whole venture was going to become once it got under way and international interest in Operation Drake began to spread. An indication of the way the scheme escalated is the fact that our original target of 216 YEs from twenty-six countries had nearly doubled to 414 before the end. At the same time, the total number of people directly involved as administrators, scientists, engineers, communications experts, fund raisers and sponsors, plus the countless others who played unofficial but often vital roles behind the scenes, rose to well over 2,000. The cost in hard cash − not counting the incalculable thousands of pounds' worth of free and cut-price travel facilities, goods and services donated by friends and supporters in commerce and industry − rose from an early estimate of £650,000 to over £900,000.

Sir Francis Drake took as his motto *Sic Parvis Magna* ('Great Things Have Small Beginnings') and this applied perfectly to the development of Operation Drake. The origins of this mammoth expedition can be traced back to the founding of the Scientific Exploration Society (SES) in 1969 when I was an Adventure Training Officer at Sandhurst. The British Army is fortunate in having a unique Adventurous Training scheme which allows its members to take part in challenging and worthwhile expeditions 'on duty', and it was my job to encourage young officer cadets to indulge in such ventures for the betterment of their characters and with the least possible detriment to British relationships overseas!

As an engineer officer, I regarded the conquest of natural obstacles as a part of my life and thus I heartily enjoyed this job.

At Sandhurst I helped to organise up to twenty small expeditions every year, and as they became more complex and far-reaching so the administrative headaches increased. Major irritations arose from minor matters such as the disposal of piles of kit and equipment remaining at the end of each expedition.

It was General Sir John Mogg, then Commandant of Sandhurst and the future Chairman of Operation Drake, who suggested that we ought to consider setting up some kind of permanent organisation with charitable status through which all such ventures could be planned, equipped, run and, most important, financed. This made such obvious good sense that a group of like-minded colleagues gathered and formulated the basic aims and ideals of the SES. Since then it has built up into an international body of servicemen, scientists and explorers, with members all over the world. It works closely with the British Museum (Natural History) and the Explorers Club in New York, and maintains a global network of valuable contacts in all walks of life.

The long-term forward planning of expeditions is one of the Society's main functions and, from the very outset, the idea evolved of doing something rather special that would combine all the different aspects of exploration and also exploit the full potential of the SES set-up. The concept of Operation Drake grew out of this notion.

The first step was when we started to consider the possibility of linking together what had originally been planned as a series of separate expeditions in South America, Panama, the Galapagos Islands, PNG and the Sudan. This was prompted by the fact that all these sites are approachable by sea, which meant that a ship could be used as a float-ing base, thereby adding a whole new dimension to the exercise, while at the same time greatly simplifying the logistical problems of moving personnel, stores and heavy equipment from one location to the next.

Then came the decision to build the entire project around the involvement of young people. This key development, which was what really gave Operation Drake its unique flavour, came about very largely through His Royal Highness The Prince of Wales. The SES has

[18]

made a point of including young people in its expeditions, normally always young soldiers, but in 1969 the Dahlak Quest team included our first civilian youngsters: two eighteen-year-old students. Five years later we were joined on the Zaire River Expedition by three sponsored teenagers – a business student, a police cadet from my home island of Jersey, and a river runner from Colorado who was financed by Mr Walter Annenberg, then the American Ambassador in London. This proved so much a success from everybody's point of view that it was enthusiastically agreed from then on that the inclusion of such Young Explorers should become a regular feature of SES ventures – not that we ever envisaged taking along quite so many as eventually joined Operation Drake.

It was Prince Charles who made the suggestion that maybe we should start thinking in terms of not just two or three youngsters but two or three hundred. Although momentarily taken aback by the prospect of planning on such a grand scale, we quickly realised that this was simply a logical extension of what we had in mind, and would not only broaden the whole outlook of the project but also give it a far greater sense of purpose.

From our meetings with international youth organisations, schools and universities, it had become abundantly clear that many youngsters these days feel the need to be stretched and challenged more severely than they can ever normally hope to be in modern society. Outward Bound and similar adventure training schemes do their best to satisfy this need and to provide imaginative outlets for natural aggression and excess energy, but for a lot of young people they do not really go far enough. Again, it was Prince Charles who pinpointed the underlying cause of their frustration and summed it up in a phrase when he told the House of Lords that what the young were really seeking were 'some of the challenges of war in a peacetime situation'.

The success of Operation Drake owes a great deal to Prince Charles. From the beginning he played a vital role, and without his encouragement and support the project would never have got off the ground. He is by nature a man of action with a great spirit of adventure who, as he later confessed, would have welcomed the opportunity to join the expedition himself.

His involvement dated from 1977 when I went to see him and explained what we had in mind. He was immediately fascinated and asked if there was anything he could do to help. When I suggested that it would be a marvellous thing if he were to become our Patron he readily agreed.

This gave us a tremendous boost. It was not only a very great honour but it also endowed the project with a prestige and credibility which would encourage the sponsors, on whose financial backing we were totally dependent. Furthermore, it would help to attract young people to take part. Although it was understood that the Prince's association could not be officially announced until the venture was financially viable and certain to go ahead, he was kind enough to send a discreet message of support in advance. It read as follows:

Colonel Blashford-Snell has explained to me the purpose behind 'Operation Drake' and I was most interested by its imaginative and adventurous approach. I hope therefore that it is given every chance to succeed, given all the ghastly problems that exist with raising large sums of money nowadays. From my historical studies I seem to remember Francis Drake managed to elicit some discreet Royal support for his expeditions, but only if the rewards from a little well-planned piracy were forthcoming! Times have changed! CHARLES

That message, with its characteristic touch of humour, was the key factor that enabled us to take Operation Drake off the drawing board and into the realm of reality.

Our main priority now was to raise the £50,000 which, we calculated, was the capital needed to launch Operation Drake with any confidence. That kind of sum is hard to come by at the best of times and in a period of world-wide recession we reckoned it would take a great deal of scrimping, scrounging and scraping of the barrel to raise it. In fact, it fell into our laps at the stroke of a pen thanks to the extraordinary generosity of one man.

Mr Walter Annenberg has done a great deal over the years to help worthy causes and, being a man of great foresight and imagination, he has always found the idea of expeditions intriguing. I discovered this when he attended the dinner held in London to commemorate the centenary of the historic meeting between Stanley and Livingstone in 1871, when Stanley had uttered his legendary greeting, 'Dr Livingstone, I presume?' We talked about the Zaire River Expedition, which was being set up at the time, and he showed tremendous enthusiasm. The next day, quite unexpectedly, I received a handsome cheque from him, along with a note wishing me good luck and expressing the hope that his contribution would help to keep the wolf from the door. He later became even further involved and did much to ensure the success of this venture and bring about even closer co-operation between explorers on both sides of the Atlantic.

In view of this, it was with a thrill of anticipation that I accepted an invitation to visit him at his home in Palm Springs next time I was in the States, so that I could tell him all about Operation Drake.

It was quite an experience. I arrived in Palm Springs with my wife, Judith, and daughters, Emma and Victoria, to be met at the airport by a chauffeur-driven limousine that whisked us to his estate on the outskirts of this remarkable desert township, where Mr Annenberg lives with Bob Hope and ex-President Gerald Ford as neighbours.

As we passed through the remote-controlled gates, we were immediately impressed by the sheer scale and magnificence of the place, which is really a private golf course with a splendid modern house in the middle. A special guest cottage in the grounds awaited us, and we were provided with a car for transport between there and the main house!

I was just coming out of the shower when Emma rushed in to announce that Mr Annenberg had arrived to see if we were comfortable. I poured him a drink and without any real preamble he said, 'Tell me about this Drake thing – and how much you need to get it started.' I gave him a brief outline of what we had planned and added as nonchalantly as possible that we required about £50,000 before we could really get under way. He asked me if I thought we could really pull off something quite so big, and when I assured him that there was no reason why we should not be able to make it work, providing we could get the finance, he paused for a moment and then said, 'I'm not sure exactly what the exchange rate is at the moment – but if I give you $100,000, will that be alright?'

It was at that moment that Operation Drake ceased to be a dream and became a reality, and from then on it all started happening at a whirlwind pace. My first task on returning to England was to assemble the nucleus of our executive team at our London HQ, which was housed in a Whitehall basement and known to all as 'Room 5B' or 'the dungeon'. This damp, dark, musty-smelling cellar two floors below ground level was a somewhat dismal place where daylight never penetrated and the atmosphere was permanently grey. But beggars cannot be choosers.

Among the stalwarts who gathered at what was to be the nerve centre of the expedition for the next four years, one of the most important was ex-Royal Engineer Captain Jim Masters. Jim, an old colleague and veteran explorer, took over the key role as Head of Logistics and Personnel, which involved the mammoth task of moving hundreds of people and tons of equipment round the world for nothing or next to nothing. One could not ask for a better man to tackle such a difficult and vital job. Jim's ability to get things done made such an impression on local government authorities when he accompanied me on the Zaire River Expedition that they went out of their way to persuade him to stay on afterwards for two years, totally reorganising

[21]

the distribution and technical supply systems within the country's medical health service – a daunting assignment which he carried out with complete success.

Former company director Mervyn Price came in as Director of Administration to keep an eye on our finances, and he was later joined by Major Roger Chapman, another long-time ally with whom I had shared several adventurous exploits. This very vital job was later taken over by George Thurstan, a tough and determined ex-Royal Marine, who gave up a career in the Police Force to join us.

Ruth Mindel, who had already proved herself a most capable Public Relations lady, was brought in to combine the duties of Sponsor PR and Procurement Officer and yet another old friend, Val Roberts, valiantly agreed to sign on as Registrar in charge of the office and the paperwork.

On the scientific side Andrew Mitchell, a young zoologist from Bristol University, came in to act as Scientific Co-ordinator and took responsibility for liaising between the Scientific Sub-Committee and HQ.

Chris Sainsbury, my chief aide and photographic expert for the past two years, gave up making films of Junior Soldiers on exercise, and was appointed as a watchkeeper on the ship and Chief Photographer.

Meanwhile, there was one more very important post to be filled, and in securing General Sir John Mogg as our Executive Chairman we had a third stroke of great good fortune to add to the two bonuses that had already come our way in the form of Prince Charles' moral support and Walter Annenberg's financial backing.

The General was a little reluctant to take on the job when first approached at his home in Oxfordshire because, as he pointed out, he was greatly looking forward to a quiet life in his retirement. But he surrendered gracefully to my appeals after I assured him – with an absolutely straight face – that the position would involve no more than two or three meetings a year and possibly a couple of pleasant trips overseas.

Of course, things did not work out quite as I promised, and he ended up spending most of his time guiding Operation Drake. Nevertheless, he seemed to enjoy every minute of it and even managed to make up for some of the fishing he had missed in England by catching some fine tuna in PNG. We were fortunate to have a Chairman of such standing. As a former Deputy Supreme Allied Commander, Europe, his international reputation and contacts were formidable and as a respected figure of the highest calibre he brought added prestige to the project. On top of that, he has a rare ability to get on extremely well with just about anybody, as well as being perfectly in tune with the young generation.

[22]

Things were now beginning to run smoothly and the money was coming in steadily, as more and more individuals and companies began to take up sponsorships or promise support in kind. A major boost came when Norman Munn, a sponsor of the Zaire River Expedition, introduced me to John Whitney, the energetic Managing Director of London's independent station Capital Radio. He reacted so enthusiastically to the whole idea of Operation Drake that he immediately decided to sponsor ten YEs from the London area as well as giving regular coverage to the expedition.

At this point Prince Charles was able to announce officially that he had agreed to become Patron of Operation Drake, and at the same time he promised not only to launch the expedition on the four hundredth anniversary of Drake's departure but also to be at the helm of the *Eye of the Wind* when she sailed out of Plymouth nearly a year later, in October 1978, to get our great adventure under way. Squadron Leader David Checketts, the Prince's Private Secretary, also became an enthusiastic supporter and formed our Public Relations Sub-Committee, which did so much to ensure that we got the best possible publicity. David also helped us to obtain a large amount of sponsorship, but one of his most valuable suggestions was to bring in Neilson McCarthy Limited as our PR consultants.

Beth Barrington-Haynes, who looked after Operation Drake on their behalf, proved to be a tower of strength and together with her colleague Jamie Neilson rapidly became a very important part of our fast expanding HQ staff.

During this busy period I was still commanding the Junior Leaders Regiment, Royal Engineers, at Dover and, of course, many of my staff became involved with Operation Drake. What we should have done without the help of Betty Starling, my PA, and Major Larry Batty, the Quartermaster, I do not know. Corporal Ray Thomas, my driver, also played a vital role not only in chauffeuring me but in becoming an expert in boat handling, vehicle mechanics, outboard engines – in short, a Jack-of-all-trades.

I began to feel I was riding a very fast horse in a steeplechase, and as we cleared each fence our confidence grew. However, we had a long way to go before the finishing post, and now the real work of selecting the YEs had started.

Chapter Two

Dateline: St Augustine's Priory, Bilsington, Kent, England,
4 February 1978

The scream of a Gibbon ape echoed incongruously from the centre of a rhododendron bush and mingled with the squawks of parakeets and other unmistakable sounds of the jungle which issued mysteriously from among the bare winter branches of a Kentish copse. 'Very tropical, I must say,' muttered one potential YE sarcastically as he contemplated the murky depths of the ice-cold pond in which, he suspected, he would very soon be immersed. He tried his best to convince himself that it really was a crocodile-infested African river. If only that were true – at least the water would be warmer.

Our attempts to add a little jungle atmosphere to the first of the special YE Selection Weekends by playing recorded sound effects from Borneo through concealed speakers might have been a trifle more convincing had the weather not been quite so Siberian. The skies were grey, the temperature near freezing and it could not make up its mind whether to rain, sleet or snow as the sixteen short-listed candidates from the south eastern area of England assembled at Augustine's Priory, kindly loaned to us by Roy Pratt-Boorman, Chairman of the *Kent Messenger* newspaper group. Ahead of the candidates lay thirty hours of concentrated discomfort and gruelling tests aimed at finally sorting the men from the boys – and the women from the girls.

Altogether Operation Drake received over 58,000 applications for the 216 YE vacancies that were originally available. A careful process of elimination gradually whittled this number down until we were left with the short-listed few who then competed directly against each other at the Selection Weekends held at eight different centres throughout the UK as well as in Australia, Canada, Iceland, New Zealand, West Germany and the USA.

The judges were on the look-out not just for the fittest, the strongest or the most obvious natural leaders. The qualities we specifically listed as desirable included zeal and energy, tempered with reliability, common sense and sound judgement; also initiative, matched with tact,

[24]

and steadiness under adverse and trying conditions. Last, but by no means least, we were looking for a sense of compatibility.

The programme of tests was carefully devised to show up the candidates' strengths and weaknesses in all these respects. What we were really after in the end was a well-balanced, mixed group. We wanted to be able to put together in the field teams that might include, for example, someone highly intelligent, well-educated and about to enter into one of the professions, along with a young person from a broken home who had possibly been in trouble with the police and might even have been to Borstal. We were also prepared to take a number of physically disabled people.

The batch of sixteen candidates – including three girls – who arrived rather apprehensively at St Augustine's Priory that bleak Saturday had no idea what to expect. They had been told simply to report to the Priory with all the personal kit they felt they would need during a weekend's camp, along with a certificate of medical fitness! All they knew for sure was that they would be facing some stiff challenges both mental and physical.

After a general briefing and a kit inspection to check how sensibly they had prepared for the rigours of the weekend, they were led off into the woods, issued with tents and given half an hour to set up camp. They were then divided into two teams of eight and marched off to Priory Pond for the first test, which had been carefully dreamt up with the sadistic intention of trying to ensure that everybody experienced the maximum discomfort at the earliest possible stage of the proceedings.

They were asked to imagine that they were being pursued through the jungle by hostile terrorists, that one of their number had been badly wounded and was a stretcher case, and that they had just one hour to get themselves and their casualty safely across the crocodile-infested river represented by the pond. They were supplied with a highly unstable single-seat canoe and also some oil drums, planks and lengths of rope with which to construct a makeshift raft on which to ferry the heavily-bandaged casualty. The main idea here was that they should all fall in and get soaked to the skin, and most of them duly obliged. It sent shivers up the spine just to watch them floundering around in the icy water, and our tropical sound effects could have done nothing to warm them up.

They were given no time to get their circulation going again before being marched off to another location where, having been divided into teams of four, they were set the task of bridging a stream with a structure strong enough to take a Land Rover. This was to be built using only the timber they could find lying around or were able to cut down.

No sooner had this been completed than they were off to a local

[25]

swimming pool to prove that they could cover the required number of lengths, and then, as exhaustion began to set in, they listened thankfully as they were told that they would now be going back to camp for a meal. The sighs of relief soon turned to gasps of anguish when they saw the menu. Hopes of being handed a tasty supper on a plate were cruelly dashed when they were given a few brace of freshly-killed, unplucked pigeons and left to their own devices. If they were lucky, they got a few unappetising mouthfuls of half-cooked, half-burnt flesh before collapsing cold, wet, tired and still hungry into their sleeping bags.

Those who fondly imagined that they were going to be left in peace for a good night's sleep were very quickly disillusioned. At one o'clock in the morning everybody was rudely awakened and despatched on a cross-country march to a map reference where, they were warned, they would be expected to deal with some kind of emergency. But they eventually got there only to find someone waiting to tell them it was all a false alarm and that they could turn straight round and go back. By the time they had stumbled back into camp and crawled into their sleeping bags once again, they were even more shattered, but still there was no respite.

At three o'clock they were woken a second time and sent off to another map reference. This time they arrived to find that there actually was a staged emergency awaiting them and they had to gather their scattered wits sufficiently to deal with it in a sensible fashion.

By then it was hardly worth bothering to try snatching a few minutes' sleep before the hard day's night was ended by a six o'clock reveille and the arrival of breakfast – a whole raw mackerel which landed with a thud on the frozen earth outside each tent. That is an easy thing to deal with in a kitchen with all mod. cons, but far from straightforward when all you have is a blunt knife and fork, a small mess tin and a box of matches – and even more so when you are being deliberately hurried along. In most cases the mangled and blackened carcases served up at the end of the candidates' desperate culinary endeavours were less than mouth-watering.

After this intentionally demoralising start to the day, the unhappy campers were plunged into a new series of tests aimed at proving mental, rather than physical, prowess. In particular, we wanted to see how well the various individuals retained their powers of concentration and original thought when they were in a state of considerable exhaustion. It was interesting to note that, for many of the youngsters, the prospect of having to get up in front of an audience and speak for three minutes on any chosen subject proved far more gruelling than any of the previous hardships.

[26]

This, together with various intelligence and observation tests and some shooting to ensure the candidates knew how to handle weapons safely, rounded off the weekend and the judges then had the task of deciding which four out of the sixteen should be declared winners and go forward to claim places on the expedition. They had all acquitted themselves well so it was no easy choice, but after long deliberations over a bottle of Scotch the names that emerged were those of Anthony Bonnick from Farnham in Surrey and Nicholas Hopkins of Alton, Hants – both eighteen years old – together with 22-year-old Nigel Lang from Canterbury and a young policewoman from Gravesend called Christine McHugh.

Christine made a good all-round impression and remained admirably calm, even when given a nasty shock by the rather alarming test of 'nerve' which we slipped in early on and which was, for just about everybody, one of the most unforgettable features of the whole weekend. Two at a time, the candidates were led to an upper floor of the Priory, handed a torch, tape measure and some bathroom scales, and warned that somewhere in the darkened room was a wild animal. 'If you handle it carefully it's quite safe,' I cautioned. 'Now you must find it, catch it, weigh it and measure it.' For the first few seconds after they entered they would not notice anything, then they would see a pile of sacks in one corner. When they lifted them, out slithered twelve feet of python, with its flat diamond-shaped head preceding it and its darting tongue seeking the way. The huge snake gave off a shimmering blue hue as it moved slowly through the torch light. Even the coolest youngster gasped. Swallowing hard, Christine tried to steer Monty, as he was inevitably called, onto the scales. All attempts to turn him into a Michelin tyre advert failed and it quickly became obvious that there was only one way to weigh him. Christine squared up to the beast, just as she might have faced a disorderly drunk on a Saturday night in Gravesend, and seized it. 'Careful, for heavens sake,' I cautioned as Monty, glad of some warmth in the freezing-cold Priory wound himself around the woman police constable. I need not have worried, for, as the reptile's body cooled, his contortions slowed down and he became sleepy. However, Monty's handler, Jean Rubenis, was clearly concerned about her valuable pet's temperature. Quickly an electric fan-heater was produced and Jean warmed Monty up. Once again he became quite lively and all was well.

Monty Python was undoubtedly one of the stars of Operation Drake. We had originally planned to confront our unsuspecting Selection Weekenders with an eighteen-foot radio-controlled crocodile which Ruth Mindel had somehow managed to unearth, but there turned out to be insurmountable problems involved in transporting this mechanical monster on the roof rack of her Mini! An inflatable dinosaur was then briefly considered before Andrew Mitchell discovered Animal Finders, a firm which specialised in providing unusual creatures for every occasion – mostly for films and television. After sifting through their fascinating catalogue of exotic and talented creatures, we settled for Monty.

He terrified the living daylights out of most of the Directing Staff the first time we saw him – and we knew what to expect! So I can well understand the horror experienced by some of the YE candidates. However, he was actually pretty harmless – at least, most of the time.

He only disgraced himself once – and that was highly dramatic. It happened during a special Capital Radio audio-visual presentation organised by Magic Lantern Ltd to give people an idea of what Operation Drake was all about. Peter Shea, a London YE, agreed to put Monty through his paces and demonstrate how one was supposed to weigh him. We decided afterwards that it must have been the heat of the footlights round the stage that made Monty unusually lively on that occasion, but whatever it was, he decided to put the squeeze on poor Peter.

The first indication that all was not well was when Peter's running commentary began to get more and more strained as Monty wound himself ever tighter round the lad's neck until all that came out was a croak! Fortunately the handlers were close by. They rushed on stage and hurriedly unwound the unruly serpent, whereupon Peter sank red-faced and somewhat breathless to the floor.

Monty was by no means the only 'frightener' we used for the quite serious purpose of asseessing how various people would react to some of the weird and wonderful creatures they could expect to meet in the jungle. At the Jersey Zoo some candidates found themselves trying to take the bust measurement of a female gorilla, while others were asked to roll up their sleeves, hold out one hand and shut their eyes, whereupon a gruesome-looking bird-eating spider with great hairy legs would be sent crawling up their arms. I learned later from Andrew Mitchell that it was 'poisonous, but rarely bites'.

Exotic and obviously intimidating animals were not always available – and not always necessary. For a city boy like Winston Bygrave, brought up in London with very little experience of the countryside, the problem of how to catch and weigh two panic-stricken sheep on a set of bathroom scales was every bit as unnerving as doing the same thing with a snake. Winston very quickly worked out the right method. 'That was the easy part,' he wrote in his report of the Selection Weekend at Machynlleth in Wales, from which he emerged triumphant as one of the chosen YEs. 'The difficult part was catching the wretched things. They were scared of me and, to be quite honest, I was scared of them. Eventually I managed to get hold of one and the surprising thing was that it became absolutely still when it was in my hands, making it very easy to do the weighing. Finally, exhausted but pleased, I found out the weight of both of them.'

The weekend's surprises had begun for Winston the moment he arrived in the village of Pennal at 7.30 a.m. having walked the three and a half miles from Machynlleth, where he had been delivered by the night train from London. As he presented himself at the rendezvous point, he was surprised to see other candidates emerging rested and well fed from the local bed-and-breakfast establishment. 'I could have cried,' he noted. 'When I received the letter telling me that I had been chosen to attend a Selection Weekend for Young Explorers, I thought that finding one's way to Pennal was part of the test. I thought that the village would consist of no more than a few houses, much less a bed-and-breakfast. I also thought that the judges would be waiting there to greet us on our great discovery of the village. I had imagined how I would tell them how I used my initiative to travel overnight so that I could arrive in the morning on time. But, alas, my preconceived ideas were shaken – and this would not be the only time.'

Winston threw himself into the tests with enthusiasm. He trudged over hills, down dales and along a freezing river, with his team and their make-believe casualty; he fired a shotgun for the first time in his life, weighed his sheep, took over as cook for his group and struggled to prepare a meal of fish, potatoes, onions and carrots over a spluttering camp fire; he helped to write and perform a short play; and, in a pitch-dark room, thrust his hands into bowls of onions in egg white, chess pieces in spaghetti, nails in oil, and sausages in beans, in an attempt to identify them by touch alone – the onions in egg white was the only mixture that defeated him.

His make-or-break moment came as darkness fell at the end of the first day. He and the others were taken in a Land Rover to a secret destination where sacks were placed over their heads and they were told to imagine that they were in the jungle at night and that, having thus been deprived of their sight, they must use their other senses to follow the route of strings and ropes that had been laid down in advance.

'I was led to the starting point and my heart began to beat fast,' he wrote. 'I began to move slowly, holding on tightly to the string. I had gone only twenty yards when suddenly I felt my feet sink into some cold, slimy mud. "That's it," I thought to myself. "I'm going back. A joke's a joke, but I think they've taken this a bit too far."

'I began to make my way back, but bumped into another candidate

[29]

who was following behind me. I stopped and he passed me. In the background I heard one of the judges say: "Number twenty – are you going to move or not?" I stood still and began to think. I thought of how tough I thought I was and here I was ready to give up the ghost. I was facing the most decisive dilemma I would encounter on this whole weekend. Shall I accept defeat or shall I take the gauntlet?

'While I stood there so many thoughts came to my mind. I began to realise what the examiners were trying to do. (This conclusion that I'm about to state was reached after a considerably long raging mental battle to convince myself that they were not just trying to kill us off!) I realised that they were sorting out the men from the boys and the women from the girls. I began to realise that these examiners looked on Operation Drake as a very serious thing, whereas up until then I had looked on it as just another cruise. I also realised that the judges were not particularly looking at how one behaved or survived in normal conditions, but how one behaved and acted in abnormal conditions. It was then that I stopped looking at the tests as carefully constructed sadistic acts against enthusiastic Young Explorers and began to see them as trials which would bring out the real you, what one is really made of. I decided that I would accept the challenge. From that time on I went out to prove to myself that I was man enough to do it.

'I moved on with new zeal and determination. Though the mud reached above my knees and my boots were filled with the stuff, I didn't care. I didn't care any more about my physical suffering. All I cared and knew about was that I was going to conquer this test. I began to use my other senses extensively and it soon became quite easy moving through the swamp. I even found that my sense of humour had returned. Finally, I came to the end and was greeted with a genuine "Well done!" which had an element of surprise in it, as if they had really expected to lose some of us in the swamp.'

When it came to the 'dreaded' three-minute talk, Winston decided to describe how his views had changed during the course of the weekend. 'I had originally planned to talk about how I found my way to Pennal, but then I thought to myself, "Big deal! Twenty-nine other candidates also found their way to the village so what's so special about the way you came?" So I decided I had nothing whatsoever to lose by telling a true, candid story of how my preconceived ideas were all shattered, one by one. I was shocked at the warm and humorous response that I received from both staff and candidates. Although I didn't plan it to be a funny talk, I must admit that there were parts in it that if Queen Victoria had heard, then even she would have been amused! The ultimate aim of my talk was to show that during this Selection Weekend I personally learned that there is more to an expedition than meets the eye, and also discovered what it is like to work with other people in situations in which it is not easy to do so.'

Fifteen months later Winston was able to put to good use some of the lessons he had learned about himself and his attitudes to other people, when he found himself in the jungles of Indonesia. And the man who was so proud of having got himself from Euston to Pennal must surely have revelled in the challenge of getting himself from London to that remote camp in Sulawesi.

Chapter Three

Cheering, waving crowds lined the waterfront and hundreds more people gathered on the Hoe to give *Eye of the Wind* a wonderfully emotional send-off as she headed out into the Sound with Prince Charles at the helm. It was a truly magnificent sight as the beautiful, white-painted brigantine eased her way gracefully out to sea. Guns were fired, Royal Navy warships piped their respects as she passed, and the armada of small boats that escorted her out of harbour whoop-whooped their farewells. From her deck, Capital Radio's David Briggs broadcast a live running commentary on the departure, which to all intents and purposes seemed to get Operation Drake finally under way. Not too many people were aware, I hope, that this was not actually the case.

Like Francis Drake himself, we had got off to a false start. The main difference was that we *knew* we were not going anywhere after that ceremonial leave-taking. *Eye of the Wind* certainly gave the impression of making a dignified and dramatic exit, but she was actually towed out to the breakwater by a tug. There, with His Royal Highness at the helm, full sail was set and we appreciated the real beauty of our flagship for the first time. Once Prince Charles had been taken off by launch and then whisked away in a helicopter, and when the film and TV cameras had stopped rolling and the crowds had dispersed, she was towed back in again. The official excuse was that she had to undergo extensive sea trials before she could actually start the voyage, but the slightly embarrassing truth was that she was far from ready to sail. Her new engine, for which the Prince himself had generously paid half the £11,000 cost, was not yet in running order, and there was still much refitting to be done and equipment to be loaded. It had been a frantic race against time to get her into any sort of fit state even for that brief ceremonial trip along the Sound and back again, with everybody, including the first batch of YEs who had joined the ship a fortnight before, slaving twelve hours a day, seven days a week. As one of the youngsters publicly consoled himself during a Capital Radio interview:

'At least it has helped us get fit in readiness for Panama!'

Thanks to the magnificent efforts of all those who drove themselves so hard to be ready against all the odds, we were able to go ahead with the big day as planned. But it was touch and go. There was even a joke circulating that it had been cut so fine that there had only been time to paint the side of the ship that would be facing the cameras and the crowds, and the other side had been left untouched! If people laughed a little nervously at that one, it was because it was uncomfortably close to the truth. The deck had certainly not been painted – that chore was not completed until Tenerife.

It would have been a tragedy if we had been forced to postpone the formal departure. For one thing, it is doubtful whether Prince Charles would have been able to fit a later date into his crowded schedule, and that would have been a major disappointment to everybody concerned, robbing the occasion of much of its significance. Apart from that, it might well have been seen as an ill omen for the expedition. As it turned out everything went remarkably smoothly.

A special service of dedication was held the previous day in the Royal Naval Church of St Nicholas at the shore station HMS Drake. During the service the skipper of *Eye of the Wind*, Captain Patrick Collis, called on the congregation to ask for God's blessing on the ship with a time-honoured chant that dates back to the embarkation of the Crusaders in the thirteenth century. Among the prayers said was the one written by Francis Drake himself on the day he sailed into Cadiz in 1587.

Many of us were offering up a few prayers of our own by the time Prince Charles arrived and the moment approached for the skipper to give the order to cast off. And they were answered. There were no awful hitches. The Prince gave a warm and witty speech which ended with some advice for the YEs. 'I have a feeling', he said, 'that those who take part in this particular expedition will enjoy themselves, but at the same time I expect there will be moments when they will wish that they were back home and had never volunteered for the thing in the first place. All I can say to them on that score is, just stick to it and when you get back you will find that, rather like beating your head against a brick wall, it's marvellous when it's over.' There were very few people involved with Operation Drake over the next couple of years who did not have occasion to recall those words and reflect how true they were.

As *Eye of the Wind* left harbour, the Flag Officer, Plymouth, followed in his launch, taking with him General Sir John Mogg, the Lord Lieutenant of Devonshire, Field Marshal Sir Richard Hull and myself. We were just beginning to relax a little and breathe a few sighs

[33]

of relief now that everything was going so well when I happened to glance at the Admiral and noticed with alarm that his knuckles were whitening as he clutched the brass rail in front of him. I followed the line of his stony gaze and experienced an awful sinking feeling as I recognised the Royal Standard fluttering in the breeze.

The Royal Navy had most specifically requested that this should not be flown until *Eye of the Wind* was well clear of the dockyard; otherwise, naval protocol required every ship present to parade bands and guards, and since it was a Sunday this would be rather awkward as only skeleton crews would be aboard. Not wishing to interfere in any way with the sailors' weekend shore leave, we readily agreed to keep the Standard furled at the masthead until we were out of the dockyard. And yet there it was for all to see and we had barely left the shore.

I discovered later what had happened: no sooner had Prince Charles stepped on board than he asked Captain Collis, 'Where's my standard, then?' When the skipper explained why it was not being flown, HRH grinned mischievously and said, 'Well, let's break it anyway and see if they have got any bands and guards!'

There was just one more anxious moment during the day, but once again the Prince's great sense of humour saved what was potentially a rather embarrassing situation. It was one of those classic clangers that had all the hallmarks of something straight out of a Goon Show script and so, as a well-known fan of that programme, he undoubtedly appreciated the funny side of it. It centred around the provision of special private toilet facilities wherever an official Royal visit is being made. We had certainly not overlooked this vital point of etiquette and a particularly handsome prefabricated edifice had been erected by the Department of the Environment near the helicopter landing pad. Sure enough, just before boarding the Wessex helicopter of the Queen's Flight on his way home, the Prince decided to avail himself of this convenience.

As he advanced towards it, an officer jumped forward smartly to open the door, only to find it apparently jammed. Increasingly harder and more frantic pulls failed to shift it. Even when a burly Petty Officer stepped up and virtually braced one foot against the door jamb, it still failed to budge an inch. Clearly, it was locked. It emerged later that the attendant who had been thoughtfully posted was under the impression that if the building was not required when the Prince first arrived then it would not be needed at all, and so he had gone off with the key in his pocket.

When defeat was finally admitted, Prince Charles, who had been observing the proceedings with some amusement, turned to the senior officer present and jokingly inquired, 'Do you have a tree, perhaps?'

[34]

'I'm sorry, Sir,' stammered the officer, indicating a fallen elm nearby. 'I'm afraid we've just cut it down!'

'Oh, never mind,' murmured HRH. And as he turned to board the helicopter he added, 'I hope you find the key.'

The Prince's presence made the day a memorable one for everybody – but particularly the YEs aboard *Eye of the Wind*, who were delighted to find him charming, relaxed and informal. From the moment that he took the wheel of the ship with the remark 'All I need now is a parrot!' he was a tremendous hit with the youngsters. He chatted to them for about two hours and posed for photographs, and showed an obviously genuine interest in what they were about to undertake. In the launch that took him off the ship and transported him back to shore, he seemed to be bubbling with enthusiasm for the whole venture and gave the strong impression that his imagination had been fired by his close contact with the YEs.

Everyone at HQ was overjoyed to see something go right after so many weeks of constant crisis. We had all been under intense pressure from the moment that Operation Drake had been officially launched nearly a year before. For the first few days after the announcement, things went quite mad and Room 5B looked like a casualty station as, hollow-eyed with exhaustion, the team worked round the clock in an effort to cope with the avalanche of press, radio and television enquiries from all over the world, not to mention the letters and phone calls from people wanting to sign on as Young Explorers. An indication of the kind of interest that was sparked can be gained from the fact that Capital Radio received no less than 10,000 applications from the London area alone for the ten places it was sponsoring. Such an enthusiastic reaction made all the hard work involved seem really worthwhile, and an added consolation was that many of the inquiries with which we had to deal came from people wanting to contribute to our funds. When we eventually counted up the cash, postal orders and cheques that cascaded in from ordinary members of the public it amounted to a very handsome bonus of over £58,000.

Even after that initial flurry of activity had died down, the pace remained hectic and we became only too well aware of the sheer magnitude of the task we faced and the vast range and complexity of the problems that had to be sorted out. As I knew from experience, organising one fairly compact, four-month expedition can be hard enough – but even I had not bargained for all the financial, logistical and administrative headaches involved in getting an international show like Operation Drake on the road and keeping it rolling.

By the time *Eye of the Wind* sailed from Plymouth we had over 2,000 friends, associates and committee members working flat out on

[35]

our behalf in nearly thirty countries. The activation of a world-wide network of local Operation Drake committees had been our first main task once we knew for certain that the venture would definitely be going ahead so that they could get on as soon as possible with the job of rousing interest, finding sponsors, selecting YEs, and, in areas where phases of the expedition would actually be taking place, making preparations for our arrival, including the forward planning of the various projects. Messages flashed round the globe as we appointed a Chairman here, a Secretary there, and so on. It all happened so quickly that Dr John Chapman-Smith, a former medical officer on the Zaire River Expedition and our contact in New Zealand, was taken completely by surprise when he arrived back in Auckland after a brief business trip abroad to be met by hordes of pressmen wanting to know more about Operation Drake. 'You tell *me*,' he exclaimed. 'I haven't the faintest idea.' It was not until he got to his office that he received the letter I had sent him explaining what it was all about and asking him to be our local Chairman.

All around the world, busy people found time to devote a tremendous amount of effort towards helping. In Australia, Denis Cordner, the local Managing Director of ICI and a tirelessly energetic man with a reputation as a fine sportsman and a fantastic organiser, headed a marvellous team that included Sir William Pettingell, Major General Tim Cape, and Colonel Reg Glanvill.

In the USA, Sir Gordon White of the Hanson Trust became our Chairman and, with the British Consul-General Gordon Booth (later Sir Gordon also) as Secretary, put together a formidable organisation. As ever, Otto Roethenmund and Vince Martinelli were in the forefront, and the contribution made by Mr William Seawell, President of Pan Am, was to prove immeasurable. Pan Am's generosity was incredible. They not only provided free air travel for many of our staff and all the American YEs but also gave Barbara Martinelli leave of absence from her job with Inter Continental Hotels so that she could work on our behalf. Dr Dan Osman, a tried and trusted ally from way back, helped to recruit medical staff and raise funds, while New York businessman John Linehan gave me the use of his office, as well as the benefit of his business experience and contacts. Ralph Barnett, head of the Gestetner Corporation in America, kindly provided an Operation Drake office for the use of our committee. Denis Lowry of Gestetner Duplicators' British Sales Organisation had given us similar facilities in London. Indeed, everywhere we went, Gestetner did everything possible to help us.

In PNG an old school friend, Nigel Porteous, did a grand job of stirring up enthusiasm for Operation Drake among the traditionally cynical Aussie expatriates, and the committee there, under Defence Force Colonel Ken Noga and the British High Commissioner, Douglas Middleton, worked ceaselessly to smooth our path. It seemed that nothing was too much trouble for people like Ray Thurecht, boss of the PNG Printing Company and the local Gestetner agent, and Major John Girling and his wife, Ida. Everywhere in this exciting land we seemed to make friends – and in Port Moresby Sandy Sandbach, Alan and Linda Musicka did much to facilitate our preparations.

The list goes on for ever – Jim Edwards, the amazing entrepreneur and hunter who became a great conservationist and now runs the unique Tiger Tops jungle lodge in Nepal and who did so much for us as friend, adviser and sponsor; John Blower of the United Nations Development Programme, who came up with such a remarkably worthwhile project for us in Sulawesi; and Robin Leonard of British American Tobacco in Djakarta, without whose help the difficult Indonesian phase could never have been organised so efficiently; Jack Davis, Billy St Mālo and Dr Reina Arauz who gave us so much support in Panama. There were countless others, but to mention everyone who helped us would require a book in itself. However, Appendix A does show how it was organised and I have tried to list the major supporters in Appendix B.

Meanwhile, at the same time as we were trying to organise and co-ordinate the world-wide activities of all the local committees from our HQ in Whitehall, we suddenly found ourselves facing our first major crisis – we did not have a ship. We thought we had struck lucky when the Dulverton Trust agreed to charter the *Captain Scott* to us for a nominal £1 a year, on condition that we undertook to pay all her costs and maintenance bills. Even though we estimated that these could add up to £100,000 over the two years, it was still a very good deal for this magnificent modern sailing ship that had been built as recently as 1971. We were not particularly concerned that the Trust reserved the right to sell the ship if a buyer should materialise before the date when she was due to be handed over to us, since the chances of this happening were considered extremely remote. Nobody could believe it when, at the very last moment, the Sultan of Oman came up out of the blue with an offer they just could not refuse. That left us high and dry at a late stage when all our other plans were advanced well beyond the point of no return.

It was a catastrophic situation. From start to finish of the expedition all our worst and most expensive headaches were to be connected in some way or another with the ship. It was never to be plain sailing, but for a while, after we lost the *Captain Scott*, it looked as if there might be no sailing at all. We had already discovered that ships of the size and

[37]

type we needed were not easy to find at the best of times. The chances of finding a replacement at such short notice were not good.

We were becoming decidedly desperate when, quite unexpectedly, I received a picture postcard from my American friend Allen O'Brien. It showed the brigantine *Eye of the Wind*; Allen wrote that he had become co-owner of the vessel, that he had heard about my 'Francis Drake scheme' through the SES Newsletter, and that if I should ever have need of another sailing ship to bear *Eye of the Wind* in mind. Such a timely offer seemed too good to be true, but hurried enquiries revealed that although the ship was in Australia she was due back in England in the summer of 1978 and would then be available. She was not quite as big as we would have liked, but it was our only hope. We wasted no time in concluding a deal whereby she was chartered to us very reasonably for £1,000 a month.

We had got for our money a flagship with a distinctly working-class background. She was built in 1911 at a dockyard near Bremen, specifically to ply the round trip from Germany to Argentina to Cornwall and back, carrying salt from Germany to Argentina, hides from there to Cornwall, and china clay from Cornwall to Germany. There is a blank in her history during the First World War years, and nothing more was heard of her until 1923, when she was bought by a Swedish concern. For the next forty-five years she spent her winters trading cargo in the Baltic and the North Sea, and her summers drifting for herring off Iceland. She was badly damaged in the late sixties by a fire which broke out while she was ice-bound in the Baltic, and after being towed back to Gothenburg she was left there to rot until the present owners, who had been searching for some time for just such a vessel, found the burnt-out hull and decided to buy her.

The syndicate of six enthusiasts – tragically reduced to five when Allen O'Brien was killed in an air crash in India in 1980 – spent six months patching her up sufficiently to get her from Sweden to England, where they laid her up for a year in Faversham while they raised the money to restore her properly. They then spent eighteen months painstakingly rebuilding her with their own hands and some volunteer labour.

Their limited funds led to some interesting improvisation when it came to materials and fittings. The floor of the lower saloon came from a dance hall that was being converted for bingo, the bench seats were pews taken from an old church, and the magnificent oak pannelling was salvaged from a bank that was being demolished. The superb teak in the deckhouse was rescued from a redundant Australian minesweeper that was being scrapped, while the compass was taken from an old trawler that had also ended its days in a breaker's yard.

[38]

The pinrail was fashioned from old sleepers that once supported the Tenterden Railway in Kent and the spars were made by the owners using adze and spokeshave in the traditional manner.

Despite all this admirable work by the syndicate – led by Londoner 'Tiger' Timbs and Leslie Reiter, who were to stay on board throughout Operation Drake as Mate and Purser respectively – it became frighteningly clear when we took delivery of the ship in August 1978 that she would need an awful lot doing to her before she met our requirements. As well as fitting a new engine, we were left with no alternative but to carry out extensive alterations below decks in order to provide adequate accommodation. These were the two major items. In addition there was an alarmingly long list of less fundamental but equally necessary repairs and refinements. And once we got started, we found that whenever we felt satisfied that everything had been thought of, somebody always managed to unearth another unforeseen complication.

Gloom and despondency began to set in as it became obvious that, in addition to the astronomical costs of carrying out all the work, there was no way that it was going to be finished in the few weeks left before we were due to sail. That the ship was sufficiently presentable to go through the motions of leaving on 22 October and that she was actually able to depart only three weeks late was largely due to Skipper Patrick Collis who used his influence and his contacts to persuade his friends in the Royal Navy to give us a generous amount of assistance, and we owe a debt of gratitude to HMS Drake who helped us out in so many ways. Although the Navy were very much in charge of the refit – through dozens of volunteers working during their leave and spare time – there were also Royal Marines, Royal Engineers, Royal Electrical and Mechanical Engineers and airmen of the RAF. In fact, the whole venture had already taken on the Joint Service-and-civilian atmosphere which was to be one of the major factors that contributed to Operation Drake's success.

Although the Services gave wonderful help, our sponsoring companies, encouraged by Ruth Mindel's Procurement Department, also gave fantastic support. Lucas provided expert advice on the ship's electrics and gave us a bank of batteries; Plessey, Marconi, MEL, Racal, and a company appropriately named Drake provided radios; Decca kindly lent us a radar, and the ship's fire protection systems were donated by Wormald International; and many more kind-hearted companies helped in hundreds of different ways. And, of course, one must not forget the YEs who sweated away like galley slaves and must have wondered what they had let themselves in for.

[39]

Chapter Four

Dateline: Aboard 'Eye of the Wind', November–December 1979

There are few experiences in life more exhilarating than the thrill of climbing the rigging of a sailing ship in a gale for the first time, or more demoralising than the sheer misery of discovering what it means to suffer from really severe seasickness. Both the agony and the ecstacy of life before the mast were very soon brought home to the Young Explorers aboard *Eye of the Wind*, as the brigantine battered her way south from Plymouth to the Canary Islands through winds that rarely subsided below a fresh force 4 and often rose to a howling gale force 8.

Everyone was apprehensive in advance about going aloft, but throughout the whole of Operation Drake less than half a dozen YEs flatly refused to have a go and there was no question of trying to bully them into it. The interesting thing is that most people, even those with no head for heights – who had been dreading the prospect of having to fight with flapping sails while swaying many feet up above the deck – soon found that it was not nearly as frightening as they had imagined. On the contrary, for most of them the sensation turned out to be so thrilling they got hooked on it to the extent of nipping up and perching there as a form of off-duty relaxation. After all, that is the one place on a small, crowded sailing ship where you can get away from it all and enjoy peace and quiet with the refreshing feeling of the wind in your hair.

The truth is that even at night and in foul weather it is not nearly as alarming and dangerous as it might appear to the average landlubber. There is plenty to hang on to and you actually feel quite secure. Of course, it is important to know what you are doing, and, before putting to sea, all the YEs were sent up the mast and literally shown the ropes so that they could tell the difference between the clews and the bunts, distinguish the sheets from the stays, and not confuse the bullwanger with the lubber hole. After that, most of them were able to look forward to their first real sail change under way with a bit more confidence. But there were still butterflies in the stomach.

Peter Shea, a YE sponsored by Capital Radio, admitted as much

[40]

when, in an interview broadcast just before *Eye of the Wind* left Plymouth, he told listeners in a slightly anxious tone of voice, 'We have heard lots of stories about how rough it's going to be in the Bay of Biscay.' Then he added boldly, 'But we don't want to cross the Atlantic with hardly any wind, not doing anything. We want to be heeled hard over, dashing up the rigging with spray pouring over the decks. This is what attracted us in the first place.'

In that respect Peter and his young colleagues were certainly not disappointed. No sooner had the ship finally set sail on 7 November than she ran into a violent storm, just as Francis Drake himself had done, and to avoid any risk of suffering the kind of damage that forced the *Golden Hind* to return home, *Eye of the Wind* spent her first night at sea moored to a buoy. Unfortunately, few of the YEs were in any condition to savour this early challenge from the elements since they were all hanging over the rail being ill. They had prepared themselves for all the more dramatic hardships, but the one thing they had not bargained for was the totally crushing effect of seasickness. The unpleasantness of even a mild attack comes as a terrible shock the first time you suffer, and there was nothing mild about what those aboard *Eye of the Wind* had to undergo during their first few hours at sea. They were quickly reduced to wretched, shivering little heaps who curled up and wished for death to bring blessed relief. It was a great leveller for a bunch of people who had begun to think that they were ready for anything.

There was no respite the following day as the ship motored on to Jersey, her bow thumping down into the waves and sending regular sheets of ice-cold salty spray whipping the length of the deck to sting and then numb the faces of those who gasped for fresh air in an effort to ease their queasiness. By the time they arrived in St Helier most of them were looking distinctly green about the gills and rather shaken.

Happily, the majority recovered sufficiently to enter into the spirit of the great send-off festivities that had been organised by the local Operation Drake committee, under the endlessly energetic chairmanship of my old friend Adrian Troy. Adrian, supported by Ray Bellows and Trevor Green, had worked miracles in drumming up the most tremendous support and enthusiasm for the expedition and, as I have always counted Jersey as my home, I was particularly moved by the way in which the island community responded to the whole venture.

We very much wanted to reward the huge crowds who gathered to see us off by making *Eye of the Wind*'s departure as memorable as possible, and this was achieved with spectacular success by setting full sail before the ship was clear of the harbour. This delicate operation

[41]

required all members of the crew to be positioned by the sheets, halyards and all the other essential ropes that have to be pulled and released in perfect synchronisation. As this was the first time that many of the YEs had ever had a chance to set the sails, some of which had never been set by anybody, there was a certain air of breathless suspense as the Mate, Tiger Timbs, and other experienced members of the permanent crew directed the performance with all the precision of a complex ballet. Everything went smoothly, however, and the effect was suitably dramatic as the sails filled and the ship breezed out into a beautiful clear blue morning. Apart from anything else, it made some marvellous footage for Al Bibby and his film crew.

There was only one moment of concern and that was when it looked as though Jersey YE Sacha Campbell was going to be left behind. Poor Sacha had been despatched to the other end of the island to acquire a length of terylene rope, which marine biologist Patricia Holdway needed to tow her plankton net. After various unforeseen hold-ups, he arrived back at the quayside and pushed through the crowd only to be greeted by the heart-stopping sight of *Eye of the Wind* disappearing out to sea. Fortunately, a fast launch was on hand to zoom back into the harbour, pick him up and deliver him to the ship.

My enjoyment of what was a wonderfully colourful and exciting occasion was marred somewhat by the bad news from Skipper Patrick Collis that it had become clear on the way over from Plymouth that the ship was still not right. The 'gypsy' and windlass had very quickly developed an extremely unhealthy-sounding knocking noise and in addition there was something drastically wrong with the anchor chain which caused it to slip alarmingly whenever it was raised, making this a slow and potentially dangerous operation. After much discussion we came to the conclusion that there was very little to be gained by hanging around in Jersey while we tried to deal with these problems. Apart from anything else, we just could not afford to fall any further behind schedule. The winds seemed set fair for the Atlantic crossing so that, with any luck, the engine should not be required that much – nor should the anchor. Once in Panama, there would be a little more breathing space in which to get things sorted out. I tried not to dwell too long on the extra expense that would undoubtedly be added to the ship's already rocketing maintenance costs. The accountants would have a fit when told of yet another enormous and unforeseen bill, and I knew that our hard-pressed fund-raisers would have to summon up even more super-human efforts.

As I returned to London with these thoughts weighing heavily on my mind, the spirits of the YEs aboard *Eye of the Wind* soared as they enjoyed their first day of fine weather sailing. There was hardly any

[42]

wind and, as the ship drifted peacefully along at about two knots, the off-duty watches basked in the warm autumn sunshine. Chris Sainsbury – whose many duties included that of Ship's Diarist – recorded in his log: 'The weeks of being messed about in Plymouth had taken a heavy toll on the morale of the whole ship's company, but as we were settling down to our second lunch at sea (most of the first went over the lee rail), I could sense the most remarkable atmosphere of comradeship which had until this point been severely lacking. None of the YEs knows quite how life at sea will affect him or her, but there is a great feeling of expectation.'

It took them quite a few days to adjust to the ship-board routine which was based around two four-hour watches and which allowed for only two free hours in every twenty-four; the rest of the time was spent working or eating or sleeping. Chris Sainsbury's watch timetable was as follows:

0730 Breakfast	1200 Watch commences	2330 Called for watch
1100 Lunch	1600 Stand down	2400 Watch commences
1130 Called for watch	1800 Supper	0400 Stand down

Meanwhile, just as the one day's calm had lulled everybody into thinking that maybe life on the ocean wave really was rather idyllic after all, the wind got up again, heavy seas started running once more, and the dreaded seasickness returned. The pills liberally dispensed by Dr Nigel Pearce only added to the lethargy which had already become very noticeable among people losing sleep as they struggled to get used to a strange new pattern of life. However, no longer could anyone be allowed the luxury of self pity and even those with the queasiest stomachs were roused mercilessly from their bunks to carry out the duties of their watches. Working up on deck in the fresh air when one is feeling grim is bearable, but carrying out chores like cleaning out the 'heads', or clearing up the debris in a stuffy galley, under such circumstances can be a stern test of character.

Most people got their sea legs after two or three days, but some took a little longer to fall in with the motion of the ship and two Gurkha soldier YEs, Dilliram and Mohan Limbu, never mastered it. This unfortunate pair had everyone's sympathy since they clearly found the environment bewilderingly alien and, as they spoke only limited English, they had to suffer in silence most of the time. Despite all this, they remained clearly determined to enjoy what they bravely described

[43]

in their end-of-voyage reports as the greatest experience of their lives.

The general air of depression at this early stage of the trip was not helped by the fact that the winds tended to be blowing in the opposite direction to that which had been hoped for, with the result that progress was frustratingly slow. Instead of the desired north-easterlies that would have hurried the ship along down the coast of Portugal, there were south-westerlies that kept pushing her out into the Atlantic. It was a case of two steps backwards for every three forwards.

After ten days everything changed for the better. The wind veered round and, as even the more delicate stomachs finally settled down and people began to feel comfortable at last, the whole atmosphere improved.

The YEs were more in the mood from then on to appreciate such delights of life aboard a sailing ship as the perfect peace of the night watch on a clear, starlit night, the playful friendliness of the dolphins which would dart alongside and ride the bow wave with an expression of sheer pleasure on their faces, and the occasional sightings of whales, sharks, tuna and flying fish that every now and again would come whirring out of the waves and crash land on the decks. At the same time they were suddenly able to laugh off such minor inconveniences as having to stand by helpless and watch a lovingly prepared meal disappear over the side as the ship lurched into a trough between two waves and an avalanche of water swilled across the deck and swept overboard two large baskets of chicken legs and peeled potatoes.

On that occasion Chris Sainsbury recorded in his log: 'The *Eye of the Wind* is, on the whole, a very dry ship and this will probably be one of the very few freak instances when we will actually have the decks awash with several feet of water. Under two headsails, lower topsail, the main and nock staysail we were doing six and a half knots close hauled. Everyone was soaked to the skin by mid-afternoon and all cameras were out to record our breath-taking progress which, as the sea conditions worsened, became all the more exciting, with waves breaking right over the deck houses. Even the Captain and the Mate, standing on the high poop deck, were not immune, and more than once the foaming white crests of passing seas were violently blown off straight into their faces or down their necks.'

There were no real dramas during the crossing of the Bay of Biscay, although there were some moments of excitement when a catamaran was spotted which seemed to be behaving in a very strange manner. She was visible on and off for several hours and at one point, after being lost to view for a time, she suddenly reappeared right in the *Eye of the Wind*'s path, rolling and pitching under a heavily reefed main. She looked to be in trouble, but a quick chat on the VHF radio revealed

[44]

that although she had been damaged she required no assistance.

After a brief revictualling stop at Santa Cruz, Tenerife, *Eye of the Wind* headed out into the Atlantic, where, for the first few days, she encountered very light winds and eased along at a gentle pace. Although in some ways it was a little frustrating to be relatively becalmed in this way, it did at least afford a good opportunity to get on, very belatedly, with the task of painting the decks and, far more enjoyable, provided a perfect excuse to heave to each day and give everyone on board the chance to experience the rather special sensation of swimming in mid-ocean.

The slower progress also suited marine biologist Trish Holdway very well, since her nets could only be trawled effectively when the ship was doing less than three and a half knots. Trish, a specialist in marine plankton from the University of East Anglia who originally intended to join us only for the first phase of the expedition and ended up staying for the whole two years, was particularly interested in making a study of neuston – the tiny organisms which live in the topmost centimetres of the water – while at the same time carrying out research into the effects of pollution on the marine environment. She was helped in the collection, analysis and classification of her samples by the YEs, who also conducted their own experiments into goose barnacles sticking to the ships hull with a view to helping oil companies in their efforts to combat a menace which loses them roughly £25,000 per tanker per year in cleaning costs and loss of revenue.

By now a big family feeling had developed on board and the various personalities had established themselves. Among the permanent crew, Skipper Patrick Collis had emerged as a rather awe-inspiring figure, while the Mate, Tiger Timbs, a Londoner who had thrown up his job as a welder to follow his love of the sea and who was senior member of the syndicate that owned *Eye of the Wind*, was easy-going and popular. His Australian friend Leslie Reiter, another of the syndicate, who acted as Purser and Nurse, fulfilled the role of a strict mother to the YEs with fearsome efficiency, and somehow managed to frighten them all into being reasonably clean, neat and tidy. Deck hand and Watch Leader Peter 'Spider' Anderson, another Australian who had been on *Eye of the Wind*'s previous voyage and had intended to stop off in England to take up a place at art school there until the prospect of Operation Drake lured him back to sea, was the quiet man who specialised in the most extravagant practical jokes.

One of his early victims was YE Kirsty Macdonald-Henderson, a young West Country policewoman to whom he successfully sold the idea of a so-called Cape Verde Oblong as the Atlantic's answer to the Bermuda Triangle – an area of ocean where ships and planes have

[45]

disappeared without trace and all manner of weird and wonderful unsolved mysteries have been logged. It all started when Kirsty pointed out an odd-shaped cloud formation on the horizon and remarked to Navigator Graham Robson that it looked very much like land. Graham kidded her that it was the coast of Africa and that this meant the ship must have sailed in a complete circle, whereupon Spider picked up on this and developed the fantastic story of the dreaded Oblong. At the same time he swore her to secrecy on the grounds that the others must not hear about it in case they panicked. From then on he arranged all sorts of strange manifestations for the poor girl's benefit. He himself crawled behind the wheel and jammed the steering gear and he got Ship's Engineer Corporal Steve Merritt, to play tricks with the engine, while Signaller Corporal Roger Secker was persuaded to make the radio and the electrics generally behave in the most unorthodox fashion. The climax to the joke came one night when Kirsty's watch were on duty and things were carefully arranged so that she would be up on deck alone. Suddenly she heard a strange noise above the lapping of the water, and as she peered into the darkness she saw, crawling aboard over the gunwale, a sea monster that would have done credit to a Hammer horror movie. As it lurched towards her, all dripping and slimy-looking with the moonlight glinting on its hideous features, Kirsty turned and fled. At that point the beast took great delight in identifying itself as Spider dressed up in a frogman's outfit and covered in seaweed and other suitably grotesque accessories.

Spider was not the only prankster on board and Kirsty was not the only girl to fall into a carefully prepared trap. Tiger and Chris Sainsbury fooled Dorset YE Mary Newman with a simple but effective ploy that involved the surreptitious placing of a plastic octopus in Trish Holdway's plankton net one night. Mary, who had been sponsored by Westward TV, was in charge of hauling in the net and collecting the samples, and when, in the dim deck-lighting, she noticed this apparent denizen of the deep ensnared in the mesh, she rushed off excitedly to consult with Trish. She then returned wearing an enormous pair of protective gloves and having removed the monster with a pair of tongs and deposited it in a bucket for closer inspection, was heard to announce triumphantly that it could not actually be an octopus as it had more than six legs! The rest of her watch, all of whom were in on the joke, could scarcely contain their glee as they observed all this from their hidden vantage points. In the end Chris Sainsbury stepped forward and pointed out the Made in Japan label, whereupon he discovered that young Mary packed quite a punch.

As was to prove the case through the whole of Operation Drake, the girls were more than able to hold their own with the men in every respect. Barbara Shopland from Ontario, a top-class long-distance swimmer who kept herself superbly fit and could often be found practising her Yoga in some corner of the ship, had amazed everybody during a drinking competition in Plymouth by sinking a pint in three seconds and drinking a yard of ale faster than some men could down a half! This ensured that she was held in the highest esteem by her male crewmates throughout the voyage!

Diana Newton from Taunranga, New Zealand, also made a big impression on everyone with her morale-boosting cheerfulness and won further admiration by somehow managing to swot up for a horticulture exam in between all her other duties. Among the other YEs who emerged as characters were Rory O'Connor from Berkshire, Kiwi Erwin Van Asbeck and John Wright from Yorkshire. Rory had everybody fooled with his slightly scruffy, tousled hair urchin look, behind which he concealed a high-powered brain. Nobody would have guessed that he was about to go up to Cambridge to study medicine. He turned out to be one of the most energetic and inquiring people on board and was fascinated by the engine room. Erwin was the great bird-watcher who would rush to the side at the merest hint of a sighting, while John was by far the most enthusiastic convert to the delights of marine biology and spent every spare moment peering at specimens under the microscope, or dissecting them in Trish's laboratory.

One of the most popular figures among the ship's company was David Briggs – the senior Capital Radio producer who had been assigned to 'live the news' for the first six months of the expedition. What endeared him to one and all was the way that, in between his reporting duties of interviewing, editing and sending back live, up-to-the-minute reports, he quite happily mucked in with the YEs and did his fair share of even the most menial chores. One minute he would be in his makeshift studio in Trish's laboratory, deftly cutting and splicing tape as the ship rolled violently from side to side, and the next he would be wallowing in the scuppers helping with the washing up. The whole experience must have represented a considerable cultural shock to an obviously suave and sophisticated media man who is one of his station's top executives, but he made it clear from the start that he expected no concessions. Just about the only thing that marked him out was that, almost alone among a ship full of increasingly dishevelled and rumpled-looking people, he did his best to keep up appearances and always managed to look reasonably smart – a commendable trait for which he was mercilessly ribbed.

David's talent as a producer proved most useful when it came to organising the evening's entertainment for the big party which was laid

[47]

on to mark the halfway point in the Atlantic voyage. This was intended as a substitute for a crossing-the-line ceremony and was a riotous success. The various watches worked for days on their songs and sketches. One lot actually called up a passing naval ship on the radio in order to obtain the full unexpurgated lyrics of 'The Good Ship Venus', only to decide, having studied them, that they were a bit too lewd and might offend the Skipper. Gudjon Anngrimson from Reykjavik taught them a slightly less rude Icelandic song instead. On the big night, David acted as MC and offered a grand prize for the winning sketch, which the judges awarded to Trish Holdway and Graham Robson, who were introduced as 'the *Eye of the Wind*'s answer to John Travolta and Olivia Newton-John' and brought the house down with a cleverly adapted rendering of the Peter Sellers/Sophia Loren song 'Goodness Gracious Me'.

The voyage continued at a fairly leisurely pace, with the winds rarely rising above force 4, and one month after leaving Tenerife *Eye of the Wind* docked at Bridgetown, Barbados, for a brief refuelling stop, during which the YEs advanced their education with a visit to the notorious Harry's Nitery! Then it was on to the island of St Vincent and Operation Drake's first land-based project.

Chapter Five

Dateline: La Soufrière, St Vincent, 24 December 1978

It is not often that one spends Christmas Eve taking the temperature of a live volcano. This point was not lost on the YEs, most of whom dwelt on it in their diaries, and the contrast between the familiar connotations of the date and the very unfamiliar environment in which they now found themselves helped to heighten the sense of adventure.

The last major eruption of the volcano La Soufrière had been in 1901 and on that occasion over 1,500 people lost their lives. Seventy years later, there was renewed, but much less dramatic, activity spread over a period of four months during late 1971 and early 1972, when a lava island was thrown up in the middle of the crater lake and the water was heated to boiling point. The local population was hurriedly evacuated, but this mini-eruption gradually subsided without any full-scale fireworks. Since then the volcano had appeared to be fairly stable, although there had been recent changes in the temperature and colour of the lake which indicated the possibility of further disturbances.

Operation Drake's purpose in going into the crater was threefold. The main aim was to undertake the first proper thermometric study of the lake for five years, and this was to be carried out in conjunction with Professor J. B. Shepherd of the Seismic Research Unit of the University of the West Indies. In addition, the fact that the lake had been effectively sterilised when it boiled in 1971 was of tremendous interest to Trish Holdway, for whom it provided a rare opportunity to get an insight into how aquatic life re-establishes itself from scratch. Finally, the recolonisation of the lava island by flora and fauna was equally interesting, and this was to be examined by the YEs on behalf of our scientists.

Clambering the 3,500 feet up to the outer rim was no easy task, especially when weighed down by scientific equipment and the Avon inflatable boat which was needed to ferry people across the lake to the island and for use in sampling the water temperatures. The boat was actually lugged most of the way by four YEs carefully selected for the job because of their sturdiness and uncomplaining natures – namely

Sapper Mark Henrys, Yorkshireman John Wright and the two Gurkhas, Mohan and Dilliram Limbu. They were part of an advance party of ten who set out the day before the main group and camped out on the lower slopes of the crater. They were justly proud of their efforts, and were quite put out when asked to wait just a few hundred feet below the summit until the others caught up with them to give them a helping hand over the final section – especially as this was largely for the benefit of the film cameras.

Peter Shea, who was with the main party, described the ascent: 'The first part of the walk took us along a sloping, narrow track which wound its way through lush green jungle – our first sight of real tropical rain forest. Although it was only seven o'clock in the morning we began to sweat a great deal almost as soon as we started walking. The sun was just coming up but we could not see much of it due to the density of the jungle.

'Our first rest point was at a lava flow, a band of volcanic rock stretching all the way down the mountainside. It was about twenty feet across and there was a small stream of fresh water running down the middle of it. From this point on, the vegetation began gradually to thin out until we came into open scrub land. By now we were very high up and had a magnificent view of both sides of the island. We climbed on and visibility dropped as we reached the level of the low cloud, and soon we lost sight of the sun altogether.

'We came upon the edge of the crater very suddenly and, despite the cloud, were presented with a staggering view. The huge crater was spread out before us with the lake at the bottom and the island covering 50 per cent of the area of the lake. The island of dull grey rock stretched up to a height of eighty to one hundred feet and in the middle we could see smoke, steam or fumes rising gently up.'

There were actually clouds swirling around inside the crater below the level of the rim, and this added to the breath-taking effect; later, when all the cloud and mist cleared, there were equally dramatic views clear across the island and down to the brilliant blue waters of the Caribbean.

The next task was to get the boat down the almost sheer 1,000 feet inner walls of the crater to the water's edge, but this was achieved in just forty-five minutes by the simple expedient of inflating it and skimming it over the top of the boulders and vegetation.

Peter Shea was one of the first people to go across to the central island: 'The first surprise when we reached the shore of the island was the composition of it. From the edge of the lake it looked as though it was made of dust and ash, but on reaching it we found that it was made up of large pieces of rock ranging in size from 300 to 600 cubic

[50]

millimetres. To start with, we had to climb a very steep slope, 50 to 60 degrees in some places, and this was not easy, due to the looseness of the rocks which kept cascading down in miniature avalanches on top of the people climbing behind you.

'Even before we finished climbing, we noticed that all the rocks were covered with a dusty green moss, despite the already strong smell of sulphur. We reached the top of our climb and saw before us a long gully stretching up the vent hole of the island. The walking became easier now and, much to our surprise, the vegetation became more abundant. Ferns, grasses, moss and small brush-type plants were observed. We drew close to the vent hole and still the vegetation was present, despite the thickening fumes and steam and the noticeable change in the air temperature. Warm steam could be seen and felt coming up between the gaps in the rocks. We rose up again about seven metres and found ourselves looking down on the very centre of the crater. It was an exciting moment for all of us and, as we gazed down, very definite sulphur deposits could be seen over an area of about ten square metres, along with strongly smelling clouds of sulphur fumes and steam. The rocks were very hot to touch and the warm wet steam could be felt on our skin. We stayed for a few minutes and then made our way back gathering samples of all the plants we could see.'

Meanwhile, the water temperatures recorded were far higher than expected, ranging between 28°C and 47°C, and this caused considerable excitement, since it seemed to show that an eruption could be more imminent than had been generally anticipated. Just how imminent was revealed three months later when, on Good Friday 1979, La Soufrière suddenly exploded and sent a mushroom cloud of grey smoke billowing nearly five miles high, while cinders were showered over a forty-square-mile area. One witness described it as being like an atomic blast, while another talked of a sound like rolling thunder and a ball of orange fire. The forests on the crater slopes were reduced to blackened stumps, while the banana and coconut plantations were covered in a film of ash that resembled dirty snow. The fallout was so bad fourteen miles away in Kingstown that the inhabitants wore surgical masks and handkerchiefs over their faces. This time nobody was killed and perhaps that was partly because of the warning which had been made possible by Operation Drake's observations. For those YEs who had gazed into the very mouth of the volcano, it was a sobering thought to imagine what would have happened to them had they been there just a few weeks later. Had they known what was to come so soon after their visit, undoubtedly they would have hurried down the slopes of La Soufrière a little more anxiously that Christmas Eve.

[51]

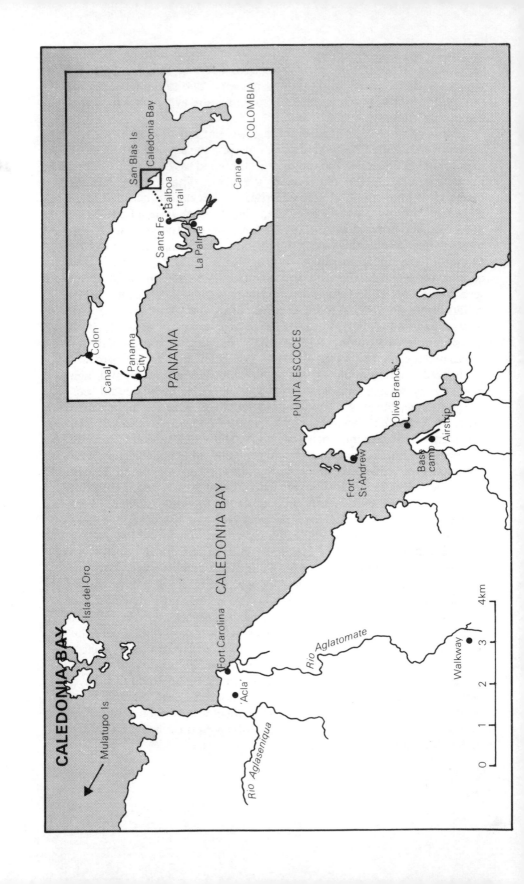

Chapter Six

Dateline : Caledonia Bay, 3 January 1979

Among the heroic failures of history, the disastrous attempt to found a Scottish trading colony on the Darien coast must rank high as a tragically misguided venture of truly epic proportions. It made an impact that is still remembered in Scotland today, and demoralised the entire nation to such an extent that it can be said to have played quite a significant part in preparing the way for the Act of Union by knocking the heart out of the opposition. And yet it seemed like a good idea at the time.

It was the brainchild of pioneering Scots businessman William Paterson. He became the leading light in a small group of merchants who boldly decided that it was time the country got involved in the very lucrative Indies trade, monopolised until then by the English and the Dutch. The Company of Scotland Trading to Africa and the Indies was established in 1695 specifically for this purpose and so great was enthusiasm for this grand masterplan, aimed at putting little Scotland in the forefront of international trade, that the £200,000 needed to finance it – an enormous sum in those days – was raised without much difficulty from private individual backers.

Panama was chosen as the location for the first outpost in this new trading empire, after Lionel Wafer, an extraordinary character who got wrecked there while operating as surgeon aboard a pirate ship, came back with tales of vast riches in gold. Paterson's imagination was also fired by the notion of a short-cut connection between the Atlantic and the Pacific. He was convinced that the narrow Panama Isthmus was 'the door of the seas and the key of the Universe', and he dreamed of creating a port that would serve as a gateway between East and West, which would enable Scotland to control the richest trade in the world.

And so it was that in July 1698 five ships set sail from Leith bound for 'some place or other not inhabited in America ... and not possessed by any European Sovereign, Potentate, Prince or State to be called by the name Caledonia'. Most of the 1,300 eager colonists who crowded aboard had no idea where they were going until they were out to sea –

[53]

a security precaution to prevent news of the enterprise leaking to the English, or other enemies who might want to ensure its failure.

The voyage across was horrific. The cramped conditons and foul atmosphere below decks guaranteed the maximum discomfort even before sickness and fever began to take a grip and the death toll started to mount. There were times when as many as three bodies had to be heaved over the side in a single day. At the final count, more than forty of those who set out failed to reach their destination and many others were in a pretty bad way by the time William Paterson himself, together with his family, led them ashore to be greeted by a scene which can have changed very little in the intervening years since then.

First impressions were good. Early reports that found their way back to Scotland enthused about the place as a veritable Earthly Paradise and, even allowing for the need to impress the shareholders at home, it seems that there was initially an air of optimism about the prospects for what was to be called New Edinburgh. But it was not too long before disillusionment began to creep in, and with the onset of the rainy season, which lasts from April to December and brings over 200 inches of rainfall, things went rapidly from bad to worse. Malaria and yellow fever cut a swathe through the colonists, whose resistance had been lowered by the combined effects of the long, harrowing voyage, poor and inadequate rations, and the hostility of the mosquito-ridden environment.

The lurking threat of the Spanish soon forced Paterson and his people to abandon plans for the township of New Edinburgh and to concentrate instead on completing Fort St Andrew. Even here, work continued at a pitiful pace since those men who were not actually dying were scarcely living, and most of their energies seemed to be devoted to grave-digging. The cemetery was the fastest-growing feature of the community and within a few months more than a quarter of the original 1,300 settlers were dead. By July 1699, when it was decided that they would have to leave the colony and sail in search of reinforcements and fresh supplies, there were only 700 left.

For them the nightmare was still far from over. Two of the ships made it back to New York – but only after a further 255 men had been lost – while a third was wrecked, and a fourth just about made it to Jamaica with 137 fewer on board than when she set out, having been chased by the Spanish. Only one of the seven ships that had left Scotland – the original five plus two resupply vessels – arrived back again and only a fraction of the settlers who had ventured forth so confidently ever set eyes on their homeland again. Paterson was left a broken man – the cruel shattering of his dreams and the shame which was unfairly heaped on all those involved drove him literally mad.

Even then the tragic saga was not over. In August 1699 a second wave of colonists had set sail from Scotland, unaware of what had been happening. They believed that they were going out to join a thriving and well-established community, and one can imagine the horror they must have felt when, having lost 160 people on the way over, they arrived to find the place deserted and empty. One wrote in his diary: 'Expecting to meet with our friends and countrymen, we found nothing but a vast howling wilderness, the colony deserted and gone, their huts all burnt, their fort for the most part ruined, the ground which they had cleared adjoining the fort all overgrown with weeds.'

Once they had got over the initial shock they set about trying to re-establish the colony but soon ran into exactly the same problems that had plagued the original settlers. Fever was rampant again within a matter of weeks, and then, to add to their misery, the Spanish moved in and laid siege to the place. Despite brave and determined resistance, it was only a matter of time from then on before sickness, starvation and enemy snipers wore them down. They finally surrendered in April 1700 when the Spanish general, who was anxious to have the whole thing over with before the rains came, made them an offer they could not refuse − a fourteen-day truce while they packed up and left.

By then they were in such a state of disarray that they had to be towed out to sea by the blockading Spanish navy, but still there was to be no salvation. Of the three ships that limped away from Caledonia Bay one was sunk off Jamaica and the other two were smashed to smithereens by a hurricane off the coast of South Carolina. As before, only a handful of survivors lived to tell the sad tale of the colony's last catastrophic days. Back in Scotland there was scant sympathy for the poor wretches who had suffered so appallingly for nothing. National pride had been badly hurt and insult was added to injury as accusations of cowardice were bandied about in the search for scapegoats to blame for the humiliating failure of the venture. The full £200,000 compensation handed out by the English as part of the Act of Union in 1707 did little to make up for the bitter disappointment of the Darien Disaster.

Nearly three hundred years after the Caledonia Bay fiasco, as the concept of Operation Drake began to take shape, my thoughts turned to this remote spot that was so steeped in history, drama and all the romance of the Spanish Main. It seemed to fit the bill in almost every respect. Not only was the terrain and the general environment suitably challenging, but there was also the prospect of exactly the kind of interesting and scientifically valid projects that we were anxious to set up. In addition, there was even a connection with Francis Drake since his 'Port Pheasant', which he used as a secret base when in the area, and the natural harbour within Caledonia Bay known as Puerto Escoces are widely believed to be one and the same.

On top of all this there was the vital fact that, thanks to the success of the 1972 Darien Gap Expedition, in which I had participated, we already had friends and connections in Panama. The government liked us and as a result of our earlier dealings with General Omar Torrijos and his officers, we had the confidence of the powerful Guardia Nacional which should prove to be an invaluable asset. We also had friends in the British Embassy and could rely on the support of such key figures as the highly respected businessman Jack Davis, and Dr Reina Torres De Arauz, Director of the Patrimonio Historico.

And so it was that in 1976 I found myself leading a party of ten people on a reconnaissance mission to find out more about Caledonia Bay and to start the forward planning for Operation Drake's proposed visit there. The team included Americans Dr Dan Osman and his friend Linda, who came as Medical Officer and Nurse, and Vince Martinelli and his explorer wife, Barbara, who shared the duties of Quartermaster. US Army Sergeant Mel Trafford was our diver for the underwater recce. From Britain there were Scientific Co-ordinator Andrew Mitchell and my faithful aide, Chris Sainsbury, who went in ahead to make some preliminary arrangements, with the help of Mr Robert John, the British Ambassador, and Jack Davis. Finally, Dr Reina Arauz kindly supplied us with an archaeologist who was also to act as Liaison Officer.

We flew into Mulatupo, the village from where we hired dug-outs and crews to take us the last ten miles to Caledonia Bay. Our first view of Puerto Escoces from the sea was breath-taking. With its coral gardens and breaking surf, golden beaches fringed by leaning palms and twisted mangrove and backdrop of green-clad slopes rising to a clear blue sky, it struck me straightaway as one of the most bewitching natural harbours I had ever seen.

Our first priority was to try and establish the whereabouts of the ruins of the Scottish settlement and so, with the help of notes made by Dr Reina Arauz and maps sketched for us by Dean Webster, an American clergyman with a specialist interest in the history of Panama, we began to cut our way through the undergrowth towards the headland where their fort was thought to have been.

I literally stumbled on what we were looking for when I fell into what had clearly been the moat. Other discoveries in the immediate vicinity confirmed this. Apart from evidence of ramparts, look-out posts and gun positions, there was a lot of pottery lying about, and Vince Martinelli soon unearthed a small cannonball. Clearly, there was plenty here to keep our archaeologist happy.

Almost as promising were the test dives which Mel Trafford and I carried out in the bay to see if we could find any traces of the several wrecks that were thought to be lying on the seabed, including a French merchantmen called the *Maurepas* (whose real name was probably *St Antony*), that was rumoured to have gone down with 60,000 pieces of eight on board. Although we did not come up with anything definite, Mel did discover a very interesting mound in the sand some fifty feet down. He estimated that it was roughly one hundred feet by fifteen, with what seemed to be projecting spars, and from this description it sounded as if it could be the hull of a ship. We did not have time to investigate more thoroughly, but we had the satisfaction of knowing that we had turned up something that would get the diving project off to an interesting start, with the added incentive of a possible treasure trove – not that it was going to be, by any means, easy pickings. Apart from the difficulties involved in breaking through the cocoon of sand and coral that was covering whatever it was down there, there was an extra complication that I had become chillingly aware of as I floated above Mel. At one point I turned round and came almost face-to-face with a Blue Shark. It gave me no more than a cursory glance with its beady, unblinking eyes, before veering away and disappearing into the underwater gloom with one flick of its mighty tail fin. But, nevertheless, I kicked swiftly for the surface and reflected that our divers would have to keep their wits about them.

The ten-day reconnaissance ended on a further note of triumph when a medicine man led us to a spot in the jungle further down the coast which seemed as though it really could be the site of the Lost City of Acla. The old man had heard through the grapevine what we were looking for and came to see us, saying that many years before, when he was a child, he had once seen a big wall in the forest. He thought he could find it again, he said. We set off in canoes and followed him along the coast and then through a narrow opening in the coral reef into a secluded inlet, from where he led us up into the mangrove swamps. He started running around like a gun dog looking for some lost bird, but after three and a half hours he had still not found anything, and as it was getting dark, we started to leave. Then suddenly a young Cuna boy appeared on the scene, and after chatting to him the medicine man got very excited and said that the boy knew exactly where the wall was. And, lo and behold, he took us no more than two hundred yards into the forest and there was a clearing where he had been burning the undergrowth ready to plant coconut trees, and right in the middle was the wall. It was built of coral blocks and was about one metre high and several metres long. Nearby were bits of pottery and glass which proved that it must be a European site. We made sketches in the fading light and Gricelio, the Panamanian archaeologist, got very enthusiastic and seemed to think that there was every chance that this was indeed Acla.

We therefore left Caledonia Bay in high spirits, having achieved just about everything we had set out to do. We had even discovered an old and totally overgrown grass air strip, which we later learned had been cleared by a Dutch plantation company that once had interests in the area, and although the lush tropical undergrowth had long since reclaimed it, we reckoned it could be made serviceable again reasonably easily.

It was on 5 December 1978 that Captain Jim Winter of the Royal Engineers led our advance party ashore through the mangrove swamps that fringe the shore of Caledonia Bay and walked straight into a most unfriendly welcome from a striking fer de lance – one of the world's deadliest snakes, which is known by the suitably sinister nickname of Mr X on account of its distinctive markings. One lightning swipe from Jim's machete and the danger was over. But this chilling little incident served as a reminder that the place chosen for our first major land phase was one of the most inhospitable regions to be found anywhere on Earth.

As Jim kicked aside the twitching remains of the fer de lance and led his men forward to start work on the base camp at Punta Escoces, preparations for Operation Drake's arrival were well under way in Panama City where we would set up our tactical HQ.

Jack Davis had worked wonders on our behalf. Major Jeremy Groves, Field Leader, along with Jim Winter and ex-Royal Marine George Thurstan, on this first phase, arrived in the capital to set up our Tactical HQ to find that the accommodation provided for this purpose was almost embarrassingly luxurious. It was a beautiful five-bedroomed house, with two bathrooms, and a kitchen equipped with everything from an electric tin-opener to a fridge and cooker with the wrappers still on them. The furniture, which included a colour television and stereo system, was all brand new and a BMW car was thrown in for good measure. All this was thanks to our good friend Eric Brewis, who ran the local subsidiary of British American Tobacco. As Jeremy noted: 'Our base outstripped the wildest dreams of even the most demanding armchair explorer. We began to wonder whether we would ever manage to pry ourselves away into the jungle!'

Many other facilities were also made available: a friendly insurance tycoon offered free use of his telex; a plastics company provided office facilities; and two more cars were loaned to us. Sponsors were found who contributed food, fuel, tobacco and beer. Camp stores were borrowed from the US Army and the ever-helpful Guardia Nacional promised men, aircraft, gunboats and a landing craft that proved particularly useful when it came to moving over one hundred tons of stores and equipment from Colon to Caledonia Bay.

Thanks to such fantastic support, everything was right on schedule, and on 3 January Piper Robert Little of the Scots Guards, cutting a magnificent, if slightly incongruous, figure as he stood silhouetted against the palm-fringed headland of Punta Escoces in full ceremonial dress, got things off to a formal start by playing a lament in memory of his ill-fated countrymen of so long ago. It was a moving moment and I reflected that the lonely ghosts of Fort St Andrew must surely have appreciated the haunting sound of the pipes again after 280 years.

The occasion was a surprise visit by General Omar Torrijos who flew in to visit us. The General, commander of the Guardia Nacional, turned out to be a tough but charismatic man who immediately made a great impression on one and all by nonchalantly shinning up a fifty-foot palm tree to fetch my daughter Victoria a coconut.

The base camp and runway had been completed two days earlier after much back-breaking labour. The main party had joined Jim Winter and his team before Christmas, and throughout the festive season had sweated in temperatures of over 100 degrees in the shade, digging latrines and garbage pits, unloading tons of stores and hauling them half a mile up to the camp site, and clearing twelve years' growth of palm trees, undergrowth and tussock grass from the airstrip. In just ten days they levelled a strip five hundred yards by fifteen, using only picks, shovels and machetes. By the end of it, blisters had grown on blisters, backs had peeled raw in the sun, and people who had thought they were fit had pushed themselves to new physical limits.

The YEs from *Eye of the Wind* arrived in timely fashion shortly after the General had touched down so that he was able to welcome them as they flew in from Panama City in a relay of light aircraft. The original plan had been for them to sail to Caledonia Bay, but this had to be abandoned when the ship's gearbox finally gave up the ghost and she had to be left at Colon to await a replacement.

The last lap of the voyage, from St Vincent to Colon, had been fairly fast and furious as strong trade winds blew *Eye of the Wind* along at a record pace. Between Christmas Day and New Year's Day she covered more than a thousand miles. There was only one untoward incident and that occurred in the very early hours of New Year's Day. There had been a fairly restrained party on board, during which a case of champagne presented in Plymouth by friends at HMS Drake was gratefully knocked back and 'Auld Lang Syne' was duly rendered on the stroke of midnight and then, at one o'clock in the morning, when everything had quietened down, a ship was sighted on the horizon. As

[59]

she approached nearer and nearer, it became clear that she was on a collision course and showed no sign of altering her bearing. *Eye of the Wind*'s sails were illuminated with a powerful searchlight so that she must have been visible to the other vessel, but still nothing happened.

As a last resort Radio Officer Corporal Roger Secker was ordered to call her up and remind her in no uncertain terms that, as a sailing ship, *Eye of the Wind* had right of way and so would she kindly take evasive action. At the very last moment she did alter course and passed just under the stern of *Eye of the Wind*, but then immediately turned round and headed straight back towards her.

At this point slight unease gripped those on the bridge. The more they altered course the more the other ship followed their every move. Just when they were beginning to fear that maybe they were dealing with one of the pirate ships that are more common on the oceans of the world today than they ever were in Francis Drake's time, she called up on the radio, wished a 'Happy New Year!' and disappeared. Clearly not everybody at sea that night had welcomed in 1979 in such a sober fashion as *Eye of the Wind*'s crew.

The next morning there was excitement of a different kind as land was sighted, but for the YEs, it was tinged with sadness as they realised that they would soon be saying goodbye to the ship that had been their home for the last two months. There were some tearful farewells as they boarded the coach that took them across to Panama City and to the Guardia Nacional air base, from where they flew to Caledonia Bay and adventure of a different kind.

Weighing and measuring Monty the Python was one of the
tests which confronted candidates on the Selection
Weekends (CHRISTOPHER SAINSBURY)

HRH The Prince of Wales at the helm as *Eye of the Wind*
leaves Plymouth harbour (CHRISTOPHER SAINSBURY)

Eye of the Wind under full sail (CHRISTOPHER SAINSBURY)

Taking an Avon inflatable boat down into the crater of
La Soufrière volcano (CHRISTOPHER SAINSBURY)

(from right to left) General Sir John Mogg, Chairman of
Operation Drake, Lieutenant Colonel John Blashford-Snell
and Captain Jim Masters with a Panamanian Guardia
Nacional escort making their way through the jungle to the
walkway (CHRISTOPHER SAINSBURY)

Claire Bertschinger and Royal Engineer Sergeant Mike
Christy constructing the aerial walkway in Panama
(CHRISTOPHER SAINSBURY)

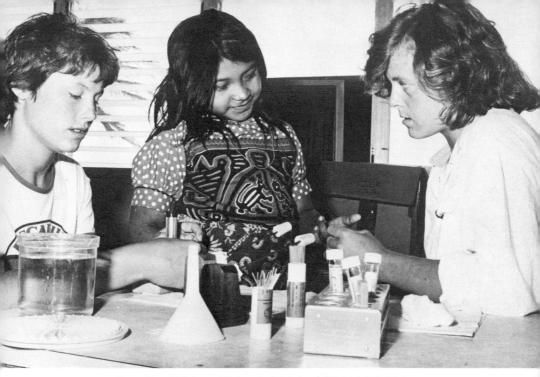

Canadian YE Anna Richards (right) and British YE Helen Mallinson (left) taking blood samples from a Cuna Indian girl during the medical project in Panama (CHRISTOPHER SAINSBURY)

The diving team who worked on the wreck of the *Olive Branch* with one night's haul of sharks caught nearby – a possible explanation for the disappearance of one diver's bucket (RAY PRINGLE-SCOTT)

Scots Guardsman Jock McGregor filtering precious water
through a millbank bag during the Balboa trek
(DESMOND DUGAN)

British YE Chye Ong (left) and Panamanian YE Irving
Bennett (right) supporting British YE David French, one of
the casualties on the Balboa trek (DESMOND DUGAN)

(inset) A Panamanian Army helicopter air-lifting out one of
the Balboa casualties (DESMOND DUGAN)

British YE Wizz Gambier, who swopped her shorts for a
grass skirt on Kwaiawata in the Marshall Bennett Islands
(CHRISTOPHER SAINSBURY)

Chapter Seven

Dateline: Punta Escoces, January–March 1979

The dramatic story of the ill-fated Scottish colonists came vividly alive for the YEs as they helped with the excavation of the site of Fort St Andrew and unearthed a wealth of finds and features that very colourfully illustrated the tragic enterprise and enabled them to visualise with great clarity what life in the settlement must have been like.

They worked under the inspired direction of 23-year-old Cambridge archaeologist Mark Horton, who rapidly established a reputation as one of the great personalities of Operation Drake. Although distantly related to that Grand Old Man of archaeology, Sir Mortimer Wheeler, he actually reminded most people more of Magnus Pyke, as he waved his arms around and enthused wildly about some point of academic interest. His involvement in his subject was so total that virtually nothing could distract him. This was proved in typical and very amusing fashion when he was giving our Chairman, General Sir John Mogg, and a party of visitors a guided tour of his excavations at Acla. A snake suddenly slithered across the path right in front of the General. I reached for my revolver, but was beaten to the draw by Major Eric Aguillera of the Guardia, who, armed with a shotgun, blasted the snake to oblivion. As the sound of gunfire died and the dust cleared and people almost literally began picking themselves up off the ground, Mark could be heard prattling on about his beloved artefacts as if nothing had happened at all.

Mark was recommended to us by Professor John Alexander, head of the Department of Archaeology and Anthropology at Cambridge and one of many top scientists who served on eye surgeon Freddy Rodger's Scientific Sub-Committees as specialist advisers on our various scientific projects. The young Peterhouse postgraduate jumped at the unique opportunity to investigate the site of the Scots colony which, although known, had been largely ignored by archaeologists because of the prohibitive expense of organising a dig in such a remote and inaccessible spot.

[61]

Following the discoveries of our 1976 recce, Mark arrived to find the remains of Fort St Andrew completely overgrown with a coconut plantation and thick impenetrable undergrowth up to ten feet high, so he and his teams of YE helpers started by cutting a swathe four hundred yards long and ten to fifteen yards wide through the middle of the area, followed by a series of parallel swathes cut at right angles to form a rectangular grid. Altogether about half the total interior area of the fort was cleared in this way, and then excavations were made in and around features of particular interest. These included a circular powder house, the well which is known to have been sunk during the siege after the main outside water source came under fire from the Spanish artillery, and a section of the ramparts and bastions where gun positions and the site of a guard room were clearly identifiable.

Vast numbers of artefacts were meticulously logged by the Finds Assistant, an amusing, intelligent American girl named Maria Mabee. Two storage houses near the main entrance to the fort yielded large quantities of green and yellow beads for use in trading with the Indians, bits of pottery were discovered all over the site, while excavations near the three-sided south bastion of the ramparts led to the discovery of a hoard of military relics, including musket balls, a flintlock mechanism, a pike end, knife blades, and a bronze sword hilt. Among some of the other more interesting items that turned up were a Spanish rowel spur, a selection of bronze shoe-buckles and a Scottish coin bearing the crown and thistle and the date 1695.

Also found were some long-stemmed clay pipes with the initials P and G imprinted on them, and these played a vital part in confirming a major triumph for the Joint Services diving team led by Flight Lieutenant Mike Cameron and Corporal Brian Ranner of the RAF. Their project, in which YEs were able to take part after being trained by Robbie Williamson, started disappointingly when the mound which had excited Mel Trafford and myself so much during the earlier recce turned out to be nothing more than a natural feature of the seabed. Anthony Lonsdale, an electronics expert who uses a special metal-detection device called a proton magnetometer to locate wrecks buried under sand, continued to check every square yard of the bay, but got nothing except false alarms. One big register on the magnetometer seemed promising, but turned out to be a barge full of railway lines – a decidedly twentieth-century relic left behind by the same ill-fated Dutch plantation company that built the airstrip.

San Antonio Reef, which was considered to be the most likely location for the *Maurepas*, proved to be devoid of anything exciting, although some sections of worm-eaten oak were found in the area. More timbers were discovered at Pink Point, where the Scots had sited

[62]

a battery of cannon to cover the entrance to the bay, but again there was no sign of a wreck. It began to look suspiciously as though the ship, along with her pieces of eight, had broken up completely or been salvaged by either the Spanish or the French after the colony had been abandoned. There is no doubt that both countries knew of the wreck and the lure of the fabled treasure would have been just as much of an incentive to them as it was to us.

At this point the search was switched to look for the *Olive Branch* – one of two resupply vessels sent out from Scotland, which, having arrived in Caledonia Bay, burned to the waterline and sank, after the ship's cooper accidentally dropped a lighted candle while tapping brandy from the barrels in the hold and caused an instant inferno.

The team made good use of the special diver propulsion unit *Sea Horse* – a one-man torpedo-like underwater tow which enabled them to cover large areas of the seabed without expending excessive air supplies. They concentrated their attention on an area close in to the shore on the eastern side of the bay. This sheltered spot was thought to be where the colony would have had its anchorage. Here, sure enough, Tony Lonsdale soon got readings that indicated something fairly substantial spread over an area roughly thirty-five yards long by nine yards wide and when the divers went down and probed in the mud they made contact with wood and coral concretion.

The site was on a steep mud slope that dropped off the edge of the coral reef. At the shallow end there was live coral at a depth of six feet, while at the other end one could go down twenty-five feet before sinking into thick ooze. Underwater visibility was bad at the best of times and became non-existent once this silt was stirred up. Not quite what one expects in the Caribbean!

The team often had to work in pitch-blackness, using water jets and an air-lift suction pump, as well as shovels and buckets to clear glutinous mud, sand and coral fragments. After some considerable time, a piece of timber was prised out and brought to the surface for close examination by a marine archaeologist, who was able to confirm that it definitely came from an old sailing ship, as it consisted of a sandwich of pine and oak with a layer of felt and tar in between. This method of protecting the hull from certain wood-boring parasites by adding a sacrificial outer casing of pine was a common feature of sixteenth and seventeenth-century European vessels – particularly those bound for tropical waters.

The next sample provoked even more excitement. It was immediately identifiable as a piece of deck planking, and it was badly burned on the underside, while the nail holes were charred right the way through, thus indicating a fire down below of sufficient intensity

[63]

to make the nails glow red hot. We soon realised that we had found a virtually complete ship and the evidence pointed to its being the *Olive Branch* − but it was another three weeks before final, indisputable proof was forthcoming. The breakthrough came when, after much careful probing, the divers uncovered a number of barrels, some of which were still intact. Down on the seabed, they sifted delicately through the silt that clogged the barrels in the hope of finding something of the original contents, while up above, on the *David Gestetner* − the giant inflatable that served as a diving platform − the results of these painstaking labours were awaited with almost breathless anticipation.

The air of tension was further increased by a hair-raising incident that had taken place a few days earlier. One of the divers, Warrant Officer Marc Moody, was down on the bottom, filling a bucket with silt in zero visibility, when there was a tug on the rope and the heavy pail was snatched away. Marc assumed that it had been hauled in by those up top on the platform, but when he surfaced he was puzzled to find that this was not the case. Nobody knew anything about it and there was no sign of the bucket.

The disappearance remained a mystery until, shortly afterwards, the Guardia hauled in the fishing nets they had set nearby, and there, thrashing around in the mesh, was a number of sharks including two man-eaters − a five-foot Mako and a ten-foot Hammerhead. It did not take too much imagination to put two and two together and come up with a chilling possibility as to who or what might have stolen the bucket.

Marc and his colleagues were understandably a little twitchy after that and every time something brushed unexpectedly against them down in the gloomy, pea-soup depths, they nearly jumped out of their wet suits. Even the excitement caused by the discovery of the barrels could not entirely take their minds off the spine-tingling thought of what might be nosing around them as they worked.

Meanwhile, the contents of several barrels were panned out like gold dust and passed up for examination. The first cask yielded a pronged fork and a few slivers of bone which suggested that it might have been part of a consignment of salt pork or beef; the next two were empty, and the fourth was full of nails. It was the fifth that provided the vital clue in the distinctive shape of three clay pipes that were identical to those found at Fort St Andrew − they even carried the same P and G initials, which, it was irreverently suggested, might stand for Porridge Gobbler. It was known that the cargo of the *Olive Branch* included a batch of such pipes, since this was listed on the manifest − which is still in existence − along with Scots bonnets, Bibles, buttons, beads, glass

[64]

drinking-cups, hunting horns, mattocks, looking glasses and pewter jugs.

Great were the celebrations that followed this positive identification. The only disappointment was that lack of time meant that it was impossible to undertake a full excavation. It was estimated that this would require a further six months and so will have to wait for a follow-up expedition in the future.

However, before the team finally packed up and left, it located the ship's rudder, which was fully intact with the shaft and pintles still attached. This discovery made it possible to plot the orientation of the wreck and piece together the sequence of events leading up to her sad end.

The team's underwater photographer, Flight Sergeant Ray Pringle-Scott, told the probable story in his report of the project. 'Everything became clear. When the *Olive Branch* caught fire, she was evidently anchored with her bows into the wind. The blaze started in the after-hold and roared downwind to engulf the stern first.

'As the inferno inched forward against the wind, the ship would have started to settle by the stern, causing all the loose gear and cannon to tumble aft. This would explain the two large magentic readings – one at each end of the site. The bow section would probably still contain the spare anchors and forward cannon, securely lashed down, while the main deck guns, with their breechings burned through, would most likely have rolled aft as she settled. The picture was complete.'

It remained only to photograph all the finds and plot them on the master plan, and then to rebury the exposed timbers so as to conserve them. This very nearly produced a last-minute disaster, when several tons of silt suddenly slid into the main area of excavation and almost engulfed two of the team.

Back on land, the total success of the historical and archaeological projects was nicely rounded off when Mark Horton and his team of YEs unearthed evidence which enabled us to prove beyond a reasonable doubt that the Lost City of Acla had been rediscovered. Acla was built in 1516 by the Spanish Governor of the area, Pedrarias Davilla, and was only the second European township to be established anywhere on the American mainland. It was from there that Vasco Nunez de Balboa, the first European ever to gaze upon the Pacific Ocean, later set out across the isthmus, taking with him the dismantled parts of four ships which were to be reassembled on the other side. It was also the place where Balboa met an unjust end, when political conspiracy resulted in his being publicly executed in the main plaza. Thereafter, Acla was never quite the same again, and although it

[65]

lingered on for some years as a gold-mining and trading community, it seems to have been finally abandoned around 1560.

Over the years, historians have often speculated about the exact location of the site, but although several went and poked about in the general area, no one managed to pinpoint it with any certainty. As it turned out, the wall which I had been shown during the 1976 recce was something of a red herring, but I was not the first to be diverted by it. It was examined in 1953 during the expedition of King Leopold of the Belgians by Dr J. M. Cruxent, who was, however, unable to come to any definite conclusion about either its date of origin or its purpose.

After clearing the area all around the wall and digging a trial trench across the centre of it, Mark Horton decided that it seemed most likely that it was part of the Spanish fort San Fernando de Carolina, which is known to have existed in the area between 1785–93. The only artefact discovered nearby – the base of a glass wine bottle of an eighteenth-century type – was evidence to support this theory.

It was at a spot several hundred yards further inland on the same headland that Mark eventually found the more conclusive evidence he was looking for – pieces of decorated Spanish pottery of a kind known as Isabela Polychrome, which was common in the early part of the sixteenth century, but which has never turned up on any site founded after 1540. This discovery came at the very last moment, only days before the archaeological team was due to pack up and leave, when Jacinto Alemendra of the Panamanian Patrimonio Historico happened to walk into an area of dense bush and spotted a small heap of pottery lying on the ground. Mark immediately concentrated his entire effort on excavating this particular location, which had been ignored up until that moment.

The Isabela Polychrome fragments taken together with other topographical, geographical and historical evidence left little doubt in Mark's mind that the site of Acla had indeed been found, and when he presented his case to experts in Panama and Britain they confirmed this. It was a major archaeological coup, which the Head of Panama's National Institute of Archaeology hailed as an extremely exciting discovery that provided a vital clue to the European settlement of America.

While all this was going on, Major Alan Westcob of the Duke of Wellington's Regiment had arrived to take over from Jeremy Groves, who returned to command a squadron in England. Life settled into a reasonably well-ordered routine at the tented base camp where our little community enjoyed the kind of facilities that, by normal expedition standards, amounted to sheer luxury. The 'mod. cons' included a wooden lavatory that was regarded with considerable pride by its architect, until the downdraught from a Guardia helicopter landing nearby blew the thing down and left some poor devil sitting enthroned in splendid and rather embarrassed isolation. There was also a bar stocked with what was originally thought to be an inexhaustible supply of beer. Someone had managed to get the order wrong – I suspected a deliberate mistake! – and the result was that we found ourselves in possession of a veritable EEC-style beer lake. It was estimated, with a good deal of satisfaction, that even if every individual in the camp consumed eight cans a day we would still be pushed to get through it all before the expedition left Panama. In the event we succeeded in drinking the place dry with six weeks still to go! Exploring can be thirsty work – especially in the hot tropical sun.

Our Scottish members were not slow in reminding us of the need to celebrate Burns Night in such an appropriate place, although the poet was born long after the colony was abandoned. So Ruth Mindel's attentions were turned to the bulk-buying of haggis, and Simon Ames, the friendly head of publicity at British Caledonian Airways, had them flown out to us, complete with a company flag bearing the Lion of Scotland.

None of us will ever forget Burns Night 1979. Our Panamanian friends, led by Billy St Malo, now one of our leading supporters, came in force and the little airstrip was soon crowded with light planes. Lily Dawson, our organiser for Scotland, was there with fifty bottles of J and B, which she had begged from the kind Senor Motta in Panama City. Billy, fearing some of his countrymen might not take to haggis, flew in an enormous paella. Another Scot, James Davidson of Shell in Panama, provided a stock of much-needed insect repellent. Carlos Patterson, a direct descendant of William Paterson, came with his relatives. Senior officers of the Guardia Nacional arrived looking very smart, as did those from the US Forces in the Canal Zone.

The dinner, cooked and supervised by Lily Dawson, Helen Cameron and Kim Batty, was served in the open. It included a haggis, piped in by Robbie Little and addressed by Desmond Dugan, the forester from Argyll, and was rounded off with all the traditional speeches. I myself was nearly lost for words when a Panamanian lady enquired quite seriously when Mr Burns would be putting in an appearance. 'It is his birthday party isn't it?' she asked.

Whether it was the haggis, the J and B, the Highland dancing or the tropical night is not certain, but by three o'clock in the morning the company was beginning to show signs of exhaustion, although there were still a few hardy souls sitting with their backs against the palm trees watching the sunrise when Alan Westcob's yells of 'Wakey, wakey' roused the revellers from their hammocks. I wonder what the ghosts of the settlers thought. Somehow I feel they would have approved.

But it would be wrong to emphasise such home-from-home comforts, which were but small compensation for a tremendous amount of hard work and a lot of real discomfort. The phase two YEs arrived in mid-January and were straightaway sent out to acclimatise on a series of seven-day jungle courses, which basically involved being despatched into the forest with no food and very little water.

Capital Radio's David Briggs, game as ever after a brief holiday in the West Indies to recuperate after his Atlantic crossing on *Eye of the Wind*, volunteered to join one of the first groups – a gesture he was soon to regret. Poor David's jungle debut was a far from pleasant experience which landed him in hospital and left nobody in any doubt about the toughness of the challenges which Operation Drake was providing for the youngsters taking part.

There is a set of before and after photographs of David which says more about the way he suffered than a thousand words of description. He presented himself on the morning of departure looking like Stewart Grainger in one of his big-white-hunter film roles. The rakish angle of the bush hat, the stylish improvisation of the towelling cravat, the buccaneering look of the well-holstered machete, the devil-may-care smile – it all added up to a picture so dashing that the photographer did not hesitate to capture it for posterity.

As it happened, David was not feeling quite as confident as he appeared. Before setting off, he had asked the Guardia escort who was to accompany his group whether, in his opinion, he was sufficiently well prepared for the venture. The man looked him up and down, grimaced and inquired whether he had thought about snakes. David assured him that he had thought a great deal about snakes. It was then suggested that one fool-proof method of making sure that one was not bothered by snakes was to put some garlic inside one's boots. Like most people, David had started off by treading very carefully in the jungle, being convinced that something deadly lurked under every leaf, and although by this time he had gained considerable confidence when it came to the well-worn forest paths, he was still a trifle apprehensive about the horrors that might be slithering about off the beaten track, so he took the advice to heart and stuffed his socks with several cloves.

A torrential tropical downpour ensured that the party, which was led by Captain Christopher Lawrence and included five YEs and two members of the Operation Drake film team as well as David, were soaked to the skin before they had gone more than two hundred yards. The first day's march ended at around 3.00 p.m. As David was having

[68]

the greatest difficulty in getting his hammock rigged securely, the others left him to get on with it while they went off in search of food to supplement the somewhat scrawny owl that had been blasted into oblivion from almost point-blank range on the way up. Their parting request to him to have a camp fire going in readiness for their return proved easier said than done, and when they trooped back dismally an hour-and-a-half later clutching five small fish, he had only just succeeded in setting light to the damp twigs he had gathered, despite the aid of a gas cigarette lighter. His humour was not improved when he took his boots off before retiring for the night only to find that the garlic had cut his feet to ribbons.

It was on the second night that they began to be obsessed by food – or rather the lack of it. The hunting party returned to camp with a few more minnows and some roots that tasted vaguely like potato, a combination that turned out to be less than totally appetising, and he spent the rest of the evening reminiscing about his favourite London restaurants.

A further disappointment awaited him when he went to turn in. Having despaired of ever getting his hammock set up properly, he had decided to experiment instead with a tent arrangement made from a groundsheet, with his sleeping bag resting on a mattress of leaves. The completed construction was so inviting that it made him sleepy just to look at it, but unfortunately, while he was eating his meagre supper and fantasising about a slap-up meal in the Savoy Grill, giant ants had munched through his leaf mattress and left him with nothing to cushion himself against the hard ground.

Meanwhile, a much more serious problem had developed. What he had dismissed on the first day as a heat rash on his arms and face had already got much worse, and by the next morning it had turned into a mass of very unsightly blisters. At the same time, his lacerated feet were raw and festering. By the end of the third day, he was only too ready to give up and go back to camp with the film team, that had all the footage it needed by then.

By the time he limped out of the jungle he was a very sorry sight, and the photographer who had recorded his departure could hardly believe it was the same person he had watched striding out so confidently. He insisted on taking some shots of the grim-faced, bedraggled figure, before David was led off to see the medics. Their diagnosis of his rash as Kissing Bug Disease seemed to add insult to injury. Later, in hospital in Panama City, it was established that he was actually suffering a form of jungle eczema, but by then it was too late to save his dignity. The original diagnosis had already been greeted with great hilarity by his colleagues at Capital Radio, not to mention a few

[69]

million listeners. Six months later, David still had the scars to prove that it really was not that funny.

We encountered another amusing problem when the representatives of a Swedish magazine arrived to do a major photo-feature on Operation Drake. They came down from New York, after first contacting me to get permission for a series of articles. Although I had never heard of their publication, I was impressed by the circulation figures they quoted and I had no hesitation in giving them the go-ahead for what seemed like some useful publicity.

They duly turned up at Caledonia Bay and were obviously decent chaps. But no sooner had they trotted off to start work on their pictures and interviews than I was notified that they were involved in an angry scene down on the beach.

I immediately raced down to find out what all the fuss was about and ran into our female marine archaeologist, fuming with indignation. Was I aware, she demanded furiously, that the publication for which these two men worked was a hard-core girlie magazine? And would I care to make it absolutely clear that no way was she going to pose for pictures clutching her artefacts!

When I inquired innocently whether she meant it was like *Playboy*, she snorted that it was far worse than that – it made *Playboy* look like a parish newsletter. Even the photographer himself admitted that his wife would not have it in the house because it was so risqué – but he added that the Operation Drake article would be absolutely serious and above board. In the end, I managed to smooth things over and they were able to get the material they needed.

It was not until some months later that I was sent the published articles. They were spread over four issues and were done very well – intelligently written and beautifully illustrated. But as for the rest of the contents! They left nothing to the imagination.

A slightly more delicate problem was posed by the fact that relations between the local Cuna Indians and the Guardia have been strained ever since the Indian uprising of 1913, during which there were some very bloody clashes. The simmering hostility between the local villagers in the Caledonia Bay area, who were fascinated by what we were doing and often came into the camp, and the forty officers and men of the Guardia, who had been assigned to us as an escort force, was often in in evidence, and at one point it came uncomfortably near to boiling over into an incident.

It all started when the Cuna complained that we had accidentally destroyed or damaged some of their banana plants and coconut trees. It was not a serious matter and was quickly sorted out when we agreed a very generous compensation tariff for that and any future damage. The difficulty came when one farmer tried to trick us and put in a claim for trees that had not been touched by any of our people – and the Guardia caught him out.

They exacted a subtle and telling punishment. The farmer was made to sit and watch while his chief, who had come with him to make the complaint, was forced to do all their washing up and to clean out their camp. The chief was seething with such a fury when they eventually let him go that he jumped into his canoe and paddled off, leaving the farmer to sit pathetically on the edge of the camp for two days before someone was sent to pick him up.

This certainly ensured that we had no further phoney claims from then on – but it did nothing to foster a spirit of brotherhood and good will between the Cuna and the Guardia, and this reflected badly on us by undermining our friendship with the Indians. Clearly some gesture of reconciliation was necessary, and after some deliberation we decided to hold a Grand Sports Festival to which everyone in the area would be invited. The various events were carefully chosen to ensure victory for all. The Guardia, for instance, spent their entire time playing volley ball, so this was included for their benefit and they duly wiped the floor with the rest of us. On the other hand, there was never the slightest doubt that the Cuna would win the canoeing races by a mile. And for Operation Drake? What else but bowls! At the end of it all, everybody seemed to be on speaking terms again, although whether this was due to the athletics or the drinking and dancing that went on afterwards until late into the night is a matter for debate.

Chapter Eight

Dateline: Walkway Camp, Panama, 8 February 1979

Claire Bertschinger was in a classic predicament. Marooned on a slippery branch more than 120 feet up in the forest canopy, she could move neither up nor down. In fact, she hardly dared breathe in case she lost her precarious balance. And yet, crawling purposefully towards her on a neighbouring branch was a particularly poisonous-looking snake. Claire did what most people would do in similar circumstances – she burst into tears.

It was the only time during her two spells with Operation Drake that Claire, a slightly built 23-year-old nurse from Hertfordshire, made any kind of concession to female frailty, despite constantly putting herself in situations where she could expect the going to be especially tough. She joined us after writing to me out of the blue to say that she had always wanted to go on an expedition and hoped that I might be able to advise her on how to go about getting involved in one. When I wrote back telling her about Operation Drake and offering her the position of Field Nurse in Panama, she leapt at the opportunity and without hesitation set about raising the money she needed to finance herself. She not only found sponsors for herself but also saved money by such personal economies as walking and cycling everywhere instead of taking tubes and buses. Then she got leave of absence from her job in a London hospital, sacrificing certain promotion in the process, and came out to fulfil her adventurous ambitions.

She arrived at Caledonia Bay with one of the advance parties and plunged willingly into the back-breaking tasks of clearing the airstrip and setting up camp, as well as tending the medical emergencies, which ranged from extracting sea urchin spines to dealing with the regular cuts inflicted by razor-sharp machetes. Then, when work started on the aerial walkway, she soon had to answer a radio SOS to go up there and tend to some minor injuries resulting from an accident with a block and tackle, and rather than have her repeatedly undertaking the exhausting four-hour march to the site every time anything happened, it was decided to station her there permanently.

[72]

This suited her well and she was happy to help with the construction work in between treating any casualties. At first she was asked to do no more than fetch and carry tools and materials, and send them up in the hoist to where Sapper Sergeant Mike Christy and his team were operating in the treetops. The only danger in that came from the nuts, bolts, screwdrivers and other bits of ironmongery that regularly rained down from above, burying themselves several inches deep in the ground with a dull thud. But most of the team had to leave after the first two spans had been completed and Claire was the only person available to go aloft and help Mike Christy with the third and final section.

Claire takes up the story in one of her long letters home, which incidentally must have had her poor parents wondering whatever she had let herself in for. 'Mike asked me if I was prepared to help him fix the block for the main rope 120 feet up. "It's a bit difficult and not too safe as you have to balance on the branches up there," he said. "But, of course, you don't have to help if you're too scared." That did it – I agreed to help.

'The tree had been pitoned with steel pegs and we had a hoist system working. Mike went up first, pulling on his own weight. When he reached the top, I clipped on to the hoist and he started hauling me up. Up and up I went, through branches full of leaves, past the hornets' nest and up among the dangling vines.

'At last I made it, and I wedged myself into the angle of a large branch and clipped on to a flimsy safety line. I then prepared to take the strain of the block and rope and other tools, while Mike worked well above my head. After about one and a half hours we finished that initial part of the job, and Mike went down to the ground on the hoist while I clung to the tree.

'Then it was my turn and I clipped myself on to the hoist and was lowered down slowly. Suddenly, when I was about twenty-five feet from the ground, the rope jammed and I was left dangling. A knot must have formed and jammed the block up above. There was nothing for it but to go up again, so up I went. At the top I had to get my weight off the rope and half-kneel, half-sit on a bough. As I grabbed for a stray line, my hold on the hoist relaxed and the rope whistled through my hand, out of control. It then jammed and jumped out of the block above my head.

'Below me on the ground the sparks were flying and they wanted to know why I let go of the rope and if I intended to stay up in the tree for the rest of the day! My eyes filled with tears, my vision blurred and I began to shake with fear. There I was, 120 feet up and perched on a wet slippery branch with no means of getting down. What's more, the ants were crawling all over me – and the flies and spiders as well – and

[73]

I couldn't even scratch myself for fear of falling.

'The air down below was still blue but I knew Mike would do something. So, for the third time that day he climbed 120 feet up the tree, pulling up his own weight on a rope which was jammed and could slip at any moment! He finally reached the top safely and set about freeing the hoist. I didn't dare look and tried to concentrate on the view. I saw the river far down below, blue and orange birds were flying nearby, woodpeckers and humming birds ... and a snake was crawling along the branch next to mine. A snake! Up there at 120 feet!

'I tried to shift my position and found that my feet had gone to sleep. I also kept a wary eye out for other creepy-crawlies. I heard a tree crashing down in the distance and became more aware that my tree was swaying from side to side in the breeze. My mouth was dry and I was dripping with sweat.

'By now Mike was on his way down again at last, but fifteen feet from the ground he lost his grip and fell, the rope tearing through his hands and burning them painfully. When he had recovered, he called out that he was ready. I clipped on to the hoist again and launched myself into space only to drop five feet before the rope and harness took the strain! Then I went down, spiralling all the time, until my feet touched the ground. It never felt so good, although my legs were shaking for some time afterwards.'

However, in typical Bertschinger fashion, she was up in the treetops again that very afternoon getting on with the job.

The aerial walkway projects were devised by Dr Stephen Sutton of Leeds University and Andrew Mitchell. Both these scientists had personally suffered the frustration of not being able to carry their researches up into the forest canopy where, scientifically speaking, it all happens. Stephen's investigations into the vertical zonation of insects in Zaire and Andrew's study of primates in Borneo had impressed on both men the need to overcome the inaccessibility of the treetops if one really wanted to find out the secrets of the jungle's complicated eco-system. And in a world in which the mighty rain forests are being carelessly destroyed at the alarming rate of fifty acres per minute, the search for such knowledge is seen as an increasingly urgent priority. The vital factor is that once the jungle has been cut down, it never grows up quite the same again, and since the rain forests provide much of the world's oxygen and a large proportion of our total fresh water supplies, there is good reason to suppose that the casual removal of such an important element in the grand global scheme of things could produce a great environmental catastrophe. We have to find out the facts before it is too late.

Quite apart from these wider considerations, the walkway project had tremendous scientific validity in that it provided botanists, ornithologists, entomologists, and specialists in almost every branch of natural science with a unique opportunity for original research amid what the nineteenth-century explorer Henry Bates described as 'an uproar of life'. Nowhere else on Earth can one expect to find such a dazzling variety of animals, insects and plants as exists in virgin jungle. In any one acre there are likely to be three hundred different species of tree compared with a mere twenty-five in an equivalent area of British woodland while a sample zone of three hundred square miles will contain anything up to six hundred different types of birds – well over ten times the British average. There was the added bonus that the project could be repeated in three separate jungle regions: Panama, PNG and Indonesia – thereby making possible an unprecedented comparative study.

From Operation Drake's point of view, the project fitted in perfectly with our other aims. The actual construction of the walkways would present our Sappers with a truly original challenge, whilst the jungle environment would serve as an ideal proving ground for YEs in search of some real adventure and a chance to test their initiative and their powers of physical fitness and endurance.

Most of the materials for the basic construction had been provided by a British company, Package Control Ltd, one of whose executives, Mike Tindall, is an enthusiastic member of SES. The actual building of the walkways involved first stringing lengths of tensioned polypropelene rope between the two trees chosen as the anchor posts for each span of 150 feet. A framework of Dexion angled metal strips, provided by a kind Panamanian company, would then be assembled on the ground before being taken up and suspended from the ropes by webbing straps. Finally, a flooring of expanded metal mesh sixteen inches wide would be bolted on. At its lowest point the resulting structure would sway some seventy-five feet above the ground, while the observation platforms erected in the trees between the spans were a dizzying 130 feet high.

The Sappers carried out a dummy run in the pine woods of Minley Manor, near Camberley, to make sure it would work and came back confidently forecasting that the job would only take a few days. But when they got to Panama, they soon found that it was not quite that straightforward.

The location of a suitable site was the first problem. What we needed was primary forest that had been standing untouched for hundreds of years – secondary forest that had been interfered with by Man was no good. At Caledonia Bay all the immediately surrounding jungle had been severely damaged by the activities of the Indians and it was not

[75]

until we climbed what we christened Heartbreak Hill and ventured into the interior that we discovered a suitable spot on the banks of the Turdi River. This was a good four-hour march away from Alan Westcob's base camp and involved hacking, scrambling and wading through some very tough terrain, so that moving in all the equipment became a major consideration. We were fortunate, in the end, to have the use of a Guardia helicopter which could fly in the gear.

Even then, there were still difficulties. Selecting the specific trees between which to suspend the walkway proved far easier said than done. One had to satisfy the twin requirements of the Sappers and the scientists, and these tended not to coincide. No sooner had the scientists picked a perfect spot where the trees were in flower and everything was ideally suited to their needs than the Sappers would have to rule it out on the grounds of impracticability. A common snag was that many of the trees were simply unclimbable, so that not even Mike Christy, with his monkey-like agility, could get up them to fix the initial ropes. Some of them were so hard that when one tried to hammer a steel piton into them, it would bend, and even if one did succeed in bashing it in, the tree would squeeze it out again within a very short space of time.

However, we eventually succeeded and sorted out a prime section of forest where three spans were completed which stretched through a perfect 420-feet cross-section of the upper canopy. For the scientists it proved to be every bit as exciting as we had hoped. Sitting in his 130-feet vantage point on the observation platforms, ornithologist Peter Hudson, from the Edward Grey Institute of Field Ornithology, looked out over the treetops and was thrilled to record twenty times more species than at ground level. Oxford University botanist Andrew Sugden was able to study at very close quarters plants that would otherwise have been maddeningly out of reach. Entomologists Willie Wint from Oxford and Caroline Ash from Leeds were able to carry out a comprehensive investigation into the vertical zonation of insects which would otherwise have been impossible. The light traps set at higher levels also attracted some interesting bats.

The combined observations in Panama, PNG and Sulawesi, especially those bearing on the process of pollination and the respective roles played by birds, bats and insects, will eventually make an important contribution towards solving some of the mysteries of life at the top in the rain forest. So much was achieved at the three separate walkway sites that Stephen Sutton, who had overall responsibility for the projects, estimates that it will take him six years to sort through all the various observations, specimens, analyses and so on before he is in a position to make a final report.

The scientists were greatly helped in their work by the YEs, who very soon discovered that even the most mundane tasks of observation became fascinating when conducted in such exotic surroundings. To sit on the walkway for a few hours, swaying in the warm breezes while surrounded by all manner of weird and wonderful creatures, turned out to be a marvellously relaxing experience, and such chores as keeping watch on one particular bloom, and noting down details of every insect that visited it during the entire day, could actually become quite enthralling.

English YE Hazel Preston spent many happy hours on the 'Brownea watch' − the tree whose spectacular pink flowers last just one day and are a favourite with the Long-Tailed Hermit hummingbirds. In her diary she wrote: 'You would sit down fifteen feet or so from the tree with binoculars and a notebook and the routine was that every fifteen minutes you would count the number of bees and insects on the flower. Every hour you would count the petal fall, and when the hummingbird came to feed, you would record the time of the visit, the number of feeds (i.e. the number of times the bird dipped its beak into the flower), and the number of calls it made. Earlier in the morning a note would already have been made of the number of the tree, the height of the flower and its position on the branch.

'It was very peaceful sitting among the trees with the sun coming through the leaves − though not quite so good if it rained. Sometimes you could sit for hours without a hummingbird visit and then have several visits close together. Before you saw them you would hear their wings making a sort of purring sound in the air.

'There were always lizards, frogs, toads, spiders and birds to be seen darting around and the birds included brightly-coloured kingfishers, macaws and toucans. At a bend downriver there was a tree hung with the long nests of oropendola birds; the nests looked like long woven bags in the shape of a droplet. The birds were black with brilliant yellow markings and they made a call rather like running water. There were also a lot of large blue Morpho butterflies and enormous flying beetles which made a loud whirring noise as they zoomed past. You would often see wasps' nests in the trees, looking like lumps of clay, and also ants' nests and one of the commonest and most amazing sights was a colony of leaf-cutter ants at work in an endless chain of fetching and carrying.'

Everyday life at the walkway camp was considerably less comfortable than at the Caledonia Bay base camp, but many of the YEs preferred it. It was a fairly idyllic setting beside the cool, crystal-clear river and there was an away-from-it-all atmosphere; these two things more than compensated for such irritations as mosquitoes, sandflies and the all-pervading damp. After a week or two of getting up each

[77]

morning and climbing into wet clothes the seasoned jungle camper ceases to be bothered by it – even when shirts and socks start sprouting vegetation! It rained a great deal, usually at night, and, as most people were sleeping out in the open in hammocks slung between the trees, this led to many a rude awakening. Those who did not rig their waterproof ponchos or groundsheets in exactly the right manner to form a roof that would withstand the tropical downpours were likely to turn over in the early hours of the morning to find themselves squelching in four inches of water. Even worse was when a puddle would gradually build up in the roof until this either split or gave way, depositing a couple of gallons of water in the face of the sleeping occupant who would let out a shrill cry of shocked surprise.

Nevertheless it was an attractive and interesting place to visit. Those who came included General Sir John Mogg, who managed the arduous approach march with little difficulty in spite of an arthritic hip. The General wore the jungle green uniform in which he had commanded the Commonwealth Brigade in Malaya many years before, but his faithful boots collapsed at the camp and he gave them to Scottish YE policeman John Wiggins, who said he would boil them up if food ran out. The General was hoisted up into the treetops and to our delight inspected the walkway. It was a pretty remarkable achievement and left everyone impressed by the toughness of British generals. Oliver Pritchett of the *Sunday Telegraph*, who also ascended the walkway, wrote a most amusing article about the visit.

Of all the VIPs, pressmen and other guests who went up to visit the walkway, the person who made the greatest impression on everyone who saw her there was handicapped Canadian YE Anna Richards. Anna, a beautiful 23-year-old blonde from Edmonton who, tragically, had to have a leg amputated to stop the spread of bone cancer, was one of two disabled people who joined Operation Drake in Panama, the other being Paul Hanson, from the Hydon Hill Cheshire Home, who is confined to a wheelchair. Anna's determination to make the journey from Caledonia Bay to the walkway, as far as possible under her own steam, was an example to everybody. Her guts, her uncomplaining good humour and her refusal to let her disability restrict her any more than absolutely necessary were never more in evidence, as she struggled on with a smile on her face, despite being, at times during the trip, inwardly near to tears with pain and exhaustion. It was a humbling experience for those who were with her that day and watched her meet and beat her own personal challenge.

That other game girl, Claire Bertschinger, made a dramatic exit from the walkway camp after collapsing suddenly with a raging fever. She had to be stretchered out, no mean feat in view of the rough terrain, and then flown to Panama City's Gorgas Hospital, where she spent a fortnight undergoing endless tests as the doctors tried to establish what was wrong with her. It was a month altogether before she was declared fully fit, and as soon as she was given the all-clear there was no stopping her from heading straight back to the walkway. And a few days later she did not hesitate to join me and a dozen others on a tough ten-day trip to the legendary gold mines of Cana. These mines, situated in a remote valley close to the Colombian border, were known as far back as the seventeenth century as the richest in the whole of Latin America, and it was not until 1928 that the fabulous seams finally petered out and the workings were abandoned.

The Cana patrol sailed to Colon in *Eye of the Wind* and then motored down in two ex-US Army trucks to Yaviza, the last outpost before the Darien jungle. The trucks, driven and owned by two friendly Americans from the canal company, were ideal vehicles. Our 180-mile journey along the rutted logging trail that passes for the great Pan American Highway at this point took us eight hours, and as we bumped and rattled along at a steady twenty to thirty miles per hour, I could not help smiling at the memory of how, just six years before, it had taken me ten weeks with the British Trans-Americas Expedition to blaze a trail through this very area.

At Yaviza we bedded down on the bare wooden floor of a small room above the local police station where the first things we saw on wakening in the morning were the giant cockroaches scuttling away into the corners. Then we all piled rather gingerly into a thirty-foot-long piragua for the trip up to Boca de Cupe. The narrow dug-out leaked and we constantly had to climb out into the water and push it off mudbanks, and it was getting very dark when we reached our destination at 8.30 p.m. that night.

Amongst the crowd of people who pressed down the steep bank of the river to see us arrive was a man I knew, who had been transported from his jungle home to take part in the 'This is Your Life' programme when I had been 'captured' by Thames TV in 1976. His curly hair turning grey and his boney old frame creaking with arthritics, he hobbled up and pumped my hand.

'Ah hear you was back,' he grinned.

'Charlie, I need somewhere for us to sleep, eight good men to act as carriers tomorrow, a guide to show me the trail to Cana and somewhere to buy you a beer.'

Within an hour all was fixed and we enjoyed a cool beer from the last fridge in Panama.

We had an old two-storey shack to sleep in − once again it was infested with cockroaches − and then, at seven o'clock the next morning we began the two-day march to the mines. It was very hot and sticky, and we rested ten minutes in every hour, but, even so, by midday our Canadian doctor was having trouble with his legs, which were sore and swollen. He could not go on, so it was decided to leave him by the river with two companions until we returned four days later. We marched until five o'clock in the evening, before pitching camp and eating our meagre rations.

Barclays Bank YE Michael Wright was in the Royal Marine Volunteer Reserve, so I really let him run the patrol. This he did with great skill, and we were just settling down on the second night of the march when all hell broke loose. The carriers started screaming and I assumed we were being attacked by smugglers (common in this border region) or wild pigs. Whatever, the best remedy might be a sharp shock, so I grabbed my .357 Smith and Wesson and blasted two shots into the night sky. As the deafening roar died away there was complete silence! No smugglers, no pigs. Apparently one of the carriers, sleeping between two others, had suffered a nightmare. He had thrown out his arms on either side and grabbed whatever his hands touched. The result had proved both surprising and extremely painful for his colleagues whose screams had started the row.

Claire noted in her letter home: 'We left early the next morning in our wet clothes − wet from the day before, and the day before that and the day before that. Trudge, trudge, trudge. The ground got steeper and steeper and it got hotter and hotter and then we heard that one of the party at the rear had collapsed. I walked and ran a mile back to revive him from heat exhaustion and then, as we moved on to catch up with the others, we found some bananas and we grabbed them and ate them like wild animals!

'Then on and on we went and it got steeper and started to rain and we crossed many rivers and the track died out and we had to blaze our way again. Higher and higher we climbed, our legs aching, our feet on fire and our tummies rumbling. The sweat poured down us, soaking our clothes. What with the stale sweat, the mud and the dirt, we smelled like sour milk − but at least we were all the same. Suddenly, high up in the mountains, we came into a clearing where the sun was pouring down and in front of us, across a small valley, were some tin-roofed shacks − Cana, at last.

'To me it seemed like Shangri-La. We soon covered the last few hundred yards to the shacks and found that one was a kind of dormitory with wooden slatted beds and we all settled in. Next to my bed was a wooden box that I kept tripping over. It seemed to be full of something and when I opened the lid I found it crammed with long, cigar-shaped objects wrapped in brown paper. GELIGNITE!! You

[80]

never saw a building empty so quickly. J.B.-S. said it was in a dangerous state (dated 1926) and very carefully it was carried far, far away. We then ate a meal of our dried rations and fell asleep exhausted.'

When we had staggered into the camp we were amazed to see neon lighting and enamel basins. Clearly the mine had been in use since 1928 – and when our Guardia escort, Moran, discovered some warm horse dung on a disused airstrip, it indicated what may have been a hasty departure of some illegal miners.

Having put my foot down a hole, I really did stagger into the camp and was extremely grateful for Claire's good nursing which reduced the sprain sufficiently for me to march back thirty-five miles to Boca de Cupe two days later.

There was still some little way to go before the actual mine shafts, and when we eventually discovered the two gaping, overgrown tunnel entrances, it did not need the fer de lance hissing a warning from the gloom just inside to discourage any more attempts to explore further into the uninviting depths. The risk of a collapse at any moment was far too great, but I made a note that it might be worth considering a full-scale operation at some date in the future which might attempt to reopen the mines.

There were plenty of interesting relics lying about, including machinery, a wooden horse-drawn gold wagon and a quantity of porcelain beer bottles. The YEs tried panning for gold in the nearby river – and actually had some success. Not that any of them were going to be able to retire on the proceeds, but it was an indication of just how rich the mine once was. Pausing only to help each other remove the loathsome ticks which stick to one's body like minute limpets and have to be burned off, we set out to retrace our weary footsteps back to relative civilisation.

At around the same time that I was leading the Cana recce, zoologist Nick Lindsay set off with a small group on a week-long trip to the Cloud Forest. This is situated high on the slopes of the continental divide separating the Atlantic from the Pacific and gets its name from the short, moss-covered trees that result from the cool but humid mountain environment.

Nick, who works with Gerald Durrell's Jersey Wildlife Preservation Trust, was in Panama principally to make a study of Geoffrey's Tamarin – a small Marmoset which is fairly common in the jungles of Darien. He managed to study several groups in their wild state and gathered information which will assist in the breeding programmes of related rare species at the Jersey Zoo. He returned from the Cloud Forest trip with an impressive collection of snakes, earthworms, lizards, frogs and toads, as well as plants and mosses.

While all this was going on, a medical team under Dr Nigel Pearce was carrying out a comprehensive health survey among the Cuna children of the island of Mulatupo. This involved a general examination and also a series of eight special tests aimed at pinpointing everything from Vitamin A deficiency to worms. This was not quite as simple as one might suppose.

Dr Pearce approached the project with caution. First he had to get the approval of the leaders of the 2,000-strong community and this required considerable diplomacy. Once permission had been granted, he had to win the people's confidence and in order to do this he organised a big party, complete with sing-along and games, which seemed to do the trick, because the next day the mothers started arriving with their children at the little medical centre that had been set up.

The first major problem came with the blood tests. This was initially done by finger pricks, but the kids screamed so much at this that there was a danger of everyone being frightened away, and a different method had to be introduced. The Vitamin A test was fine since this involved putting on a special mask which was used to measure the patient's ability to see in the dark – the level of one's night vision indicates one's Vitamin A reserves – and this was considered great fun.

The real difficulties arose with the sugar absorption test, a completely new method of discerning various blood, urinary and intestinal diseases which had never been used in the field before. It seemed simple enough. The children were given a special drink and five hours later had to provide a urine sample. The trouble was that five hours is a long time and a lot of the children tended to wander off and forget all about the bottle they were supposed to urinate into. Those who remembered too late would often get their friends to top up their bottle for them.

In order to combat this, the YEs had to keep the children entertained for the whole five hours, so that they would stay around the medical centre until it was time to give their samples. Sing-songs and dances were organised – colouring books were even imported in an effort to amuse them. It seemed to work and a vast number of samples were eventually despatched to eleven medical departments in Britain and France for analysis. The work was part of a comparative project examining malnutrition and resistance to disease in Panama, PNG and Sulawesi.

As for the health of the expedition members themselves, this was reasonably good. A few, like Claire Bertschinger and David Briggs, had to be evacuated with fevers and heat-stroke, while skin infections were common, aggravated by the bites of the sandflies which were everywhere, and which are so small that they can penetrate even a mosquito net.

There was just one real emergency – and that was a frighteningly dramatic affair. It happened along the notorious Balboa Trail ...

Chapter Nine

It was a ragged bunch of individuals who staggered from the jungle, blinking like moles as they emerged into the glaring sunlight after twenty long days in the shadowy depths of the forest. Their clothes were torn, grimy and sweat-stained, their bodies were a mass of cuts, sores and festering insect bites, and they were hollow-eyed with exhaustion. But as they stumbled out thankfully into the open they seemed almost delirious with excitement. They had made it. Their commander, George Thurstan, called for one last effort. Spurning the offer of transport for the last couple of miles into Santa Fe, at the end of an epic 130-mile trek, he gave the order to 'Form a rabble!' and, led by Cathy Davies – the amazing seventeen-year-old Scottish YE sponsored by Prince Charles – they jog-trotted along the hot, dusty road into town. It was an impressively defiant finish to one of the most arduous of all Operation Drake's adventures.

There were twenty-two people in the party that set out from Acla on 25 February aiming to follow the route of the long-vanished, 450-year-old Balboa Trail across the Panama Isthmus. Four of them never reached the other side. They collapsed under the combined strain of prolonged discomfort, fatigue and dehydration and had to be air-lifted out in a life-or-death emergency rescue mission which led to some highly dramatic and extremely anxious moments and provided the expedition with its first taste of real danger.

The idea of trying to follow in the early sixteenth-century footsteps of Balboa had not featured among our original plans for the Panama phase and did not come up until the last moment, when we were desperately looking for something to replace the Membrillo River project. This involved locating and studying the dreaded Buffalo Gnat – an insect so unpleasant that even the local Indians have surrendered and moved out of the area on the Membrillo River where it is most commonly found. Owing to circumstances beyond our control, the project had to be cancelled at a late date which left us just seven days to set up an alternative. After poring over an old historical map of

[84]

Panama for some hours, George and the Phase Leader, Major Alan Westcob, hit upon the notion of the Balboa Patrol.

The Guardia Nacional were not at all keen on it. Their first reaction was to rule it out, and this was quite understandable since their main concern was to make sure that nothing too awful happened to us while we were in the country, and there was not the slightest doubt that what was being contemplated here was very risky. Previous attempts had ended in disaster − particularly a nineteenth-century international expedition during which several men lost their lives. The last thing the Guardia needed was a repeat of that kind of tragedy.

The Guardia only reluctantly agreed to let us go ahead when we pointed out that we were not about to take any silly chances and that, anyway, there were factors involved that reduced the hazards considerably. For one thing, we would be going in the dry season, when conditions were not nearly as difficult as they might be when the rains had swollen the rivers into raging torrents. Apart from that, we had a very good back-up organisation in the event that something did go badly wrong. The Guardia's Major Eric Aguillera shrugged his shoulders somewhat dubiously and immediately showed how seriously he was taking it by flying in some of his very top men to advise us. These included the Commanding Officer of their equivalent of the SAS, the Commandant of their Recruit Training School and their most senior signals officer.

George Thurstan had no illusions about what he was letting himself in for. Even in the dry season, with a back-up force of helicopters and with the latest and most sophisticated communications systems, it was still going to be very tough − much tougher, strangely, than it would have been for Balboa back in 1513. Not only did the Spaniard have five hundred bearers and guides to ease his progress, but it is also a fact that the Panamanian jungle was far less impenetrable in those days than it is now. There were many more Indians living in the interior at that time, more villages and a lot more well-worn trails. Later the Cuna and the Choco fought each other and the Cuna withdrew to the coastal areas, leaving the forest to close in again. We knew that our patrol could expect to be hacking its way through dense undergrowth for much of the time and they would probably go for days on end without seeing another living soul.

Despite this, George had no real reservations about going through with it. After all, Prince Charles himself had talked about 'the challenges of war in a peacetime situation', and George, in particular, felt very strongly that this was precisely what the YEs were looking for. He believed that we should not be afraid to spice the adventures we set up for them with an element of real danger. This attitude was typical of a man who, as a tough, no-nonsense, ex-Marine Commando, delights in driving himself to the very limits. But he was dead right. The most common complaint about Operation Drake from the YEs was that we did not make things hard enough for them a lot of the time. Nobody who was on the Balboa Patrol made any protests on that score!

George picked his team very carefully. Everybody had to pass a rigorous medical test in which everything was checked from their teeth to their blood pressures. Several people were turned down because they were not fit. The final party was made up of twelve YEs – including three girls – plus five Guardia, film cameraman Rik Gustavsen, radio operator Sergeant Alex Gill of the Scots Guards, photographer and diarist Desmond Dugan, a Choco guide, and a hunter with the delightful name of Jesus Zuleta. They travelled as light as possible, carrying with them clothing, rations and medical equipment that had been pared down to the minimum safety requirements.

With everyone fresh and in high spirits, the first day's march had the easy-going atmosphere of a Sunday afternoon nature ramble, even though they were forced almost immediately to leave the beaten track and push into the thick of the forest. They had time to study with interest some tapir tracks and to observe from a safe distance a pit viper which Guardia Sergeant Juan Diaz spotted and pointed out as one of Panama's deadliest snakes.

Mid-afternoon is the time when one starts looking for a suitable camp site on this sort of trek and at about 3.00 p.m. they found an ideal spot near a small stream. After a meal of dehydrated rations, everyone was in a relaxed mood and the camp fire gossip continued late into the evening. Jesus Zuleta, meanwhile, disappeared quietly with his ancient shotgun and returned some time later with two large rodents called agouti.

Throughout the trip, Jesus was to prove an efficient hunter who kept the pot well stocked with jungle turkey, pig, the occasional monkey and even snake. There is a lot of meat on a six-foot python – and it is surprisingly tasty. It was interesting to watch how people gradually changed their attitudes towards living off the land in this way. Some of them found difficulty at first in eating an animal that had been slaughtered and butchered before their very eyes. The next stage was that common-or-garden turkey was all right, but pretty little monkeys or exotic and beautiful parrots and toucans were not fair game. However, it was not too long before hunger began to remove all hang-ups.

On the second day, the patrol started walking in a small river. Although it was not very comfortable to splosh along in the water for

[86]

long periods, and despite the fact that they had to concentrate hard to avoid slipping and stumbling on the uneven bed of the river, it was still far easier than having to hack their way through the heavy, tangled undergrowth.

The next few days were largely uneventful. Heads went down as the novelty wore off and the pace hotted up, and the cumulative effect of long hard spells on the march in testing conditions began to sap reserves of energy. People flopped exhausted into their hammocks in the evenings and the camp fire chat sessions grew shorter and shorter.

The unavoidable minor irritations also began to set in − the sweat rashes and insect bites, the blisters and the scratches that refused to heal in the tropical humidity. Young Scots Guardsman Jock McGregor developed what looked ominously like impetigo and Guardia medic Daniel Rodriguez was having a lot of trouble with his leg.

Apart from that, there was mild annoyance of repeatedly straying off course − easily done when maps are necessarily very basic and identifiable landmarks are hard to find − and the excitement of spotting the tracks of some big cats which Jesus reckoned could be either jaguar or puma. There was also a moment of alarm when the powerful radio started to pack up, but Alex Gill got a message to HQ requesting a replacement to be flown out on the resupply helicopter which was scheduled to rendezvous with the patrol at the village of Surcurti on 3 March − day seven.

It was at this point that the first major crisis developed. The village of Surcurti, on the Surcurti River, had been picked out as the ideal spot for the resupply drop during an aerial recce shortly before the patrol set out. When George Thurstan first looked down from the air onto the area he was about to venture across, he did experience a momentary flash of doubt. Spread below him was an unbroken sea of green that stretched in all directions as far as the eye could see. It all looked exactly the same, but after a while the pilot identified the Surcurti River, along which the patrol's route lay, and, having followed it for some miles, came upon a large village which he confirmed was Surcurti. It was close to a bend in the river where a broad gravel bank formed what would serve as a perfect landing pad.

Major Aguillera made a point of stressing that, whatever happened, the patrol must be sure that it went to Surcurti and not to nearby Morti, which was located on a very similar river. He was vague about his reasons for emphasising so strongly the need to avoid Morti, but later that evening George wheedled out of him the somewhat startling information that the villagers there were very hostile and had once captured a Guardia patrol and held it hostage. It had taken a major operation to go in and rescue them.

The Balboa Patrol picked up the Surcurti on the afternoon of the fifth day and immediately pitched camp. They got going again earlier than usual the next morning to ensure that they reached the village and got settled in with plenty of time to spare before the helicopter arrived. Eventually they arrived at a bend in the river around the corner of which lay Surcurti, according to the map. This seemed to be confirmed by the presence on the bank of a banana plantation – although this appeared to have been neglected so that the fruit was rotting on the trees.

George called a halt and, having warned people not to take pictures of the Indians in case it frightened them, led an advance party forward round the bend. The sight that met their eyes was totally unexpected. There was nothing. Obviously there had once been a village, but it had long been deserted. What was more, one glance was enough to tell George that this was not the place he had been shown from the air.

Morale immediately plummeted. Everybody had been looking forward keenly to the boost of getting fresh supplies and to the prospect of a couple of days' rest in the relative luxury of a village environment. There was also the worrying mystery of what, exactly, had gone wrong. For once there was no doubt at all about their position. They were definitely on the Surcurti River and the abandoned village was certainly the one they were supposed to be aiming for. To complicate matters further, the radio had by now completely ceased to function, so there was no way of contacting headquarters to let them know what was happening and to seek advice.

They pitched camp for the night, and after a good meal of US Army patrol rations supplemented with freshly picked bananas, their spirits rose once more. They decided that in the morning they would hoist a marker balloon and hope that the resupply aircraft would spot it.

They got up early and sat for some time, straining their ears for the unmistakable thud of helicopter blades – but in vain. Eventually they accepted that they must move on and they left the marker balloon, along with a giant arrow of leaves pointing in the direction they were travelling. Then they headed off towards the next village up the river.

Progress was slow because they had to leave the river and take to the jungle where the undergrowth was so dense that visibility was down to a few yards. By the time they had to stop for the day and make camp, they had still not reached the second village. They were further delayed the next morning when they awoke to find that Jesus and Sergeant Arsimodo Jaen of the Guardia had failed to return from the previous night's hunting trip. They walked into camp minutes after a search party had left to look for them, explaining that they had got lost while chasing a pig and had decided to wait until daylight before trying to find their bearings again.

The second village was finally reached after another couple of hours' hacking through impenetrable undergrowth, but it was obvious before they got there that it was going to be just as dead as the first one. However, no sooner had they arrived than a helicopter flew over and, although it was very high, they managed to attract attention with a smoke flare. There was nowhere very suitable for it to land, but the pilot gave a brilliant exhibition of controlled flying and slotted it in above the river bank, with its rotor blades clipping the trees, and hovered there long enough for the supplies to be off-loaded.

The mystery of where the carefully planned rendezvous had gone wrong was now cleared up. The village which the pilot of the original recce flight had identified as Surcurti was actually the very Morti which George had been warned to steer well clear of and this was where the aircraft had duly been despatched. The pilot had actually landed there, but realised the mistake in time to lift off again just as the hostile villagers were advancing menacingly towards him.

The patrol stayed put that night, and the next morning the helicopter returned with a new radio. There followed another lazy day during which everyone took the opportunity to wash themselves and their clothes, and generally take stock of the situation. A number of people had started suffering from foot rot – which had probably been picked up at the Choco hunting camp where the party had spent the night two days previously – and others had gone down with dysentery. George Thurstan had a particularly bad dose and was feeling so rotten that there was even a suggestion that he should rest up for a day or two until he improved, but characteristically he pooh-poohed any such notion.

Less debilitating, but equally unpleasant, were the ticks with which nearly everybody was now infested. The patrol sometimes resembled a tribe of baboons as they helped to rid each other of these loathsome lice that resist removal like limpets and produce the most awful sensation as they crawl up between the hairs on one's legs during the night. The daily tick count became quite an event as people vied for the record of having the largest number embedded on his or her person. At one point the average per person was nearly forty!

A more delightful entertainment was provided that day by a tree snake which passed through the camp. It cruised through the branches at an incredible speed and never for one moment lost its smooth rhythm as it moved easily from one tree to the next. Attempts to catch it proved futile and it soon disappeared purposefully on its way at the same steady pace.

[89]

On 6 March – day ten – the patrol got moving again and pressed on to the Chucunaque River, of which the Surcurti is a tributary. They reached it the following day without any major incident, although there was momentary alarm when, without any warning, two of the Guardia men at the rear of the column suddenly opened up with a barrage of rifle and shotgun fire apparently aimed at nothing in particular. Everyone stopped and gaped in amazement as they blasted away at the water, and then all became clear as an ugly serpentine head broke the surface only to become an instant target for a final volley from the shotgun. Mr X once more!

For two more days, the patrol followed the course of the Chucunaque, and it was here that they encountered some of the most impenetrable jungle of the entire trek. Progress at one point was reduced to less than two miles in a whole morning and there were times when it took an hour to advance just a few yards. But when they eventually had to strike out away from the river they soon found themselves facing an even more severe problem – lack of water.

At first it was quite a novelty to be without it, having been actually wading through the stuff for so long. It was a matter for jokes when rationing had to be introduced as the level in bottles that were filled before the move away from the Chucunaque began to drop. People were still fairly light-hearted about it when they had to start filtering the contents of stagnant pools through Millbank bags to get rid of the solid impurities, before boiling it and then spiking it with purifying tablets. But the novelty very quickly wore off, and before too long it got to the point where George Thurstan had to alert HQ to the possibility that another urgent resupply flight might be necessary, as even the brackish puddles had dried up. The next morning, after his radio call, cameraman Rik Gustavsen woke up with a fever.

They broke camp two hours earlier than normal that day and moved out without any breakfast at 6.30 a.m. with the intention of covering as much ground as possible and thereby increasing the chances of finding water. But it soon became clear that they now had yet another problem. The old timber trail they had been following in the confident expectation that it would lead them to Sante Fe was gradually taking them further and further in the wrong direction. The Guardia kept insisting that it would eventually turn and put them back on the right bearing, but every bend seemed to push them further and further off course. George was becoming increasingly anxious – yet there was nothing he could really do about it. They were past the point of no return. With such an acute shortage of water, the alternative of plunging back into the thick of the forest and hacking their way along on the correct bearing was out of the question. Not only would the

[90]

extra effort dry people out even quicker, but their progress would be so slow that they would greatly reduce their chance of finding water.

Meanwhile, Rik was rapidly getting worse. The only way to keep him on his feet was to share his kit among the rest of the party and, as he grew weaker and weaker, he soon had to be half-carried. By the time a halt was called in the early afternoon he was semi-conscious and the whole patrol was mentally and physically drained. Then came the last straw. As they sat resting and trying to resist the temptation to gulp down the half-cup of water that was all each of them had left, the Guardia para-medic, Silvester, suddenly collapsed with giddiness and vomiting.

Now that he had two sick men on his hands, George no longer had any choice but to signal for a rescue helicopter. I had just returned to my Tactical HQ in Panama after a spot of fund-raising at the Navy League's weekly lunch, when George's curt message came through. Sarah Everett, my efficient PA, pulled out the file marked 'Search and Rescue − Emergency Instructions'. It was now up to us to co-ordinate the operations, but Alan Westcob was also monitoring the situation from his base in Caledonia Bay. This was when we really blessed the PRC 320 radios that Plessey had loaned us, for at once all interested parties were in touch.

Although totally exhausted, the members of the patrol somehow managed to galvanise themselves into action and got stuck into the seemingly impossible task of clearing a landing zone. Using nothing but their machetes, they felled trees that were up to two feet thick, and within four hours they had levelled an area roughly fifty yards square. In the circumstances it was an astonishing feat − but it inevitably took its toll. Two YEs collapsed with heat exhaustion − David French from England and Ulsterman Miles Clark, who had kept everyone amused with his endless fantasies about food and who was found to have lost twenty-five pounds when they eventually got him back to base. It could have been worse. At one point a tree toppled unexpectedly and nearly crushed Cathy Davies. As the cry of 'Timber!' went up and she turned to run clear, she caught her foot in some loose branches and went sprawling. One of the Guardia soldiers grabbed her hand and dragged her out of the way, just a fraction of a second before the eighty-foot tree came crashing down. He probably saved her life.

Meanwhile I had despatched Jim Winter with a Guardia helicopter to try to liaise with the various elements involved in the rescue which were now concentrating on an area over one hundred miles away. Doing it all by radio gave me a remote feeling, but Kim Batty, who ran Tac HQ for us, administered coffee all round and Guardia Bradley, our driver, acted as interpreter when required.

[91]

As soon as George radioed for help Tac HQ had got spotter planes and helicopters scrambled from the US Air Base in the Canal Zone, whose previous emergency had been the mass suicide of the Reverend Jim Jones and members of his religious sect in Guyana.

Although George could not be sure of his location, he had worked out an estimated position, but we knew full well that even if he was spot on – which he very nearly was, as it turned out – it would still be quite tricky trying to pinpoint him.

I told him to expect the planes to start arriving around 4.50 p.m. As that time approached, he called on his team to rouse themselves for yet another effort in keeping a bonfire well-stocked with greenery to create as much smoke as possible. This they did, but as the appointed hour came and went and straining ears were unable to pick out even the vaguest hint of an aircraft engine above the chatter of the parrots and the parakeets, numbed minds were no longer able to spur aching limbs into action and everybody finally flopped. Keeping that fire alight was quite beyond them even though they knew it could be vitally important.

An attempt to launch a marker failed, because there was no water to spare to pour on the chemical which then reacted to produce the gas to fill the balloon. Urine, it was soon discovered, did not work! As a last resort, Guardia private Luis Murillo, was despatched to shin nearly one hundred feet up the highest tree in the vicinity, where he perched clutching a brace of red smoke flares which he was ordered to fire off if he saw anything flying his way.

Just as hope was fading, along with the light, Luis let out a triumphant yell and ignited the first of his flares as a US Army helicopter tracked across the sky about a mile away. The plume of red smoke was spotted by the crew and within seconds it was hovering 180 feet above the little clearing where the members of the patrol were jumping up and down, waving and cheering with delight and relief.

The chopper then flew off and circled at about 2,000 feet while the pilot tried to get a fix on the position, and there was another moment of panic on the ground when it lost them again – further evidence of the needle-in-a-haystack problems involved in picking out a clearing just a few yards square amid thousands of acres of identical jungle. An added frustration for those on the ground was that although they could see the plane, they could not easily talk it in on the radio because no direct link-up was possible. Communication had to be relayed first from the jungle to Caledonia Bay and then on to Tac HQ in Panama City, from there to the control tower at the air base by telephone and from the control tower to the plane. The consequent delay in getting instructions through added to our difficulties, but without those communications we could well have had a death on our hands. As it was, our Plessey and MEL radios gave us tremendous flexibility and enabled me to discuss everything with George, who although under great stress remained utterly cool, calm and collected throughout the drama.

After ten agonising minutes the helicopter re-established visual contact and returned to hover again at about 180 to 200 feet. The pilot was reluctant to land among the tree stumps and decided instead to have Rik winched aboard. The winch was shaped like an anchor and the dazed and delirious cameraman was strapped to the flukes before being hoisted up. It was just as well that he was too ill to appreciate exactly what was happening to him, otherwise he would probably have died of fright!

Pausing only to promise that further flights would come out the next day to collect the remaining sick men and to bring out fresh water supplies, the helicopter headed back to base. An offer was made to fly in another chopper that night, landing it by torchlight, but George would have none of that. With Rik safely away, things were no longer quite so desperate and there was no point in taking any further risks. The patrol settled down for a very thirsty night.

Amazingly, the first helicopter out the next morning again failed to locate them. It circled round and round the general area, but was unable to pick out the smoke of their warning bonfire from among other forest fires smouldering nearby, and eventually returned to base. On the ground, dark despair set in again. Once more they had been forced to endure the frustration of being able to see the plane clearly, without being able to attract its attention. Worse still, their frantic efforts to build up the fire in order to make more smoke had not only further exhausted them but had also caused them to sweat out extra precious liquid. They cut down vines in the hope of adding to the dregs of foul-tasting water that was all they now had left, but even those were all dried up and yielded only a few drops of moisture which did no more than dampen cracked lips.

George was seriously thinking of breaking out the one full bottle he had kept hidden at the bottom of his pack as a final emergency measure when, after four hours, one of the searching aircraft homed in on the Guardia's treetop smoke flares. Even then the wait was not over. The helicopter had almost run out of fuel and only had time to get the fixed-wing plane that was now circling at a higher altitude to mark the spot while it raced back to base to refuel. The circling marker plane did not let the clearing out of its sight, and within forty-five minutes a succession of helicopters winched up the other sick men and whisked them off to join Rik in the Gorgas Memorial Hospital. They also dropped in six jerry cans of water. The crisis was over.

The relief that flooded through the group is reflected in Desmond Dugan's diary entry for day eighteen, made after he and the rest of the team had collapsed into their hammocks when the drama was finally played out. He wrote:

'The events of the last few days will give me and, probably, most of us a whole new slant on life. We should now appreciate all those things we have taken for granted simply because they were at our fingertips. I will think back to today and remember it well every time I turn on a tap. Also, we should not forget how much effort has been put into the whole evacuation programme and the water drop. If it is not already expressed then I put it in the records now: from the depths of our hearts we thank all involved in coming to our aid. It was not a life-or-death situation but it so easily could have been.'

But still it was not quite over. There was another ten miles to go to Santa Fe and, as the route lay through dense jungle, it was once more bound to be hard going. Furthermore, the level of water in the six jerry cans had dropped alarmingly in the first few hours after the drop, as people slaked their thirst, and rationing had to be reintroduced almost straightaway.

The following day was spent hacking relentlessly through thick undergrowth again until, about midday, they hit upon a dry river bed that followed their route, and progress speeded up. Even so, they had still not reached their goal by the time they camped that night, despite having been on the go for twelve solid hours.

Along the way, they had replenished their water supplies from two pools that Jim Winter had spotted from the air. The contents of both of them were enough to turn the stomach. The first had dead fish floating in it, while the second had obviously been wallowed in by a herd of peccary – a type of wild pig – and stank to high heaven. However, with the experiences of the previous few days very fresh in everybody's mind, the murky liquid which they happily proceeded to filter and boil somehow seemed as welcome as a crystal-clear mountain stream.

The evidence of peccary was interesting. Rather like piranha fish, these small pigs are harmless individually, but can be deadly when hunting in a pack. Locals take to the trees if they hear a herd coming through the jungle, and they say that, if they besiege you in the branches, your only means of escape is to throw down an article of clothing in the hope that they will attack that, thinking that it is you, and then move on. People who have been caught in the path of a fast-travelling herd say it is a terrifying experience.

Fortunately, the herd that had visited the pool was no longer in the neighbourhood.

There was a truly relaxed atmosphere in the camp that night for the first time for many days, as people contemplated the pleasing prospect of an imminent end to their ordeal. After a meal of turkey and rice, they chatted round the camp fire and then retired to their hammocks, where they gazed up at the stars and reflected on what they had been through.

For those who had made it, there was a great feeling of achievement. Suddenly all the hardships were something to remember with pride, and there was satisfaction in the knowledge that dangers had been faced and overcome.

The experience had provided some interesting insights into human nature under stress. For instance, it was seen that those who were physically the strongest did not necessarily have the greatest mental resilience and therefore cracked up more easily.

One thing which stood out a mile, and which was remarked upon by everyone, was the way the three girls came through it all. No concessions were asked or given, and they not only matched the men stride for stride but also showed a calmness under pressure that proved an invaluable steadying influence on everybody else. Cathy Davies, in particular, proved to be a tower of physical and mental strength. When some of her male colleagues were wingeing at the thought of having to hump a heavy jerry can full of water, she just stepped forward without a word, hefted it onto her shoulder as if it weighed nothing and moved on. Despite being the youngest member of the party, she emerged naturally as one of the leaders and was generally so impressive that she was asked to join us again on a later phase of the expedition as one of the staff.

Cathy, who is now at university in Scotland, said later that she never for one moment regretted getting involved in the Balboa Trail project — 'not even when I had dysentery and felt really ghastly. There was a lot of discomfort — some might use a stronger word — but I expected that. And although it was dangerous at times I was never afraid that I wouldn't get through in the end.'

Canadian student Ann Smith and English secretary Denise Wilson also made deep impressions on everybody with their strength of character, their determination to see it through on equal terms and, not least, their feminine charm. It was generally agreed by the men that it was the three girls who held them together at times of crisis.

'It doesn't surprise me that we were able to cope as well as the fellows,' said Cathy. 'I do a lot of mountaineering and it is a known fact that though men have superior physical strength, it is the women who can keep going longer under stress.'

The day after their triumphant entry to Santa Fe, the members of the party either flew or sailed down to La Palma to await transport back to

[95]

Caledonia Bay. Dreams of hot showers and clean clothes at La Palma were shattered when they arrived to find that there was a severe water shortage there, as well as in the jungle, and baths were banned. As a consolation, they were loaded into a truck and taken some miles to a quarry where a couple of pipes had been rigged up to provide a pathetic dribble of water from a natural spring – hardly the thing to wash away the ingrained grime of three weeks on the trail. But somehow it seemed a fitting end to an exploit in which physical discomfort and hardship had been a key factor, as those taking part drove themselves into the ground to such an extent that most of them did little except sleep for a fortnight afterwards. George Thurstan admits that it took him six months to recover fully. But that, as he adds with a certain masochistic pleasure, is what it was all about.

The party arrived back as the rest of the expedition was being wound up in Caledonia Bay. This was a laborious task that involved packing up over one hundred tons of stores and arranging for the transport back to Panama City England of a huge quantity of delicate archaeological finds and biological specimens. The job was completed just as the rains came and turned the little airstrip into a quagmire. The last few representatives of Operation Drake were happy to get out in time and leave the place once again to the ghosts of Fort St Andrew.

Chapter Ten

Dateline: New Orleans, Easter 1979

The slightly scruffy-looking individual curled up asleep for the night on a bench in the New Orleans bus depot was no Bourbon Street drop-out – it was Major Frank Esson of the Army Air Corps and he was in the middle of a somewhat unusual errand of mercy for Operation Drake.

Frank had arrived in Panama to take over as Senior Watch Leader aboard *Eye of the Wind* during her voyage across the Pacific only to find himself pitched straight into the middle of a crisis. As if the need to fly out a new gearbox from England had not caused us all quite enough headaches, it now emerged that the reason the anchor chain kept slipping was that it was completely the wrong size and did not fit the 'gypsy' around which it was wound in. There was no alternative but to get a replacement, yet that was very much easier said than done. We were not at all certain that we could find one, but we knew for sure that if we did, it was likely to be terrifyingly expensive. And the cost of transporting something weighing several tons promised to be pretty frightening, too. All this at a time when we were already in danger of going into the red, thanks to the gearbox. On top of everything else, we had the problem that the ship was due to sail in a matter of days and any further delays would put us desperately behind schedule.

Doom and despondency began to settle as we contemplated the hopelessness of the situation. And then Frank stepped in. The story of how he saved the day by finding a chain and getting it to *Eye of the Wind* in time for her to sail right on cue, and all for next to nothing, has already passed into expedition folklore.

He quickly established that there are only a handful of chain yards in the world where he could reasonably expect to find what he was looking for, and he then set out prepared to try them all if necessary, starting with the nearest one in New Orleans, moving on up the east coast to New York if he had no luck there, crossing over to San Francisco after that, and in the last resort even travelling back to England.

The prospect of embarking on what could turn out to be a world-wide wild goose chase was quite bad enough by itself. But it was not that straightforward. There was the added complication of one enormous handicap – he had to take the 'gypsy' with him!

There was no way this could be avoided since it was the only foolproof method of making sure he got a perfect fit. And he had to take it on the plane with him as personal baggage because we just had not got time to air-freight it from one place to the next. As one man could hardly lift the 120-pound lump of ironmongery off the ground, Frank's ability to charm airline staff was clearly going to be stretched to the limit.

With Easter weekend approaching and *Eye of the Wind* due to sail on the following Tuesday, he was in too much of a hurry to brood over such potentially insurmountable obstacles. It was probably just as well because, if he had thought about it long enough, he would surely have talked himself out of it. As it was, he had no sooner decided to go than he was on his way. He left so quickly that there was not even time to go to the bank and get some money for him, and we had to have an instant whip-round which yielded only a fistful of dollars. His personal belongings consisted of no more than a toothbrush tucked into an inside pocket, but with the 'gypsy' crammed into his hold-all he was hardly travelling light!

The first stage of his journey, from Panama to Miami, went very smoothly. We had already learned by experience that if you wore uniform and acted with an air of authority you could bluff your way past most officials, so George Thurstan simply marched down to the airport with him and made a big fuss about how vital it was for Frank and his unlikely piece of equipment to get on the first plane out. Prince Charles' name was dropped into the conversation several times for good measure. Eyebrows shot up when Frank's innocent-looking hold-all sent the indicator on the baggage scales right off the clock, but no objection was raised.

The real fun and games started when he got to Miami and tried to arrange a connecting flight to New Orleans. After some twenty hours and ten different airlines, he eventually managed to persuade someone to accept him and his luggage. The negotiations must have been hilarious to watch. All the check-in desks were situated along the same concourse and after the first couple of flat refusals, Frank developed a system whereby he would slide the hold-all along the marble floor until he reached a pillar near the desk he was planning to approach next. He would then pause for a few moments to catch his breath and summon his strength before lifting the bag and waddling the last few feet as nonchalantly as possible. Nobody was fooled, and in the end he became aware that his progress up the concourse was being observed

[98]

with amused interest by those who had already turned him down. He finally dropped all pretence and threw himself eloquently on the mercy of one of the smaller national airlines with a suitably embroidered tale of woe that would have brought a tear to the eye of a company sergeant major. Even so, they only agreed to take him with extreme reluctance. They must have been desperate for custom.

Frank eventually arrived in New Orleans late at night, and, because he had so little cash with him, he elected to put himself up at the bus terminal, where he fell asleep cuddling his precious 'gypsy' for safety – though it is hard to imagine who could possibly want to steal a thing like that. When the gates of the chain yard opened at six o'clock the next morning Frank fell in and he could hardly believe his luck when, after rummaging around for a couple of hours, he found a chain that fitted.

That was a real turn-up for the book – he had quite expected that he really would have to go all the way back to England to find exactly what was required. To round off a perfect day, he even managed to get the several tons of chain aboard the Panama Canal Company ship *Cristobal* before she sailed that afternoon, with the result that *Eye of the Wind* was able to depart as planned. And as a final extra bonus the Panama Canal Company generously decided that, as they were about to give away the canal itself, it really would not make too much difference to them if they were to donate one old rusty anchor chain to Operation Drake, so we were saved an expense of several thousand pounds into the bargain.

Poor old Frank, meantime, had to spend a couple more nights on bus-station and airport benches, as he had spent virtually his last dime telephoning us to request that we organise his ticket back to Panama. He informed us when he returned that he had been forced to live for three days on a diet of beer and cigarettes, but by the look on his face he had not found that too much of a hardship!

The total success of his mission came as a huge relief to me and, even more so, to Frank Taylor, Operation Drake's Treasurer, who had again been forecasting imminent financial disaster. It was a relief, too, for General Sir John Mogg, who bumped into Prince Charles at Badminton and said he hoped he would not end up in the Tower if we went into debt. 'No, you'll probably go to Carmarthaen Castle – that's mine and it's much worse,' replied the Prince of Wales.

From start to finish we lived from hand to mouth and, as inflation alone made a mockery of our original budget estimate of around £650,000, we constantly had to rev up our already frantic fund-raising activities in order to keep up with soaring costs and to stop ourselves slipping back too far into the red.

Every month Frank Taylor, a shrewd and hard-headed Scotsman, who is Financial Controller of Esso, would hold a meeting with our Director of Administration for a full and frank discussion of our commitments and expenditure, and every month this invariably seemed to result in a terse and somewhat alarming memo full of coldly calculated figures that showed us precisely when we would run out of cash and exactly what our projected debt would be at the end of it all. By the half-way stage of the expedition this latter entry on the monthly balance sheet had crept up past the £100,000 mark.

Frank's little reminders would always lead to a hectic redoubling of efforts to squeeze even more blood out of stones already hardened by the worst world recession since the 1930s. Miraculously, we would claw our way back to solvency again – but never for long. In such circumstances a sudden unexpected expense, like that incurred in replacing the gearbox and so narrowly avoided in finding a new anchor chain, would cause the kind of panic that traditionally has businessmen leaping from skyscraper window ledges. It is probably just as well that our offices were in a basement!

Our main bread-and-butter source of income was the sponsorship fees for YEs. This was originally £2,000 per head, but had to be raised to £2,300 later on as we struggled to keep pace with inflation. In addition, we had a steady flow of cash coming from the sale of T-shirts, maps, brochures and a series of commemorative covers for stamp collectors specially designed for us by artist Anthony Theobald and franked in various places visited by Operation Drake. The franking of these covers on each phase was regarded as something of a chore by the YEs, but we consoled them with the thought that it was all helping to pay for their adventure.

The fees from occasional lectures, radio interviews and television appearances could also be guaranteed to produce a small amount for the kitty, and whenever really hard times were seen approaching, I would hurriedly arrange a quick lecture tour to bring in a few extra pounds. These talks can sometimes be fairly soul-destroying affairs which involve flogging two hundred miles in the car to some unheated village hall where, if you are lucky, forty people turn up to sit there sniffling with colds while you show slides and wax lyrical for a couple of hours, and then end up collecting little more than the price of your petrol. But every little bit counts, and many members of Operation Drake spent much of their free time helping in this way.

To keep the Operation Drake show on the road, we relied very largely on being able to raise support in cash and kind as we went along, by any means available, and as a result we soon became expert scroungers, masters of both the hard sell and the soft touch. A mercenary streak is an essential quality for anyone involved in organising this kind of venture and I must confess that experience has taught me to be quick in taking advantage of people's generosity and quite shameless in my readiness to exploit their good will. One of the largest donations we received was the £5,600 we got from the St George's Day Club in London. This largely resulted from a table collection after I had spoken to the twelve hundred guests at the Club's lunch on St George's Day 1980 and is a tribute to the generosity of these patriotic gentlemen.

I have never hesitated to use a pretty face to further a cause which, however good it may be anyway, will always sound much worthier when charmingly explained by an attractive young lady. 'Blasher's Blondes' or 'Charlie's Angels', as they were variously known, played a vital role in securing sponsorships, goods and services for the expedition. Lisa Van Gruisen, Barbara Martinelli, and Maria and Barbara Szpak, Ruth Mindel, PA Sara Everett, and later 'Margot' Barker in Britain, and Sara Spicer-Few and Jeanette McKeague in PNG were among those who did a marvellous job of selling the idea of Operation Drake to companies and individuals who might otherwise have thought twice about backing it.

Of course, there are times when that kind of approach does not cut any ice and there was one occasion when we feared it might actually work against us. An American contact had lined up a big corporation for a major cash contribution and the company president was invited to a party at which the deal was to be clinched. The word was that this gentleman was quite a swinger, so the scene was carefully set for a real rave-up at the luxurious home of a friend – plenty of booze, lots of lovely ladies and a nice relaxed atmosphere around the pool-side terrace. Most of the men were wearing slacks and Hawaiian shirts, and I was beginning to feel very awkward and out of place in my dark suit, collar and tie – which was all I had with me at the time – until our star guest arrived. He was very soberly dressed in grey suit, white shirt and black tie and it was immediately evident that whoever had done the homework on what he was like had got it all wrong. Instead of the hard-drinking jet-set executive with an eye for the girls and a taste for the good life that we had been expecting, we found ourselves being introduced to a small, balding, rather timid little man. As a stunning red-head sidled up and asked him what he would like to drink, he revealed that he never touched hard liquor and later he let slip that he had never married because he found that most women were only after his money! I had visions of him tearing up his cheque in disgust, and stepped forward smartly in my pinstripe to inject a bit of stiff-upper-lip British reserve into the proceedings. Happily, we got our donation in the end.

[101]

My old friend Dan Osman, a marvellous fun-loving character who is a surgeon by profession, would stop at nothing in his efforts to raise money for Operation Drake. Once he actually extracted a promise of a sizeable contribution during an operation. He was chatting to his patient while waiting for the anaesthetic to take effect, and when it emerged that the man was in a position to influence the distribution of the funds of a large charitable trust Dan wasted no time in pressing our case. The patient's last words before he passed out were: 'Operation Drake? What is that, doctor – some kind of duck hunt?'

Slow-talking Tulsa oilman John Linehan was equally enthusiastic in his support of Operation Drake and even spent some time in the Panama jungle with us. He kindly let me use his New York office and provided introductions to many very useful contacts. He also helped to drum up a considerable amount of financial backing, even throwing a party for us which produced donations of $15,000. He himself presented me with $5,000 in typically flamboyant fashion, arranging for a radio-controlled jeep to roll to a stop in front of me, whereupon the bonnet lifted automatically to reveal a cheque.

Not all our benefactors were quite as flamboyant as John and Dan, but there were many who were just as wholehearted in their support.

Elaine Hoeflick, Gordon Booth's secretary in New York, must have given up all her spare time for two years to ensure that the YEs from the USA were efficiently organised.

Viscount Gough was another generous sponsor, and he twice joined us in the field – in PNG and Kenya.

Businessman Colonel John Hines not only gave us money out of his own pocket but also worked incredibly hard on our behalf to raise a small fortune from other sources. A great man of action, in his earlier years he had directed his energy and drive towards making a huge success of his business career and, having done all that, felt the need in his sixties to escape from the boardroom and do something that would take him out of his comfortable rut.

Apart from the individuals who backed us financially there were also the charitable organisations that turned up trumps from time to time. Every now and again we would get a windfall like the £5,000 that arrived from the Bernard Sunley Fund quite unexpectedly.

Over and above the cash contributions we received, donations in kind worth hundreds of thousands of pounds were made by commercial sponsors offering free or cut-price goods and services. These ranged from the loan by Plessey of a number of their amazing PRC 320 portable radio transmitter/receivers, each worth several thousand pounds, to the twenty-four toothbrushes given by the Lion Brush Works Ltd of Newcastle. Halls Barton Ropes offered us a

[102]

discount on ropes and rigging for *Eye of the Wind*, and the Maidstone Tarpaulin Co. Ltd did the same with sails. We got free typewriters from Smith Corona, tape recorders from Philips and tools from Stanley Tools Ltd. Batchelors supplied enough Farmhouse Stew to keep an army of 40,000 men going for a day, while Foremost Catering Disposables Ltd provided the means to give each one of them a cup of tea or coffee. For those with a taste for something a little stronger there was Scotch from Dewar's and Grant's, stout from Guinness and even mead from Merrydown. Everything from pencils and pillowcases to maps and medical supplies, from boots and beefburgers to calculators and chewing gum, and from towels and toilet paper to rockets and rabies vaccinations was provided by companies large and small. The list of sponsors – printed in full at the back of this book – goes on and on, and I only wish we had the space to pay full tribute to each one individually. Without their help we could never have done it.

There are a few who must have a special mention because of their overwhelming generosity and endless assistance. British American Tobacco, for instance, did so much for us in Panama, Sulawesi and Kenya. We are also particularly indebted to the many airlines who gave us free and cut-price stand-by travel facilities, without which the cost of moving personnel around the world to faraway places with strange-sounding names would have been prohibitive. British Airways, British Caledonian Airways, Pan Am, Kenya Airways, Garuda Indonesian Airways, Air Nuigini, Qantas, Air New Zealand and Cathay Pacific were all astonishingly magnanimous in this respect.

We also benefited in all sorts of ways from the support of the Armed Services, not only the Royal Navy, the British Army and the Royal Air Force but also the Guardia Nacional in Panama and the PNG Defence Force. We were also indebted to the Armed Forces of Australia, Ecuador, Egypt, Fiji, Kenya, New Zealand and USA. It has always been my experience that, especially in developing countries, the local Armed Forces tend to be very keen to get involved with expeditions that give them opportunity to get men and equipment out in the field in an adventurous situation, and this was certainly the case in both Panama and PNG where the large amount of assistance was almost embarrassing.

Our Director of Logistics, Jim Masters, had one of the toughest jobs on Operation Drake in trying to organise the transport of personnel and hundreds of tons of equipment from one distant and inaccessible spot to another, and the fact that he managed it so brilliantly had a lot to do with the wonderful co-operation of the RAF.

When Jim first approached his contacts there, they took him out to lunch and broke the news to him very gently that they could not do anything to help him because of the general economic climate – and then proceeded to give him everything he asked for over the next two years. It did not cost the taxpayer a penny because their assistance never involved them in anything they would not have been doing anyway. It was just a matter of arranging things in such a way as to be of mutual benefit to themselves and Operation Drake. So it was that Hercules transport aircraft on routine training flights flew stores between the UK, Panama, PNG, Sulawesi and Kenya. It actually helped them because their crews were given the opportunity to practise in more realistic circumstances than normal, and it was a God-send to us.

The RAF were not the only people on whom Jim relied to keep Operation Drake on the move. He also got tremendous help from the civil airlines and also from the Pacific Steam Navigation Company and then the East African Shipping Conference, where he gained a valuable contact through the fiancé of one of the YEs.

The favours Jim arranged for us were amazing – he always managed to find someone with whom to hitch a lift for our stores and personnel. But it was sometimes touch and go. As he himself will admit, with a sparkle in his eye, there were times during the preparations for each of the four land phases when it looked as though there really was no way of getting everybody and everything together in the right place at the right time, but invariably something would turn up at the last moment and, miraculously, we would manage to muddle through.

However, it was not just due to luck. Jim worked very hard at establishing a credibility for Operation Drake with the individuals and organisations who could help him by making it very clear that we were not out just to grab, grab, grab, without the slightest intention of trying to give anything back. Not that we often had much to offer apart from the possible satisfaction of being involved with a genuine and worthwhile venture – but for many people that was enough. 'It's not until you do something like this that you discover just how many fine people there are about,' says Jim.

Chapter Eleven

Dateline: Aboard 'Eye of the Wind' on the Equator, 21 May 1979

The strange and unearthly air of silent calm that descended over *Eye of the Wind* as she approached the Equator was not wholly due to the light winds, constant swell and heavy current that reduced progress between the Cocos Islands and the Galapagos archipelago to a wallowing four knots. It had more to do with the fact that the entire ship's company had become totally wrapped up in secret preparations for a grand crossing-the-line party. It is probably true to say that at no other stage in the whole expedition were YEs seen to muster as much mental concentration as was brought to bear on the task of thinking up lewd limericks to accompany each 'initiation' planned as part of this traditional ceremony.

One could almost hear the whirring of cerebral cogs as people retreated into corners and sat there with knitted brows, chewing pencils to the lead in the quest for inspiration. Otherwise, the peace was only occasionally shattered by Tiger gleefully rubbing his hands together and cackling with delight for no apparent reason as he dreamed up another suitable 'punishment'. Spider, meanwhile, spent long hours working on props and costumes, and in her laboratory Patricia Holdway took time off from analysing the contents of her nets to mix some truly revolting concoctions to be poured over the heads of the thirty hapless victims who would be crossing the Equator for the first time in their lives.

The line was actually crossed in the early hours around dawn, but the 'court' did not sit until after breakfast when the important chores of the morning had been completed. The part of Neptune was taken by 21-year-old YE Gillian Rice from Bickley in Kent, while Chief Petty Officer Richard Shrimpton, the ship's engineer whose Royal Navy blue verses had to be heavily censored, made a spectacular appearance as Queen Amphritos. Watch Keeper Robert Clinton was Clerk to the Court – very apt since he is a lawyer by profession – and YE Bruce Buckley, aged nineteen, from Hove, Sussex, was appointed Court Barber. Tiger and Leslie Reiter were Court Attendants, and the role of

Davey Jones was taken by twelve-year-old Miranda Kichenside, the much-travelled daughter of the ship's new skipper, Mike Kichenside.

The ceremony went off in predictably boisterous fashion, complete with rude rhymes, duckings and the exaction of some truly humiliating forfeits. One of the first to suffer was Capital Radio YE Linda Batt-Rawden, who was wired for sound by Capital reporter-on-board, Pam Armstrong, so that listeners back in London could share her misery as she was tarred and ducked. Linda, who was to rejoin Operation Drake at a later stage as a fully fledged Capital reporter herself, entered gamely into the spirit of things in characteristically extrovert style, but the verses citing her 'crimes' had to be drastically edited before being allowed on the air!

Among the more disgusting 'punishments' were those meted out to 23-year-old New Yorker Dan Rikleen, who was forced to swallow a particularly revolting brew of cold porridge, and twenty-year-old Tyrone Spence from Loughborough, who had to be held down while a pilchard-and-tomato-sauce sandwich was crammed into his mouth. How Chris Sainsbury ever managed to survive the nauseating ordeal of being force-fed with a mixture of gin and cooking oil, administered by means of a plastic tube shoved down his throat, remains a mystery. As somebody rather cruelly pointed out, it just went to prove that he really would drink anything! Nobody escaped totally unscathed and even the new skipper, who had taken over from Patrick Collis in Panama, gracefully submitted to a ducking.

By the end of it all, everybody was in such a mess that the only satisfactory way to clean up was to dive over the side for a swim in the inviting, clear blue water. The day ended on a further note of excitement when the ship anchored within sight of the twinkling lights of Wreck Bay, Chatham Island – the first port of call in the Galapagos Islands.

The Pacific phases of the expedition had started a little over a month earlier when *Eye of the Wind*, with expensive mechanical problems temporarily behind her, sailed through the Panama Canal and headed up the coast on a three-week expedition to Costa Rica. She returned to Panama to collect Mike Kichenside before setting out on the 8,000-mile South Seas voyage to PNG. During the trip to Costa Rica, Tiger, the Mate, took over as Acting Skipper and was obviously delighted to be in command of his own ship for the first time.

For the new batch of YEs, who had flown into Panama only days before the ship sailed, the first thrill came when Tiger hove to and allowed them to swim in the ocean. Tyrone Spence had only once in his life swum in the sea, and that was during a holiday at Butlin's in Skegness, and so, for him especially, the experience of diving from the deck of a sailing ship into the warm Pacific was overwhelming. It proved extremely difficult to lure him back out of the water and when eventually he clambered reluctantly aboard again, to be greeted by a stern reprimand, he was spluttering with excitement. 'It's so deep, so blue, so clear – wow!' was all he could gasp.

Francis Drake got to know these waters well. It was here, four hundred years previously almost to the month, that he sought refuge among the sheltered islands and hidden bays while he prepared the *Golden Hind* for what was expected to be a return trip to England across the Atlantic, back the way he had come. The success of his voyage had already been more than assured by the capture of the Spanish galleon, *Cacafuego*, on 1 March 1579, as a result of which the hold of the *Golden Hind* was bulging with treasure. But then, in April, another Spanish vessel fell into his clutches, which yielded a very different, yet in some ways even more valuable, prize in the form of two pilots fully equipped with the charts of the so-called 'China Run' which the Spanish had established across the Pacific between Mexico and the Philippines.

This windfall caused Drake to change his plans completely. He may well have been worried anyway about the dangers of retracing his route around the Cape since his escapades on the way out had left hornets' nests of angry Spaniards who would no doubt be waiting to intercept him on his return journey. Now he had been presented with an exciting alternative that combined the convenience of a safe escape route with the pioneering challenge of finding a new way home. Being the kind of man he was, Drake did not hesitate to go for the main chance. Pausing only to lay a false trail by continuing northwards up the coast of America to the site of modern-day San Francisco – where he claimed what is now California for the Queen and named it New Albion on account of the white cliffs that reminded him of Dover – he turned westwards and set sail into the unknown. It was at this point that he started thinking seriously in terms of a round-the-world voyage.

It was from a hiding place in the lee of the Isla de Cano that his men sallied forth in a pinnace – 'blowing trumpets and firing arquebuses in the air', according to a contemporary report – and captured the two pilots from the passing Spanish cargo ship. During the twelve days that he remained in the area, careening *Golden Hind* and searching for fresh water and other supplies, he also spent some time in a secluded bay situated on the Osa Peninsula, which juts out from the south-western corner of Costa Rica.

The picturesque inlet is known to this day as Drake's Bay and one of our main purposes in going to Costa Rica was to take part in the ceremonial unveiling of two special plaques – one presented by the

Costa Rican government, the other by the Lord Mayor of Plymouth – to commemorate the visit of *Golden Hind*.

Torrential rain delayed the arrival of the light aircraft bringing myself and various VIPs down from the capital, San Jose, and then there was a further slight hold-up when it was discovered that the entire gathering of sixty people would have to be ferried across the river Agujitas in canoes. But all went well in the end as the British Chargé d'Affaires, Jerry Warden, and the Costa Rican Director of Tourism, Senor Guardia, shared the formalities. The memorial, with the two plaques set into it, looked very impressive and this was a tribute to the do-it-yourself skills of Mr Gordon Rayson, a representative of the Ministry of Overseas Development, who stepped in and took on the job when it was discovered that there were no local workers to tackle it.

Afterwards everybody lunched aboard *Eye of the Wind* and the white-painted ship looked particularly magnificent as she rode at anchor, framed against the startlingly bright shades of blue of the sea and the sky and the vivid greens of the jungle rising behind her. It was easy to imagine *Golden Hind* in her place and to picture Drake and his men taking small boats up the cool, tree-shaded Agujitas to fish for the plentiful needlefish, from which the river takes its name, to hunt for fresh meat and to gather exotic fruit.

On the way up to Drake's Bay, a party of eighteen YEs, under the leadership of Trish Holdway and Frank Esson, had been dropped off at San Pedrillo to complete the last few miles of the journey overland with a walk through the Corcovado National Park, and during the ten days after the unveiling ceremony and before *Eye of the Wind* sailed on, a series of groups went out on further treks into the interior, each lasting from two to four days.

Although the Costa Rican National Parks conservation system was only started in 1970 it already takes in 3.5 per cent of the country's total land mass. This is a greater proportion than is found in any other Latin American country and, indeed, there are very few nations anywhere in the world which can boast such impressive concern for their natural resources. The 14,500-acre Corcovado Park provided the YEs with a perfect introduction to the jungle.

They were accompanied on their patrols by Park guides who pointed out and explained the wealth of wildlife, and at night they stayed either at the homes of Park wardens, whose hospitality was memorable, or slept out in the forest, using the giant fronds of banana plants for shelter. Five of the Park's eight stations were visited and most of the main trails walked. The going was not too tough and the purpose was a purely observational task on behalf of the Park, yet everyone found the

[108]

experience tremendously rewarding.

It made a deep impression on many of the YEs. 'The rain forest was enthralling,' wrote young Chris Goy from Australia. 'There were huge hardwoods, entwined with vines, and I was struck by the tremendous variety of trees, so different from the uniform continuity of the Australian eucalyptus forests.

'All the trees and shrubs were very broad-leaved and some of the leaves were positively gigantic. We were generally walking along well-defined tracks in the damp and steaming gloom with towering trees blocking the sun. We had to skirt around huge splayed tree trunks, stepping among tangled masses of roots and spongy leaf litter. We passed through abandoned plantations and partook gratefully of the pineapples, bananas, sugar cane, sweet lemons, mangoes, coconuts, limes, cashews, avocado and breadfruit.'

Cathy Lawrence, a twenty-year-old Canadian from Toronto, found it hard to believe it was actually happening to her. 'Being in the jungle was like being in a dream world,' she noted. 'I could never quite relate to the magnitude of the foliage, brushing past leaves that were larger than me and seeing the vines hanging from the trees almost as if they were trying to stop us from getting past. The fairy-tale situation of me being posed by the local press back home behind a plastic philodendron in my front hall suddenly became reality when I found myself in a jungle which previously I had only been able to imagine from the impressions I got from Tarzan magazines.'

Bruce Buckley got a bit of a shock when he set about selecting a spot to bed down for the night in a hut at one of the Park stations. 'I picked what I thought would be a good place, but one of the guides didn't seem so sure. He kept pointing at the ceiling above my head and saying something I couldn't understand at all. I thought he must be explaining that the rain came in through the roof until I looked carefully and suddenly noticed a boa constrictor curled up on one of the beams! I immediately moved my gear to the other end of the hut despite being assured that the snake was quite harmless. It was the closest I had ever been to a snake and I didn't like it one little bit.'

Julie Barlow, a 23-year-old Australian from Brisbane, also had several brushes with Costa Rican wildlife. 'On our third day in the jungle I looked a snake in the eye. Our guide disturbed it and it immediately turned round, curled, with its fangs exposed. It was four feet long and green and I can vividly remember the whitish colour of its open mouth. My immediate reaction was to jump backwards, knocking over the person following me, and the snake skimmed away.

'On two nights we were attacked by bats. The first time I was washing up by the sea and I heard what sounded like a splashing sound in the water. I shone my torch in that direction and suddenly two bats headed straight for me and the light. The guy who was helping me wash up jumped behind me for shelter and I was left to fend off the bats with the torch.

'The second encounter was when we bunked down in a loft at one of the hill stations. It was very late when the bats returned to their roosts to find three people asleep under their mosquito nets. There was a great scuffle, which woke us up, and they fluttered around trying not to get caught in the nets before escaping out into the dark.

'Coming through the jungle one day the guide suddenly stopped us and ordered us to be quiet. He had heard quite a rustle in the scrub ahead and thought we were about to be charged by peccary and you could see his eyes darting around looking for suitable trees in which to take refuge. However, within a few minutes they fortunately moved away and we were able to continue.'

Mark Creer, twenty-two years old, from Vancouver, Canada, had an unnerving experience of a very different kind. 'We heard a roaring sound approaching us at one point. It started deep in the jungle and gradually came nearer and nearer and it was quite scary because of the intensity of the sound. At first we thought it might be a very large group of monkeys coming our way and it was several minutes before we realised it was actually the sound of heavy rain beating down, and then it rained harder than I would have believed possible, a real tropical downpour.'

New Yorker Chris Downs was even more bothered by a mysterious sound that kept him awake as he lay in his hammock one night. 'It was a strange hissing, scraping sound,' he recalled. 'First I heard it by the door of the hut we were sleeping in, and then in the extreme corner, and then, to my utmost consternation, it was immediately below my hammock. I was petrified and afraid to move for fear that this animal would take my life. The noise kept up for two to three hours and the unseen creature was moving backwards and forwards, round and round the tiny room. I was on the verge of tears and would have screamed out to Trish, the group's scientist, except that I was more afraid of the ribbing I would get from my fellow explorers than I was of the unknown danger below. I remained totally motionless for what seemed like an eternity, beseeching the gods to come to my aid, until finally I realised, to my relief and embarrassment, that the sound was caused by nothing more menacing then my companions turning over in their nylon hammocks!'

It was quite understandable that Chris, being a city boy, viewed the jungle with considerable suspicion. 'Entering it for the first time, I felt like Alice going through the looking glass,' he noted in his diary. 'A whole new world was opened up to me, one that was completely foreign to me, filled with strange noises and decaying smells. The only impression I had had of jungle before was the stereotype image I had seen on television, luxuriant vegetation infested with all types of insects, snakes hanging from trees, and all kinds of dangerous animals staring out of the undergrowth. I walked with extreme caution because I expected danger at every bend. But gradually I began to realise that this was an exaggerated fear. As time went on I got to feel very relaxed as it became clear that the jungle was a very peaceful place.'

When they were not coming face to face with the denizens of the jungle, either imagined or otherwise, the YEs helped Trish Holdway with a coastal survey on behalf of the Costa Rican government. This involved examining the effects of coastal erosion and tidal sediment disposition, as well as investigating the plant and animal communities of the shoreline which teemed with all sorts of life, including sand crabs, skinks, basilicus lizards, parrots, scarlet-rumped tanagers, Sally Lightfoot crabs, and a myriad of butterflies and moths. It was a good excuse for some wonderfully exotic beachcombing and there was the added element of excitement in going ashore in a dug-out canoe through heavy surf and Pacific rollers, which turned out to be an exhilarating experience.

The Costa Rican visit ended with a farewell party aboard *Eye of the Wind*, during which the guides from the Corcovado National Park watched in wide-eyed amazement as the more energetic YEs gave an impressive exhibition of high-diving from the ship's rigging, and then it was on to the island of Cano for a brief stop-off before heading back to Panama.

The anchorage chosen by Tiger at Cano was almost certainly the same as that used by Francis Drake himself. There is a coral reef surrounding the island and it is largely unapproachable except by entering this one small bay. With its sandy beach and backdrop of tree-clad cliffs rising sharply to a height of well over four hundred feet, the location was exquisitely beautiful.

The island is uninhabited, apart from a National Park warden, a few domestic pigs long since run wild, and the ghosts of the many Indians buried there. The mainland tribes used it as a burial ground some eight hundred years ago and, although hundreds of the graves have been opened and robbed by treasure hunters hoping to find gold and jewellery interred with the bodies, many more remain untouched.

Eye of the Wind spent a day there and in the afternoon a Costa Rican gunboat came to investigate and sent a boarding party over to her. They were recalled even before they had come alongside and the gunboat left as suddenly as she had arrived, presumably because some more pressing emergency had arisen. It was probably just as well since Tiger might have encountered some difficulty in explaining how he and his very piratical-looking crew happened to be there without the proper immigration papers or cruising permit. Operation Drake's presence in the area was covered only by the vaguest form of diplomatic immunity, and the fact that the Costa Rican equivalent of the British Admiral of the Fleet had attended the unveiling ceremony at Drake's Bay might not necessarily have cut any ice with suspicious security forces who probably did not speak much English.

A few hours before docking at Balboa in Panama, *Eye of the Wind* made an ocean rendezvous with the BP supertanker *British Resolution*. To see *Eye of the Wind* and *British Resolution* side by side put the development of sea power into startling perspective. *Eye of the Wind* seemed like a child's Serpentine model as she sailed around the giant tanker. BP were among our leading supporters, providing not only fuel for *Eye of the Wind* – a very welcome gift – but also the valuable assistance of their agents around the world. In return, teams of BP's deck cadets visited *Eye of the Wind* when our YEs were ashore on land-based projects and used the ship as a training base.

Mike Kichenside's arrival on board was eagerly awaited. We had been lucky to secure his services at short notice since qualified sailing-ship skippers are not exactly thick on the ground. There was the added advantage with Mike that he was familiar with *Eye of the Wind* having captained her for part of the round-the-world voyage that immediately preceded Operation Drake. He was only too happy to join us – as long as we would allow him to bring his daughter, Miranda. We had no objection to that and so Miranda, who has accompanied her father everywhere since her mother died in a car accident, moved into a special berth next to Mike's cabin, complete with a vast quantity of schoolbooks. She turned out to be a far more accomplished sailor than any of the YEs and was a positive boon to the expedition.

Everyone on the ship was greatly impressed by Mike from the moment he stepped aboard, but he must have got an awful shock when he first set eyes on his crew. They resembled a walking casualty department as they limped on deck nursing cuts and bruises and sporting a selection of sticking plasters, bandages and slings. The reason for their sorry state was a rugby match that had taken place the previous day, following a challenge from the local army club. The encounter resulted in more injuries than had been sustained in the whole expedition up until then. And they were the winners!

The trouble was that among *Eye of the Wind*'s international crew of YEs only three knew anything about the rules of English rugby, while the rest operated on the simple basis that if a member of the opposition was unlucky enough to get the ball he should be brought down as swiftly as possible, using whatever technique came naturally. With Australians, Americans, Canadians and Tasmanians among the Operation Drake Fifteen, the other side were ruthlessly felled with tackles that combined the roughest features of rugby league, American football and ice hockey. It was not long before they resorted to similar tactics, and the pitch soon resembled a battlefield, with the injured littered from end to end. The Operation Drake team crawled away from the battle claiming victory, while their stunned opponents suggested that maybe the local Special Forces side would be a better match for them.

The first six days of Mike's command were largely uneventful as *Eye of the Wind* motored sluggishly through a heavy swell towards Cocos Island. One innovation that he introduced was the idea that the Sunday service should in future be conducted by volunteers from among the YEs rather than by himself. Tyrone Spence and nineteen-year-old Jerseyman Anthony Houiellebecq came forward and offered to officiate on the first Sunday, when an unusually attentive congregation assembled expectantly on the foredeck, wondering whether they were about to have the fear of God instilled in them by the two meekest and mildest of all the YEs. In fact, they both performed admirably and Tyrone displayed a surprisingly professional pulpit manner.

Cocos Island has an air of mystery and romance about it, which is one reason why it has become something of a Mecca for the more adventurous European beachcombers, artists and drop-outs who want to get away from it all. It got its name from the coconut groves which puzzled the earliest explorers, who found them already flourishing despite the lack of inhabitants. It is still not known for certain who planted the trees, although Thor Heyerdahl has speculated that it may have been Polynesian sailors. His theory is that the Polynesians used the island as a natural storehouse where they could drop in whenever they were passing and harvest the coconuts, which would give them a source of liquid, locked in a natural and easily manageable container, ideal for tiding them over on long voyages.

The other great attraction of Cocos is its reputation as a real-life Treasure Island. Such bold buccaneers as the legendary Henry Morgan and the famed Benito Bonito, also known as Bennett Graham, are rumoured to have used it as a hiding place for millions of dollars' worth of booty looted from ships and cities along the South American coast in the early nineteenth century. Even more specific are the stories about the 'Treasure of Lima' – a fortune in gold, silver and jewels said to have been entrusted by the city authorities to the safekeeping of Captain William Thompson of the *Mary Dear* during a revolution in

[113]

Peru. Thompson supposedly buried it somewhere in Cocos's Wafer Bay and never got a chance to go back for it. Over four hundred bounty-hunting expeditions have since gone in search of this treasure trove, but nothing has ever been found.

Arriving in Chatham Bay, where the water was so crystal-clear that Mike Kichenside was able to pick out a sandy spot amid the rock and coral and drop anchor precisely upon it, it was easy to conjure up visions of a colourful past peopled by characters straight out of pirate fiction.

Apart from the handful of Europeans who had 'gone native' – including an Englishman who claimed to be writing a book about being marooned on a desert island – and a small detachment of Guardia Civile from Costa Rica, the place is uninhabited. This is not really surprising since, despite its colourful history, it is a fairly inhospitable spot. There are two seasons – wet and wetter – and the terrain is harsh, with just one steep and muddy inland path linking the two main bays. The flora and fauna are by no means abundant – although there are one or two interesting lizard species peculiar to the island – and the surrounding waters are shark-infested. Tiger and Spider were confronted with alarming proof of this latter fact when they dived down to inspect the ship's propeller, only to find themselves under unpleasantly close scrutiny from five of the brutes, including two which they estimated to be about fifteen feet in length. When they came back on board, a large frozen fish was dangled over the side as bait and within a few seconds there was a dark blue blurr in the water and the hook was left bare. Nobody showed any desire to go swimming after that.

During their thirty-six hour stopover at Cocos, the YEs divided into three groups. The more energetic ones went off with Frank Esson to climb the island's highest peak, in search of an American fighter plane which had crashed there during the war and had instantly vanished from sight on the densely forested slopes. This exercise was carefully designed by Frank to wear out the more zestful individuals whose restlessness after being cooped up on board the small ship might otherwise present slight problems, but although he threatened 'utter misery and total deprivation and a diet of salt tablets and rice', he had no shortage of volunteers. Clearly, this was exactly what a lot of people were looking for. The exhausting march worked perfectly in so far as it succeeded in burning off the excess energy of the fit and youthful YEs – the only problem was that it reduced poor Frank to a state of near collapse.

Meanwhile, the other two groups either busied themselves with a survey of the coastal wildlife or accompanied Trish Holdway on a

[114]

mission requested by the Smithsonian Tropical Research . were keen to get hold of specimens of a particularly rare known to inhabit the island and were also interested in hea the spread of earthworms from their point of introductio. northern coast. The stick insects proved frustratingly elusive migratory progress of the earthworms was successfully moi. thanks mainly to 23-year-old New Zealander Dianne Bear, exhibited an unusual sixth sense for discovering the things. Acting like a water diviner, she would walk along with her head on one side and then suddenly stop dead in her tracks, start digging furiously and invariably produce a worm. This unlikely talent caused great amusement among Dianne's fellow YEs, who had already had reason to rib her over the extraordinary incident involving her future mother-in-law. Dianne was already engaged to a Costa Rican before she joined Operation Drake, but she had never met her fiancé's family – until his mother made a surprise appearance at the Drake's Bay unveiling ceremony. Dianne had no inkling in advance that this was going to happen and the shock was considerable.

More appealing than the earthworms were the blue-footed and red-footed boobies, and an added advantage was that they were not nearly so hard to find. Huge colonies of these birds were resident all over the place and were so tame that one could walk right up to them without any reaction other than an occasional warning hiss. But it was as well to be wary of the hoards of land crabs that surrounded every nest waiting for an opportunity to steal either the one egg or the young chick which each pair of birds produces.

Just before the ship weighed anchor and departed, Spider added her name to all the others carved on the rocks of Chatham Bay – the traditional visitors' book of the island since 1757, when a passing mariner first obeyed the age-old urge to leave his mark – and then *Eye of the Wind* sailed away into the sunset.

Chapter Twelve

Dateline: Galapagos Islands, May 1979

Charles Darwin was just twenty-two years old, and therefore younger than quite a few of our YEs, when he visited the Galapagos Islands aboard the *Beagle* in 1835 and made the vital observations that were to lead, over twenty years later, to the publication of his revolutionary theories about evolution in *The Origin of Species*. This added great relevance to Operation Drake's ten-day programme of study, research and observation in the group of sixty-one islands which straddle the Equator six hundred miles off the coast of Ecuador and which Darwin pinpointed as a unique natural laboratory. It gave the YEs a meaningful perspective in which to view those very oddities among the local flora and fauna – the famous finches, the sunflowers that have developed into trees, the gulls which forage at night, lizards that feed on seaweed and cormorants that have forgotten how to fly – that had so excited the young scientific explorer who went there under such similar circumstances nearly one hundred and fifty years before.

Eye of the Wind put in briefly at Chatham Island, the administrative centre of the group, in order to complete customs formalities, and then sailed straight on to Academy Bay on Santa Cruz. Here the YEs visited the Charles Darwin Research Station, whose director, Dr Heindrick Hoeck, had arranged an itinerary that would take them to several islands and involve them in a series of projects that would aid the Station's conservation work. This was started in 1962, since when most of the archipelago has been designated a National Park, where strict environmental control is exercised in an effort to protect the wildlife from the various outside interferences which were threatening to destroy it. Much has been done to repair the damage caused over the years by indiscriminate slaughter and the introduction of alien animals such as pigs, goats, dogs and rats, but, even so, some endemic species are on the verge of extinction. Entry to the islands is now rigidly regulated and Operation Drake was privileged to be able to go to places and see things not readily accessible to the average tourist.

During a guided tour of the Research Station, the YEs were shown the incubation pens where giant tortoises are reared in perfect conditions as part of the campaign to replenish stocks of these extraordinary lumbering creatures on whose backs Darwin and his colleagues from the *Beagle* used to ride. Several subspecies are already extinct and a rather sad fellow known as Lonely George was introduced as the only surviving Pinta tortoise left in the world.

Certain subspecies of the prehistoric-looking land iguana are also becoming alarmingly rare and, once again, the Station is doing its best to save them by breeding them in captivity and then releasing them in specially protected areas where they cannot be got at by the wild dogs which are largely responsible for the drastic reduction in their numbers. American research scientist Howard Snell gave the YEs a crash course in how to identify the different types of iguana, in preparation for one of their projects, which involved searching for specimens of a particular endangered species. It was thought that very few, if any, still remained in their natural habitat, but a female was urgently required for breeding purposes.

YE Chris Downes, meanwhile, had already discovered a large number of the plentiful marine iguanas living in a very *un*natural habitat. While walking through the town, he had spotted dozens of them sunning themselves on the roof of a house. Inquiries revealed that this was the home of a local celebrity called Carl Angermeyer, who kept these miniature dinosaurs as pets and loved nothing better than to show them off to visitors, so Chris went along with Jim Heck, radio operator on *Eye of the Wind*, to investigate further. Sure enough, they got a big welcome from the amazing Mr Angermeyer, and when they approached the house they were astonished to find it literally festooned with the big lizards. They were hanging from drainpipes, stretched along window sills, even lounging in the living room. It turned out that there were 125 of them altogether and many of them answered to their own names. Mr Angermeyer explained, as Chris helped him to feed them their daily ration of white rice, that when he built the house forty years previously the iguanas were already in residence on the site, and rather than chase them away he had decided to let them settle in with him. They were, he insisted, charming and gentle creatures to have around the place.

The remarkably harmonious way in which the Galapagos animals lived in peace with themselves and with human beings was something that made a deep impression on the YEs. They were surprised to see birds, sea lions and iguanas happily sharing the same small rock, and were delighted to find that they could get within touching distance of many of these exotic creatures without them taking fright. Most of all, they were enchanted by the way the sea lions joined them for a swim.

This happened on South Plaza Island and was mentioned by almost all the YEs as one of the most memorable experiences of the expedition.

'They showed a sense of trusting communication that I would not have thought possible,' wrote Julie Barlow. 'It was such a captivating temptation to stay underwater with them that I kept on forgetting to surface for air before diving down again. Their lithe bodies, their light gliding through the water made one realise the limitations of one's own limbs and admire their ability to dart off in all directions with the slightest flip of their tails. They would swim straight towards me and look me right in the eye before turning quickly in their tracks and dashing away. One young sprite even circled my waist with a few quick circuits before heading off.'

Naomi Person, a 22-year-old New Yorker, found that the seals were just as playful when she went swimming in a lava pool. 'The lava had created a sort of natural sculpture garden, pillars rising up out of the water and all around the sides. I stepped out onto a rock and heard a strange groan and in a cavern underneath me were some fur seals, and as we walked round the edge it became apparent that the whole area was filled with caves inhabited by the seals. We wanted to go swimming there, but were not sure if the seals would be as friendly as the sea lions. Finding a pool filled with tropical fish, we decided to try there. The purple and blue fish were making a strange clicking sound that was perfectly audible underwater. And then suddenly the seals appeared and it quickly became apparent that they were very playful. It wasn't long before there were eight of them around me. They would wait upside down until I approached them and then flip over, somersaulting down to the bottom. Their expressions were really cute, large, wide eyes and little ears that stuck out. After an hour I was ready to go and swam over to the edge to get out of the water. They all followed me and popped their heads up, staring at me. I could not resist those pleading little eyes and went back in for another five minutes.'

Mike Kichenside had adopted a policy of sailing between the islands during the night so that the maximum number of daylight hours could be spent ashore and, after leaving South Plaza at 8.45 p.m., *Eye of the Wind* arrived off Marchena at seven o'clock in the morning. So startling was the contrast between the two islands that those aboard could have been forgiven for thinking that they must have been whisked to a completely different part of the world during the hours of darkness.

To call Marchena inhospitable would be a gross understatement. It is dominated by a 1,125-foot volcano and most of its eight-by-six mile area is covered with a field of lava broken only occasionally by scrub-covered hills. But although far from inviting, the scenery was certainly spectacular. The lava flows looked like swollen, rushing rivers that had suddenly been turned to stone at the wave of a magician's wand.

The YEs' task was to carry out a census of the goat population that had been first introduced in the 1960s. As they started climbing up towards the crater rim, they soon found that the solidified cascade of lava was both tough and treacherous to negotiate, with many razor sharp edges that sliced through the soles of their shoes and threatened an extremely painful landing to anyone who stumbled and fell. It proved to be an exhausting day as they scoured the island in the blistering sun for signs of the elusive goats, and most of them were greatly relieved to get back down to the beaches where, once again, the magic of the Galapagos wildlife was captivating.

Capital Radio's Linda Batt-Rawden was one of those entranced. 'After five hours of climbing I was shattered and to see the sea lapping gently on a white beach was fantastic. We stopped to eat our oranges before setting off along the beach and while we sat there birds appeared from everywhere as if to see who was intruding on their domain. Flycatchers, cactus finches, ground finches, Galapagos doves and mocking birds – they all came, as if from nowhere, to chatter and stare.

'As we walked back along the shoreline to where *Eye of the Wind* was anchored, I felt like a child set free in a sweet shop as I came across one after the other of the most incredible scenes.

'On the tideline lumpy black volcanic boulders jutted out into the ocean and, on first glance, it appeared as if the whole of the rock surface was liquid and mobile. But on closer inspection I discovered that it was actually covered in metre-long, black, marine iguanas basking in the hot afternoon sun.

'Among the rocks, where the sea had receded, deep pools of Walt Disney fantasy magnified tiny shoals of fish that darted among spiny sea urchins, bright anemones, delicate starfish and soft rippling ribbons of weed. Each pool had some hidden treasure, each rock some secret resident. Lava herons fished in the pools, stealing stealthily on long, slim legs – bright eyes watchful. I surprised a sleeping seal and watched as it joined its friends in a deep pool with a huge, sloping rock. As the sea rushed in over the rock, the seals used it as a helter-skelter slide, playing, chasing and leaping out of the water in sheer exuberance.

'There were birds everywhere, perched on rocks or squatting in shady spots. Night herons, their soft grey plumage blending into the rocks like shadows, and great grey herons all of four feet tall, perched on long stilt legs, Galapagos hawks, dark-feathered with cruel beaks – all of them completely approachable.

'Each tiny bay or rocky headland along that shore offered a glimpse of Galapagos wildlife. Sunbathing iguanas crowded, often one on top of the other, by the tideline; bright red Sally Lightfoot crabs scurried sideways for shelter beneath a rocky outcrop; tiny, velvet-coated seal cubs, doe-eyed and unafraid, rested in the shade. All of them seemed secure in a world that had evolved without fear of man's interference.'

The next stop was at James Island, where the contrasting highlights of the day were provided by the delicate beauty of a flock of pink flamingos and the awkward comedy of a pair of blue-footed boobies indulging in a courtship ritual. This involved much neck-stretching and slow backwards-and-forwards stepping that made the birds look even more stupid than usual. It is amusing to think that the booby was so-called because of its dim-witted look. It tends to spend long hours gazing fixedly at its bright blue feet with a mixed expression of surprise and disgust on its face, as if wondering how they ever got to be that colour.

From James Island *Eye of the Wind* returned to Santa Cruz, but put in this time at Conway Bay, on the eastern side of the island, where the search for the rare land iguana, *Conolphus subcristatus*, was to be launched. Not much hope was held out since the scientists at the Charles Darwin Research Station were pretty certain that every last one of the very few survivors of a once-thriving colony had already been rounded up. There was therefore great excitement when Gillian Rice peered down a burrow to find her gaze returned by a glinting pair of beady yellow eyes.

After an hour of frantic digging in the hot sun with their bare hands, the YEs were apparently no nearer to extracting the iguana from its den. The more they dug, the further it retreated down its tunnel. And the hisses and growls that issued forth were a trifle disconcerting. Just as they were all beginning to wonder whether it was worth bothering to go on, their quarry made an unexpected exit – backwards. Pausing only to give everybody a very nasty look the three-foot long creature complete with bared teeth, spat furiously at them and made a bolt for the undergrowth. It would probably have escaped but for the prompt action of Mark Creer, who threw his jacket over it and then dived on top of it. The catch was transported triumphantly back to the ship in a haversack and thence to the Research Station where it was confirmed as a much-needed female of the sought-after species. This success brought the Galapagos visit to a perfect climax, affording relief to the scientists and joy to the male Santa Cruz iguanas already in captivity.

This short phase of Operation Drake had proved, diplomatically, the most difficult that Tac HQ had to arrange and I was thankful that it had gone so well. Before finally departing from these enchanted islands *Eye of the Wind* dropped in at Post Office Bay on Floreana and picked up the mail in time-honoured fashion. There is a gaily-painted barrel on the quayside which passing ships have used as a postbox for nearly two hundred years. The way the system works is that each vessel deposits her own mail and picks up whatever is addressed to any of the places she is headed for. *Eye of the Wind* duly left behind forty letters and postcards, and collected everything that was addressed to the South Sea Islands. And then she headed out into the wide blue yonder of the Pacific.

Chapter Thirteen

Dateline: Fiji, 18 July 1979

Seven weeks after leaving the Galapagos and three months after she originally set sail from Panama, *Eye of the Wind* brought phase three of the expedition to an end when she docked at Suva, Fiji. For all those on board it had been a memorable voyage which, more noticeably than perhaps any other phase of Operation Drake, succeeded in achieving the aim of uniting an international bunch of complete strangers into a team of friends. A remarkable spirit of comradeship developed naturally among people living and working together so closely for such a long time, sharing hardships, adventures and new experiences along the way.

Once they had bid a fond farewell to the Galapagos, it was a month before they set foot on dry land again. They enjoyed some superb sailing as consistently strong south-east trade winds combined with the Humboldt Current to send *Eye of the Wind* creaming along at an average speed of seven knots. Those who had anticipated sun-bathing conditions were soon disillusioned – sweaters and even oilskins were very much the order of the day as the fresh breezes whipped stinging spray across the decks. But it was so invigorating that nobody had any complaints – except, possibly, Trish Holdway who was rarely able to put out her sampling nets while such a cracking pace was being maintained, for fear of them being ripped to shreds. And at one point she tried every day for a week to give a lecture, with slides, on the plight of the whale, only to be forced to abandon the attempt each time because there was no way of keeping the projector and screen level as the ship lurched through the waves. However, there was eventually ample compensation for this disappointment when she was able to give her talk with 'live' illustrations provided by several schools of sperm whales that passed nearby.

Back in Australia, Britain, Iceland, New Zealand and USA frantic fund-raising was in progress to keep the show solvent, and at the same time recce parties visited Fiji, Indonesia and PNG. Not only were we having to raise money for the Operation as a whole, but as the world

[122]

recession bit deeper it was clear that many of our directing staff also needed help. Contrary to what many people thought, they were having to find their own air fares plus £5-a-day subsistence. Some of the best instructors and scientists are paid very meagre salaries and simply could not afford to take part. However the Nuffield Trust and the H. and M. Charitable Trust gave us some magnificent help for the servicemen, and many kind individuals came forward to assist the civilians, and so another crisis was averted. Nevertheless, I began to feel more and more like a man trying to stop a dyke collapsing whilst desperately short of sand bags to shore up the weak points.

Aboard the flagship, life soon settled into a smooth routine. When not actually on watch duty or rushing to answer the summons, 'All hands on deck', that heralded the need for a rapid change of canvas, the YEs found plenty to keep them occupied. The lectures on navigation proved to be particularly popular and a number of scientific projects were carried out, ranging from a comprehensive listing of all bird-sightings to a study of the various organisms found growing on the hull of the ship and the effect of different anti-fouling substances upon them. A regular diversion was supplied by the frequent torrential downpours, during which everyone would race on deck with every available receptacle in order to replenish fresh water stocks. These storms also served as extremely welcome natural shower baths in which to enjoy a very satisfactory shampoo.

The ship's social life came to centre around the weekly Saturday night dinner parties laid on by successive watches at the end of their seven-day stints on duty in the galley. The first of these was a French Evening, when amazing gastronomic delights were conjured up in the cramped kitchen, and this was followed by a Trappist Monks' Evening, when nobody was allowed to speak a word. On this occasion the night ended on a hilarious note with a joke session conducted entirely in sign language and with cue cards. Almost as funny were the bread-making efforts of the various watches.

The days passed quickly in this fashion, and then there was the excitement of waiting for the cry, 'Land ahoy', that signalled the first sighting of the Tuamotu Islands. The excitement was tinged with nervousness, since Tiger had been working hard at building up an aura of menace around the name Tuamotu with a series of terrifying yarns about the many ships that had come to grief among the treacherous atolls that often protruded only a few feet out of the water, like sets of jagged teeth. But if the atolls were indeed a lurking threat to the unwary, the islands themselves were quite breath-taking. With their golden, palm-fringed beaches, they lived up to everyone's expectations of what South Sea Islands should be like.

Eye of the Wind's arrival in Tahiti's Papeete Harbour was also wonderfully romantic. She sailed in out of a perfect sunset with her crew aloft and a welcoming escort of ten-man canoes and an armada of other small boats, in which the traditional dusky beauties were conspicuous by their toplessness. Even the sudden rude and noisy obtrusion of the twentieth century in the shape of a jumbo jet taking off from the nearby airport and climbing low over the harbour could not entirely spoil the magic of those moments.

The whole of Tahiti was buzzing with preparations for a big forthcoming festival and the ship's company enjoyed a lively three-day visit. Also in town was Erwin Van Asbeck, a phase one YE whose life seemed to have been transformed already by his Operation Drake experience. Erwin had enjoyed his Atlantic crossing in *Eye of the Wind* so much that he had jumped at the chance to work his way back home from Panama by joining the crew of a yacht that was to be delivered in New Zealand. With a twelve-month delivery period, he and his colleagues were taking their time and making the most of a South Sea odyssey. It sounded like the trip of a lifetime, but just when everyone was beginning to feel a little envious, Erwin confessed that he would give anything to be back on *Eye of the Wind*.

Meanwhile, Tiger made an alarming discovery when he donned his diving gear and went down to inspect the bottom of the ship. The latest mechanical problem involved the prop shaft, which had been rattling and banging ominously all across the Pacific. When Tiger peered at the propeller, he saw to his horror that the vibrations had shaken it loose to the point where it was only held on by one bolt − and even that had been worked loose down to the last couple of threads! It was an amazingly lucky escape. Just a few minutes more motoring and the whole thing would have dropped off − there was no doubt about that. And then we would have been in a terrible fix, because *Eye of the Wind*'s propeller was unique and the chances of finding a replacement would have been nil. As it was, the danger was still not over, because the job of adjusting the thing and bolting it on underwater was an extremely tricky operation, during which the slightest slip could have sent the heavy unit plunging to the bottom of the harbour. Everybody held their breath while the repairs were carried out, but happily there were no further disasters. This was small consolation for the fact that the ship would obviously have to go into dry dock as soon as she got to Fiji, so that the prop shaft could be fixed properly − something that seemed certain to strain even further our overstretched finances.

Between Tahiti and Fiji, the fair winds deserted us and the ship experienced both the roughest and the calmest weather of the entire round-the-world voyage. First it was rough, with a long series of

The giant inflatable *David Gestetner* being used as a diving platform during the search for the wreck of the *Olive Branch* in Caledonia Bay. *David Gestetner* was also used on the Zaire River Expedition (CHRISTOPHER SAINSBURY)

(from left to right) American Robert Roethenmund, Canadian YE Anne Smith and British YE Peter Whitehouse excavating on the site of Fort St Andrew in Caledonia Bay (CHRISTOPHER SAINSBURY)

Marine iguanas in the Galapagos, with *Eye of the Wind* anchored in the background (CHRISTOPHER SAINSBURY)

A PNG highlander (CHRISTOPHER SAINSBURY)

Scientists at work on the aerial walkway in Sulawesi
(RUPERT RIDGEWAY)

Marine biologist Dr Patricia Holdway (centre right) with two YEs carrying out a survey of Vesuvius Reef off the coast of Sulawesi (RUPERT RIDGEWAY)

Camels leaving the El Kajarta Gorge, with Mount Kulal in the distance (CHRISTOPHER SAINSBURY)

squalls during which steady force 10 winds gusted force 11, whipping up mountainous seas and tossing *Eye of the Wind* about like a cork. For anyone who has never previously weathered storms like that, such conditions constitute a stern test of nerve – especially when one is constantly having to go aloft to change sail. There is the breath-taking moment as the ship climbs up each forty-foot cliff of water, followed by the stomach-wrenching lurch as she crests the wave before surfing down the other side. At that point, she is almost impossible to steer and there is the fear that she will slew sideways and get swamped.

As suddenly as the storms had broken, so they abated and *Eye of the Wind* found herself becalmed and drifting backwards in a heavy swell. Although anxious about the state of the prop shaft and the possibility of shaking the propeller loose, Mike Kichenside once again had no option but to start motoring. The rolling motion this produced in a lumpy sea was far more uncomfortable and inconvenient than the pitching and tossing that accompanies a fast drive through the waves, and even Leslie Reiter, such a stalwart throughout the expedition, was brought near to tears of frustration as her galley was reduced to chaos around her, with the contents of every cupboard showering onto the floor. The final straw was when a beautiful apple pie was catapulted out of the oven to become instant apple crumble underfoot.

As the ship laboured on, she began to fall behind schedule to the extent that proposed visits to Palmerston Atoll and also Tonga – where the King had hoped to come aboard – had to be cancelled. This was unfortunate but unavoidable. The YEs had been looking forward to both stop-offs and had become particularly fascinated by the strange history of Palmerston Atoll.

It was originally discovered by Captain Cook in 1774, but remained uninhabited until the middle of the nineteenth century, when it was colonised by an extraordinary character called William Masters, who settled there with his three Polynesian wives. Masters was an adventurer who had left England to join the California Gold Rush of 1849 and it was only after much globe-trotting that he finished up on the remote atoll – seven miles long and fives miles wide – and decided to stay there until the end of his days.

Before he eventually died in 1899, he had founded a considerable family and his children carried on the good work, so that by the time an American round-the-world sailor called in in the 1920s, the little community was over one hundred strong. Masters' eldest son, having followed dad's polygamous example, was at that stage in the interesting situation of having one wife who was younger than his grand-daughter. Some of the relationships within the colony were mind-bogglingly complicated, but, strangely, the in-breeding had not caused any obvious degeneration. Another fascinating feature of the little society was its language – an antiquated form of English that was a century out of date.

The whole bizarre story is fairly well-documented by various people who visited the place periodically, including one person who reported that, during a freak hurricane in 1926, a vast tidal wave forced everyone to seek refuge in the trees and while they were up there one of the women gave birth to a daughter!

It was a great pity that *Eye of the Wind* was unable to put in at the atoll, where Masters is still the most common name, but a radio call was made announcing her approach and some of the islanders came out to meet her in their canoes, and presents were exchanged.

As the 8,000-mile voyage from Panama to Fiji drew to a close, the YEs had time to reflect on the highlights of the long weeks at sea. In their final reports, most of them picked out the thrill of clinging to the yardarms with numbed fingers while changing sail in a strong wind, the fascination of the exotic wildlife they had encountered along the way, and the warmth of the friendship that developed among the ship's company. And then there was the deep satisfaction of being on watch in the hours just before dawn when the stars were at their most brilliant and the silence at its most profound. That was the time when many of them found themselves looking at their lives in a new light.

Gillian Rice summed up the special enchantment of those moments.

'The weeks at sea brought me closer in contact with nature and the elements than at any other time in my life,' wrote the young medical student. 'Never before have I had the opportunity to ponder over wind and waves, stars and sky, the clouds and the moon, the rising and setting of the sun. But for three months they were my constant companions whose beauty thrilled me over and over again, as if a veil had been lifted from my eyes, blessing me with increased awareness and a new appreciation of nature's artwork.

'Night time held special magical qualities for me and I would gaze contentedly at the celestial inhabitants keeping their long vigil until the encroaching light of dawn appeared. While the glittering constellations moved slowly across the velvet sky in their predestined orbital paths, the moon shed glowing beams of lunar brilliance which lit the ship in her pure white radiance. Moonlight danced on the billowing sails and, as she descended slowly towards the horizon, crested a shimmering pathway of illuminated wavelets stretching across the ocean, whose calm surface, on a windless night, was disturbed only by the gentlest of heavens and sighs. Never before have I experienced nature's beauty with such immediacy, nor gained so many hours of sensual fulfilment.'

[126]

Chapter Fourteen

Dateline: Moala Island, August 1979

Hurricane Meli brewed up out in the Pacific, north-east of Vanua Levu, and on the morning of 27 March 1979 burst upon the eastern Fijian islands of the Lau group with relentless fury. Mature coconut palms were snapped off and carried across the islands like straws in a breeze, buildings were flattened, boats were smashed to matchwood and forty-nine people lost their lives, while many more were injured – those who were not crushed under collapsing buildings were killed and maimed by flying debris, including sheets of corrugated iron that scythed through the air like giant razor blades. At Nayau and Ono, the devastation was so total that the two islands were left desolate and uninhabitable, and the surviving population had to be evacuated. What had not been flattened by the wind during a four-hour battering was washed away by the tidal wave that followed in the hurricane's wake. At Moala, the destruction was not quite so final, though it was terrible enough, and the stricken islanders did have a little left on which to start rebuilding their shattered lives. It was here that Operation Drake was eventually sent to help out with relief work.

It is interesting that our offer of assistance was at first turned down by the central Fijian authorities and it was only after some delicate negotiations by our lawyer-turned-explorer, Rupert Grey, and the personal intervention of the Fijian Prime Minister, who happened to come from the Lau group, that we were permitted to go in. It may seem strange that a gift-horse should be looked in the mouth in this way, especially as very little had actually been done at that stage in the way of relief work, but there was a reason for the hesitation. There is normally a strict ban on casual visitors and foreign yachts in the area, in a sensible effort to protect the islanders' way of life from possibly detrimental outside influences. So it was understandable that we were regarded with slight suspicion initially. Once we made it obvious that our motives were genuine, there were no problems at all.

Our allotted task was to erect prefabricated classroom blocks and

[127]

teachers' quarters in the two villages of Keteira and Vunuku. It promised to be back-breaking work, carried out in heart-breaking circumstances, and yet it turned out to be one of the most rewarding of all the projects tackled throughout the expedition. What made it so was the overwhelming charm and hospitality of the local people, whose infectious warmth and friendliness came shining through, despite the tragedy they had suffered. They managed to transform the entire exercise into a uniquely happy experience which was quite unforgettable for all those lucky enough to take part.

The ninety-mile trip across from Suva to Moala did not get things off to a very good start. The new phase four YEs had hardly stepped off the plane before they were shepherded onto an ancient, flat-bottomed landing craft, which took thirty-six hours to wallow its way through gale force 6 winds and a stomach-wrenching swell. The stewed fish heads which were served up as a great local delicacy did nothing to ease the awful misery!

But from the moment the party of twenty-eight YEs and directing staff stepped ashore, things began to improve dramatically. They were immediately invited to a *sevu sevu* − the traditional Fijian welcoming ceremony, which gave them their first taste of the social formalities and protocol that is such an important part of life on these outlying islands. Wizz Gambier, aged eighteen, from Somerset described the procedure:

'We gathered outside a tent, sitting cross-legged in a circle one half of which was composed of the village chief, his spokesman and the village elders. In the centre of the circle was a large wooden bowl carved from the kauri tree, into which was poured fresh water. Beside the bowl a man was pounding yaqona roots, and when these were shredded, they were placed in a fine cloth bag and steeped in the water to produce the traditional drink of *grog* or *kava*. To look at, this drink is like muddy water and at first taste it resembles matchsticks and numbs the end of the tongue. After drinking a reasonable quantity it begins to numb one's lips as well.

'After the chief's spokesman had said a few words and our leader had replied, gifts were exchanged. We were presented with a prized *tabua*, or whale's tooth, and gave a quantity of yaqona in return. And then the grog-drinking began.

'A server who is seated at the bowl fills half a coconut shell (*bilo*), and this is handed to another server who waits for the village spokesman to announce who to serve it to. When one is offered a bilo of grog one claps one's hands once, cupping them so as to make a hollow sound, drinks the grog and then returns the bilo. The grog has to be drunk in one breath, and while one is drinking it the server claps three times. On returning the bilo, the drinker then claps three times

[128]

and the Fijians say such things as "mother, mother, mother", and clap three times, too.

'After our first taste of their customs, one feeling was uppermost in all our minds and that was how friendly and warm the people were. One only had to walk out of the house to be greeted by broad ear-to-ear grins.'

Work on the buildings started straight away and the local men, once they had got over the surprise of seeing our girls labouring with picks and shovels and carrying heavy loads, joined in enthusiastically.

From then on a tremendous bond was forged between Operation Drake and the local people. Although they slaved away every bit as hard as the YEs did, they continually poured out their thanks with touching sincerity. And the whole community worked hard to make their working guests feel at home. The women and girls appeared regularly with tea and Fijian doughnuts and the young boys shinned up the tall palms to provide a treat of cool, fresh coconut milk to slake terrible thirsts. The womenfolk also served up the most sumptuous meals of crab, crayfish, curries, chicken and pork, rounded off with a mouth-watering dessert called Fijian pudding, made from ground coconut, casava and tapioca steamed in banana leaves and covered with a golden syrup made from coconut milk and brown sugar.

Every night was party night, with much grog-drinking accompanied by exhibitions of traditional dancing, which included the delightful custom whereby the girls come and touch the toes of the men they wish to dance with them.

Hardly surprising, then, that when the time came to leave, the YEs found it a real wrench to tear themselves away and the Fijians were equally sorry to see them go. As they handed over parting gifts, the tears were rolling down their cheeks and soon there was not a dry eye anywhere. The final departure, as recalled by nineteen-year-old Christopher Richardson from Newcastle-upon-Tyne, was highly emotional.

'We had our last little grog session and our last dances and then the entire village escorted us down to the beach, where the punts were waiting to take us out to the Prime Minister's private yacht, out of our dream-like villages and away from our newly made friends.

'The scene down on the beach could have been taken straight from a novel, the villagers wading out into the water with the band still playing, dancing as they went. They climbed into punts as well and followed us right out into the bay where the ship was anchored. It was such a magnificent and magical scene that it brought tears to my eyes.'

The Prime Minister had kindly sent his private yacht to ensure that the return journey to Suva was quicker and more comfortable than the trip out. While the YEs had been away, *Eye of the Wind* had been in dry dock having the damaged prop shaft replaced. Thanks to the magnificent combined efforts of the Royal Fiji Navy, the local shipyard, government officers and local supporters, the job was done much more quickly and efficiently than we had ever dared hope was possible. And then, just when we were gloomily counting the cost, we had a rare stroke of luck. Columbia Pictures were filming a remake of *The Blue Lagoon* in Fiji and they asked if they could hire *Eye of the Wind* for a few days, complete with crew, to use in some of the scenes they were shooting. Not only did this provide an interesting diversion for the YEs – but the handsome fee offered by the film company helped considerably towards paying the repair bills.

After this rather novel interlude, the ship set out on the last lap of her voyage to Papua New Guinea. There were brief stops along the way at a series of islands and atolls, each of which seemed more Utopian than the one before. Two days were spent at Tikopia Island, where the YEs got their first glimpse of real grass skirts, and it was near there that they sailed through a sea of pumice, which was the result of underwater volcanic activity that had also thrown up a new island in the Tonga area. The island remained visible for two days before vanishing again as eerily as it had appeared.

At Guadalcanal in the Solomon Islands, the locals came out to meet *Eye of the Wind* and took the YEs on sight-seeing round trips in their canoes. And then it was on to Kwaiawata in the Marshall Bennett group, where no other ship had been for ten years. This was another enchanting spot, a forgotten speck in the ocean, away from all the normal sea routes and consequently passed by unnoticed by the rest of the world. There the YEs traded rice and fish hooks for shells and souvenirs, and *Eye of the Wind* came away with the foredeck covered with paw paws, mangoes and every imaginable variety of exotic fruit.

It was on 5 September that the ship finally came alongside at Lae, Papua New Guinea, to be greeted by a marvellous welcome that will long be remembered by everyone concerned. It augured well for Operation Drake's stay in the mysterious island chosen as the theatre for our second major land phase – a place that more than lives up to its reputation as the 'Last Unknown'.

Chapter Fifteen

Dateline: Lae, Papua New Guinea, 5 September 1979

There was a time when no sailing ship was welcome in Papua New Guinea. The approach of any such vessel to the reef-bound shores of the island was regarded with suspicion and hatred by the coastal villagers and landing parties could expect to be greeted by a hail of spears and arrows. This was hardly surprising, since, for many years, European visitors had only one use for the wild, remote and exotic land named by the first Portuguese explorers *Ihlas de Papuas* – Island of the Fuzzy-Haired – and that was as a source of strong young slaves to be carried off and sold on the world's very lucrative labour markets.

Attitudes have changed since then, happily, and *Eye of the Wind* sailed into Lae to a fantastic reception. However, although the people are friendly these days, the environment remains just about as hostile as it ever was.

The island, second largest in the world after Greenland, is shaped like a giant turtle swimming in the South Pacific seas just above the northern tip of Queensland, Australia, and is divided neatly down the middle by a straight north-south border, between the Indonesian territory of West Irian in the west and PNG in the east.

It is an untamed tropical wilderness in which soaring mountain peaks rise out of stinking mangrove swamps, mighty rushing rivers gush through plunging rocky gorges, and baking arid scrubland gives way to wide delta quagmires. And, overall, it is shrouded in dense, impenetrable jungle, which is why it is still one of the least-explored areas left on Earth. The inaccessibility of the interior meant that nothing at all was known about it until the first aircraft flew over it in the 1920s, and existing maps, compiled from aerial photographs, still contain blank spaces marked, 'Cloud – Relief Data Incomplete'. That is the modern equivalent of the mythical creatures, the gogs and magogs, with which the old cartographers used to fill the unknown areas that nobody had been able to reach and chart.

It is not just the terrain that makes PNG so inhospitable. The climate and the creepy crawlies – which seem to be bigger, nastier and more

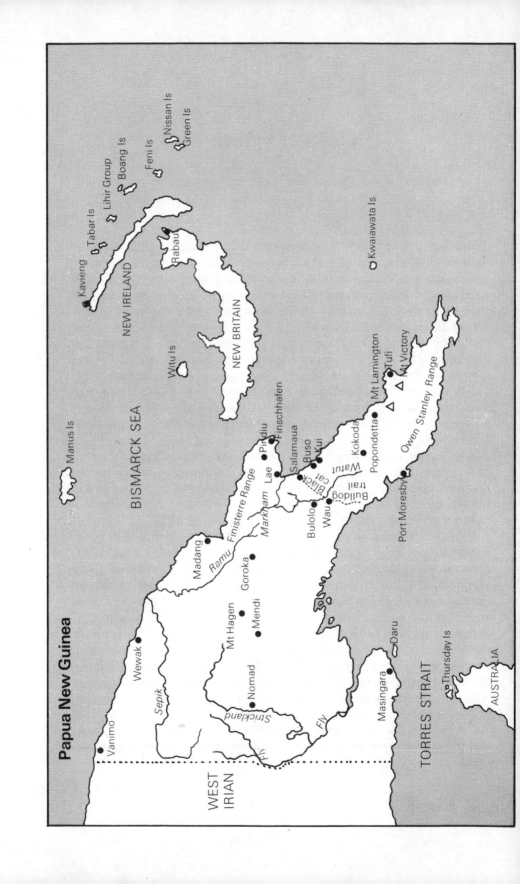

Papua New Guinea

plentiful than anywhere else in the world – add further dimensions of discomfort and danger to life outside the few air-conditioned townships. The feverish, steam-heat humidity of the lowlands soon leaves one limp with exhaustion, and the catalogue of lethal wildlife includes the world's largest crocodiles, enormous pythons that can break every bone in a full-grown pig's body and then swallow it whole, and small snakes just a few inches long with a bite so poisonous that they can cause death within a matter of minutes. These are out-size lizards, scorpions and spiders the size of your fist. Mosquitoes, which I personally regard as the greatest threat of all, are also particularly virulent there.

One way and another, it is a real battle against the elements to survive in PNG. Everything stings or bites or causes rashes and infections, and the best that twentieth century technology can provide in the form of salves, lotions and repellents seem powerless to protect one's skin against continual attack. Your clothes rot and the most rugged jungle boots crack up in half the time it would take anywhere else. Even my pith helmet, which for twelve years had kept me cool, dry and safe from falling coconuts in some of the most God-forsaken corners of the world, finally surrendered to the atmospheric extremes of PNG and sprouted a terrible green mould. (Fortunately, news of its sad demise had no sooner reached England than offers of replacements flooded in from old colonials all over the place, and the *Daily Mail* very kindly went to the lengths of having a new one made to measure by Moss Bros, who had presented me with the original one back in 1968.)

What all these horrors added up to was, without doubt, the finest Adventurous Training area in the world! My attention had first been drawn to this fact by Mr George Baker, a former British High Commissioner in PNG, who also happened to be the father of my one-time PA Pam, and became a great supporter of the SES, and a valued adviser on all matters diplomatic. He was always enthusiastic about the tremendous potential of the country as the site for an expedition of the kind that interested the SES, and as soon as Operation Drake began to take shape, he started to lay the groundwork and forged what was to be an invaluable contact with Brigadier Ted Diro, Commander of the PNG Defence Force.

At around the same time, an army colleague, Chris Barnes, came to see me, saying that he was leaving the services and was looking for something to keep him busy for a few weeks. I gave him £100 and told him to go and have a look at PNG for us. Chris is an incredibly tough, adventurous character and that was just the kind of brief he relishes. He went out there and undertook a one-man recce, sizing the place up and sussing out some of the main problems we would have to face in terms of logistics and so on. His report backed up George Baker's view that PNG was ideally suited to our need for some really challenging projects.

I then led two further advance recces, the main one – in August 1978 – being chiefly remarkable for the extraordinary flying of Noel Frewster the young pilot of the PNG Printing Company who chauffeured us round the island. Light aircraft are used like buses in PNG, hopping over jungle from one outlying community to another. It is the only way to travel in a country which has few roads, and one soon gets used to endlessly hair-raising landings and take-offs from bumpy grass airstrips that are usually no more than small clearings on the jungle hillsides. So great are the thrills and excitement of flying in PNG, it is hardly surprising that the pioneering local airline Tal-Air – which executes more landings and take-offs in an average year than British Airways world-wide – has recruited quite a number of its pilots from among Vietnam war veterans who have developed a taste for danger and for whom straightforward civilian flying would seem rather dull.

To cover all the areas that we needed to see, I split the reconnaissance party into three groups. Robbie Roethenmund and Lisa Van Gruisen joined a gunboat of the PNG Defence Force at Rabaul to investigate the outer islands; Vince Martinelli looked into the problems of the Wau Trails; whilst Noel Frewster, Barbara Martinelli and I flew up to Wewak to try to make a low-level air reconnaissance of the notorious Strickland Gorge. PNG, surprisingly, has the most extraordinarily widespread and efficient telephone system, so it was quite easy for us all to keep in touch.

The island recce party soon had a problem. Robbie went down with colic and Lisa's gunboat broke down. Another gunboat was sent to take over the task and soon that, too, had engine trouble. A third vessel arrived and Lisa completed the job, having temporarily put out a large part of PNG's Navy in the process.

In the jungle of the Owen Stanley Mountains, Vince was learning to appreciate the toughness of the going, whilst on the north coast at Wewak we waited for the weather to clear and allow us to get in to the high-altitude valley of the Upper Strickland River. We were in luck, for within a day of our arrival favourable weather was indicated and Noel decided to have a try. Barbara had the still cameras and took the rear seat, whilst I held the Canon 8mm cine camera in the front. The twin-engined Cessna 301, named 'Olivetti' after the company who sponsored it in an air race, was an ideal aircraft for the job and we were soon climbing south into the cloud-shrouded mountains.

At twelve hundred feet we crossed a rocky ridge and winged our way through the crags and peaks of this little known land. Suddenly Noel pointed. 'Look, it's clearing,' he shouted. Sure enough, ahead of us the clouds were rolling back to reveal an emerald-green valley surrounded by towering cliffs and dark mountains. Barbara's camera was already in operation as I raised my cine. Noel took the Cessna through the valley at one thousand feet, and we got a good view of the river winding its way fairly gently at first and then tumbling over rocky ledges in foaming fury before it plunged into the narrow, vertical-sided gorge. I felt the aircraft bank sharply and looked up to see a wall of rock racing past a couple of hundred feet away. Blasts of wind shook the Cessna as it flew twisting and turning through the mountain pass. The river had almost disappeared in the dark green foliage which now covered the entire valley bottom and seemed to close over the top of the canyon. Eventually we emerged from the mountains and saw the endless flat swampland of the Lower Strickland ahead. 'That's fine, Noel,' I yelled, 'can you take us back at low level?' The Australian pilot made a funny face and we reloaded our cameras. The return journey was the most exhilarating flight of my life. Manoeuvring his aircraft like a fighter, Noel hurtled through the great cleft in that green wilderness. Barbara and I concentrated on filming, but the gravitational forces on some of the turns were such that my arms felt like lead and I could hardly lift the camera. Cliffs and jungle shot past the wingtips. We saw underground rivers emerging, huge caves, strange trees and then a single rope bridge across the river. 'So someone does live down there,' I thought. Even so, there was no other obvious sign of any human habitation. Back at base that night, we worked on our reports with enthusiasm because we knew that we now had the vital information which would enable Roger Chapman, the experienced explorer who had been awarded the MBE for gallantry whilst with us on the Blue Nile Expedition, to tackle another fearsome river exploration task.

By this time our local Operation Drake committee, under the leadership of Colonel Ken Noga of the PNG Defence Force and Donald Middleton, George Baker's successor as High Commissioner, had already begun the job of rousing interest, selecting projects and finding sponsors – no easy task in a community still largely dominated by Australians who have never been famous for their charitable feelings towards anything associated with the 'bloody Poms!' Despite this, they succeeded so brilliantly that no less than forty-one PNG YEs were sponsored to join us during the phase. It is hard to resist the enthusiasm generated by people like Nigel Porteous, fellow Jerseyman and long-time friend, who, along with his wife, Jenny, co-ordinated all the advance work with such boundless energy that the local newspaper

[135]

Niugini Nius was moved to remark shortly before *Eye of the Wind* arrived in Lae: 'The level of activity surrounding preparations for the four-month PNG phase has increased so much as to leave one quite breathless.'

The generosity of some supporters was quite overwhelming. Major John Girling, the Chairman of Rice Industries, for instance, not only sponsored two local YEs but also paid for two chalets at the Lae Lodge in which to house our Tac HQ; he also provided the office furniture to go in them, put a car at our disposal and made space in his warehouses for us to use as a central stores. On top of all that, both he and his wife, Ida, worked ceaselessly on our behalf before, during and after our stay. Ray Thurecht of the PNG Printing Company was another stalwart who helped us in many ways, and we also owe a great debt of thanks to Alan and Linda Musicka, who threw open their house in Port Moresby as a transit station for Operation Drake personnel arriving in the country. For four months they were never able to call their home their own, as a succession of strangers passed through it. Without such marvellous people the venture would never have been possible. A great many local companies also offered valuable help and the assistance of Air Niugini and Tal-Air was to prove of special importance.

Meanwhile, I had decided that I personally would have to take charge in PNG, simply because our operation there had rapidly escalated into such a large and complex affair that I felt it would be unfair to push the overall responsibility onto anybody else. We had so many different things going on, spread over such a wide area, that our resources were stretched to the limit, and I anticipated, quite rightly as it turned out, that there were likely to be more everyday organisational headaches than on any other phase.

Our advance party, under Major Roger Chapman and including Quarter Master, Warrant Officer Len Chandler RE, started arriving in the island almost two months before *Eye of the Wind* sailed into Lae to mark the formal launch of the phase. They were followed by tons of stores and equipment that came in by sea and RAF Hercules, and that included everything from rations sufficient for 160 people for six months to the six-foot Avon Sea Raider craft which we transferred from Panama via Britain. Then the sixty-odd scientists and Directing Staff began to fly in, and preparatory work on the various projects got under way. These were hectic weeks and, as the pace hotted up in our Lae Lodge Tac HQ, Operations Officer Captain Mike Knox of the Royal Highland Fusiliers, dealt coolly and efficiently with the endless succession of minor crises which are really what an expedition like this is all about. Warrant Officer Les Winterburn REME, who had been with us on the Zaire River Expedition, and Corporal Ray Thomas,

[136]

quickly set up a workshop to maintain a fleet of vehicles that the PNG government had generously lent us. Third Officer Clare Downham, WRNS, became my Adjutant and organised the office with my new PA, Cathryn Barker, whom we nicknamed 'Margot', because she reminded us of the character played by Penelope Keith in the popular television series *The Good Life*. In Port Moresby, Sara Spicer-Few, our bonny PR lady, plunged into the problems of procurement. Sergeant Peter Lavers and his signallers established communications with our rear link that 30th Signals Regiment ran at Blandford in England, and we were all set.

As the YEs stepped ashore from *Eye of the Wind* everything, miraculously, seemed to be ticking over very smoothly. Four years of planning was about to come to fruition in four months of concentrated activity.

Chapter Sixteen

Dateline: Buso, 18 September 1979

The site eventually chosen for the PNG aerial walkway was totally idyllic. Situated on the east coast some sixty miles south of Lae, it was virtually inaccessible except by boat and this meant that the scientists were able to carry on with their work undisturbed by a constant stream of visitors. Indeed, much as we loved the Buso Camp, it was one of the major logistic headaches for Len Chandler. Local boats were hired to take supplies down and Corporal Ray Thomas eventually wore out the fast Avon Sea Raider on the Buso run. The PNG Defence Force helped with landing craft, but often it was local businessman Harry Pelgen who came to our rescue with his superb twin-engined 'Swordfish'. I do not know how we should have managed without Harry, who generously never charged for his wonderful service. The actual camp was set up within ten yards of the sea on the edge of a beautiful palm-fringed sandy beach, where dugongs, strange seal-like creatures, would fearlessly come into the shallows to feed. Not far away, in some of the most picturesque jungle one could ever hope to find, was a deep, clear river in which to cool off at the end of a hot sweaty day in the tropical humidity.

From the scientific point of view, it was also very satisfactory. Finding a tract of primary rain forest ideal for everyone's branch of research is not at all easy, as we had already found in Panama and were to find again in Sulawesi. But the Buso location fulfilled Dr Mike Swaine's scientific requirements. Mike, a botanist and climber from Aberdeen University, had arrived early to assist with the siting of the walkway. Apart from the pleasantness of the surroundings, it had the further advantage that it was part of a reserve owned by the Bulolo Forestry College, who were only too happy to loan us the two permanent huts, the cookhouse and the ration store they had built there and which formed the nucleus of our camp site. Two more huts, one of them a laboratory, were erected with the help of Mr Marcus of Buso and some of his villagers, along with Captain Mike Kuwi and four men from the PNG Defence Force and, what with the introduction of a generator to power electric lights, a cooker and even a fridge, the luxury was enough to make any true expeditionary blush with embarrassment. Not surprisingly, the walkway proved a very popular project and, after a stint there, most of the YEs were understandably reluctant to leave.

The three spans of walkway – one of which was left behind at the end of the project so that further research could be carried out by the Bulolo Forestry College – were constructed under the supervision of Sergeant Louis Gallagher, a wiry Glaswegian sapper, who emerged as one of the 'characters' of the phase, and who regarded his structures with great, and justifiable, pride. Like Mike Christie in Panama, Louis found that his only real problem was how to make the initial ascent one hundred feet up into the treetops, but he was provided with a solution to this in the nimble form of PNG Defence Force Sergeant Robbie Aki, who displayed an astonishing ability to shin up the sheerest trunk with the greatest of ease. To get lines from one tree to another Andrew Mitchell had obtained a crossbow which also proved useful.

Botanists, entomologists and zoologists alike were all delighted with the walkway, which gave them their first opportunity to study PNG's extraordinarily rich variety of flora and fauna high in the forest canopy. The island boasts over ten thousand plant species, including more types of orchid than any other country in the world and an exceptionally wide range of mosses and ferns, and also harbours virtually every known insect group – a fact of particular interest to the team from the Queensland Institute of Medical Research who carried out projects on parasitology and insect vectors of human disease. But it is the birds which are most obviously and spectacularly prolific. More than six hundred and fifty different species have been recorded – almost as many as in the entire North American continent – and in many cases their names are almost as colourful as their brilliant plumage. Among the 401 specimens that were trapped and tagged by ornithologist Peter Driscoll from the University of Queensland were a chestnut-backed jewelbabbler, a glossy mantled manucode, a lemon-cheeked honeyeater and a red-capped flowerpecker.

Also netted were several different kinds of birds of paradise. Of the forty-three species of this most breath-takingly beautiful of all birds known to exist, thirty-eight are to be found in PNG. Their dazzling plumage brought them close to extinction at one time, as they were hunted ruthlessly for the feathers that were much in demand as decoration for ladies' hats, but they are now flourishing once again, thanks to changing fashions and a rigorously enforced protection policy. The YEs were warned that the penalty for being caught with just one of the magnificent tail plumes is a hefty fine and up to two

[139]

years in prison – so, no souvenirs!

Not quite so attractive as the birds of paradise were the bats, which were collected with outstanding success by Ben Gaskell, our resident batman, or chiropterologist, working on behalf of the British Museum (Natural History). By coincidence, Ben managed to trap exactly the same number of specimens as Peter Driscoll – 401 – using fine-mesh nets suspended among the trees around the walkway and in a nearby mangrove swamp. Ben also suspended mist nets from the walkway in the canopy of the forest to trap bats there for the first time ever. This work has opened up a new perspective on the distribution of bats in the forest. As many as ten times the number of bats were found flying in the canopy as at ground level and some species thought to be rare were found to be common high up in the forest. A previously undescribed species of tube-nosed fruit bat, that was twice the normal size and had totally different markings, was discovered. Ben was delighted with this exceptionally loathsome-looking creature that gets its name from the tube-like nostrils that protrude from its frighteningly ugly face. 'This is the greatest moment of my life,' he enthused to a representative of his local newspaper back home in London. And then, as if sensing the reporter's disbelief that anyone should want to spend his life chasing after something so disgusting, added: 'People think I'm a bit batty myself to spend my time up to my knees in smelly mud in a swamp full of malarial mosquitoes, but to me bats are the most misunderstood creatures in the world. They have always had a bad press, what with Dracula and vampires and ridiculous stories about them getting caught in women's hair. They are actually beautiful, gentle creatures – even though they do keep biting my fingers when I pick them up.'

Ben, who joined us again in Sulawesi, turned out to be a marvellously eccentric character, who insisted on dressing for dinner in the middle of the jungle in full tropical evening dress, including a white tuxedo and white shoes which he somehow managed to keep white, despite the ravages of life in the forest that left most people looking like badly dressed scarecrows. He also kept everybody amused with his conjuring tricks and his pranks, the most successful of which involved his suddenly hurtling out of the jungle one night heavily disguised as Dracula, complete with a cape and false fangs. After terrorising all the girls around the camp fire, he disappeared back into the forest with much flapping and screeching, whereupon a carefully positioned stooge dashed out of the shadows shouting for Ben and saying that he had just been passed by an enormous bat. Instantly, Ben materialised casually and not at all breathless from the other side of the camp, attired in his normal collecting gear and asking what all the fuss was about. At that point someone else dressed in the Dracula gear went flapping past on the edge of the clearing and Ben gave chase, eventually capturing this second accomplice and returning to camp with him enmeshed in his collecting net. It was all very cleverly set up and caused much hilarity.

Such fun and games added to the charm of life at the Buso camp, which was run with easy-going efficiency by Captain Anthony Evans of the Coldstream Guards. The daily routine of the little community was enlivened by a full programme of scintillating do-it-yourself social events that brightened the camp-fire night-life scene. There were regular dinner parties hosted by different groups, each of which tried to outdo the others in working culinary wonders with the limited army rations available. Elaborate and mouth-wateringly misleading menus would be written out and the meals were served with great style on the camp's rickety wooden trestle tables, that were decorated on these occasions with orchids and other exotic plants. Formal wear was occasionally required and, although nobody could match the high sartorial standards set by Ben Gaskell with his white tuxedo, some of the improvisations showed tremendous imagination. The ladies donned long dresses fashioned from bits of sacking and other unlikely materials and looked most attractive with the flowers of the forest in their hair, while all the men managed to find something that would make do as a black dickie bow. After dinner, people would sing, or recite poetry, or perform sketches and plays.

During the day, much painstaking and valuable work was carried out and it will be many years before all the specimens, samples and data that were amassed can be fully processed by the universities and other institutions around the world to which they were despatched for examination and analysis. A botanical team from the University of Queensland led by Dr David Lamb studied the physiology of tropical forest at Buso. The walkway enabled them to take measurements of the nitrogen intake of leaves from the high canopy to ground level and these samples were processed in a futuristic array of tubes, bottles and electrical instruments set up in the camp laboratory.

Other scientists continued the study of the distribution of flying insects in the forest, hauling four ultra-violet light traps up into the trees each night. The thousands of insects collected are now being sorted out in Britain, providing the first information on their vertical and horizontal distribution in PNG's forests. Dr William Wint continued the work he had begun with us in Panama, studying the way in which insects attack leaves in the canopy. The YEs helped him crate no less than one hundred kilos of leaf samples alone. And the British Museum's Jon Martin, whose specialist interest is in aphids, which cause millions of pounds' worth of damage to crops the world over,

[141]

went home with enough samples to keep his department happy for many months. Detailed research such as this is a vital first step in understanding the immensely complex workings of the tropical rainforest ecosystem. It is like adding another piece to a seemingly impossible jigsaw puzzle.

Apart from the unwelcome but almost unavoidable attentions of mosquitoes, sandflies and other insects, which had everyone itching and scratching and whose bites often turned septic and festered in the humidity, the discomforts of Buso were relatively few and there were not many close encounters with creepy-crawlies of a really dangerous kind. There were one or two close shaves. YE Lynda Thompson, from Swindon, came within inches of treading on a Papua black – one of the deadliest snakes on the island – and Cathy Hignell, a nurse sponsored by Capital Radio, had a nasty experience when she climbed into her hammock one night, felt something wriggling under her back, and jumped out again to find a poisonous scorpion lurking there. Queensland scientist Dr Ian Fanning had the distinction of being one of two people bitten by a snake – and that was a twelve foot python. Ian had been summoned to the neighbouring village of Kui by the inhabitants, who had found the snake preparing to attack one of their pigs. He was bitten on the hand as he tried to catch it and, although such snakes are non-poisonous, their bite is, nevertheless, extremely painful and can still cause a serious infection. The sharpness of its fangs was proved by the fact that it managed to eat its way out of the canvas bag in which it was imprisoned by our reptile expert, Ian Redmond, after Ian Fanning had brought it back to Buso for examination. It was never seen again.

Five YEs – Joppa Johns, Julius Violaris and Boniface Buloti from PNG, Glenda Watson from the UK and Channel Islander Caroline Buxton, who was sponsored by best-selling author Jack Higgins – spent over a month at Buso, and others went there for two to three weeks. In his final report Anthony Evans concluded: 'Apart from visiting a new and relatively inaccessible tropical country, I consider that the YEs learned five particular lessons while at Buso. They had the opportunity to do many things that are taken for granted by some but never done by most, such as using generators and inflatable power boats, abseiling, snorkelling and cooking for over thirty people. They became more familiar with natural environments that they may not have known at all, such as the sea, the jungle, the hills and nature herself. Some YEs visibly benefited from this during their stay, developing their self-confidence and their ability to adjust to the situation and the problems encountered. Learning to use one's eyes to look at the beauty, orderliness and intricacy of nature I consider to be a lesson in itself. So

[142]

is the appreciation of a single-minded but apparently haphazard approach to the collection of scientific data – particularly to those who did not study science at school; this approach may help them cope with the rat race in the big wide world outside. Perhaps the most important lesson, however, was given to all by the ability of people of both sexes of appreciably different ages, backgrounds, races, cultures and interests to work together towards communal goals in a friendly and harmonious atmosphere. For this reason many people were sad to leave Buso Scientific Camp.'

Chapter Seventeen

Dateline: Imbinis, West Sepik, Papua New Guinea,
November 1979

In a small, isolated village deep in the interior of the remote northwestern province of PNG, Dr Hugh Savill and the Operation Drake medical survey team found themselves caught up in the middle of a frightening drama. They had awoken that morning to discover that, quite out of the blue, their native bearers had been accused of some grave and deliberate insult against the villagers, who had worked themselves up into an angry mood and were now demanding retribution. The elders had gathered to sit in judgement, and while they held court, the young men hovered menacingly in the background, waiting impatiently for the verdict and the go-ahead to carry out whatever punishment was decided.

Hugh and his colleagues watched the proceedings with dismay. Before they set out on the ten-day patrol in the backwoods of the West Irian border country they had been well aware of the traditional enmities that exist between tribes and villages in the outlying areas of the island and which can explode into open violence at the slightest provocation. The bearers themselves had been a little anxious about venturing so far out of their own territory, but, as they were going to be with a party that included members of the PNG Defence Force as well as white men, the risk of any trouble had seemed slight.

Everything was fine when they arrived in Imbinis, the most distant point of the patrol's itinerary. A big party was in full swing and they were given a very friendly welcome before being shown to a large, vacant hut in which to live during their four-day stay. The trouble arose a couple of evenings later, in the most innocent circumstances, when one of the PNG Defence Force soldiers started strumming the guitar which he carried with him everywhere and the bearers got up to dance to the music. It seemed harmless enough, but the villagers somehow got it into their heads that the bearers were mimicking the dancing of their womenfolk, which they had seen at the party. They were accused, quite simply, of 'taking the mickey'.

As the elders considered this very serious charge, an ugly situation was clearly brewing. A 'guilty' verdict, which seemed very likely, would mean, at the very least, the immediate expulsion of the bearers from the village and probably a fairly severe beating up to hasten them on their way. It could be even worse if things really got out of hand. And, although there was no hint of hostility towards the rest of the patrol, they would nevertheless be left in a difficult position, if the bearers were kicked out. They would be left stranded without any means of carrying their mass of equipment and, as they had no radio with which to contact Tac HQ in Lae, they would have no way of summoning assistance.

In the end there were some extremely tense moments before a Defence Force medic, who came from the opposite end of the island and was therefore accepted as an independent arbiter, managed to defuse the situation by persuading the elders that no insult had been intended by the bearers. It took a great deal of diplomatic wheeling and dealing on his part before the young men rather grudgingly relaxed, and the crisis was over. From then on, until the patrol finished their survey, packed up and left, the bearers remained very subdued and stuck close to the rest of the party.

This was by no means the only evidence of fierce inter-village hostility encountered in the West Sepik region by the medical teams. A second patrol, with another medical officer, Dr David Bowdler, penetrated much further into the interior and came close to witnessing an even more violent incident. They had just left the village of Mamambra, where Lieutenant Richard Bampfylde of the 15/19 King's Own Hussars had remained to collect some extra samples, when a fight broke out involving four men, one of whom was hit in the face and knocked to the ground. He quickly picked himself up and rushed off into the jungle only to return some time later with twenty friends, all armed to the teeth and spoiling for a fight. 'There was then a great shouting match between these men and the elders of Mamambra, as a result of which it was agreed that the matter would be settled by a formal battle to be held in three days' time,' recalled Richard. 'I was told that the argument which led to the fight had started over the local school, which was supposed to be maintained jointly by the three neighbouring villages that it served. One of these villages – the one from which the man who was knocked down came – had decided, for various reasons, that they didn't believe in schooling and were therefore going to opt out of their share of the maintenance. I left the village almost immediately after the battle challenge had been issued, so I never did find out whether or not it actually took place. I sometimes wonder how it all turned out in the end.'

The answer to that is that there was almost certainly a fairly bloody confrontation. Such tribal fights, which are more like organised brawls than battles, are commonplace even in the more closely policed parts of PNG and often take place on such a scale that the government has to declare an official Fighting Zone – a state of emergency procedure that enables them to introduce curfews and other measures in an effort to curb the violence. This actually happened in Lae while we were there. The problem springs from what is known as 'pay-back' – the deeply rooted philosophy of an eye for an eye, a tooth for a tooth. Most disputes are settled on this basis. Tribal rivalries tend to be particularly intense in a country where geographical and environmental barriers have divided the people into many small communities so completely isolated from one another that there exist in the island more than seven hundred different languages – one seventh of the world's total!

Apart from their own first-hand experiences of these hostilities, the medical teams heard many reports of inter-tribal killings from the villagers of the West Sepik whom they interviewed as part of their survey, and who talked about such things in a rather matter-of-fact way. Hugh Savill wrote in his report: 'It was not uncommon when taking down family histories to hear of relatives killed by other villages. Some villages even have a "hired killer", a post which may be passed from father to son. Anyone with a grievance against another village, or person from that village, can hire him to take revenge. This is often directed not against the actual culprit but against anyone from his village. Women are usually picked as being easier victims. They are attacked, sometimes when working in their gardens, stunned with a stone and then, while they are unconscious, poison is rubbed on the tongue and on other parts of the body and the area is then pricked to introduce the poison, so that they come round but then die a few days later. We were also told of killings with spears and knives, and there are still strong beliefs in death from magical powers, although it seems that natural causes are often mistaken for such. Tragically, these innocent deaths can sometimes lead to revenge killings.'

Despite such alarming indications of fighting, feuding and murder, the Operation Drake teams were welcomed with friendliness wherever they went. They also found that once they had explained their project to the chiefs and elders and had got permission to go ahead, the villagers submitted quite willingly to the indignity of being examined, the unpleasantness of having a needle shoved in their arms for the purpose of taking blood samples and what must have seemed like the utter stupidity of providing stool and urine samples – and all this even though most of them had no idea what a doctor was, and had seen few, if any, white men before. The medical team examined villagers for evidence of malnutrition and its effects on health and resistance to

[146]

disease. Specialised tests were used to measure vitamin A deficiency and the efficiency of the intestinal tract in absorbing nutrients from the limited food available to them, continuing the comparative work begun in Panama. Strangely, this was not quite so easy in the more sophisticated villages around Buso, where the medical project started off. Although the people there offered almost overwhelming hospitality, they were definitely not keen to offer themselves as medical guinea pigs. This was put down to the fact that they were, on the whole, very healthy and probably saw no reason to get involved, on top of which they were understandably reluctant to give up a day's fishing or farming. After several weeks only about two hundred people had come forward in Buso, Kuwi and Lababia, and the project was in danger of losing momentum.

It was at this point that Andrew Mitchell attended a medical conference that happened to be in session up in the highlands at Goroka at the time, and met doctors and officials from the local Medical Research Institute who suggested that Operation Drake would be more than welcome to move its medical team into the West Sepik. The whole area, with an estimated population of over 112,000, was served by just three doctors and had never been the subject of a proper health survey. The Institute itself was urgently in need of information concerning the spread of certain diseases and would be very grateful for any help we could give in that respect. And so it was that, after an advance recce by Andrew and Dan Osman, Hugh Savill and David Bowdler headed up to Vanimo with Barbara Martinelli and ex-Panamanian YE Elba Guardia and a handful of YEs, plus a small detachment from the PNG Defence Force. Barbara, a very tough lady in spite of her slim build, was no stranger to working with primitive people in difficult terrain. She had spent four months treating the sick in a remote part of the Himalayas. Elba had won her spurs with us in Panama, where she had worked amongst the Cuna on Mulatupo. Alan Fila, one of the American YEs, had useful medical training from his time in the US Army, and he also joined the team.

With immense assistance from Dr Subhas, the Provincial Health Officer, they started work in the coastal villages of Vanimo and Yako, where, as at Buso, they found that the people were relatively wealthy, healthy and well fed – to the extent that, as Dr Savill noted in his report, for the first time since they had started their surveys in PNG, the word 'obese' began to appear in case histories. But as soon as they moved into the interior, standards of material and physical well-being rapidly deteriorated and there was much evidence of malnutrition and a high infant mortality rate.

The inland patrols found their marches through the jungle

[147]

reasonably easy. There were always paths to follow and, although the few sketchy maps in existence were rendered fairly useless by the way in which villages tend to move on from one location to another whenever their gardens become overworked and the soil exhausted, they had very little difficulty in finding their way around. The only real problems were presented by river crossings. No boats or canoes were available in which to ferry themselves and their equipment over, so there was no alternative but to wade across. As some of the rivers are not only wide, deep and fairly fast-flowing but are also known to be crocodile-infested, this could occasionally be a tricky and somewhat nerve-wracking manoeuvre. Hugh Savill's team, who were further handicapped by having one bearer who could not swim, found in one case that the water was above their shoulders and that the only way to keep their feet on the ground was to have their packs on their heads weighing them down.

Wherever the medical team went, there was a welcome from the people who were quick to appreciate the value of a doctor's skill. Barbara Martinelli remembers their stay at one small village. 'It was just after dark and we were about to have dinner when a commotion broke out amongst the people,' she relates. 'Four men carrying an injured person on a home-made stretcher arrived at our hut. As they entered, I saw to my horror that the patient's face was a mass of dried blood from which his eyes stared vacantly. There was no sign of movement and as I looked more closely I could see a deep wound in his forehead.' At this point one of the stretcher bearers handed Barbara a piece of tree branch which he indicated had caused the wound. Apparently the victim was a tree cutter who had made the classic mistake and had been struck by the falling timber. Hugh bent over the victim and found that he was still alive. There followed a difficult operation to clean up the wound and stitch back the various layers of skin. All this was performed by the flickering light of paraffin lamps, and it was three hours before the weary team fell into their hammocks. The grateful villagers bore the patient away.

Some of the villagers they visited were very primitive, with the men wearing nothing but a hollowed-out gourd over the penis and the women dressed in grass skirts, and they even came across a few cases where the main medium of communication was still by drum. And yet the air of happiness, harmony and social stability was most striking. 'Their village societies are enormously civilised in the broadest sense of the word,' noted Hugh Savill. 'Their elders are democratically elected and they have a great sense of natural justice. There seemed to be no crime and one never saw discipline being exercised over the adolescents, because it was simply not needed. It is only in their

[148]

relations with enemy villages that their normally strong sense of right and wrong unfortunately deserts them and they become uncivilised.'

The information and samples that were collected in the West Sepik during the six-week project were of great interest both to the Institute of Medical Research at Goroka and to Operation Drake's own comparative studies. Malaria and TB were found to be common, leprosy and elephantiasis were a problem in certain concentrated areas, and influenza and measles epidemics tended to flare up with particular virulence. There was no sign that cysticercosis had spread over the border from West Irian — something the Institute were particularly anxious to find out about — and only a handful of cancer cases were discovered. Just one serious psychiatric case was encountered and that was a young unmarried mother. She did not know who the father of her five-month-old baby was and, from its birth, had rejected the child and had suffered outbursts of irrational, violent behaviour. When seen by the medical team, she was lying down, completely withdrawn, talking of not feeding herself and apparently oblivious of everything going on around her. Despite support from her family, it was considered that she would probably die from self-neglect.

Although witch doctors are known to practise in these regions, and there are documented cases of perfectly healthy young people dying for no reason within forty-eight hours of being told that a curse had been put on them, the patrols did not come across any hint of this. But some of the older generation are suspicious of white man's medicine. David Bowdler managed to save the life of one man almost against the wishes of his family. He found him suffering from a ghastly, deep-rooted infection all the way down his back which was so agonising that he could only lie still on his stomach. His only chance of survival was to be taken down to the hospital at Vanimo, where he could be cured with a fairly straightforward course of treatment, but his family sat round in a huddle and were reluctant to let him go. In the end David managed to persuade the patient that it was the best thing for him, and he then had him stretchered out quickly before his relatives got him to change his mind.

The medical team really hit the local headlines when they helped to stem a cholera outbreak, and from everybody's point of view the Vanimo medical project was a tremendous success. One of our HQ photographers, 22-year-old Nigel Lang, joined the patrols and wrote of his experience: 'It provided us with a unique opportunity to live with the tribesmen, which no ordinary visitor to the island could ever have. It was a fascinating experience which gave me an insight into the people which otherwise I would never have had, and there was the feeling that we were really doing something positive to help them.'

[149]

Chapter Eighteen

Dateline: Finisterre Mountains, 20 September 1979

US Air Force Colonel J. W. Harris was not at the controls of his P47 fighter when it took off from Nadzab Air Base on the morning of 29 April 1944 – it was flown instead by First Lieutenant Marion C. Lutes, who took it up to test the guns. Lieutenant Lutes' radio message to that effect was the last that was ever heard of the aircraft. It never returned to base and was listed among the 325 Allied planes that went missing without trace during the heavy fighting that went on for three years in PNG during the Second World War. And it stayed on that list for just over thirty-five years until a team of five YEs, led by my second-in-command, ex-Royal Marine Mike Gambier, discovered it buried in the jungle on a hillside in the Finisterre Mountains.

One of the YEs – 24-year-old solicitor's clerk Sarah Budibent from south London – later described the search. 'It all started when we went to the village of Tauta to join in the Independence celebrations and got talking to a hunter called Paul, who told us how he and his brother-in-law had stumbled on the wreckage of an aircraft while out hunting wild pig. Nobody else knew about it, he said, but he would be prepared to guide us to it.

'The next morning we set out and trekked for four days through rugged terrain and thick jungle. Our route covered steep ascents and descents and at one point we climbed 10,500 feet up a mountain so that we were actually above cloud level. At other times the undergrowth was so dense that we had to crawl. On the afternoon of the fourth day we reached the brother-in-law's hunting hut and then, at 0700 the following morning, he led us out on what he promised was the last lap. We scrambled up and over two high ridges, down across two rivers and eventually found the aircraft half-buried in the mountainside. We would never have found it without Paul whose sense of direction was uncanny. He told us that the tribesmen in the area wouldn't go near it because they were afraid it was haunted by evil spirits.'

The wreck was quite well preserved and the name J. W. Harris was still clearly visible painted on the side, along with four Japanese flags indicating the number of enemy aircraft he had shot down and a beautiful pin-up. On my return to Britain, I passed through the USA and telephoned the Colonel at his home in Texas. He was fascinated to hear of the find and sent us photographs of himself taken with the plane shortly before the crash.

The instruments revealed that the doomed fighter had ploughed into the hillside at precisely 12.20 plus forty seconds, but it was not clear what had caused the crash. As there were no bones around, it seemed probable that the pilot had made a soft landing and climbed out.

Meanwhile, it seems likely that the P47 will remain undisturbed for another thirty-five years – and possibly for ever. Towards the end of Operation Drake's stay in the island, the film crew decided that they would like to film the wreck and a second patrol was mounted to retrace the steps of the first. Unfortunately, all the original members had left by then and at Tauta there was no sign of Paul the guide. After waiting around for several days, they found another guide who said he knew where the plane lay, but he then led them to a completely different wreck which was later identified as a rare B16 bomber, only four of which served in PNG. Colonel Harris's one-time pride and joy could not be rediscovered – and perhaps it never will be now.

Some of the most unpleasant fighting in the whole of the Second World War took place in PNG. General Douglas MacArthur described the island as the most inhospitable arena in which Western troops ever fought. More than 170,000 men died as the Australians and the Americans struggled desperately to prevent 200,000 Japanese troops from overrunning the place – and a very high proportion of those succumbed to the terrible hazards of the environment rather than to enemy action. The Japanese got within a few miles of their goal before the dogged resistance of the Allies finally turned them back. Had they taken Port Moresby, they would have had a perfect base from which to launch an invasion of Australia, just a short distance away across the Torres Strait, and who knows what might have happened then.

The search for war relics, not only on land but also in the sea, and the reopening and signposting of the old war trails provided the motives for testing jungle patrols and some very interesting diving. These projects were all carried out for the PNG government, who are trying hard to preserve these grim reminders of their recent history.

Captain Tony Molony's diving team located and charted no less than forty ship and aircraft wrecks in the separate areas of Salamaua, Madang, Finschhafen and Rabaul. The waters around PNG provide some of the best diving in the world since the water is warm and generally very clear, while the reefs are untouched by either pollution or over-fishing. However, there are also plenty of hazards. Sharks, stonefish and sea snakes abound, and you can never be quite sure what denizens of the deep you will find lurking in the shadowy, sheltered corners of old wrecks. Also, the coastline shelves very sharply in most areas, with the result that there is some very deep water close in-shore and, although this provided challenging diving for experts, it was at the same time a potentially dangerous situation for the unwary diver whose concentration might lapse. The need for extra special care was underlined by the limited availability of surface decompression facilities.

Irving Bennett, a former Panamanian YE who had worked with the team in Caledonia Bay and rejoined them in PNG as a fully-fledged member, witnessed at close quarters one of the strange effects of diving that can disorientate even the most experienced diver. He described in his diary what happened when he went down with two others to investigate the *Yokohama Maru*, one of the biggest wrecks in the Salamaua area.

'It measures 300 feet in length and is virtually intact,' he wrote. 'It was sunk by means of an explosive charge placed on the propeller at night and this was the only area where there was any real damage. It has been visited very little by divers as the highest part is at a depth of 150 feet while the rest continues down to 280 feet. At these depths the time one can stay down is drastically reduced – a dive of ten minutes requires twenty minutes of decompression while coming up. And we couldn't afford to make any mistakes because on this occasion we had no decompression chamber.

'Another thing you have to watch out for, common at these depths, is nitrogen narcosis – an intoxication of nitrogen which produces an irresistible urge to laugh together with a sensation like drunkenness. Its danger lies in the fact that it reduces the diver's capability of reasoning and has an adverse effect on his reactions. The leader of our trio came under that effect during today's dive just as we arrived at our agreed depth of 120 feet. At this point he suddenly departed from our plan and started swimming away from the ship. Without thinking, we followed him and it was a little while before we realised what was happening and decided to make for the surface again. Now that I am out of the water it seems funny – but at the time it wasn't so amusing.'

Young Irving completed seventy-three dives altogether and investigated a total of nineteen ships, eight barges and three aircraft, in nine different ports and harbours. The team included RAF divers, Chief Technician Dave Whitehall and underwater photographer Corporal Dave Clamp, as well as Robbie Williamson, and they were joined by a selection of YEs with diving experience. All were fascinated by their tour of what amounted to an amazing underwater war museum. Sharks and giant barracuda nosed watchfully along the coral-encrusted decks of warships that had come to rest at crazy angles in these ghostly graveyards of Second World War machinery, their guns silhouetted in the hazy blue water, and shoals of brightly coloured tropical fish darted hither and thither through the cockpits of bombers whose bomb bays had spilled their deadly cargo onto the seabed.

Meanwhile, much more war debris and other poignant reminders of the bitter fighting in PNG were discovered and investigated by the various land patrols. In Uberi, Lieutenant Desmond Monteith of the Coldstream Guards led a party which located and retraced part of the legendary Kokoda Trail, along the sixty-mile length of which the Japanese and the Australians had been locked in a terrible campaign. The patrol hacked its way through dense undergrowth and tall kunai grass to the long-deserted village of Ioribaiwa, where the Japanese advance finally ground to a halt, while another group explored Imita Ridge where the Aussies had dug in and faced the Japanese across the valley in a last stubborn and successful stand. The sheer enormity of their feat in dragging up the two heavy and awkward twenty-five-pounder field guns that played such a vital part in turning the enemy back became frighteningly obvious as the patrols sweated their way through the exhaustingly rugged terrain. They stumbled across many entrenchments and, among the relics they found, there were both Japanese and Australian helmets, live mortar bombs and hand grenades, a rusty magazine filled with rounds, hundreds of ration tins and a very large quantity of Australian beer bottles!

The Wau war trails – the Bulldog, the Skindewi and the Black Cat – were all tackled by groups under the command of Lieutenant Colonel Robin Jordan of the Royal Engineers. His brief from the National Parks Department was to map and mark them from end to end with special signs provided by the PNG Printing Company, and to provide sufficient information about suitable camp sites, reliable water sources, outstanding views, and the location of interesting war relics to enable the Department to produce detailed guide booklets for future trekkers.

The eighty-mile long Bulldog, which was originally blazed by the Royal Australian Engineers in 1943, and the Skindewi, which dated back to the gold rush days of the 1920s, were both relatively easy to follow, despite being heavily overgrown. But the Black Cat – which, like the Skindewi, runs from Wau to Salamaua and was originally pioneered in the gold rush – was so challenging that Robin Jordan, himself an exceptionally tough parachute engineer, thought when he did his initial recce that it would be beyond the capabilities of the YEs. But that, as he later admitted, was before he had met the YEs and realised the high calibre of these young people. What made the Black Cat so demanding was the fact that it constantly ascended and descended the very steep sides of the Bitoi River valley and crossed the river several times. At times the gorge-side path was barely six inches wide, with a drop of several hundred feet into the valley below. And with a sixty-pound pack on your back that is a daunting prospect.

Back in the mountains south-west of Lae, a group led by Robbie Roethenmund, the rugged young American who had been with us on one of the early recces, discovered another aircraft wreck, this time a DC3 troop carrier of the USAF which had a particularly macabre aspect in that the fuselage was found to contain human bones as well as weapons. The same kind of haunted air hung over the Japanese army hospital, hidden deep in a series of caves in the jungle of the Salamaua Peninsula, which was located by a patrol led by Richard Bampfylde. Roof cave-ins unfortunately ruled out any possibility of venturing very far into the caves, and the presence of a death adder just inside the main entrance served as a further deterrent. But a narrow-gauge railway and rusting hospital beds were seen before the patrol reached a point where the tunnel was completely blocked by a rock fall. To try and clear it and penetrate further would have been far too risky.

People from the local villages claimed that the whole hillside was honeycombed with tunnels, and this was borne out by the fact that a ventilation shaft was found some way from the entrance. We were also told that when the Japanese cleared out they went in such a hurry that they left dying men still in their beds and that before the rock falls you could still see skeletons lying on rotting mattresses.

A search of the surrounding area revealed a car, a motorcycle and a searchlight – all riddled with bullet holes – and on top of the hill there were four heavy guns, one of which turned out to have been built in Newcastle-on-Tyne in 1899 by the Armstrong Whitworth Company. It still had a shell case in the breech and the shell was just poking out of the barrel; clearly a dud.

We were fortunate to meet Richard Leahy, son of the famous explorer Mick Leahy. Richard ran a local airline and knew as much about PNG as anyone. He had a great interest in the war and was able to give us valuable clues to the sites of interest.

After his strenuous exploration of the Wau trails, Robin Jordan found himself facing an even more formidable assignment when he set out to lead a patrol up into and right across the crater of the semi-dormant Mount Victory volcano – something that had never been done before. His group included a government vulcanologist and the main aim of the project was to take temperature and magnetometer readings in the crater in an effort to gauge the stability of the volcano, which

[154]

erupted violently in 1890, spluttered intermittently during the next forty years, and has shown no real sign of activity for the last half century.

The patrol started out, very appropriately, on Guy Fawkes Day and after climbing for two days they were left in no doubt about the difficulty of their mission. They were still a long way from the summit of the 6,315-foot mountain and the going was getting tougher all the time. They frequently faced precipitous slopes of up to seventy degrees, where loose rocks avalanched as they scrambled up, making it necessary to scale these sections one at a time, so that those following behind would not be caught in a dangerous hail of stones. This slowed their progress even further and it was not until the fourth day that they eventually reached the crater lake.

Not far away from there, they came across some of the 'hot spots' where there was a very strong smell of sulphur and green fumes could be seen rising through cracks in the rocks. It was an eerie sight – and one that greatly interested PNG vulcanologist Ben Talai. He assured everyone, however, that there was no immediate danger of the volcano bursting into life.

As the party prepared to descend, illusions that it was going to be an easy downhill trip from then on were swiftly shattered. Going down proved to be even more difficult and dangerous than coming up. They repeatedly found themselves teetering on the edge of sheer drops and had to back-track in search of an alternative route. This happened at least twenty times in two days, with the result that in one ten-hour period they actually advanced less than one kilometre. Frustration and despair began to set in, aggravated further at one point by a lack of water, and Robin even considered giving up and calling in a helicopter to lift everybody off the mountain. But they decided they were not going to be beaten and pushed on. It was seven days after setting off that they arrived triumphantly at Butu Point Mission, their task completed. The locals were amazed to see them coming down from the mountain which they considered to be the home of evil spirits and referred to as *Itambu* – forbidden! After their experiences, the exhausted patrol could think of some more down-to-earth reasons for keeping away.

Major Frank Esson, now having a spell ashore, led a similar project on Mount Lamington, where a vulcanologist again took readings, but this patrol did not have such a hard time as the Mount Victory group. They still had enough energy left afterwards to walk the Kokoda Trail to Port Moresby.

At about the same time, Robbie Roethenmund led a ten-day patrol in search of the coal seams which Tom Richards, a well-known local prospector, believed existed somewhere in the area of Pindiu. The group included two geologists from the University of PNG and among the YEs who took part was Lorna Gibbons, from England, who told of her adventures in a series of letters to her family.

On the second day, as she trudged up a steep, narrow, muddy path, Lorna had her first confrontation with the loathsome leeches that are an almost unavoidable feature of jungle life. 'They were much smaller than I had imagined,' she wrote. 'They were like tiny worms, sitting half off the ground, bending this way and that as though they were watching us. We seemed to draw them to us like magnets and every five minutes or so we had to remove them from our boots as they attempted to get inside. For once, no one particularly wanted to stop for rests on the way and so we walked continuously, flicking off the leeches when we saw them.

'Our carriers, however, were barefoot and were immediately attacked. We watched in fascination as they casually pulled them off – obviously used to them. It was at this point that I took a closer look at my own feet only to discover that the leeches had taken a liking to my woolly socks, had crawled through them and were busily feeding! My immediate reaction was, I should think, identical to that of anyone else in this predicament for the first time. "Agh, leeches, where's a lighter, get the salt – do something." A lighter was quickly produced and within seconds I was leech-free. All that was left were a few trickles of blood.'

Lorna was surprised how quickly she and her companions grew accustomed to the attentions of the leeches, casually flicking them away without any fuss. The pace of the march was gruelling. 'Uphill we walked and downhill we walked, never on the flat for very long and continually stumbling over stones and roots. At times it was hard to see which way the track went and occasionally it was so overgrown that there was no track at all. Often we would see huge spiders, bigger than our hands, sitting in their webs by the side of the track, sometimes scurrying away and sometimes sitting there in open defiance.'

That night the patrol stayed in the village of Hamomeng, where they were allocated a hut in which to sleep. 'In the evening we sat outside on the "village green" eating platefuls of hot *taro* and *sago* round a lantern with the villagers,' wrote Lorna. 'Despite the fact that we had two different languages to contend with, everybody ended up in hoots of laughter as both sides described their way of life, which ranged from high-rise buildings and Concorde to the spirits living in the nearby jungle. When sign language failed, the three members of our group who were from PNG were always happy to translate, adding their own views on the conversation as they did so.'

[156]

Two days later the patrol stayed the night in the village of Kobea, where Lorna had a sore on her foot treated by the local medicine man. She was reluctant at first to entrust herself to his skills and would have preferred to avail herself of the patrol's first-aid kit. But she submitted suspiciously and, when he squeezed a brown liquid from some leaves he had picked from the jungle and applied it to the sore, the pain and throbbing stopped almost immediately. It was an impressive demonstration of the powers of herbal medicine – all that is available to the tribesmen of the forest.

There was more magic to come. 'I awoke in the morning to the sound of drums, which had apparently been playing right through the night. We had been told the previous evening about the spirits of the area and now we were about to see a spirit ceremony. It was conducted by the spirit man of the village who appeared wearing what looked like nappies held up with a beaded belt and adorned with necklaces and a mask which, with its feathers and pointed nosepiece, gave him the appearance of a bird. Brandishing an axe in one hand and a spear in the other, he danced around a wooden bowl filled with a black liquid, chanting all the time. Eventually, he scooped up handfuls of the liquid and threw it up into the air. When he had finished he stood there, chest blown out, looking very pleased with himself. With the aid of our translators, we discovered that the aim of the ceremony had been to send away all the evil spirits in the area since they were believed to be hiding the coal from us.'

By searching along all the stream beds in the most appalling terrain, Robbie's party eventually struck lucky and the next day Tom Richards and I flew in to inspect the discovery. Landing in Pindiu, we seemed to march forever in the pouring rain until we reached a leech-infested gully, and there it was – glistening black coal. A seam at least ten feet thick. Tom was overjoyed to find his theory had been correct. To celebrate, he produced a cold roast duck and a bottle of Australian claret from his pack! This was the first significant discovery of coal in PNG and Tom estimated the seam could contain 45–50 million tons. This may turn out to be of immense value to the country and plans to start mining it are already under way. It would be nice to think that it was the spirit man at Kobea who made it all possible – and why not. In this extraordinary country such things seem somehow less far-fetched.

Chapter Nineteen

Dateline: Tigaro, Central Highlands of Papua New Guinea,
October 1979

'Explorers Find Stone Age Tribe,' shouted one headline. 'The Tribe That Time Forgot,' screamed another. News of the encounter between an Operation Drake recce party led by Roger Chapman and a small group of nomadic Pogaian natives who had never before come into contact with white men was given predictably sensational treatment by the world's press and this unfortunately caused us some embarrassment. It was not that the newspapers got the facts wrong – just that they put them together out of context in such a way as to create a highly dramatic and rather misleading impression that did not go down too well with a newly independent local government that was anxious not to emphasise the primitive side of life in PNG.

Roger's original report of the meeting, which he gave us in a radio message from the tribe's tiny village deep in the remote central highlands, was relatively matter-of-fact. He was fascinated, but not unduly surprised, to have come across people who had never seen white men before in a region where white men rarely venture, and where the more isolated communities are known to have little or no contact with the tribes in the neighbouring valleys, let alone the outside world. Indeed, one member of the patrol, Bob Woods, an Australian working with the PNG government, had quite expected to make some 'first contacts'.

But when a visiting reporter picked up the story, he did not hesitate to include all the local colour he could muster, including references to cannibalism, before filing it to London in a form guaranteed to catch the jaundiced eye of any news editor. By the time the sub-editors and headline-writers had finished with it, the final version that reached the world's breakfast tables had been blown up into something only marginally less miraculous than the discovery of Conan Doyle's 'Lost World', complete with real live dinosaurs!

Immediately all hell broke loose. We were inundated with calls from radio and television stations around the globe all wanting to follow up the story. A Japanese television company was ready to spend millions of yen on flying a news team out to get exclusive film coverage of the tribe. The big American networks were also keen to get in on the act.

When the story hit the headlines, I was in Port Moresby awaiting the arrival of our Chairman, General Sir John Mogg, and George Baker, the ex-High Commisioner. They could not have arrived at a better moment and next day were able to placate the Honourable Michael Somare, PNG's Prime Minister. The diplomatic way in which the General and George handled the situation solved the problem and, I felt, greatly enhanced our image. Nevertheless, the PNG government, whom we could not afford to offend, made it clear that they were far from happy with the prehistoric image of their country which, they felt, the story projected. They were particularly upset by suggestions of cannibalism. As far as they are concerned, there is an important distinction to be made between cannibalism and the offence known officially as 'interference with the human body'. This latter involves eating flesh from a body that is already dead – as against going out and killing somebody specifically with a view to eating him – and was once quite common practice in PNG, as it was in several other parts of the world. It is now outlawed, but old customs die hard and cases still occasionally come to light. It is a subject about which the government is understandably sensitive – especially as it is doing its best to encourage a tourist trade!

In view of all this, we had to go out of our way to play down the more sensational aspects of the story which had even excited the interest of Sir Robin Day and the BBC's 'World at One' radio programme. Roger had a telephone interview with Sir Robin and did his best to put things into perspective. Even so, it remained as one of the highlights of the entire expedition.

It all happened as Roger led a gruelling twenty-six-day patrol through the largely uncharted Strickland Gorge in preparation for a first-ever attempt at tackling the white-water challenge of the Upper Strickland River. Only a handful of white men had ever set eyes on the seventy-five-mile stretch of foaming rapids and cataracts that come cascading through a cleft in the mountains 2,500 feet deep, and nobody had ever thought seriously about trying to ride these swirling waters in a boat. Roger's plan was to take a party of eight men through in two inflatables, but first he needed to go and have a close look to make sure that the venture was at least vaguely feasible. The aerial survey that we had already undertaken was no good by itself, because you cannot really judge the severity of a rapid from the two-dimensional view you get from above, and, apart from that, some sections of the river are permanently obscured by low cloud.

His thorough preliminary research showed that only four white patrols had ever before penetrated these wild and inhospitable regions – the first one a mere twenty-five years previously. All four were led by Australian Kiap officers – the equivalent of the British colonial District Commissioners – in the days before PNG was granted independence.

The real pioneer was Des Clancy, who, in 1954, went in with three representatives of the Australian Petroleum Company and one hundred and fifty bearers, guides and armed escorts to search for oil shales. They followed the course of the river as closely as possible along the Gorge and eventually carried on through to the lower reaches where it broadens and meanders more sedately for some four hundred and thirty miles before joining up with the Fly River. They never did strike oil, but Clancy came back with some interesting information about what lay hidden under the umbrellas of low cloud that had always frustrated the aerial map-makers.

At one point, a location known as the Kagwesi Crossing, the whole of the mighty river is channelled through a crevice in the granite no more than ten feet wide. It was, he reported, an awe-inspiring sight. Later he was forced to climb out of the Gorge because of the impassability of the terrain, but, from a vantage point three thousand feet up above the river, he got a distant view of the gap where the water gushed out of the mountain ranges into the plain below. The mist and cloud that rose like steam from the raging torrent caused him to christen the spot the 'Gates of Hell', while the churning white water rapids beyond it he named the 'Devil's Race'.

Two years later another experienced Kiap officer, J. P. Sinclair, set out with one white companion and one hundred and six bearers intending to cross the river at Kagwesi Crossing. But when he arrived there he was greeted by a sight even more astonishing than that which had taken Clancy's breath away. It was the rainy season and the river had risen more than twenty feet, so that the water level was actually above the narrow fissure – but the line of it was clearly and spectacularly marked by a fantastic mare's tail of spray that was hurled many feet into the air by the tremendous forces created under the surface. So great were these forces that hefty logs were being thrown up and then bobbled like feather-light table-tennis balls on the crest of the fountaining jets of water.

The two other patrols that ventured into the area between 1968–72 struck out into the interior of the Muller Mountains with the specific aim of trying to contact the native inhabitants for the purpose of completing a national census. Roger actually managed to track down members of each of these teams and they were able to supply useful briefings about both the conditions and the people he could expect to meet.

[160]

They confirmed that the terrain is as harsh and inhospitable as one is likely to find anywhere in the world. When you are not scrambling and hacking your way up and down almost sheer-sided ridges covered in dense undergrowth, you are having to pick a careful path across limestone rock so sharp-edged that the soles of the toughest boots will be shredded after a few miles. Even seemingly open areas, that appear from the air to be smooth carpets of green turf, usually turn out to be covered in kunai grass fifteen feet high that is so difficult to cut through that a fit man can be reduced to sweat-soaked exhaustion within a matter of yards.

Roger also learned that the interior tribesmen were often extremely primitive and that their reactions to outsiders would be unpredictable. The early patrols had adopted a policy of sending ahead shouters – native guides who would go forward and literally bellow out advance warning of the party's arrival in the area and call in any tribes in the locality for a meeting. Salt and tobacco would then be handed over as a gesture of friendship and, once the ice had been broken, impressive shooting displays with rifles would be laid on to discourage any hostile notions. There had never been any attacks although one of the census patrols had narrowly avoided an ambush.

It was against this background that Roger led out his ten-strong recce party, which included ex-SAS Sapper Staff Sergeant Dave Weaver, the Australian expatriate government lawyer Bob Woods and American Bill Neumeister, a strong, silent character who normally makes his living as a smoke jumper in Alaska – a job that involves being parachuted into the heart of forest fires to put them out before they really get started. There were also four native bearers and two members of the PNG Defence Force, who were to act as liaison officers.

The bearers were recruited from villages around Lake Kopiago, where the base camp for the expedition was sited. Finding suitable men was not too easy. There was a marked reluctance to venture deep into the mountains, partly because of the punishing conditions and partly owing to the risk of straying into enemy territory. However, with the help of the District Officer and a show of hard cash, resistance was finally overcome and four fine, strong-looking individuals were taken on.

They were all from either the Duna or the Huri tribes otherwise known as the Wigmen on account of the extraordinarily elaborate head-dresses they wear. To see the males strutting around like peacocks on market day, while their womenfolk get on with the business, is quite an experience. It is like watching an exotic Easter Bonnet Parade. Each crowning glory seems more extravagant than the one before –

towering structures of hair, feathers, fur and flowers that are often shaped rather like Napoleonic hats. Quills or bamboo are traditionally worn through the nose, but since the advent of Western influence, ball-point pens are very much in vogue!

It did not take long to discover that the going was every bit as tough as everybody had warned it would be. Within three days – before they had even reached the Strickland River – the party lost the services of the two local soldiers, who had to return to base when their legs gave out under the strain and badly-swollen knees threatened to bring them to a complete and painful standstill. Everybody else was suffering, too, as they sweated, slithered and clawed their way through the forest, stumbling under the weight of their fifty-pound packs as their feet caught in the tangle of roots and creepers. Even the bearers found it hard to cope at times as the patrol pressed on at a murderous pace. They were on the march by 0645 every morning in an effort to make the most of the cool part of the day and did not call a halt until 1600. They then had just about enough energy left to set up camp and cook a meal before collapsing, exhausted, into their hammocks by 1900. By that time they were normally so tired that neither the mosquitoes nor the regular drenching downpours disturbed their slumbers.

Once they reached the river it was a matter of following its course as closely as possible, carefully charting every feature and grading each rapid on a scale of one to six depending on the degree of danger and difficulty it presented. After three weeks they reached a point just north of the Bulago River junction. They had already passed the Kagwesi Crossing a few days before – and found it every bit as awesome as Clancy and Sinclair had promised. Now they were about to enter one of those tantalising and mysterious blanks on the map.

Having camped for the night on a narrow ledge above the river, they awoke to find that the torrential rain that had bucketed down while they slept had transformed their surroundings. The level of the water had risen so dramatically that they were effectively cut off on their ledge and could neither advance nor go back the way they had come. There was only one way out – and that was upwards. It meant climbing a hair-raising three thousand feet up the side of the gorge, which was almost sheer in some parts, but there was no other alternative.

It took nearly ten hours to claw their way to the top. They had to move with the utmost caution, hauling themselves up on vines, roots and the most tenuous handholds in the crumbling rock. By the time they eventually made it, they barely had the strength to rig their hammocks and swallow a hurriedly prepared meal before flaking out.

[162]

The next morning they decided to strike inland, away from the gorge, in search of a suitable clearing in which to land the planned resupply helicopter. After cutting through the jungle for about three hours, they picked up an old hunting track and followed that for a further couple of hours until they reached a stream which provided a welcome excuse to stop for a cup of tea. It was as he bent to scoop a billycan of water for the brew that Roger noticed something he had not expected in such a remote area: the distinctive smell of wood-smoke — from someone else's camp fire.

The patrol immediately crept further along the track until, around a bend, they glimpsed through the trees a small clearing in which stood two low, rectangular huts with wisps of blue smoke filtering through the thatched roofs. Then figures were seen moving about and the sounds of children playing and pigs squealing floated across the forest.

Roger sent ahead two of his Duna bearers — Harirega and Ayape — as an advance party, and when he saw that they received a friendly welcome he led the rest of the patrol forward into the clearing. As he did so, Ayape directed towards him one of the men with whom he had been conversing in a strange dialect, and when Roger extended his hand the small bearded man grasped it firmly and held on determinedly, clearly not wanting to let go.

There then followed a bizarre four-way conversation. Roger spoke in English to Bob Woods, Bob translated into Pidgin — the nearest thing to an official language in PNG — so that Harirega could then rephrase the message in Duna for the benefit of Ayape, who was the only one familiar with the dialect spoken by the tribesmen.

In this rather tortuous, roundabout way, it was established that the village was called Tigaro and that the inhabitants were nomadic Pogaians. There were five families in the group which numbered fifteen altogether. The man who was hanging on to Roger's hand so affectionately was called Kiwanga and the chief, who was away working in the village 'gardens' but was due back at sunset, was named Kemba. When he eventually made an appearance, he confirmed that nobody in his small tribe had ever seen a white man before — a fact which seemed to be rather amusingly borne out by the way in which Roger, Dave, Bill and Bob were subjected to close scrutiny and the occasional curious prod.

The fascination was mutual. Kemba and his people were clearly untouched by modern civilisation. Their most sophisticated and prized possessions were two steel axe heads which they had traded with other tribes in the Bulago Valley, where they had been originally introduced by one of the later Kiap patrols. Otherwise, they had only stone tools and implements.

[163]

The women wore grass skirts, while the men covered themselves with a loin cloth in the front and over their backsides a hanging bunch of leaves known evocatively in Pidgin as 'arsegrass'. They exist on a diet of root crops, which they grow in their forest 'gardens', augmented with whatever they can hunt down with their bows and arrows of sharpened bamboo. Their precious domestic pigs are only slaughtered on very special occasions and are otherwise treated with loving care. The women walk around clutching piglets as if they were their own children and will even suckle them in emergencies.

Friendship was further cemented with gifts of salt and tobacco, and then it was agreed that the patrol would spend the night in the village before clearing a landing site for the helicopter the next morning. The villagers watched spellbound as Dave Weaver prepared the powerful Plessey radio and called me up in Tac HQ three hundred and fifty miles away in Lae.

My arrival next day in a giant RAAF Chinook helicopter brought the stone age face to face with the twentieth century in the most spectacular fashion. The idea of a simple supply drop was changed at the last moment because film man Al Bibby was aboard the chopper and wanted to land and get some footage of the 'Lost Tribe', and it was then decided that the patrol might as well take advantage of the situation and hitch a lift back to the banks of the Strickland. Alas, the stone axes had not cleared the last few feet of tree stumps and landing proved impossible, so we had to remain in the hover, but Roger's patrol managed to clamber aboard.

As the Chinook lifted off and rose above the tiny jungle clearing, with a deafening roar from its powerful engines and the downdraught from its twin rotors creating a mini-hurricane that raised a swirling cloud of dust and whipped the surrounding foliage into a frenzy of dancing branches and wildly fluttering leaves, fifteen near-naked brown bodies prostrated themselves on the ground, their hands clamped over their ears, their foreheads pressed to the earth, their eyes not daring to look up. As the scene receded out of focus below them, the members of the patrol peered down anxiously at the prone forms and wondered what must be going through their minds.

Fifty years previously, when aircraft first arrived in PNG, similar encounters had given rise to the cargo cults among the primitive peoples, who understandably concluded that the strange white men who descended from the skies in the bird-like machines packed with wonderful goods must surely be gods. It was fascinating to speculate about the legends that might grow up around the meeting between Chief Kemba's people and Roger Chapman's patrol. The event would surely pass into local folklore as the tribal storytellers raised their sing-

[164]

song voices over countless camp fires and spread the news in the traditional way to the remotest corner of the forest.

After some tense manoeuvring, we dropped the patrol at the Bulalo River junction to continue the recce on to the 'Gates of Hell', but the nearer they got, the tougher the going became, and they began to realise why Clancy had been content to view this fascinating spot from a distance. When they did eventually reach it, they were all in a very sorry state. Dave Weaver's face was puffed and swollen from insect bites and his lips were cracked and bleeding, so that he looked as though he had just taken a hiding from Muhammad Ali, while Bill Neumeister was covered in cuts, sores and a blistering rash caused by brushing against a leaf with a sting many times more powerful than a normal nettle. Bob Woods' arms and legs were a mass of festering tropical ulcers resulting from open sores that refuse to heal in the humidity, and Roger had a particularly uncomfortable variety of complaints. A spider had bitten him on the hand, causing his whole arm to swell up, he had a nasty abrasion all down his right shin which just would not heal and, to cap it all, he had a bad dose of diarrhoea. No wonder that he wrote in his diary towards the end of the trip:

'Frankly, all of us will be pleased to see the back of this miserably wet, tangled stretch of river. It is only cups of tea and a sense of humour which keep us going. Our main problem is that we have to cut every inch of the way with machetes. There are no trails on the steep, muddy banks because no one has ever been here before. And, as I listen to the torrential rain on the waterproof sheet above my hammock, I can well understand why!'

Despite this, he started making plans for a return visit. The verdict at the end of the recce was that the proposed river-running venture was perfectly possible. It would be hard and there would be times when they would have to get out of the water and by-pass some of the worst rapids. But, as long as everybody knew what they were doing and did not get careless, there was no real reason why they should not get through.

Having assembled back at Lake Kopiago, the two four-man teams who would be crewing the Avon inflatables *British Caledonian* and *Cathay Pacific* went into white-water training on the Watut River. Roger, Bill Neumeister and Dave Weaver had now been joined by Jim Masters and Yogi Thami, a young professional river runner from Nepal, and the party was completed by New Zealand film cameraman 'Waka' Atwell, a PNG Defence Force warrant officer, and Jerome Montague, an American scientist attached to the United Nations Development Programme in PNG.

Both Roger and Jim had considerable white-water experience from the Blue Nile Expedition of 1968 and the Zaire River Expedition of 1974–5. They had had some close shaves on those rivers, so no one needed to tell them that a fast-flowing river can turn into a killer the instant you relax your concentration. They had learned the hard way that you have to treat rivers like the Strickland with the greatest respect, and they made sure that everyone else on the team knew exactly what they were up against.

There were plenty of thrills and spills on the Watut, and by the time the teams were ready to walk in to the Strickland to start the descent in the last week of October, none of those taking part had any illusions about a quick paddle down a picturesque mountain stream. Having descended into the remote, steep-sided valley, they reached the river and selected a dropping zone where the PNG Defence Force Dakota would deliver the deflated boats and all the heavy stores by parachute. So it was in brilliant sunlight that the twin-engined transport roared into the valley, then, directed by Dave Weaver on the VHF radio, the PNG pilot made perfect runs from south to north. The parachutes, pushed out with great skill by the Defence Force despatcher, came in right on target. As we headed back to Lae, our mission accomplished, Roger pumped up his boats and prepared to tackle the mighty Strickland.

The first few hours were easy enough and there were opportunities to enjoy the spectacular scenery, but then the white-water stretches began to get gradually more and more severe and soon the adrenaline was flowing as fast and furiously as the water. Before long, they were going into rapids that on the recce had been rated five on the scale of one to six. And there was always the knowledge that, however closely a rapid is surveyed from the safety of the bank or from an aircraft, you can never tell exactly what it is going to be like until you are in the middle of it.

The first major mishap came when Jim Masters' boat just slipped off the tongue of clear water that arrows into the start of any rapid. It immediately turned broadside on and then capsized, spilling the crew into the foaming waters. It all happened so fast that cameraman Waka was still filming as he went under. For a few seconds he bravely held on to his camera, but then realised that he would have to sacrifice it in order to save himself, and several hundred pounds worth of equipment, plus what would have been a very exciting clip of film, disappeared for ever.

Meanwhile Jim Masters had also gone under and had surfaced underneath the upturned boat. He could hear Dave Weaver anxiously shouting out his name, momentarily convinced that Jim was lost, and memories flooded back of a particularly horrific experience on the Blue

[166]

Nile. He had been hurled into an exceptionally violent stretch of water under a small waterfall and the force created by the turbulent whirlpools and swirling eddies sucked him down and pinned him to the river bed. He said afterwards that it was like being trapped in a giant tumble drier. He lost control of his arms and legs as he was rolled over and over and bounced helplessly against the boulders and rocks on the bottom. As consciousness began to fade, he somehow managed to locate the ring-pull on his life jacket and, when inflated, this provided just enough extra buoyancy to pull him clear and throw him to the surface. But he knew he had been close to death.

On this occasion it was not nearly so desperate. Coming up under the boat was the best thing that could have happened to him, even if it did give his colleagues a scare, because it not only gave him something to hang on to but also provided a pocket of air.

After that there were no more accidents until the one mighty catastrophe that brought the expedition to a final, premature halt. And that was caused by the one tiny lapse in concentration, the one moment of carelessness that they had all known could be their undoing and which they had tried so hard to avoid.

It happened shortly after they had negotiated the Kagwesi Crossing. This in itself had been fairly nerve-wracking, since they knew as they approached that if they once got sucked into the current and funnelled into that narrow fissure it would be worse than going over Niagara in a barrel. Happily, they avoided that particular hazard, got out of the river in time and portaged round the Crossing. It was a couple of days later, as they were 'lining' the boats through another impossibly difficult stretch of water, that disaster struck.

Where they went wrong was in pushing themselves just a bit too hard at the end of a long day. They had made a strict point up until then of always packing in for the day by 1500 hours specifically to avoid the risk of getting overtired and making silly mistakes. But on this occasion, they broke their own golden rule and carried on until after 1800 hours. The reason was that they wanted to get that difficult section behind them so that they could look forward to a fresh start and some easier going the next morning.

It was pouring with rain as they rigged the line and sent the first boat down the five-hundred-yard rapid. It went through like a dream. This helped to lull them into a false sense of security, and they hurried on with the second boat. The mistake they made was to leave just a bit too much slack in the bowline so that the boat was able to float out too far into mid-stream, where it turned sideways in a big stopper wave and was swamped. As it filled with water the extra weight put an intolerable strain on the five-thousand-pound line, which eventually

[167]

snapped with a twang like a breaking guitar string. The boat was swept away in an instant.

The team dismally took stock of the situation while sitting round their spluttering camp fire and it soon became obvious that they could not go on. They thought briefly about pressing on with all eight men in the one boat, but dismissed this possibility as too risky. They reluctantly decided that the only thing to do was to sit tight and wait for the RAAF helicopter that was due to resupply them in three days' time.

Just to make matters worse, their radio was on the blink, so they could not call the chopper in any earlier. On top of that, a considerable proportion of their rations had disappeared down the Strickland in *British Caledonian*, and they were therefore very short of food. For poor Jim Masters, there was the added misery that he had lost all his personal kit – including his passport and £75 in cash. All he was left with were the shorts and shirt he stood up in – and they were soaking wet. He was reduced to a rather macabre form of makeshift clothing. He took one of the black plastic body bags, which they had with them just in case of a fatality, cut arm and head holes in it and wore it like a dress. He looked like some kind of ageing punk rocker. It is not often that Jim finds himself so much in the height of fashion. All he needed to complete the picture was a safety pin through his nose!

But nobody could see the funny side of it at the time. The whole team were totally depressed as they bedded down for the night on the convenient flat ledge that was to be their home for the next seventy-two hours and lay there in the dark and the rain listening to the eerie crash of boulders avalanching down the crumbling cliffs on the other side of the gorge.

Three days later I came in with two RAAF helicopters. As the Australian Squadron Leader swung his Iriquois out of the gorge of the Devil's Race, Alan Bibby shouted, 'There's the boat', and sure enough, there it was, still fully inflated, lying upside down on a sandbank in mid-river. 'We'll go to Nomad to refuel and I'll bring you back to collect the boat,' said the pilot. An hour later Alan and I leapt out onto the sandbank and the Iriquois flew off in a whirl of spray to collect Roger's patrol. 'Any crocs about, John?' enquired Alan. 'I doubt it – too far upriver, but luckily I've got a .357,' I said, tapping the heavy Smith and Wesson that John Longstaff, the Yorkshire gundealer, had given me before I left England.

As we righted the Avon, we were amazed to find it undamaged and almost all the stores in place, thanks to Jim Masters' careful packing and securing, no doubt. To get the inflatable into the helicopter, we deflated it and then threw out the water-logged rations.

'Now we're really stuck if the river rises,' I thought, 'We've thrown

[168]

away the food and the foot pump is missing.' At that moment rain began to bucket down and low cloud filled the valley, reducing visibility to one hundred feet.

'Do you think the chopper will find us again in this?' murmured Alan. I did not think the pilot would even fly in such conditions, but said, 'Yes, they're pretty experienced.'

An hour went by, the rain pelted down, visibility got worse and the river began to rise. I found some distress flares in the boat's kit, but they were soaking wet. It would be dark in an hour.

Just when I was beginning to get really worried, we heard that wonderful 'thwacker, thwacker, thwacker' of approaching rotor blades. What a comforting sound it is! How many people in a tight corner must have blessed it! I managed to get one flare alight and then the Iriquois burst out of the cloud. We piled the boat and the kit aboard as the crew hauled us in.

'We were a bit concerned about you,' shouted a flight sergeant in my ear, 'Couple of effing big crocodiles round the corner.' And as we turned the bend, two enormous reptiles slid hurriedly into the river.

With certain members of Roger's patrol, disappointment at the failure of the mission gradually turned into festering discontent during the following few weeks, when, having been airlifted from their ledge, they linked up with a group of eleven scientists, YEs and others at Nomad, as planned, and progressed down the lower reaches of the Strickland and on to Daru, carrying out a number of scientific research projects along the way.

From a psychological point of view, it is an interesting fact that the two men who seemed to have the greatest difficulty in coming to terms mentally with the setback were, in fact, those who were physically the strongest and most resilient of the team by far. It is a syndrome with which all expedition leaders are familiar. The explanation is, perhaps, that for people whose physical strength and single-mindedness have always enabled them to win through, the taste of defeat is that much harder to stomach.

After the helter-skelter exhilaration of the action-packed ride down the Strickland Gorge, the month-long cruise through the calmer stretches of the river, into the Fly and on to Daru, must have seemed like a bit of an anti-climax to the members of the white-water team. But for the scientists and YEs there was plenty of interest. They travelled in four Avon inflatables to which we had fitted our Seagull engines – including the ill-fated *British Caledonian* which we had recovered from the sandbank. They also had a massive forty-foot dug-out canoe that Rupert Grey had purchased in Nomad, and which was now powered by a 25hp Johnson outboard.

[169]

They passed through idyllic scenery, the river slow-moving and dark green, with the forest hanging over the banks and great roots growing out into the water, which was so crystal clear that one could see right to the bottom. This was just as well, otherwise the submerged tree-trunks and fallen branches would have been much more of a hazard to the outboard engines. As it was, one was able to see well in advance where such obstacles lurked and take the necessary avoiding action. In some ways it was quite a pleasure to have to cut out the engines and raise them out of harm's way, paddling along on the current instead and, in the silence, enjoying the exotic sounds of the jungle. The bird life, in particular, was both prolific and spectacular – giant hornbills, common as blackbirds, whose appearance was heralded by a noisy wingbeat like the thud of distant helicopter blades, egrets, storks, small eagles, brilliantly coloured parrots and, very occasionally, a stunning bird of paradise with its breath-takingly brilliant plumage. There were also several sightings of colonies of flying-fox bats, hanging from the trees like great ripe fruit until they were disturbed and took to the air, darkening the sky with their four-foot wingspans.

Five different scientific camps were set up at intervals along the seven-hundred-mile route, and at each of these, between two and five days were spent carrying out the first-ever detailed research into the local flora and fauna. The main continuous project was a crocodile count on behalf of the United Nations Development Programme. PNG is the only country in the world which is legally allowed to export crocodile skins and the farming of these fearsome creatures, based at Lake Murray, is a flourishing local industry. Information about the crocodile population of the Strickland was urgently needed to help plan further development of the industry and we were happy to assist Jerome Montague in carrying out a survey.

Jerome's midnight croc hunts were not for the faint-hearted. Crocodiles are most easily located at night and, as he explained, the only way to count them is to paddle quietly down the river in the pitch dark, shine powerful torches along the mudbanks until you can see the reds of their beady little eyes and then divide by two. Each night Jerome and his intrepid team, including New York YE Stan Glass, Yogi Thami and Sapper Corporal Bill McGuiness, would slip away into the eerie blackness of the night-time jungle for between four and six hours, visiting those spots where they had noticed crocodile tracks on the mud during the day. Nosing up narrow tributaries in the dark, jumping at every sudden ripple that breaks the silence or overhanging branch that brushes against you, can be fairly nerve-wracking. There were one or two heart-stopping moments when, instead of being mesmerised by the torches as they are supposed to be, the crocodiles

[170]

took fright and dived under or – on one never-to-be-forgotten occasion – right through the boat! Sharing a small inflatable with a panic-stricken eight-foot croc when you can hardly see your hand in front of your face is the kind of experience that very soon sorts out the men from the boys. Altogether during the trip they logged 845 crocs ranging in size up to fifteen feet.

YEs Sally Mountford from New Zealand and Canadian Kurt Foellmer assisted Jim Croft and Osia Gideon, two scientists from the Department of Botany in Lae, in collecting and sending back over three hundred specimens of plants and seeds, while YE Pauliasi Vakolomo, a Fijian boxing champion, worked on a Rural Life Development Survey on behalf of the government. This involved interviewing the heads of families in the villages along the river, one of the most interesting of which was Igibira. Rupert Grey led a party there – the first outsiders to visit the place for more than two years – and found that the settlement had moved from its original location, as marked on the map, for rather sinister reasons. There had suddenly been a spate of sickness and death in the old village which nobody could explain, but which the inhabitants immediately put down to sorcery. As a result, they had abandoned the village and built a new one less than a mile away. In this way it was hoped to avoid the curse which had been put on the place. The hold which superstition and magic still have over these people was further demonstrated to the patrol before they left when they witnessed a witch doctor ministering to a sick woman. For two hours he waved the bark of a special tree over her head, chanting all the while.

Zoologist Ian Redmond also worked mainly at night, collecting a considerable variety of frogs, fish, lizards, snakes and insects by torchlight. Ian had a field day in every sense of the phrase, and would often get so involved in what he was doing that he would quite forget what was going on around him. This nearly got him into trouble one day when he wandered off into the jungle with YE Kurt Foellmer during a brief stop to search for lizards, and was inadvertently left behind. It was not until the rest of the party had been motoring down the river for fully five minutes that the absence of Ian and Kurt was noticed. For various reasons, it was difficult to go back for them, but fortunately they suddenly appeared running frantically along the bank trying to catch up and eventually jumped into the river and swam out to be picked up. They admitted rather sheepishly that it had given them a very nasty turn when they got back to find the boats gone – and they were not late again.

There were no major crises as the party forged on towards Daru, although heavy rain at night and the unwelcome attentions of mosquitoes, sandflies and other stinging, biting insects ensured the usual

[171]

discomforts. There was also one weird and unsolved mystery.

At 0130 one morning Roger was awakened by a hoarse voice shouting repeatedly for help. Later Roger said, 'My immediate thought was that Ian Redmond might have taken one of the boats out late and had either got stuck in mid-river or been attacked by crocodiles. I leapt out of my hammock to find other members of the party doing likewise. Amongst those most concerned was Ian. So who was it in trouble? I took a roll call of everyone in the camp and they had all heard the cries. There was only one remaining possibility. Dave Weaver was sleeping away from the main camp down near the boats. Jim Croft and I doubled across towards his *basha*, our imaginations alive with possibilities, only to find Dave indicating that the shouts had come from the main camp. Everyone was checked again. Had anyone had a nightmare? Could it have been a cry from the subconscious? Eventually, with no proper answer to our many questions, we all retired to our hammocks once again with the cries still ringing in our ears. Strange – and very unnerving.'

Chapter Twenty

Dateline: Masingara, December 1979

Many years ago a young Papuan warrior staggered breathlessly home to his village in a state of shock after a lone hunting trip and blurted out an amazing story. His grandchildren still recall it vividly and they will repeat it, word for word, to anyone who penetrates far enough up the Binatori River to reach their isolated but idyllic village of Giringarede.

It seems that their grandfather was feeling rather weary after hours on the trail and went to sit down and rest on a fallen tree trunk only for the 'tree' to rear up under him and reveal itself as a dragon! It stood over ten feet tall on its hind legs and had wicked-looking jaws like a crocodile. The old man did not wait to see if it breathed fire at him – he ran for his life and never once looked back to see if the monster was pursuing him.

It all sounds a bit far-fetched until you consider that stories about creatures fitting very much the same description have been coming out of PNG since the end of the last century – and many of them have come from very reliable sources. During the Second World War, Allied and Japanese patrols operating deep in the most remote parts of the jungle reported catching glimpses of what was most often described as a 'tree-climbing crocodile'.

An Australian called K. R. Slater – at one time an animal ecologist with PNG's Department of Agriculture, Stock and Fisheries, and later Senior Wild Life Officer of the Fisheries and Game Department of South Australia – was so intrigued by the legends that he started his own investigations in 1952 and wrote an article in which he stated that once he began looking into the matter his original scepticism vanished.

He came to the conclusion that what people had seen was a giant lizard of the type first officially identified in 1978 as Salvador's Monitor (*Varanus Salvadori*) – a close relation of the famed Komodo Dragon of Indonesia. A number of very large specimens of Salvador's Monitor have been caught in PNG over the years. One, seven foot in length, was trapped near the mouth of the Fly River in 1936 by a scientific

[173]

expedition, while a trader named John Senior – who runs a general store on the Kikori River – has a skin nailed to his wall which, in life, must have measured a good ten feet. On this evidence, there seemed every reason to suppose that somewhere in the most inaccessible recesses of the jungle there might lurk one or two outsize freaks – the equivalent of those 'grandfather' pike and other big fish that anglers sometimes hook from deep, dark pools. As Slater wrote: 'Stories of specimens of fifteen feet seem reasonable. It just remains for somebody to produce one.'

That was a challenge I found hard to resist and, when Dorian Huber, a Swiss YE, accompanied by our PNG government liaison officer, Miss Somare Jogo, came back from a recce with photographs of a seven-footer and reports of others even bigger, I decided to mount a search for what would undoubtedly be the longest lizard in the world.

We planned to base the expedition at Masingara, Somare Jogo's home village, and have Ian Redmond, a tough young zoologist, join us from Roger's patrol, when they reached Daru.

Masingara is just up the coast from Daru, in the area between the Fly River and the Pahotori River, that is generally considered the most likely haunt for any monster lizard.

Things got off to a suitably dramatic start even before my twenty-strong patrol reached Masingara, when we contrived to get lost in some of the most treacherous waters in the world. The Coral Sea is a wonderfully romantic name for a bit of ocean full of deadly reefs, strong currents and shifting shallows. We never really gave this a second's thought as we set out from Port Moresby, bound for Masingara in the MV *Andewa*. Through some excellent liaison by my WRNS adjutant, the little vessel and her crew had been put fully at our disposal by the government – another example of the incredibly generous help and co-operation given to Operation Drake throughout our stay.

The three-day voyage began well enough. Everybody was sunbathing on the afterdeck, while dolphins played in the bow wave and large juicy baramundi obligingly swallowed the hooks which the crew trailed out astern, assuring us of some excellent eating. It was around dusk on the second day that things went wrong. There was no sign of the lighthouse which was a vital landmark, and although everybody aboard strained their eyes through the growing darkness it was to no avail. At this point the skipper casually confessed that he never bothered with charts because he was used to sailing in waters that he knew like the back of his hand. Unfortunately, he had to admit, this part of the ocean was quite new to him and he really did not know where we were!

[174]

After haphazardly changing course a few times in the hope of hitting upon some identifiable landmark, our position was even more confused. I did have a chart with me, but it was not a lot of help since we could not pinpoint our location. To make matters worse, the compass was not working properly. We were literally going round in circles, when Chris Sainsbury, the only real sailor amongst us, suggested that as we were in such dangerous waters it might be a good idea to throw a plumb line overboard just to be on the safe side, and this revealed the startling fact that we were over a sandbank with less than two feet to spare!

The skipper inched into slightly deeper water before anchoring for the night in the hope that we would be able to get our bearings in the morning, when we would at least be able to see what we were doing. What I really feared was that we were too far south and were heading straight for the Great Barrier Reef.

Dawn broke to reveal that the water, which the day before had been the deepest blue, was now a murky, muddy brown, while large clumps of natural flotsam, including whole palm trees, floated by in a strong current. This gave us the vital clue that we must be somewhere near the mouth of the wide Fly River and enabled us to chart a course which eventually led us back to safety.

Even so, there were some more tense moments before someone spotted the faint outline of a volcanic island on the horizon which made it possible for us to fix our position exactly.

We came into Daru, the provincial capital, at midday, and whilst the good ship *Andewa* refuelled, I rushed off to find Somare and meet her uncle Mr Tatty Olewale OBE, the Premier of the Western Province. We found him at home having lunch, and reading from a gigantic leather-bound Bible, whilst his pet parakeet hopped about on his shoulder. The premier rose to greet us with the words, 'Colonel, it is the Lord who has brought you to us.' After the adventure of the previous night, I was inclined to agree. In no time Mr Olewale summoned his brother, the head postman, who was able to tell us a great deal about Artrellia, as they called the monster. The Premier wished us well and loaded us with small gifts, before sending us off with his niece, Somare, and a wizzened old pilot to guide us up the rivers.

Next day we anchored off Masingara and marched the half mile inland to Somare's well-ordered home village of traditional stilt-supported bamboo huts. There I was ushered by her brother, Seyu, towards a hundred-year-old woman, who was the most senior citizen and who was said to know more than anyone about the Artrellia, having seen several in her lifetime.

The white-haired old lady confirmed many of the things we had

[175]

already heard: that these creatures grew to over fifteen feet in length; that they often stood on their hind legs and so gave the appearance of dragons or, to our minds, mini-dinosaurs; also that they were extremely fierce.

This last point brought much nodding from the village hunters, who made it quite obvious that they treated even the smaller six- or seven-footers − which they said were quite common − with the greatest respect. This came as no surprise, since we had already been told of an incident in another village where a captured Artrellia had smashed its way out of a stout cage and killed a large dog, before escaping back into the forest. Now we learned that the creature's method of hunting was to lie in wait in the trees before dropping onto its victims and tearing them to shreds with its powerful claws. Apart from that, it possessed a very infectious bite as a result of feeding on carrion and this could bring death within a matter of hours. There were plenty of stories of men who had been attacked and killed by the Artrellia.

During the next few days, we split into four patrols and combed the surrounding jungle, but, although everyone we met understood immediately when we explained what we were looking for and claimed that they themselves had seen such creatures, the nearest any of us got to a sighting was when the local dogs that accompanied one patrol put up something that crashed off heavily through the undergrowth without showing itself.

The patrol that ventured up to Giringarede, and heard about 'a dragon disguised as a tree', got the local hunters to take them out to the spot where the incident occurred, but found nothing. There was a flurry of excitement when they returned to the village to be told that the dogs had killed a big lizard while they were away − but it turned out to be a three-foot Monitor of a well-known species. There were certainly plenty of Monitor Lizards about and I was pretty sure that Artrellia would turn out to be a giant version.

At this point I decided to offer a reward to the local hunters. Sure enough, the mere mention of money was followed by a mass exodus into the jungle of every able-bodied man in the village, armed with everything from bows and arrows to an antique blunderbuss.

In the meantime, Somare showed us some interesting snakes that she claimed were caught in a nearby swamp. They were almost jet black, more like eels, and apparently quite blind. Their skin lacked scales, but was covered in a mass of tiny pimples. Ian Redmond had never seen anything quite like these reptiles and Alan Bibby was anxious to film them being caught. 'That is not possible,' said Somare, looking very serious. 'They are only caught by the women at a certain time of year − it is a kind of ritual.'

[176]

'Goody, bags I go and catch some,' enthused Margot.

'Make sure you bring me a pregnant fully grown female,' said Ian, with scientific motives in mind.

So we left the all-female expedition to their task.

On arrival at the swamp, Margot noticed the almost naked village ladies plunging into waist-deep mud covered by a thin layer of grass. The women chopped at the grass with bush knives, peeled back the top layer and feeling around with feet and hands, found a great variety of lung fish, long-necked turtles, lizards and snakes. They hurled their catches to other ladies who waited on the bank. Margot learned that those on the side lines were pregnant and were not allowed in the morass 'because they would drive away the mud-dwelling creatures'. Eventually Margot, reduced to battle order of bra and pants, plunged in, causing much consternation because only pregnant ladies wore bras in Masingara. However, Margot explained, amid much hilarity, that she was not expecting, and the strange ritual continued. Eventually she felt something rather large squirming past her legs, and seized it. Out came a very heavy, fully grown, black, eyeless snake – almost six feet in length and full of eggs. So Ian Redmond got his wish.

It was as we steamed back down the Pahotori in the *Andewa*, after a trip upriver that had produced no actual sightings but many more confirmations that what we were looking for did indeed exist, that Corporal Mick Boxall, my signaller, got a message over the radio reporting that a hunter had managed to shoot a big lizard somewhere deep in the forest and was on his way back to Masingara with it. We returned to the village at full speed and by the time we arrived there, a large crowd had already gathered in a circle around a strange-looking lizard which was lying at their feet roped to a bamboo pole.

It was no dragon, but even so, it was still a pretty fearsome-looking specimen at just over six feet from head to tail. Once Ian had performed his post-mortem, he was able to confirm that it was only a youngster which left plenty of room for speculation about what size an overgrown adult might reach. Meanwhile, a small patrol that had been keeping vigil beside a remote water hole, which we had been told was a favourite haunt of the creatures, came back with reports that they had seen several quite sizeable specimens coming down to drink at night, but had been unable to get near enough to photograph them in the dark.

By the time we had to leave, we had still not seen anything that could be thought of as a dragon, but we were more than ever convinced that such giants did exist. Ian Redmond was so excited by the possibility that he stayed on for some time after the rest of us had gone, and he succeeded in making several sightings of more impressive

[177]

specimens which he estimated as being up to twelve feet in length.

Since my return to Britain I have read an interesting account of a sighting in the 1930s of a similar creature in West Irian. I am confident that had we had more time in which to penetrate deeper into the more remote and undisturbed corners of the forest we could well have met up with the kind of monster that gave the man from Giringarede such a fright. A further, better-prepared attempt to flush out such a wonder is high on my list of future projects. In the meantime, Dorian Huber is already planning to mount an expedition to track one down.

While the thought of coming face to face with a fifteen-foot lizard may be somewhat alarming, I doubt whether it would be quite so disconcerting as a run-in with an angry fifty-foot sperm whale – the most alarming experience I had during the entire expedition.

It happened as I was aboard *Eye of the Wind*, after visiting our underwater team at Finschhafen. A school of some forty whales was sighted, many of them leaping awesomely clear of the water, and we decided to get closer to them in order to film. So, using an Avon inflatable, we approached to within thirty yards of the school and cut the engine so as not to disturb them. We got some excellent photos and were heading back to the ship when we saw three whales nearby and decided to get one last close-up. Frank Esson cut the engine and we paddled gently towards the leviathans. I was filming with my 8 mm cine which has a zoom lens, when I saw a gigantic tail rise out of the leaden sea, then fall and disappear with a great splash. Then, as I adjusted the zoom, a dorsal fin appeared, coming straight at us. 'Shall I start the engine?' asked Frank. But I was concentrating on filming and looking through the view-finder, and felt strangely detached from the world around me. The dorsal fin came on. 'Shouldn't I start the engine?' shouted Frank, and, without waiting for an answer, he did. It was just as well because by now the bull whale's massive head was right beneath us and beginning to rise. The 'dorsal fin' was still fifty feet away. It was the fluke of its tail! Luckily the OMC engine fired first time and we shot away, pursued for a short distance by the huge creature.

It was a close shave. A second more and we would have been lifted out of the water and probably smashed to death by his tail. We were very happy to find ourselves back aboard *Eye of the Wind*, where the crew had enjoyed a grandstand view of the drama.

The ship was kept busy throughout our stay in PNG, either moving stores and personnel around or serving as a floating base for projects carried out among the small islands off the east coast. The most interesting of these was a survey of traditional medicinal plants on the Bismarck Archipelago Islands of Lou, Manus, New Hanover and New

[178]

Ireland. During the course of this fascinating two-week exercise, supervised by Dr David Holdsworth, Head of the Chemistry Department at the University of PNG, eighty-five different plants were collected of which eighty-one were positively identified.

The traditional names and uses of the plants were recorded, and they were tested in the field for the presence of alkaloids which are known to have healing properties.

The World Health Organisation was particularly interested in plants used to treat malaria and also those used as contraceptives. The contraceptive Pill was developed in the first place from tropical forest plants and during the 1980s it is hoped that a Pill can be produced that is totally plant-based.

At Lou, a volcanic island seven miles long and three miles across, a party of five YEs from PNG, the UK, Canada and the USA were led ashore by Dr Holdsworth and Osia Gideon to the village of Solang, where they were greeted by government medical orderly Mr Robert Pam. He helped them collect and identify ten plants used in the treatment of tropical ulcers, cuts, sores, coughs, headaches, diarrhoea and sterility. Later, they were shown the thermal area of the island, where the springs are so hot that you can cook food in them. They also discovered the nests of megapode birds, which lay their eggs in the warm thermal sands, and as a result of this find scrambled megapode eggs were served aboard *Eye of the Wind* – and declared to be very tasty.

Then it was on to the Plitty Aid Post – the extraordinary hospital on the south coast of Manus run by Luke Silih Tau and his wife, Sokolo. It was started without any outside government or private financial assistance, and even now receives only a very small grant from the Office of Village Development, and yet about five hundred patients are treated there every year. Only traditional plant medicines are used and these are collected in the surrounding jungle and prepared under the supervision of Mr Silih Tau. Plants and barks are dried, milled and stored, and when required the powder is boiled with water, which is then strained through muslin to provide an extract. This is administered by the nurses under the watchful eye of Mrs Silih Tau.

The Aid Post has a tremendous local reputation. It claims to have had no fatalities in its entire existence and expects to effect a complete cure in most cases. This seemed to be borne out by the fact that many of the seventy patients who were in residence when the Operation Drake party arrived actually took part in the traditional Manus welcome party that was laid on, joining the nurses in the singing and dancing! It would be hard to think of a better advertisement for the power of these plant medicines, but further testimony is to be found in the readiness of Lorengau Hospital – five hours away by outboard canoe – to refer patients to Plitty.

After explaining the uses of his natural medicines, Mr Silih Tau helped our party to collect twenty-two different plants, including several that could be used to treat more than one complaint. Cures for hookworm, asthma, backache, swollen spleen, venereal disease, pneumonia, malaria and even mental illnesses were added to those which had been found in Lou.

In Taskul, New Hanover, the medical orderly Mr Pitalai Lambes, who happened to be the uncle of one of the PNG YEs, Miss Bospidik Pilokos, made a survey of the island's medicinal plants in readiness for the arrival of *Eye of the Wind*. As a result, another twenty-two specimens were added to Dr Holdsworth's collection, and the list of ailments covered was further extended to include dysentery, abdominal pains, earache, skin rashes, abnormal lactation, jaundice and gonorrhoea. Mr Lambes was also able to point out one of the fabled contraceptive plants.

Another thirty-one plants were collected at Pidikidu, Lamussong and Konos on the island of New Ireland, and constipation, gastric ulcers, TB, sore throat, vomiting and mental stress were added to the growing catalogue of diseases and disorders that responded to these natural treatments.

Eye of the Wind's arrival at Pidikidu coincided with a traditional Malangan mortuary ceremony and feast in the village, and everyone aboard was invited to attend. They joined in a Mamu feast of pigs and taro and watched the performance of Malangan dances which are rarely seen by outsiders. The next day, a hundred specially fattened pigs were killed, singed, butchered and distributed to all the villages in the area.

The event brought this very successful project to a colourful close. Dr Holdsworth was delighted with the results which he hopes will not only lead to the development of new drugs but may also serve to stimulate further research into the use of medicinal plants, both in PNG and in other tropical areas.

The second islands project involved a comprehensive survey of native fishing methods in the area, to determine whether or not it would be feasible to organise a commercial fishing industry there. Mike Gambier organised parties of YEs, accompanied by officials from the PNG Department of Fisheries, to visit islands and atolls in the Tabar, Tanga and Green Islands groups and, although the programme had to be curtailed slightly when *Eye of the Wind*'s main cooling pump broke down and she was forced to stay at Kavieng for six days while repairs were carried out, it nevertheless gave a fascinating insight into the everyday lives of these remote communities. The three-man groups spent their nights going out with the fishermen in their tiny boats, and their days visiting the villages.

One party was lucky enough to be given a demonstration of the art of shark-calling. This involves a great deal of chanting, but the secret of the success with which sharks are apparently summoned from nowhere lies in the use of a coconut-shell rattle which is shaken underwater. Sharks can sense pressure waves caused by sound or violent movement over very long distances. That is why so many people fell victim to sharks in the early days of scuba diving. They would shoot a fish with their harpoon guns and then strap them to their sides, and the sharks would pick up the vibrations of the struggling fish and come to investigate. The trick of the shark-callers is to produce the right kind of vibrations.

Another part of the fisheries project, which was funded by the New Zealand government, was based on the MV *Gastalla*, which acted as a freezer ship, travelling around the islands teaching the locals to fish and then buying up their catch. The experiences of *Gastalla* and the findings of the groups based on *Eye of the Wind* led to the conclusion that it would not be possible to organise the local fishermen on a commercial basis. They fish when they require food, and to get them to fish to a plan would involve changing their whole way of life. Apart from that, the problems of storage and collection presented another major obstacle on islands where there is no electricity to run cold stores.

As Christmas approached, our thoughts turned to the mammoth task of packing up and getting ready to move on. At the best of times this is always a thankless chore, but in PNG it presented more headaches than usual. Not only were tons of stores and equipment spread around all over the island but the lack of road transport added further to our problems. Alas, Len Chandler, my stalwart Quartermaster, had been flown home suddenly when his wife became ill. However, we were lucky in getting a Territorial Army Lieutenant named Nick Ray, who took over at short notice.

Thanks to a lot of hard work and also the help and co-operation of our many friends and supporters in PNG, everything was successfully collected together and shipped out on schedule. On 30 December, *Eye of the Wind* left the Steamships' dry dock in Port Moresby, where she had been routinely overhauled, and set sail for Sulawesi. Thanks to Pan Am, I had a first class ticket back home via Sydney, Auckland and the USA. Knowing I had months of fund-raising ahead, I took a few days off to thank our Australian and New Zealand committees for their magnificent support – and spent a most enjoyable New Year's Eve

[181]

with Reg and Myrtle Glanvill in Sydney. A meeting with John Linehan in New York also turned out well and we sold the world TV rights on the Operation Drake project to ABC.

Chapter Twenty-One

Dateline: Kaipoli, Sulawesi, Indonesia, January 1980

Spine-tingling terror froze Dave Smith into corpse-like stillness in his sleeping bag as the awful realisation dawned as to exactly what it was that had woken him in the middle of the night. His first thought had been that it was simply indigestion that was weighing so heavy on his stomach – after all, that evening's compo rations had been rather stodgy. But as his hand moved down to give his belly a soothing rub it touched something smooth and leathery, and instantly he knew with sickening certainty that for him the ultimate jungle nightmare had come true. There was a snake in bed with him. And, to judge by the thickness of the coils with which his trembling fingers had briefly come in contact, it was a very big one.

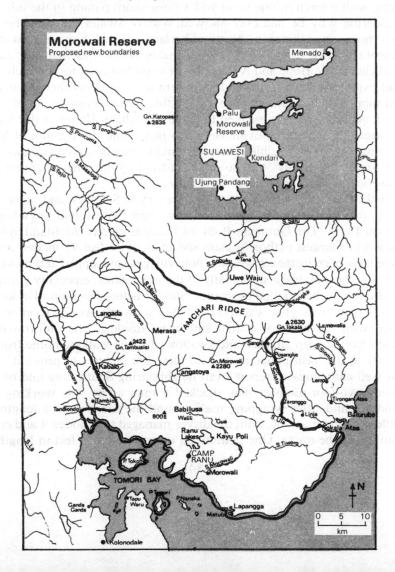

For a few seconds he just lay there in the pitch darkness of the palm-thatched village hut, hardly daring to breathe. He knew he could not hope to slide out of the narrow confines of the sleeping bag without disturbing the monster; at the same time, he could not go on lying there motionless for ever. There was only one thing to do, he decided. Galvanising himself into action with a scream of 'Christ!', he somehow managed to leap from the bag, grab the snake and hurl it as far away from him as possible, all in one swift movement. The sudden commotion had the other members of the long-distance jungle patrol who were sharing the Wana native hut with him sitting bolt upright, wanting to know whatever was going on. When Dave, still shaking like a leaf, explained what had happened, everybody else jumped up and somewhat nervously carried out a torchlight search of each nook and cranny of the room. No sign of the snake could be found, but Dave was not taking any chances. He sat up, wide awake, for the rest of the night, with a torch in one hand and a razor-sharp parang in the other, wondering why he had ever allowed Wandy Swales, his neighbour back home in Alnmouth, Northumberland, to talk him into taking temporary leave from his very comfortable position as manager and head chef at the Hope and Anchor Hotel to go and cook for a bunch of mad explorers, deep in the Indonesian rain forest. His other regulars had supped their Newcastle Brown and told him he must be out of his mind, and now he was inclined to agree with them. He never did find out precisely what kind of snake it was that found the warmth of his sleeping bag so irresistible – but he remains firmly convinced that it was something deadly. And he still shudders to think what might have happened had he turned over in his sleep!

Snakes are very much a part of the scenery in Sulawesi and, what is more, they tend to be bigger and nastier than those found anywhere else on Earth. The Guinness Book of Records credits the island with the world's largest python, a giant specimen of 32 feet 9½ inches, and there have been instances where whole villages have upped and moved to a new location because so many of the inhabitants, especially young children, have been killed by snakes. Shortly before Operation Drake's arrival there was great excitement when a twenty-foot python was killed with the body of a man still intact inside it, the unfortunate victim having been attacked and swallowed while walking home from a party at the local police post. And there are pictures to prove it. A less well-authenticated report from neighbouring South Java told of a twenty-two-foot monster that attacked a man as he was working a bulldozer and, after wrapping itself around the cab, fought a lengthy battle with the machine, until the driver managed to dislodge it and cut it up under the tracks. One python, an estimated fifteen feet in length, and instantly nicknamed Hissing Sid, was regularly seen swimming in the river near one of our camp sites, and an even larger one was brought into camp, dead, having been cleanly shot through the eye with a poisoned dart from a blowpipe.

However, for the leader of this phase, Derek Jackson – the Chairman of the British Schools Exploring Society, who had been with me on the Zaire River Expedition – snakes were the least of his worries, even though he does personally have a horror of them. The setting up of the Sulawesi operation involved greater problems of logistics and organisation than perhaps any other part of the entire two-year venture. It is probably just as well that the ultimate turn-on for any explorer worth his salt is when people purse their lips, shake their heads and murmur with an air of finality: 'It can't be done.' Because it was with that gloomy forecast ringing in their ears that Derek and his second-in-command, Wandy Swales, faced the challenge of making Sulawesi work – and triumphed to the extent that it ended up as one of the most popular and successful of all the phases.

The spot near Morowali village which Derek picked off the map as a likely base camp site was so remote that just getting there in the first place presented considerable difficulties. When it comes to internal communications, Indonesia in general – and Sulawesi in particular – makes even PNG seem sophisticated by comparison. Roads are virtually non-existent in much of Sulawesi, and there is no network of light aircraft routes. When Wandy was despatched on an advance recce aimed primarily at finding ways and means of reaching the place, he soon found himself involved in a journey of epic proportions.

It started smoothly enough with an RAF VC 10 flight to Hong Kong and then an onward connection with Cathay Pacific to Jakarta. He stopped off there to witness the local Highland Games – an extraordinary event laid on annually by the Jakarta branch of the St Andrew's Society, and proudly claimed to be the biggest get-together of its kind outside Scotland – and he made a lot of valuable contacts among the expatriate business community. Then it was on to Ujung Pandang, capital of Sulawesi, and from there to Palu with the Indonesian airline Garuda, before catching a Twin Otter light plane down to Poso. There he managed to hitch a lift on a jeep as far as Tentena, where he was introduced to an airborne Pentecostal missionary named Paul Huling, but known locally to one and all as 'Pilot Paul', who agreed to fly him down to Betelemi. That really did seem to be the end of the line and he set out to walk the twenty-odd miles to Kolonodale, the next stop on his meandering itinerary. He had not gone very far down the road before he was approached by the local 'taxi' – an ancient and highly dangerous-looking motorcycle driven by

[185]

a young man who was happy to offer his pillion seat for hire. As it happened, he would probably have been better off on foot, since the road soon became a track, the track turned into a quagmire and he spent most of the next three hours helping the driver to push the machine out of the mud. However, he eventually phut-phutted into Kolonodale, where he chartered a dug-out canoe with an outboard engine to ferry him the final fourteen miles across the bay to Morowali – at a cost of £60 return! After all that, he arrived on the other side to find that Morowali had moved, as is the wont of villages in Sulawesi, and was actually several miles away from where it was shown on the map.

Wandy's wanderings left him in no doubt about the complications that were going to be involved in moving personnel and over seventy tons of equipment into the area. Clearly, the tortuous route he had followed was totally impractical and the chances were that if the YEs had to come that way, half of them would probably never get there. After much frantic reappraisal and on-the-spot consultation, it emerged that a much more straightforward alternative was to fly from Jakarta to Kendari as directly as possible, allowing for the vagaries of local air travel, and then to go down to the quayside where, for a few pounds per person, a fishing boat could be chartered for the three-day voyage up to Kolonodale.

Although this was obviously much simpler and more satisfactory it still provided a testing introduction to the delights of Operation Drake for those YEs who did not come in the easy way, aboard *Eye of the Wind*. That part of the journey from Jakarta to Kendari tended to be plagued with delays and uncertainties, as one waited for the opportunity to acquire stand-by seats on the few available flights, while the conditions on the boats up to Kolonodale ranged from uncomfortable to downright suicidal.

There were never any proper toilet facilities on board, and the only food on offer was that which the crew lived on – an unvarying and unappetising combination of fish heads and rice soaked in red hot chilli sauce. The boats would often be overloaded to the point where they were wallowing along with no more than a few inches of freeboard, so that if the sea got up, it could be very dangerous. This was brought home forcibly and tragically when one of the leakier old tubs turned over and sank, with the loss of several lives, during her very next trip after bringing up a load of Operation Drake people.

Inaccessibility was by no means the only factor that made life extra-specially difficult for Derek and his team as they struggled to get the Sulawesi phase off the ground. There was also the frustration of having to deal with a ponderous and multi-tiered bureaucracy that demanded

[186]

permits in triplicate for even the most minor facilities. For a long time, radio contact between the jungle base camp and the outside world had to be confined to essential messages sent over with all the secrecy of a wartime spy transmitter behind enemy lines, because of delays in getting a licence. On top of all that, a slightly delicate political situation meant that one had to tread very warily the whole time.

It is hardly surprising, in the circumstances, that poor Wandy Swales suddenly keeled over with what amounted to a minor heart attack just as advance preparations in Jakarta were reaching a climax. Wandy, a 44-year-old North Shields businessman and ex-paratrooper, who had been specially recruited by Derek as his second-in-command because of his toughness and his organisational genius, had gone for two weeks immediately prior to the attack without ever having more than a couple of hours' sleep per night. In view of the pressure under which he was working, it was surprising that the results were not more serious. Happily, his collapse turned out to be less dangerous than was at first thought, and he was back on his feet within a matter of days.

Two days after Wandy was taken ill and admitted to the Coronary Care Unit of the Central Hospital in Jakarta, Bob Powell, also an old hand from the Zaire River Expedition, flew in, expecting to take up his duties as our Chief Engineer only to find himself running the whole show. As Christmas came and went amid an escalating whirlwind of activity that left precious little time for any kind of celebrations, Bob, an architect from Newcastle, began to worry that he, too, would end up in a hospital bed if the killing pace continued. But he drove himself on relentlessly, twelve hours a day and more in the stifling humidity, in his efforts to overcome an endless series of crises.

One thing that continually drove him mad as he laboured to get things organised was the local equivalent of the Spanish *mañana*. 'The immediate characteristic that has struck me about Indonesia is that there is no such thing as "now" or "no",' he wrote in his diary. 'It is apparently considered a loss of face to refuse anything, so that any requests are usually met by evasion. The word *belum* sums it up. It means, "not yet", and is typified in a story of two old Indonesians standing by the road watching a coffin go by. One turns to the other and asks if he knew the deceased. The answer comes back, "Belum"!'

Despite this and the many other enormous problems – including an embarrassing lack of funds, which resulted from delays in opening an Operation Drake account locally, and which forced him to beg loans from our long-suffering supporters in Jakarta – the formal launch of the phase went ahead on schedule at a big press conference on 3 January. This tremendous success in getting things ready on time, against all the odds, owed a great deal to the endlessly patient and generous assistance given by a handful of local backers whose commitment went far beyond what we had any right to expect. Once again, BAT were absolutely marvellous and their President Director Robin Leonard, along with Vice President Mr Lie Purwadi, and Marketing Services Manager David Grime, always seemed to be on hand with invaluable help and advice. Rudy Schouten not only gave us rooms in the Hilton but also provided conference facilities and allowed us free and unlimited use of the hotel's typing, printing, photographic and telephone services, without which it is hard to imagine how we could have operated so efficiently. And Dr Julius Tahija, President of Caltex, whose donations had already ensured the participation of so many Indonesian students and scientists, was another tower of strength whose local knowledge and prestige enabled us to short-circuit many otherwise long drawn-out complications. Our friends in Garuda, Cathay Pacific and the Indonesian Nickel Corporation also deserve special thanks.

The arrival at Kendari on 10 January of the big RAF C130 transport plane that was bringing 19,000 pounds of stores and equipment, carefully packed by veteran expedition administrator Sandy Evans in PNG, was watched with some anxiety, since the little runway was barely big enough to accommodate such an aircraft, but the pilot made a perfect landing. Then it was a matter of transporting all the gear to the quayside and transferring it onto a boat for the last lap of the journey up to Morowali, where a small advance party had been working for some weeks on the construction of the base camp huts, and making other preparations.

A coaster named the *Surya Alam* was duly chartered, but before she sailed two things happened which gave a colourful insight into the Indonesian way of life. First of all, before she could be loaded, there was a delay while a special ceremony was carried out to bless the new engine which had just been fitted. A goat was sacrificed and there followed many incantations on the foredeck and readings from the Koran, and then the dedication was rounded off with a huge feast and a ritual circumnavigation of the bay.

The second incident caused some annoyance to Bob Powell and the other Operation Drake personnel who had assembled in Kendari and were sailing to Morowali with him – although in the end they saw the funny side of it. When they went to board the *Surya Alam*, which they had supposedly chartered on an exclusive basis, they were somewhat irritated to find no less than twenty-eight people already comfortably settled on board in all the best berths. At this point Leading Aircraftsman Gary Brindle, a member of the diving team, mentioned that he had spotted a notice board, discreetly displayed on the quayside,

Army Air Corps Major Frank Esson (standing centre right) with YEs and
and Fijians rebuilding a school destroyed in a hurricane on Moala Island
(CHRISTOPHER SAINSBURY)

After an Operation Drake team spent two weeks in the jungle, a specimen
of Artrellia, thought to be a Salvador's Monitor lizard, was found. Salvador's
Monitor lizards are known to grow to great length, and a large one was said
to have killed a man two years before our arrival (JOHN BLASHFORD-SNELL)

A previously unlocated P47 fighter found by a group of PNG and British YEs led by Major Mike Gambier (centre right). Details of the aeroplane were sent back to the US Army Records Office, who were able to trace its history. On 29 April 1944 the fighter was not flown by its usual pilot, Colonel J. W. Harris; First Lieutenant Marion C. Lutes took the fighter up to test its guns, and crashed. Through the US Army Records Office we were able to contact Colonel Harris to tell him of our find (ADRIAN PENNY)

(inset) Colonel Harris kindly sent us photographs of the P47 fighter taken at the wartime airport of Nadzab, PNG, prior to the crash (COLONEL HARRIS)

An awesome encounter with a 15-metre sperm whale. Fortunately the whale dived under the Avon dinghy from which this photograph was taken, and the Operation Drake team was able to motor back to *Eye of the Wind,* leaving the whale and its family in peace (BILL NEUMEISTER)

The *Cathay Pacific,* an Avon inflatable, manned by Major Roger Chapman (left), Nepalese YE Yogi Thami (centre) and American scientist Dr Jerome Montague (right), who was working on the United Nations Development Programme in PNG (BILL NEUMEISTER)

Major Roger Chapman (right) and Australian Bob Woods (left), who acted as interpreter and guide in PNG, with members of the Pogaea tribe, who had never seen white men until Operation Drake sent a reconnaissance patrol down the Strickland Gorge. The patrol's carriers are in shorts (BILL NEUMEISTER)

WOII Keith Crawford, Devon and Dorset Regiment (left) with American
YE Ernie Jones (right) on the Morowali Nature Reserve survey
(RUPERT RIDGEWAY)

YEs disturbing terns so that they can be photographically counted, on an
island in the African Banks during the Seychelles phase of the expedition
(BORKUR ARNVIDARSON)

Kenyan YE Charles Langat climbing down into the moat of the Susua
crater (CHRISTOPHER SAINSBURY)

An aerial view of the Susua crater (KENYA WILDLIFE CONSERVATION
AND MANAGEMENT DEPARTMENT)

(from left to right) Kenyan YEs Benedict Kisilu and Richard Mangoka
and Jersey YE Hamish Pettigrew measuring the wall of the central mosque
at Shanga (CHRISTOPHER SAINSBURY)

Eye of the Wind and the Goodyear airship *Europa* carrying out air and sea pollution studies in the Mediterranean (RICHARD SAILER)

The overseas committee members with HRH The Prince of Wales at the World Trade Centre: (left to right) Dick Barkle (Pan Am), Billy St Malo (Panama), HRH The Prince of Wales, Sir Gordon White (Chairman of the US committe), General Sir John Mogg, Major John Girling (Chairman of the Drake Fellowship, PNG), Ray Bellows (Treasurer of Operation Drake Jersey), Lieutenant Colonel John Blashford-Snell – and on the table the replica of Sir Francis Drake's sword that was presented to Mr Walter Annenberg, Operation Drake's President (R.J. DAVIS)

YEs manning the yardarms as *Eye of the Wind* returns to St Catherine's
Dock, London (R.J. DAVIS)

advertising the trip north. When confronted with this, the skipper did grudgingly admit that he was carrying one passenger — a soldier in full uniform who was carrying a bulging suitcase and who could clearly not be passed off as part of the crew — but he remained adamant that everyone else was an essential member of the ship's company. The aged couple crouched in the bows? They were his parents and they always went everywhere with him, he insisted. And then there were his sons who had to come along to learn the route and the handling of the boat. Five cooks were necessary to prepare fish heads and rice, and there was a relief crew of eleven! Obviously there was no point in arguing — they would just have to settle for a cramped journey. It was noticeable, however, that a large proportion of those on board did nothing throughout the voyage except sit and stare at the white men in their midst.

After docking at Kolonodale, the next task was to arrange for the transport of the gear across the bay to Camp Ranu in small boats. The camp was situated in a clearing about a mile up the Ranu River and the first view of it was impressive. Bob Powell, describing his arrival, wrote in his diary: 'The mouth of the Ranu opens in the mangrove-covered shoreline and beckons us in. The river closes in — narrow and shallow with low, thick mangrove coming right down to the water's edge. It twists and turns and we navigate carefully around fallen and half-submerged logs. The camp appears around a bend and it is a magical sight, with engineers Mike Prior, John Rimmer and Bob Hooper waiting on the jetty they have built, looking for all the world like characters out of *Apocalypse Now* — bronzed, a little tattered and sporting a variety of headgear.'

The new arrivals pitched enthusiastically into the work of building the camp, which, with the help of some hired labourers, was already by that stage well advanced, and, although they soon found that hard physical toil in temperatures of up to 100°F in the shade can be totally exhausting, it was completed in time for the arrival of the main party.

Camp Ranu eventually consisted of four large dormitory huts, each capable of accommodating up to sixty people, a science laboratory, a survey office, a medical centre, a signals centre and a cookhouse — all of them solidly built around wooden frames with roofs of thatched leaves. It was, all in all, a very cosy set-up — and why not? There was a great deal of serious scientific work to be done in Sulawesi and the environment guaranteed that life would be sufficiently uncomfortable without introducing extra unnecessary hardships.

The pattern of our activities in Sulawesi was different from all the other land phases. Instead of being spread over a variety of unrelated projects, our efforts were concentrated almost exclusively on a single

[189]

grand purpose – the preparation of a detailed and comprehensive management plan for the proposed nature reserve at Morowali. The inspiration for this came from John Blower, an old friend from my days on the Blue Nile, who lived in Indonesia, where he was head of the FAO National Parks Development Project. When I approached him for advice about possible projects in the area, he drew my attention to the fact that the Indonesian government had an outstandingly enlightened attitude towards conservation and proposed to make 5 per cent of the country's entire land area into nature reserves and National Parks. The one at Morowali was ready to go ahead as soon as the 2,000-square-mile jungle wilderness in the southeast of the island had been surveyed and a proper plan produced. This was a fairly daunting task, since the region was largely unmapped and unexplored, apart from the coastal strip and the principal valleys leading to the interior, but any asssitance that Operation Drake could offer would undoubtedly be most welcome.

We jumped at the opportunity to get involved in something that promised to mix research, exploration and adventure in such a worthwhile way – especially when Scientific Co-ordinator Andrew Mitchell pointed out that Sulawesi was of paramount zoological interest since it lies on the Wallace Line, the watershed of animal life that separates Asia from Australia in the evolutionary process. Alfred Russel Wallace, the nineteenth-century naturalist and explorer who first pinpointed this natural border, said of Sulawesi:

'Situated in the very midst of an archipelago, and closely hemmed in on every side by islands teeming with varied forms of life ... it is yet wonderfully rich in peculiar forms, many of which are singular or beautiful and in some cases are absolutely unique upon the globe.'

Excluding bats, more than 90 per cent of Sulawesi's mammals are endemic, including the anoa, a dwarf buffalo just thirty inches high; the babirrusa, a pig-like creature with curving tusks that emerge through the top of its snout; and the island's own special monkey, the Celebes black macaque. Because of its geological isolation, Sulawesi is similar to the Galapagos Islands in that it provides a fascinating living laboratory in which to carry out scientific research and observation.

After consultations with John Blower and the Indonesian authorities, I asked Derek Jackson to lead the phase and to come up with a detailed programme of activities. Basically, a large number of YE patrols would be sent out to undertake the socio-economic and medical surveys which, along with the findings of the scientists, would be used in the preparation of a management plan to be written by Dr Andrew Laurie, who was financed by the World Wildlife Fund. In addition, the YEs were to be responsible for going out and plotting

[190]

river courses, tracks and other geographical features that would enable Royal Engineers Sergeant Phil Maye to produce the first really accurate map of the region. In addition, a vegetation map was to be produced in a fascinating project carried out by Robert Warwick-Smith from the Geography Department of London University's School of Oriental and African Studies, and the YEs, with a little help from outer space. Special photographs taken by the Land Sat 1 satellite use different degrees of reflected light to produce a relief-type impression of the Earth's surface which can differentiate between various types of vegetation. Once 'ground truth' has been established, by correlating the different patterns on the photograph to actual vegetation, a comprehensive map can be built up.

All this was going to be a formidable job of work, but, as it turned out, the overall sense of purpose helped to make it more rewarding than some of the more obviously dramatic adventures that featured in other phases.

While the final preparations were being made at Camp Ranu, the first batch of YEs were on their way from PNG in *Eye of the Wind*. They were unfortunate in that the monsoon season had started, bringing with it an endless succession of short, sharp squalls and a prevailing northwest wind that was dead against them for the whole of the three-and-a-half-week trip, with the result that the ship had to motor almost continuously.

However, the mainsail, jibs and staysails were set most of the time to give added stability and there were plenty of chances to go aloft. Like many others before her, 22-year-old Susan Mattsson from South Australia's Coffin Bay viewed this prospect with alarm. 'The day before we left Port Moresby, we went aloft while at the wharf and I got only as far as the course yard,' she recalled in her final report. 'I remember being filled with fear and breaking out into nervous laughter – I was sure I would never be able to make it any higher. Little did I know that the bug of wanting to go up at the smallest opportunity was about to bite. It was when the lower and upper topsails were set in a rain squall and then had to be taken down again almost immediately that I learned of my hidden love for working aloft. Furling the sails in a thirty-knot wind or more, with the boat beneath us pounding into the sea, is an experience that is hard to beat. While rolling and lurching about high above the decks, your fear suddenly disappears and you start to relax and roll with the waves and, yes, you even enjoy it up there and can't wait for the next time. One has a great sense of pride and achievement after climbing down from the rigging when the work is completed.'

Susan, along with her crewmates, also learned to welcome the sudden squalls, when the wind reached speeds of seventy miles per hour and the rain sheeted down, as the chance for a refreshing showerbath. 'As soon as it starts to rain, everyone races on deck in bathers with shampoo and soap in hand,' she wrote. 'You soon become expert at lathering up and washing the suds off in a short period of time. Being too slow means that you are left all soaped up when the rain stops and you have to wash down in salt water, which leaves you feeling very sticky.'

It was between Thursday Island and Ambon that a particularly violent squall produced the one major drama of the voyage when the main boom, forty-two feet long and over twelve inches thick, snapped like a matchstick. It was an awesome sight to behold as the sail billowed in the wind, arching the boom until the great timber finally split under the tremendous pressure with a crack like a pistol shot. It all happened so suddenly that there was nothing anyone could do, and those on watch stood rooted to the spot, helplessly waiting for the inevitable splintering crash.

The loss of the boom was uncomfortable rather than catastrophic since, without the mainsail, the ship lost stability and started rolling in a manner that was, quite literally, sickening. A replacement would have to be found as soon as possible and this seemed likely to prove easier said than done. In the end, a growing tree was selected and purchased in Ambon. It was then felled and towed out to a logging vessel owned by an extraordinary character – half-German, half-Indonesian, and known to one and all locally as Captain Billy – who kindly offered his ship as a floating workbench on which to shape the tree roughly with a chainsaw. After *Eye of the Wind* reached Sulawesi, Spider spent hours honing it into perfect shape by hand.

Nobody was too sorry to see Ambon fading over the horizon as *Eye of the Wind* sailed on to Kolonodale. The memories they carried away of the world's fourth most densely populated city were of oppressive, feverish heat, stinking open sewers and frantic, overcrowded streets. It was a blessed relief to get back out to sea and the fresh air.

Three days later, the ship arrived just off the mouth of the Ranu River to be greeted by a scene of breath-taking beauty. From the clear blue water's edge the emerald green jungle backdrop swept upwards to meet an azure sky in which hovered the most incredible fluffy white cloud formations.

[192]

Chapter Twenty-Two

Dateline: Tomari Islands, Sulawesi, February 1980

Many people daydream about how they would face up to the romantic challenge of being marooned on a desert island, but very few ever actually get to live out their Robinson Crusoe fantasies. The YEs on the Sulawesi phase, however, were offered the chance to do just that when, as a dramatic climax to the Jungle Survival Course, each of them was invited to spend three days and nights alone, in splendid isolation on one of the tiny uninhabited islands scattered in the Teluk Tomari Bay. Nobody was forced to do it — apart from anything else, there was obviously a real element of risk, in that members of the Directing Staff would certainly not be hiding behind the nearest palm tree waiting to pop out and come to the rescue in the event of a sudden emergency. Despite this, nearly everybody jumped at such an exciting, once-in-a-lifetime opportunity. In this modern, overcrowded age, the experience of being absolutely and completely alone, cut off from the outside world in a back-to-nature situation, is rare indeed.

This great adventure was preceded by a week-long visit to what was known as Eddie's Beach — the little cove near the mouth of the Ranu River where survival expert Eddie McGee had set up his camp. From Eddie — an ex-paratrooper- and former instructor with the Army Physical Training Corps who normally runs a Survival Centre in the somewhat less awesome wilds of Yorkshire — the YEs learned such secrets of improvisation as how to make rope out of grass, turn animal fat and hot water into soap, use ash from the fire as a sterile dressing, and produce a gourmet meal out of nothing but ferns and bamboo. They also picked up all sorts of useful titbits of information, including the fascinating fact that a brazil nut will burn like a candle for up to an hour, that a feather is unbeatable when it comes to cleaning out open wounds and that a condom is probably the most versatile product known to man, serving every imaginable purpose from storing water to keeping one's matches dry. It can even be used to attract the attention of passing aircraft — all one has to do is blow it up and spray it with water; it then becomes irridescent and can be flown like a marker balloon!

Having familiarised themselves with these and many other equally handy hints, and having also been taught vital skills like how to make fish and animal traps, where to look for fresh water, and how to distinguish between edible and poisonous plants, the volunteer castaways were considered to be in a fit and ready state to 'go solo'. They were each taken to a separate island by boat and dumped there with a basic survival kit that included not much more than a knife, a torch, a compass, a packet of biscuits, a packet of Spangles and a litre of water. Once again, anyone who wanted to make things a little easier for himself or herself was quite at liberty to take extra rations or equipment, but nobody did. They all entered bravely into the spirit of the exercise.

Most of them admitted afterwards that as the sound of the boat's engine faded into the distance and they found themselves alone, they did begin to feel a bit twitchy, especially when darkness fell. One girl wrote: 'At first I seemed to jump at nearly everything – leaves falling, hornets buzzing past, the waves booming or sounding like footsteps in the creviced rocks. Once I put my hand within an inch of a scorpion that was sitting on a rotten log and had to give myself five minutes to recover.'

Jan Morton, a student teacher from Glasgow, walked straight into an even more unpleasant welcome on her particular island. 'I was dropped on a dream beach, about a mile of sand fringed by palms, but the first thing that happened when I went up into the jungle was that I bumped into a massive web and a giant spider dropped on me and ran down my back before scuttling away. Its body was about three or four inches across and, if you included its huge red-and-yellow legs, it must have measured nearly eight inches in diameter. It gave me a real shock, because I suddenly realised that if it had bitten me and it was a very poisonous variety there would have been very little I could have done.'

One or two people decided to play it safe and sat tight in one spot, eking out their meagre food and water supplies until the boat came back to pick them up again, but the majority were much more enterprising. A lot of them built fish traps and baited them with limpets, mussels and – in one case – Spangles, but even this unlikely offering failed to tempt the passing shoals, and dreams of juicy barracuda steaks were always cruelly shattered when the traps were expectantly checked and invariably found to be empty. Jan Morton was, in fact, the only person who succeeded in catching anything at all, and even then it was only a tiddler that was so small that she had not got the heart to eat it.

Other people concentrated their search for food in the jungle, with varying degrees of success. One lucky young man stumbled on an

[194]

overgrown melon plantation and gorged himself for the entire three days, while another spent hours contemplating a coconut, nestling way out of his reach at the top of a slender fifty-foot palm, before the answer came to him in a flash of inspiration – and he chopped the whole tree down with his machete! This earned him full marks for faultless logic, but nought out of ten for conservation awareness.

Quite a few people found absolutely nothing at all, not so much as a nut or a berry, and they experienced real hunger and thirst, probably for the first time in their lives. One girl got so ravenous that she gave serious consideration to the possibility of cooking and eating a lizard before deciding that she was not quite that starved.

The psychological effects of even such a short period of isolation were very interesting. There were those who confessed that by the last day they were praying for the pick-up boat to arrive, and Jan Morton recalls that she was horror-struck when it did not arrive on time. 'It occurred to me that maybe the final, most important part of the test was that, just when we thought it was all over, we were actually going to be left there for four days instead of three. I really would have found that hard to cope with. I don't think I could have lasted another day – I was so geared up to the fact that I'd made it.'

Even so, Jan remembers it as by far the most exciting and rewarding part of the entire phase. 'A lot of the others felt the same. One had an awful lot of time to think, and it was a unique opportunity to learn things about yourself. It was very noticeable that afterwards everybody was very warm towards each other, as if the experience of being thrown back on themselves had made them appreciate other people more. In the end nobody did actually crack up and I think everybody got tremendous personal satisfaction out of seeing it through successfully.'

Survival training was, of course, an essential feature of all Operation Drake's land phases, but particular emphasis was put on it in Sulawesi, and there was a very good reason for this. Derek believed strongly that the secret of success as far as the YEs were concerned would be to leave them, wherever possible, to their own devices and to keep supervision to a minimum. Having put them all through a rigorous programme of training and preparation, he felt totally confident about following through with this policy, even to the extent of sending out patrols deep into the jungle without any Directing Staff to chaperone them. This added responsibility was gratefully accepted by the YEs, who more than justified Derek's trust in their ability to look after themselves by coping extremely competently with every situation that arose.

They were given an early taste of this independence as soon as they arrived at Camp Ranu, when, as part of the initial acclimatisation scheme that preceded their stint with Eddie McGee, they were split into small groups and despatched to one or other of four local villages, where they lived for ten days while carrying out the socio- economic and medical survey among the inhabitants. As a method of breaking in newcomers to a completely strange environment, it was as successful as it was imaginative. The YEs reacted with great enthusiasm to the challenge of finding their own way about, and the villagers were delighted with the novelty of having them and welcomed them into their homes. By the time they returned to base camp, they had not only adjusted physically to living in the tropics but had also learned at first hand a great deal about the country and its people, and had even picked up a bit of the language. At the same time, they were doing something useful.

They went armed with questionnaires which had to be answered by every inhabitant, and which covered every aspect of village life. On the basis of this information and their own observations, they were able to write comprehensive reports that made a vital contribution to the overall management plan, since the integration of the local communities into any National Park area is a major consideration for the planners.

The job was made easy by the friendliness and openness of the villagers, who treated them like honoured guests and were only too happy to provide all the necessary information about their daily lives. The headman could always be relied upon to recite the history of the village from its foundation, while others talked freely about everything from local traditions to intimate details of family life. During the day, the YEs would accompany them on fishing trips, to their plantations and on hunting expeditions, so as to see for themselves how they lived and worked.

The group that visited the village of Tapu Waru were fortunate enough to witness the launching of a new dug-out canoe – called a *perahu* – an incredible process which started nearly three quarters of a mile inland and three hundred feet up a mountain! That is where the best mahogany trees grow to a height of two hundred feet, and having been felled and roughly shaped on the spot, the twenty-five foot 'hull', which can weigh anything up to half-a-ton, is sent skidding down a slipway of logs, right through the forest and all the way to the sea. It is an amazing and rather alarming spectacle, which, for sheer drama, matches anything you are ever likely to see on Clydeside.

Richard Tarlov, the young American who emerged as project leader for Tapu Waru, described in his report how he and three other members of his group first climbed up to where the village boat-builder

[196]

was chopping away with his light, small-headed axe, hollowing out the log and neatly carving supports for the seats and a post-hole for the mast. It takes him ten days altogether to fell the tree, chop out the segment he wants, slice the top portion off, hollow out the inside and roughly cut the outside, and then, after the launch, one more day is needed to complete the job. Richard and his colleagues marvelled at the deft skill with which the boat-builder wielded his little axe. They were invited to try their hand at it, but failed miserably. 'His swings of the axe were full, overhead and very powerful in comparison to ours,' wrote Richard. 'But his ability to lay the blade precisely in the cut he last made was something to behold.'

The slipway was formed out of tree trunks felled across a dry gorge to act as rollers, with leaves spread across them as a lubricant. When everything was ready for the launch, long ropes were hitched fore and aft on the craft and belayed round the stumps of the trees that had been cut down to provide the rollers. Then the rope men took the strain, while four or five others rocked the log to get it moving. 'A great deal of excitement is generated in this job,' noted Richard. 'The thrill of getting the canoe sliding smoothly over the rollers for fifty or sixty feet can be likened to a good run on the ski slope. The danger involved, however, is enormous. One can imagine the forces at work when a half-ton load starts gathering speed down an incline of up to forty degrees. The men worked frantically to keep the sliding hulk from crashing into the limestone boulders that line the gorge. Most of the time they ran alongside, but every now and again, when there was too little room to spare, they would nimbly leap aboard and hitch a ride.

'It took two hours to descend in this manner. The myriad problems encountered on the way down were dealt with swiftly and safely by the crew of thirty, many of whom had assisted in the launching of the previous twenty perahus that had used this particular set of rollers (these get washed away in the seasonal torrents that come cascading down the gorge in the monsoons of June and July).

'At the bottom there was still several hundred metres of forest to get through before the shore was reached. Here the log rollers had been laid along a jungle path and now on the level, the belaying ropes were dispensed with and the fun really began. The entire work force pulled the craft along, while just a few guided its progress, and to the accompaniment of screams, shouts and chants the hefty mahogany hull was soon racing through the jungle at an almost uncontrollable speed.

'Eventually we reached a point near the beach where a river intersects the jungle path, and here the perahu was set afloat and rowed over to the boat-yard outside the boat-builder's house, where the finishing touches would be put to it. These included shaping the bows

[197]

and the outside of the hull, which had been left rough to protect it on the downhill trip.

'The whole parade from top to bottom was like a ritual, which ended with a feast on the beach. Everybody who had been involved in the exhausting job sat down to a fifteen-foot spread that had been prepared by the wives, and included a number of different fish dishes, mixed beans, rice, noodles, sweet potatoes and tea.'

After their period of acclimatisation and their survival training, the YEs were more than ready to venture into the jungle on their own, and patrols started ranging far and wide over the Nature Reserve area, logging minutely detailed geographical data for Phil Maye's map, and gathering information on every aspect of the forest environment and ecology for use in the formulation of the management plan. Altogether, more than eighty reports were prepared on the flora, fauna, people and places of Morowali.

The people of the region proved especially interesting. The local Wana tribesmen are generally categorised under three headings, depending on the degree to which they have become civilised in the modern sense. There are the settled Wana of the coastal towns and villages, the wild Wana of the interior, and finally the Kayu Merangka – the wild, wild Wana who roam the deepest backwoods areas. The name Kayu Merangka, literally translated, means, 'leaves that are blown on the wind', and that perfectly describes the unsettled nature and silently drifting ways of these rather mysterious people who are known for their ability to melt away and merge into the shadows of the forest as soon as outsiders approach.

All over Indonesia they are talked of with awe as primitive, head-hunting savages who are quite likely to murder, with poison darts from their blowpipes, anyone who dares to stray into their territory. We were given stern warnings by various local officials who insisted that they could be dangerous – particularly towards people dressed in green, military-style uniforms who might be confused with the army patrols that had allegedly come to be regarded with special suspicion and hostility as representatives of hated authority.

It did not take long for us to discover that the fearsome reputation of the Kayu Merangka is largely undeserved. The first tentative contact was made when Bob Powell led an early recce party up to the remote village of Uewaja. The coastal Wana were as nervous as anyone else about venturing too far into the territory of their notorious inland cousins, and guides were very hard to find. Because of this, it began to look as though they would get no further than Ratobaye – the last outpost of coastal civilisation – but there, in the end, they secured the services of a travelling damar collector who happened to be passing through and agreed to take them there for the price of a week's collection of damar – the gum-like substance that is tapped from trees and which forms the basis of one of the main local industries. Andreas, the group's interpreter from Camp Ranu, remained extremely edgy about the whole trip and pleaded with Bob to heed the warnings about the Kayu Merangka. 'They are in league with the Dewa [the Devil],' he insisted. 'They have a book and they have known for seven days that we are coming. They knew even before we left Ranu, and even now they are preparing for our approach.'

The patrol – which also included Lance Corporal Alan Bretherton of the survey team, Signaller Bob Hooper and Sergeant John Cornish of the 14/20th King's Hussars – reached Uewaja after a two-day march, and were given a shy though friendly welcome by those villagers who were not away working in their forest gardens or hunting. While Alan Bretherton got on with the job of taking bearings on all the main geographical features before the lurking mist obscured them, the others spent the day chatting to the old men, women and children, finding out as much as possible about their life-style and admiring, among other things, the craftsmanship of the ornately carved blowpipes that were stored in the rafters. Conversation flowed freely with the help of Andreas as interpreter, and the patrol, who learned to their surprise and delight that they were the first white men ever to visit Uewaja, were invited to share a meal of sweet corn, potatoes, tiny tomatoes and cucumber, and to stay the night.

As the evening wore on, more and more people arrived back in the village, including several who were slightly different from the rest – men with beards who wore only loincloths and carried blowpipes. It did not take long to establish that these were indeed the dreaded Kayu Merangka. They accepted sweets and cigarettes and talked about themselves quite happily, and Bob Powell noted in his diary: 'They clearly were not so much aggressive as frightened of outsiders, protective of their isolated gardens and suspicious of intruders. This may, at some time in the past, have led them to kill coastal people or even the 'green-shirted' soldiers for whom they seemed to reserve a special mistrust. And if they no longer did so, the perpetuation of the myth was in their interest because, so long as they were regarded as dangerous, their way of life would be likely to remain unaltered.'

Despite this, and although they were not shown the slightest hint of hostility, Bob and his colleagues understandably experienced a twinge of apprehension as they settled down for the night, heavily outnumbered. 'Any qualms we may have felt were not helped when a particularly wild-looking male Wana arrived and slipped into the glow of the flickering fire, and, as if on cue, the sky was lit by a bright flash

[199]

of lightning, followed by a thunderous downpour of rain.' But nothing happened. Andreas reported later that he had awoken at four o'clock in the morning to find six men sitting around the fire, discussing the patrol – who they could be and why they had come. They apparently came to the conclusion that they were indeed there purely out of curiosity and posed no threat.

As they left, the patrol were presented with a white chicken that had been ceremonially slaughtered before their very eyes. Its neck was plucked and then it was held up towards the rising sun as its throat was cut. 'It is for you, Mr Bob, for all of you – because you came with peace in your hearts,' explained Andreas.

An even more dramatic meeting took place later on when another patrol penetrated deeper still into Kayu Merangka territory. This group – which included Captain Ray Lloyd-Jones, Operation Drake's Chief Signals Officer, British YE Noel English, American YE Chris Cotton and Indonesian student botanists Emil Reppie and Lucky Lumingas – pushed on north of the Solato River into the extremely inaccessible regions around the headwaters of the Sabuku and Bongka Rivers. Their main aim in doing so was to climb Mount Tokala, but after several determined assaults on this peak, they had to admit defeat in the face of hunger, thirst, exhaustion and quite impossible terrain. Their final attempt ended when they ran so short of water that they were reduced to living on what they could squeeze from vines and pitcher plants. They were forced to give up at eight thousand feet and came down to replenish their water supplies in the valley below. It was as they were marching out of the valley, along the riverside, that they became aware that they were being followed.

'We didn't actually see anyone, but we could definitely hear them,' recalled Noel English, the bright young Cockney who took time off from his job as a diamond sorter in Hatton Garden to join Operation Drake. 'Apart from that, we had become quite adept at tracking by that time, and there were all sorts of giveaway signs. We detected the odd footprint in the mud beside the river and, more alarming, found that attempts were being made to obliterate the trail we were following. This was done at points where it crossed the river. The crossings were often staggered and one would have to walk along the river for a small distance before picking up the track again on the other side and what was happening was that the gap in the dense undergrowth along the bank was being filled in with branches and creepers so that there was no sign of where the path carried on.' Noel admitted that this was rather disconcerting, especially in view of the reputation of the Kayu Merangka. 'We were certainly a bit on edge, but we were resigned to the fact that there was absolutely nothing we could do if we were attacked. There were only five of us, we had no weapons and we were weighed down by heavy packs. So we just pressed on regardless.'

The confrontation came early in the morning in a clearing with a small shelter in it, under which the patrol had flopped, exhausted, the evening before. There was a breathtaking view over the surrounding hillsides, and Noel and Ray Lloyd-Jones got up at sunrise to take some photographs. It was actually in his viewfinder that Ray first spotted an old man standing in the shadow of the trees, watching him intently. Once he realised he had been seen, he started mumbling and grunting, but it was obvious from his manner that he was nervous rather than threatening. It was discovered later that what he was mumbling was, 'Please don't kill me', while his grunts were a form of verbal punctuation – rather like 'er' or 'um'.

Noel put on his friendliest smile and the old man advanced hesitantly, having first summoned his two sons, who had been watching with him, but had run off and hidden in the jungle when they saw signs of life. The ice was soon broken to the extent that the old man, whose name was Solo, invited the patrol back to his village. This turned out to be about three hours' march away and consisted of five bamboo- and palm-thatched huts, in which lived a total of twenty people who were all part of one big, happy family.

Here, once again, it soon became obvious that, far from being murdering savages, the Kayu Merangka are gentle, shy people who have got their bad reputation simply because they are timid and shrink away from contact with civilisation. Noel and his colleagues were overwhelmed with hospitality. They feasted on corn on the cob, which was roasted in the fire, and sweet potatoes dipped in wild honey, which everyone agreed was one of the nicest combinations they had ever tasted. Honey is a treasured luxury and yet, when Noel made it obvious how much he enjoyed it, Solo immediately filled a three-foot section of bamboo with it and presented it to him. And when the time came for the party to leave, he sent along his two sons, Mote and Ra'a, to guide them back to Uewaja. As a reward the boys were given Operation Drake T-shirts, with which they were absolutely delighted, despite the fact that they looked rather incongruous when worn with loin-cloths!

Such clashes of style never bother the Wana, as another patrol discovered when they went in search of the rare Impoc tree and were guided for part of the way by a gentleman who insisted on donning his Sunday best – namely, a very ancient pair of patched trousers, a denim jacket, Wellington boots and, to cap it all, a red construction helmet. When he reached a river that had to be forded, he made a great point of taking off his wellies before he walked across! His reward included some much-prized empty sardine cans.

[201]

This patrol, which included David Hudson from Australia, Dan Etter from the USA, Sammy Manning and Susan Richardson from Britain, and Ram Pi Tantu from Indonesia, got on the trail of the Impoc tree − from which the Wana milk the powerful poison used to impregnate their blowpipe darts − while investigating the Sumara River valley on behalf of Phil Maye. Their main aim was to establish whether or not the Sumara River linked up with the Ula River system in Central Sulawesi, but during their travels they were befriended by the people of Langada, who revealed the whereabouts of two of the trees − normally a closely guarded secret. Very few outsiders have seen an Impoc and the group decided that this was an opportunity not to be missed.

It took them three days to march to Bintana, the nearest of the two locations, and when they got there they soon found the tree on the outskirts of the village. It was over one hundred feet high and more than a yard in diameter and was surrounded by bamboo scaffolding. The spongy brown bark was covered in scars and fresh V-shaped notches, and the YEs discovered that when it was slashed with a machete it released a fountain of milky white sap. Bearing in mind the stories they had heard concerning the potency of the poison − which is said to kill a man in less than a minute! − they exercised extreme caution while gingerly collecting a sample for later analysis by the scientists. They returned to Camp Ranu in a state of high excitement, having located one of the legendary Wana Impoc trees.

Meanwhile, the problem of finding an area of trees suitable for the erection of the third and final aerial walkway had proved as much of a headache in Sulawesi as it had been in Panama and PNG. It seems ridiculous on the face of it − that with so much to choose from one should have difficulty finding what one wants. But it really is not that easy to find a section of undisturbed primary forest that is ideal in every respect. Several possible sites were considered and then rejected before a spot was selected some two miles away from Camp Ranu. Corporals John Rimmer and Mike Prior, with the help of Bob Powell and the YEs, then did a marvellous job and made up a lot of lost time by putting up the three spans of walkway in under three weeks. Altogether it gave access to nearly six hundred feet of the jungle canopy.

A total of twenty-three scientists joined Operation Drake in Sulawesi and, with the enthusiastic assistance of the seventy-one YEs, they studied everything from the sex life of the shorea tree − painstakingly investigated by Dr Peter Kevan from Colorado Springs University and Dr Andrew Lack of Swansea University − to the ancestry and evolution of Sulawesi rats, which was probed by Dr Chris Watts from the Institute of Medical and Veterinary Science, Adelaide.

Entomologist Dr Stephen Sutton was so delighted with the success of

[202]

the research he was able to carry out that he went home in a state of academic euphoria, claiming that Operation Drake was the best scientific expedition he had ever been involved with. Using ultra-violet light traps and suction traps, which 'hoovered' insects from the air, he studied the vertical and horizontal distribution of flying insects in the forest. By suspending traps from the upper canopy to ground level and along the walkway, he produced some very exciting new results to be used in conjunction with those obtained in Panama and PNG. It was the first time these techniques had been used in combination in tropical forest.

Butterfly expert Anthony Bedford-Russell, a marvellous character who was a great boon to the expedition in all sorts of ways, wielded his net to such good effect that he was able to collect nearly three hundred different specimens including a new species, with a six-inch wing-span. British Museum entomologist Martin Brendell amassed a 'bag' of literally thousands of beetles, whilst Batman Ben Gaskell also enjoyed tremendous success and discovered seven species previously unknown in Sulawesi. His total collection amounted to over three hundred specimens and, combined with that which he made in PNG, added up to what the British Museum believes to be the most valuable collection sent to them since that of the legendary Wallace in 1900.

Bird and reptile expert Bill Timmis, from the Harewood Bird Garden in Yorkshire, spent endless happy hours observing such quaintly named specimens as the dark-chinned fruit pigeon and the pink-breasted cuckoo dove, and when he was not doing that, he was observing such rare sights as that of a four-foot lizard robbing eggs from a nest. His work was only slightly marred by one grave disappointment, which, when he related the sad tale, brought smirks to the faces of all but the most sympathetic of fellow naturalists.

While on a scientific patrol to Mount Tambusisi he happened to spot the nesting place of the rare imperial pigeon and excitedly marked the spot so that he could return later to study at his leisure the bird's breeding behaviour, which had never previously been observed. He duly hurried back at the earliest opportunity to notch up this very prestigious ornithological 'first', only to find the nest deserted and an ominous scattering of feathers underneath the tree. He returned, crestfallen, to camp, where he was greeted with the awful revelation that one of the Indonesian guides – Harim – had also earmarked the nest for future attention and had nipped back shortly before poor Bill and bagged the bird for his supper! To make matters worse, he insisted on describing in some detail exactly how he had plucked it and boiled it up in a pot, and how very tasty it had turned out to be.

[203]

Chapter Twenty-Three

Dateline: Vesuvius Reef, Sulawesi, March 1980

Mike Kichenside, who skippered *Eye of the Wind* with a cool, calm and kindly professionalism that won the respect and admiration of all those who sailed under him, is a quietly modest man of few words who would have you believe that, from his point of view, the entire round-the-world voyage was as simple and routine as a ferry-crossing to the Isle of Wight. If that is so, then it is only because of the skill and experience that enabled him to deal competently and confidently with everything that the oceans and the elements could throw at him. Even when pressed hard to recall some moments of danger and drama along the way, he will admit to only one occasion when he was vaguely uneasy – and that was when the ship ventured into the treacherous waters in the vicinity of the notorious Vesuvius Reef.

The reef – due west of Sulawesi in the Banggai Archipelago – is like a vast table-topped underwater mountain, so huge in area that it took a whole day to motor around its perimeter in *Eye of the Wind*. It lurks just a few inches below the surface and when the sea is calm there is nothing to indicate its presence. And because it falls away almost sheer-sided into deep water around its edge, instead of shelving gradually, one can come upon it with alarming suddenness.

We believe that Francis Drake found this out to his cost at precisely eight o'clock on the evening of 9 January 1580. His visit to the fabled Spice Islands had been highly successful – the Sultan of Ternate had just fallen out with the Portuguese, and Drake seized the opportunity to step in and make a very valuable trading agreement, as a result of which, six tons of precious cloves had somehow been crammed into the already bulging hold of *Golden Hind*. And now, at last, he was on his way home. He had spent a month at Crab Island – just off Celebes, as Sulawesi was then known – while he recaulked the ship's timbers and checked her rigging, and he had then set sail on a westerly course for what he undoubtedly hoped would be an uneventful final lap of the journey back to England. It was not to be.

He was creaming along under full sail before a fresh trade wind, when there was suddenly a sickening, timber-jarring crunch and everyone aboard was thrown violently forward as the little vessel's progress was brought to an abrupt, grating halt. It was instantly obvious to one and all that she had fallen foul of the hidden menace that every seamen dreads – a submerged and uncharted coral reef. The initial reaction was that it was all over, that it would be only a matter of minutes before the ship broke up and went to the bottom, along with her crew and her priceless cargo. However, a hurried inspection showed that she had miraculously survived the impact against the jagged rocks without being holed. Even so, she was stuck fast and there did not seem to be a lot of hope. Drake threw eight cannon and half the spices overboard in a desperate attempt to lighten the stricken ship, but she remained hard aground. Characteristically, he refused to jettison any more of the spoils that were weighing her down. He preferred to take the risk of never going home at all rather than play it safe and end up getting back empty-handed.

Fortune favours the brave and, at the very moment when *Golden Hind* seemed about to keel over, a sharp gust of wind from an unexpected quarter was just enough to dislodge her and refloat her in deep water. The only person who did not have cause to feel relieved was the ship's chaplain. He had been prophesying disaster, which he blamed squarely on Drake's past sins, so the miracle of salvation rather took the wind out of his sails. Drake excommunicated him in front of the assembled crew – claiming that, as the Queen's representative on board, he had the power to do so. However, once his humour had been restored, he relented and reinstated the unfortunate cleric.

It was the exciting prospect of locating and raising Drake's discarded cannon that drew us to this dangerous spot. We had been alerted to this reef's being the most likely site of Drake's grounding by a fellow member of the Explorers Club, Bob Silver. Together with his friend Ray Aker he had hoped to organise a search, but instead they had generously passed all the information to us.

No sooner had *Eye of the Wind* arrived than she became involved in an emergency which not only proved how easy it is to fall foul of the reef but also provided an almost uncanny re-enactment of what had happened to *Golden Hind*. During a violent fifty-knot squall, lights were observed one and a half miles away on the other side of the reef, and when the weather quietened down and an inflatable was sent over to investigate, the MV *Sinar Haratan* was discovered hard aground. She was carrying one hundred and fifty tons of cement and some metal reinforcing rods, and she eventually had to jettison the rods in order to free herself.

It was the continual series of squalls during *Eye of the Wind*'s stay in the area that made life particularly difficult for Mike Kichenside. He had a big enough problem anyway finding a suitable anchorage, because of the way the reef dropped away so sharply into impossibly deep water, but he eventually managed to find a spur of coral coming out of the main reef at right angles on which to drop the anchor. However, with sudden gusts of up to sixty knots threatening to blow the ship round onto the reef, the skipper was forced to keep the engines ticking over most of the time in an effort to hold the bows into the wind and thus prevent the anchor from dragging.

Meanwhile, the search for the lost cannon continued with help from the Royal Australian Air Force, who sent up an Orion reconnaissance aircraft from No. 10 Squadron with a magnetometer aboard to overfly the area and pinpoint possible targets for the diving team to investigate. Down below, visibility was very good, but vicious currents swirling through the coral meant that divers Robbie Williamson, Peter Durey, Lieutenant Robin Bacon and Gary Brindle had to be on the alert the whole time. The Orion's first strike, needless to say, turned out to be the metal rods thrown overboard by the *Sinar Haratan*, and the only other sufficiently positive reading was obtained from a location right in the middle of the reef where nothing could be found and which seemed anyway a rather unlikely resting place for the guns since *Golden Hind* would have dropped them nearer the edge.

The exercise was, nevertheless, far from being fruitless. While the divers were looking for the cannon, they also assisted our marine biologist Trish Holdway and some of the YEs in carrying out a survey which produced unexpectedly exciting results. The reef, named *Vesuvius* after a warship that came to grief there in the nineteenth century, has been so well protected over the years by its isolation and its fearsome reputation as a place to be steered well clear of at all costs that a rich variety of marine life has been able to flourish there undisturbed. The environment proved to be so outstanding in this respect that Trish had no hesitation in recommending the spot as an underwater conservation area – a suggestion which has since been taken up by the authorities.

In particular, it is hoped that the reef may become a haven for dugong, the extraordinary and increasingly rare creatures that are supposed to have given rise to legends of mermaids. Seen from a distance, reclining on a rock, they could perhaps be mistaken for sea sirens by imaginative mariners, although they are anything but beautiful. There were once huge numbers of them in the seas around Indonesia, but because of their placid nature and their lack of natural defences they have been easy prey for hunters, who relish their meat and seek their valuable ivory teeth, with the result that their numbers

[206]

have been decimated. *Eye of the Wind* sailed throughout the Banggai Islands in search of them, as part of the survey started by John Blower and his wife, Wendy, on behalf of the World Wildlife Fund, but not one specimen was spotted. However, Vesuvius Reef seemed to be an ideal habitat, and we found evidence that dugongs do still exist there.

Back at Camp Ranu, a string of VIPs took the trouble to come out and see for themselves how Operation Drake was getting on in the back of beyond. Among these were Mr Emil Salim, the Indonesian Minister for the Environment, and the British Ambassador Mr Terence O'Brien and his wife. Mr and Mrs O'Brien scored a big hit with everyone because of the tremendous enthusiasm they showed during their four-day stay – especially Mrs O'Brien, who even insisted on being winched up to the aerial walkway, while other less adventurous visitors made it quite clear that in no circumstances were they going to move one foot above ground level. Clearly Ambassadors' wives enjoy heights, for Mrs Sanders, a keen bird-watcher, had eagerly ascended our Panama walkway.

Life at the camp – where the number of people in residence fluctuated up to 127 – soon slipped into an easy and efficient routine. For comfort, Camp Ranu probably surpassed even Buso. The high standard of the accommodation, the away-from-it-all atmosphere and the air of easy-going informality combined to boost morale sky-high. Ranu River, though rather warm and fetid, was ideal to bathe away the sweat and grime of a hard day's work. There were sing-songs and other self-made entertainments in the long evenings – and there was even a camp mascot to keep everyone amused, a Jersey cow who was inevitably christened Daisy. She soon made herself at home to the extent of wandering nonchalantly around the dining hut during meal times, helping herself to any morsel of food that took her fancy. Despite such bad habits, she was tremendously popular and when, as a practical joke, *Eye of the Wind*'s engineer, Fleet Chief Petty Officer Bob Coupland, announced very seriously that she was to be slaughtered for the ship's deep freeze, and proceeded to make a point of ostentatiously sharpening a set of butchery knives, there was an almighty outcry. Some of the girls burst into tears and even the tough, hard-bitten Aussies were indignant. They were the ones, in fact, who spirited Daisy away and tethered her in the jungle out of harm's way. Of course, Bob had no intention of carrying out his threat, and the silly cow was still there, looking sleek and overfed, when the time came to pack up and leave.

Thankfully, especially in view of the remoteness of Camp Ranu and the lack of airlift facilities, there was only one serious emergency that had to be dealt with, and that came at a time when the Governor of

Sulawesi was paying us a visit and had a helicopter standing by at Kolonodale. The patient was one of the Signallers, Corporal Kelvin Cunningham, who developed a very bad ear infection which rapidly got worse and worse until he was almost unconscious with the agony. Dr Margaret Long, who was taking part in the comparative medical survey, and Nurse Clair Bertschinger, who had joined us for a third phase, were in no doubt that he would have to be evacuated immediately. Clair accompanied him on the journey to the nearest big hospital at Soarko, nearly a hundred miles away to the south, and her diary paints a vivid picture of the dramatic dash.

'The sun is already climbing high in the sky as we go down river in the *David Gestetner* inflatable. Kelvin is on a stretcher on the floor of the boat and we rig up a sun-screen for him with the help of a poncho and someone's bootlaces. We reach the sea and head across to Kolonodale, passing *Eye of the Wind* with a wave. A cool breeze brushes our faces as the two big outboard motors speed us across the open sea and the whole trip takes one hour. As usual, a crowd of people meet the boat at the quayside, but this time there is no "Hello Mister, Hello Miss Claire" – only "Oh, Mister Kelvin sakit (sick)". I give Kelvin another shot of pethidine with stemetil and go and discuss the flight with the helicopter pilot. The flight needs to be at as low an altitude as possible to avoid the ear-drum being perforated due to the change in air pressure. The helicopter is too small for the stretcher and Kelvin is propped up, leaning against the door with his head supported by life jackets.

'It is 10.15 a.m. as we take off and skim over the treetops climbing slowly to one thousand feet. Ahead of us are mountains four thousand feet high and the pilot has to use a map as he has never been that way before. Up the valleys we fly to the mountains ahead. Up a bit, up a bit, slowly, slowly and – oops! – we are over. I know I said as low as possible and he did just that, but – phew! – we only just made it. Kelvin sits very quietly, the pethidine having taken effect. Now the clouds are closing in around us and there is a storm ahead. I watch the altimeter drop to nearly six hundred feet and then it starts to rain, making a thundering noise on the roof of the helicopter. Visibility is now almost nil and we are flying by instruments only and climbing again slowly to one thousand feet. Gosh! We've just skimmed the treetops of another mountain. If we did fall out of the sky, I suppose the jungle would cushion our fall to a certain extent and we'd hit the ground quite softly, though still a bit mangled, no doubt.

'We're now at seventeen hundred feet and climbing slowly. What an excellent pilot – and Kelvin is doing fine, considering. The rain comes through a few gaps in the fuselage, but what does that matter! We dodge another mountain which looms up beside us and then the rain stops and visibility returns. Suddenly we see in front of us an enormous lake and, on the far side, straight ahead, a rambling community – Soarko. That's good navigation for you. The flight has taken just forty minutes, but it seemed much longer.

'We circle the town, looking for a helipad. It's a neat little township – houses all in lines, cars, buses, a church and a school. This could be the USA except that it's right bang in the middle of the Sulawesi jungle. There's no helipad in sight, so the pilot decides to put down in the school playing field. We'll disrupt a few lessons, no doubt, but no matter. I jump out and, while the rotor blades continue to turn, I run to the buildings to ask where the hospital is. The teachers come out, not a little surprised at seeing a female in jungle green uniform and red-spotted scarf drop in on them out of the blue. One of them points the way, half a mile further down the coast. We lose no time and touch down again a minute or so later. A car comes out to meet us and Kelvin and I are taken to the emergency room.'

For Kelvin the crisis was over – although it was five days and several massive doses of antibiotics later before the infection cleared up completely. Then there was the question of how to get back to Camp Ranu. There were two choices. Either he and Claire could cadge a lift to Kendari on one of the light planes belonging to the International Nickel Company, and then get a boat from there on to Kolonodale, or they could walk! They reckoned the journey would take anything from seven to ten days by plane and boat, and only two or three by foot. So they decided to walk.

'We set off one morning at 5.30 a.m. We crossed the lake by speedboat and then, at 6.00 a.m. we started walking. There was a path to follow across the plain and through the jungle-covered hills. We had been told it was an easy trek as far as Beteleme. Unfortunately, it had been raining for almost a week on and off, and the track was a mass of mud. We got stuck knee-deep sometimes and had to pull each other out. This was certainly no way for my patient to convalesce!

'But we struggled on in the sweltering tropical heat, and daren't let on to each other how we really felt. Many times during the day, with my eyes blurry and stinging with sweat and my brain wanting to burst out of my skull, I thought to myself: "Why do I do this? Let's stop, let's sit down." But I kept smiling at Kelvin to keep his spirits up and said out loud: "I'm fine, we're doing well, we'll soon be at Beteleme." To make matters worse, we were only wearing plimsoles and they had shrunk in the wet mud and were crippling our feet. So we took them off and walked the last few hours in bare feet! By 5.30 in the evening, just before dark and after thirty-five miles, we reached the small jungle

[209]

village of Pono and decided to stay the night there, as we were completely exhausted. Next day we set off again at 5.30 to complete our walk to Beteleme, and there we were lucky enough to find a landrover which took us on to Kolonodale. We finally made it back to Camp Ranu the following day.'

Although this was the only real emergency in Sulawesi, there was a highly melodramatic incident towards the end of the phase which very nearly led to a major disaster. It all happened when a patrol made up of Sergeants John Cornish and Bob Hooper, Lance Corporal Alan Bretherton and Dr Ian Gauntlett marched out into the interior to investigate a possible 'Lost World' – a flat-topped, sheer-sided plateau that reared up out of the surrounding jungle very like the one in Conan Doyle's famous story. It had been spotted by an earlier patrol who were not able to spare the time to take a closer look, but were fascinated by the spectacular waterfall which cascaded from a point halfway up the cliffs on the side facing them, hinting at the existence of a hidden lake. It was all very tantalising, and clearly somebody ought to try and find out what was up there.

Right from the start Signaller Bob Hooper had problems with the radio, but this did not cause too much concern. The patrol was accompanied by two Wana guides and a young local interpreter, and not too many difficulties were anticipated. Everything went fine until, on the fifth day, a terrible row broke out between John Cornish and the interpreter. Dr Ian Gauntlett, who was taking time off from leading the medical research project, noted in his report: 'The cause of the altercation was trivial. The interpreter had been put in charge of the group's one luxury – a large bag of sweets. When we stopped to set up camp in the afternoon, cold, wet and tired, to discover that he had eaten all but six of them himself, tempers frayed. John became angry and reprimanded the interpreter, who obviously felt very humiliated at being told off in front of the Wana guides, whom, he had previously told me, he considered to be inferior to him. He first of all put up his fists and challenged John to a fight – which was clearly ludicrous since John was twice his size – and then, in a fit of rage, grabbed a parang and hacked his own kit to pieces. He stood there shaking and crying, and at one point made a move towards John with the parang raised, but some rapid talking defused the situation slightly and he calmed down. He then turned to the Wana guides and, speaking in Indonesian, apparently told them that we had come into the area intending to annihilate the Wana tribe.

'We slept uneasily that night. In a small jungle clearing in the middle of God knows where, the possibility of being murdered in our sleep seemed less ridiculous than it does in retrospect. We awoke the

[210]

following morning alive and in one piece – but the interpreter and the guides had gone, taking with them all our rice, and cooking pots and some of our protein rations.'

This left the patrol in a very awkward predicament. They did not know precisely where they were, they were low on rations, and, with the radio by then totally useless, they had no means of sending out an SOS. They considered the various alternatives open to them. They ruled out the idea of simply trying to retrace their footsteps, because, without the help of the guides, they doubted whether they would be able to keep to the faint and often non-existent track, and felt that they might well end up getting even more badly lost. They also dismissed the possibility of cutting across country as being far too risky. The most sensible choice seemed to be to follow the course of the nearby Solato River until it led them to civilisation – at least that way they would be assured of a constant water supply.

Although this seemed like the obvious solution, it was easier said than done, as they soon discovered. The problem was that the river frequently passed through stretches of deep gorge and when this happened they had to make detours, hacking their way slowly and painfully through dense undergrowth where the sharp, jagged thorns of the rotan plants tore at their skin. Then they came upon an even more difficult obstacle – a major tributary flowing into the Solato on their side. It was as they marched up it, searching for a place to cross, that an extremely dangerous situation arose.

Ian wrote: 'John was leading us up a near-vertical slope, with nothing to cling on to but clumps of grass, when he came to a rocky overhang. As he grasped it, the rock crumbled away and, with no hand grip, his feet began, very slowly, to slip. He was unable to move and two of us had to climb round and up above him to lower a rope. With difficulty, we hauled him up to a safe ledge. I am convinced that another ten minutes would have seen him fall the fifty feet into the rocky river below.

'This incident brought home to me the hazards we faced. If one of us had fallen and broken a leg or an ankle there would have been no way the others could have carried him. Food supplies would have been insufficient to last until help came and almost certainly he would have died.'

After this narrow squeak they decided they would have to go back and wade or swim across the river – a tricky procedure, as Bob Hooper was a weak swimmer. A rope was tied around his waist and he was hauled across at a furious pace so that he would not have time to sink!

The patrol took to the water again later on, and on that occasion it was Ian's turn to get himself into another fine mess that could easily have ended in tragedy. Progress had once more been interrupted by a section of gorge, but as the water was fairly slow-flowing and the jungle on each side was particularly dense it seemed like a good idea to swim through, with Bob roped to John for safety. Ian was the first to launch himself into the icy-cold water, and he was followed by Alan. He aimed for what, from a distance, looked like a conveniently flat stretch of bank, but which turned out, when he got nearer, to be the brink of a fifteen-foot waterfall!

'I could not go back the two hundred yards I had come because the current was too strong and the sides were too steep for me to climb out. For a few minutes I really thought I was finished. By a stroke of fate, however, John and Bob had fouled their rope right at the beginning and had not yet set off. Fortunately for me, they were able to hack their way along to a point about sixty-feet above us and lower a rope. Alan was the first to get out as he was directly below them. I had to swim twenty yards upstream and, with fingers that were by this time numb with cold, I secured the rope around my waist. I was pulled out and, with considerable relief, reached the safety of the trees, where I flopped down exhausted.'

When they eventually climbed up out of that gorge, they stumbled on a well-worn path that led them to a village they knew and, seven days after they had been deserted, they walked back into Camp Ranu. In the twelve days that he had been away, Ian had lost a stone in weight.

It turned out that the interpreter had come back nursing a black eye and insisting hysterically that John Cornish had tried to kill him. This could well have caused ill feeling between Operation Drake and the locals, souring the success of the whole phase, but the affair was happily sorted out with the minimum amount of fuss, thanks largely to the on-the-spot intervention of Colonel Johannes Prasanto, the official Indonesian liaison officer. Colonel Prasanto had been seconded to Operation Drake specifically to deal with this type of situation, should it arise, and he did the job superbly. Right from the start, he was more like a friend to the expedition than simply an official trouble-shooter and he proved to be a tremendous asset in every way.

As the Sulawesi phase drew to a close and the time came to repack all the tons of equipment once again before moving on, a dozen YEs accepted a final challenge which enabled them to round off their spell with Operation Drake in truly adventurous style. Armed with only a small amount of money, they were given just three weeks to get themselves from Camp Ranu right across the island to the capital, Ujung Pandang – carrying out a special project in the Lore Kalimanta

National Park on the way – and then on to Jakarta. How they made the fifteen-hundred-mile journey was entirely up to them – but they had to be in Jakarta by 28 April at the latest.

In the end everybody managed to beat the deadline, after what was, for most of them, an epic journey. Every imaginable form of transport was used. They wangled cut-price flights on light aircraft, hitched rides on lorries, buses, motorcycles and even ox carts, borrowed mules and ponies and, of course, did a lot of walking. Along the way they met many interesting people, saw all sorts of sights, and had a whole lot of fun in putting their initiative to the test.

The special project was in itself fascinating and involved locating and mapping the ancient megaliths that are strewn around the Lore Kalimanta area. A certain amount of mystery surrounds the exact purpose of these stone images which vary in size from eighteen inches to twenty feet and are up to five hundred years old. Each one apparently represents a particular person – usually a tribal leader. They are scattered about, seemingly at random, and are often in very remote spots. In many cases their whereabouts have been long forgotten and they have become lost and overgrown. The YEs, who split into two groups so as to cover as much of the area as possible, managed to rediscover quite a number that had been swallowed up by the undergrowth over the centuries, just by talking to people in the villages and getting them to remember where they had seen sites years ago. It is hoped that by pinpointing as many of the megaliths as possible, the YEs may have helped the experts to see if there is any pattern in their arrangement, which might provide a further clue as to their true purpose.

Among some of the other fascinating distractions they encountered during their travels was an out-of-the-way village where the people had a unique way of honouring their dead. After sacrificing livestock and burning rice, they would place the body in a hollowed-out tree trunk and place it in one of the caves in the cliffs above the village. They would then make a life-sized effigy of the deceased, which would also be placed in the caves at a spot where limestone water would drip onto it and gradually calcify. Once the effigy was sealed in this way the soul of the departed was believed to be preserved for ever.

In another village the headman was a professional python hunter, and he took the YEs on a snake hunt. They were hoping that he might lead them to a specimen that would beat the world record and win them a 50,000 dollar reward offered by a certain American university, but unfortunately he was unable to find anything spectacular. However, he was full of terrifying stories about the monsters he had killed in the past.

[213]

Everybody eventually assembled in Jakarta in time to attend a major scientific seminar held under the auspices of the local Institute of Sciences and attended by many of Indonesia's top scientists, at which some of Operation Drake's research activities were discussed. And afterwards the country's Director General of Forestry paid a warm tribute to the expedition's aims and achievements in Sulawesi. He said:

'It is four hundred years since Sir Francis Drake reached the shores of Indonesia, four hundred years to the very week that Operation Drake arrived. Without putting too fine a point on it, it is unlikely that Drake or any other buccaneering European sailors were welcome among the local inhabitants. Local people no doubt regarded them with considerable fear and suspicion, in some cases with good reason! Drake came in search of riches and left little behind apart from the cannons he was forced to jettison to get his ship off the Vesuvius Reef.

'You, today's circumnavigators of Operation Drake, are much more welcome than your illustrious predecessor. You come in peace and friendship and leave behind something of far greater value to the world than those rusted, coral-encrusted cannons still on the Sulawesi reefs. You have amassed a great deal of valuable scientific information, as today's seminar testified, on what is ecologically one of the most interesting and least known islands. You have also worked and collected more assiduously than anyone in Sulawesi since the great British naturalist Alfred Russel Wallace.

'But Operation Drake's most significant contribution during its four and a half months in Indonesia has, in my view, been twofold: firstly, the bringing together of so many adventurous young people of different nationalities – including twenty-seven Indonesian scientists and Young Explorers – in such an imaginative and worthwhile enterprise; and secondly, the preparation in collaboration with our Directorate of Nature Conservation of the management plan for the newly created Morowali Reserve.

'Morowali will now be safeguarded for the future as part of the natural heritage which will be passed on to future generations of Indonesians. It is something of which you, the scientists and Young Explorers of Operation Drake, can take real pride in having helped to create. I thank you on behalf of the government of Indonesia for all you have done, and I wish you and the *Eye of the Wind bon voyage* and all the very best for the future.'

Five days later *Eye of the Wind* weighed anchor and headed out into the Indian Ocean, bound for Kenya.

Chapter Twenty-Four

Dateline: Krakatau, West of Java, 5 May 1980

With less-than-poetic licence, the film-makers who based a blood-and-thunder disaster movie on the 1883 eruption of one of the world's most spectacular volcanoes showed scant regard for geographical truth when they entitled their epic *Krakatoa − East of Java*. Still, what is a few thousand miles when a hint of oriental mystery is needed to help guarantee a box-office hit!

For those aboard *Eye of the Wind*, fact proved almost more dramatic than fiction as they sailed within twelve miles of the still-active crater and witnessed an impressive display of natural fireworks. Smoke and flames had been belching forth thousands of feet into the air for a month or more before they arrived on the scene and, as they approached in the hours immediately before dawn, the horizon was lit by brilliant orange flashes on the starboard bow. This fiery spectacle gradually faded as the rising sun bathed the sky in the dazzling brightness of an equatorial morning and revealed a cloud of grey smoke and ashes billowing above the half-submerged volcano.

Meanwhile, upheavals of a different nature had been playing havoc with Operation Drake's plans. We had originally intended to have a very brief African land phase in the Sudan, but as the expedition progressed and gathered momentum, so enthusiasm and interest increased and offers of sponsorships started flooding in, with the result that we had to rethink everything and quickly plan new ways of expanding our activities in order to accommodate the extra personnel. Recce teams were hurriedly despatched to start organising additional projects and they came up with a marvellous archaeological site at Aqiq, just on the borders of Ethiopia and the Sudan, where the remains of the most southerly city in the Greek Empire were thought to be located, and also camel treks and other ventures in the interior, to go with the Red Sea survey into the coral-eating starfish which was the centrepiece of the original programme.

However, although these plans seemed fine in theory, it soon became clear that they were not going to work out in practice. For various reasons, the Sudanese were not keen on the idea, and their lack of enthusiasm frustrated all efforts to get things definitely arranged. By the time I returned to England from PNG in January, the situation was already giving cause for concern, and by March, with the scheduled start of the phase looming closer and closer, we were still no nearer to getting things finalised. At that point we resigned ourselves to the fact that we would very likely have to write off the Sudan altogether, and started looking round for a substitute. Once again Room 5B took on the air of an emergency control bunker. People pored endlessly over maps and the international telephone lines hummed as we alerted our contacts world-wide about the probability of a last-minute change of plan and sought advice from them about possible alternatives. Eventually I met with General Sir John Mogg and we discussed a short list of suggested venues.

Oman had to be ruled out because it was the wrong time of year and the weather would be against us; Namibia was considered and then rejected on the grounds that the political situation was difficult; and South Africa was discounted because, apart from anything else, it would take too long for the ship to go right round the Cape of Good Hope. Zaire was near the top of our list because we had good contacts there. But in the end, we kept coming back to Kenya. It seemed the best place for many reasons – it was politically stable, there were a lot of people living there whom we knew we could rely on for support, many major British firms were represented in the country, the RAF and all the main airlines flew to Nairobi, and it meant that *Eye of the Wind* would have to deviate only slightly from her original route. On top of all that, the environment and the terrain would provide an ideal contrast with that of the other land phases – bush, desert and even a snow-capped mountain, instead of jungle. There would also be wildlife that we had not seen anywhere else.

Having settled on this choice, we then found ourselves facing a rather delicate diplomatic problem. Since we were still technically committed to the Sudan, we could not approach the Kenyan President formally for permission to move into his country, and yet if we waited until the Sudanese gave us their decision before approaching him, it would be too late. We had to have a firm unofficial indication in advance that he would give us his blessing, so that we could go in and get on with the job of setting things up on a provisional basis.

Luckily a friend of a friend knew President Moi and asked him privately if he would welcome Operation Drake in his country. The answer was an enthusiastic yes.

Shortly after that, we reached the stage where we could not wait any longer for a final decision from the Sudanese, and Plan B immediately

[216]

went into operation, our advance parties flying into Kenya to start liaising with the local committee. The fact that we were able to get everything together at such very short notice owed an awful lot to the knowledge, experience and hard work of that committee and the inspired leadership of Chairman John Sutton. We made contact with him originally through the good offices of Sir David Checketts, the Chairman of our Publicity Committee and a former Private Secretary to Prince Charles, who said as soon as Kenya was selected that John was the man we needed. An ex-white hunter, safari film-maker and leading figure on the Kenyan social and business scene, he is also a very fit, adventurous, outdoors man who is a wildlife expert and who knows the bush intimately.

It would have been quite understandable if he had harboured slight reservations about taking on such a demanding job, but thanks to the timely intervention of our Patron, Prince Charles − whom he knew personally, having taken both Prince Charles and Princess Anne on safari in the past − he was hardly given the chance to think about what he was letting himself in for. He was standing with me in Nairobi when the Prince − who was passing through on his way to attend the independence celebrations in Zimbabwe − happened to spot us and came over to say hello. He chatted to me for a few minutes about Operation Drake and then turned to John and said in a matter-of-fact way: 'I hear you're going to be our Chairman here in Kenya?' This must have come as a considerable surprise to John, who had not really made his decision about the matter. If he felt that his arm had been ever so gently twisted, he certainly never showed it. He worked tirelessly on our behalf and must take much of the credit for turning a hurriedly arranged operation into a smooth-running success.

We were also very fortunate that my old friend Lieutenant Colonel Tim Illingworth was commanding the British Army Training and Liaison Staff Kenya (BATLSK). Tim's tented camps at Kahawa would be empty during our proposed visit and he generously put them at our disposal. This was to prove of the greatest value to us, and the support of Tim and his small staff was highly appreciated. Their good humour and patience in putting up with us for over three months is a great credit to the British Army.

Once it was under way, the phase began to snowball fast. Prince Charles was keen to get some Zimbabwean YEs involved and personally sponsored two to join us. Following his example, and thanks to some brilliant fund-raising by John Hines, the finance for a further thirteen was soon forthcoming. In addition there were twenty-six Kenyan YEs and this meant a total of nearly ninety youngsters from thirteen different countries were eventually involved in what had been planned originally as a brief African stop-over between Sulawesi and the UK. Fortunately, with the help of the Kenyan government, we were able to organise a wide variety of projects spread throughout the country, and I planned that all YEs would take part in two of the tasks.

The finishing touches were still being put to the programme as *Eye of the Wind* sailed on across the Indian Ocean towards Mombasa. It was an eventful voyage that got off to a somewhat comic start during the short haul between Camp Ranu and Jakarta with what became known as 'The Great Pig Boat Incident'. The rust-bucket cargo vessel *Harapfimbaru* was smelled almost before she was sighted, drifting helplessly and showing the black ball which means 'not under command'. As *Eye of the Wind* approached nearer, the pungent odour grew stronger and stronger and was accompanied by a cacaphony of yelling, shouting, grunting and squeaking which baffled even the Indonesian YEs on board.

Everybody held their noses as Mike Kichenside manoeuvred alongside, and the source of the stink was identified as a deck cargo of pigs. It then emerged that the *Harapfimbaru*'s engine had broken down, that she had been drifting for 'one month and one week', that water was running out, and that the crew, as Moslems, wanted nothing to do with their cargo. The *Eye of the Wind* obliged with a tow to Surabaya, motoring as fast as possible in order to keep the appalling stench downwind, but the crew of the *Harapfimbaru* were far from effusive in their thanks – in fact, they complained bitterly that they were not being lugged all the way to their home port in Kalimantan! As it happened, they were lucky to find anyone who was prepared to help them – something that became clear when *Eye of the Wind* arrived off the entrance to Surabaya Harbour and tried to get someone else to take over the tow. One Indonesian vessel flatly refused, before a tug very reluctantly agreed to accept responsibility for the floating pigsty and the constant sound of arguing and the powerful aroma thankfully faded into the distance.

After the changeover of YEs in Jakarta, the new crew did not have to wait long for their first taste of the kind of dramas that are part and parcel of life before the mast. During the first night out of Tanjung Prijok, a squall blew up and the novice sailors – who, for various reasons, had had no chance to practise their seamanship in port – suddenly found themselves scrambling up the rigging in the dark to furl the jibs, the nock and main staysails, the mainsail and the course and lower topsails. To complicate matters further, this little emergency took place in waters crowded with small boats that never bothered to put on any navigation lights until *Eye of the Wind* was almost on top of them. However, the manoeuvre was carried out without mishap and the

[218]

permanent crew looked on this latest batch of eager landlubbers with new respect. They very quickly learned the names and purposes of the seventy-five ropes that control the sails of a brigantine, and memorised the positions around the deck of the belaying pins, where each rope is secured, so that they could go straight to any particular one at the bark of an order from the poop.

Meanwhile, an early crisis had emerged when the ship's engineer came on deck to report that the level of water in the bilges was well above normal at the same time that a rather damp YE appeared to announce that the deck of his cabin was awash. It did not take long to discover that one of the three water tanks had sprung a leak, and everybody then rushed round madly with buckets and dustbins, trying to salvage as much as possible of the remaining contents. Strict rationing had to be introduced until some heavy storm clouds were spotted on the horizon and the ship pursued the showers around the ocean for a couple of hours, collecting eighty gallons of sweet, fresh rainwater.

All this, and the sighting of Krakatau, took place in the first three days and thereafter everything settled down a bit – everything, that is, except the YEs' stomachs. Seasickness once again took a sad toll as *Eye of the Wind* rolled along through an Indian Ocean swell caused by the steady southeast trade winds. But people soon got their sea legs and then they were able to enjoy fully the thrill of some superb sailing as the stiff breezes hurried the ship along. There were the usual lectures to prepare them for the tasks at the next stop and plenty of home-made entertainment to enliven the evenings – including no less than fifteen birthday celebrations! There was also a lot of hard work.

The many sea birds which roosted in the rigging during this stage of the voyage provided much interest and amusement – especially the comical boobies, one of which attached itself very firmly to the head of a YE while he was up aloft and then showed extreme reluctance to be dislodged from this perch. Equally friendly was a brown noddy which collapsed exhausted into the jolly boat after being blown further out to sea than it would ever normally venture. It posed tamely for pictures on people's shoulders before sadly, but inevitably, passing away.

Among the YEs, the personalities began to emerge. There was Englishman Wesley Lowdon, who suffered more than most from seasickness but always managed to come up smiling, bespectacled Canadian laboratory technician Howie Nisenbaum, who complained that Operation Drake could not have come at a worse time since it had robbed him of the chance to work on the research into a new virus that his team had discovered just before he left, and American girl Deirdre Macleod, who always insisted on wearing a dress or skirt – even when

[219]

climbing the rigging – and who would frequently burst into snatches of opera while on watch.

Cornishman John Poskus was another interesting character and the story of how he came to be part of Operation Drake is fascinating. A builder by trade and one of the few married YEs – his wife gave birth to a baby while he was on the expedition – he had not realised until after he came through his Selection Weekend with flying colours that, as our central fund had dried up, he would have to raise the £2,300 sponsorship fee himself. At that point he virtually gave up all hope of taking up his place – but his friends and neighbours back in the little Cornish village of Portscatho, near Truro, had other ideas. The entire community set about helping him to raise the money. Whist drives were organised by the WI, the local pub laid on special darts evenings and held fund-raising raffles, the rugby club put on a disco and the village primary school arranged a sponsored walk, and as a result of these activities and many individual contributions John got his £2,300 – plus £30 spending money. It was a magnificent effort by everybody concerned and, when their young hero returned to regale them all with exciting tales of his adventures, it was proved without doubt to have been well worth while. With his extrovert nature and his tremendous enthusiasm, John will surely have given value for money in the telling of it.

Eye of the Wind's first port of call was in the Cocos Keeling Islands – a group of coral atolls that were for many years privately owned by the Clunies-Ross family. They settled there back in the nineteenth century and developed coconut plantations with Malay workers, whom they formed into an independent self-governing community. Later the islands were granted the status of a British Protectorate and then, in 1955, they were taken over by the Australians. The family still lives on a small five-acre estate on Home Island, where nobody is allowed to go without their express permission and that of the Malay Council.

Mike Kichenside and Tiger were invited to go and visit John Clunies-Ross and his son to discuss Operation Drake's projects on the island, which were to include the demolition of an old copra drying shed on the quayside and also help with the construction of a new Council meeting house nearby. The professional expertise of John Poskus came in very handy on both these jobs – particularly the laying of one-inch-square tiles in the Council house. Meanwhile, on West Island – the only other inhabited island in the group, where the Australian administration is based, and where such modern amenities as an airstrip and a post office have, perhaps rather sadly, spoiled the utter seclusion of this remote coral paradise – the chore of franking five thousand commemorative covers had to be tackled. This was never a

[220]

popular task, but it was an important one, helping to bring in much-needed cash for the expedition.

Considerably more enjoyable was the experience of snorkelling over the reefs off Direction Island in an area known locally as the Rift. 'As soon as I looked beneath the surface, I couldn't believe what I was seeing,' wrote 22-year-old Joan Dank from Wyncote in Pennsylvania. 'Watery exclamations kept escaping through my snorkel in a series of glugs and one look at everyone else's face was enough to tell me that they were all equally astounded. To say that it was like swimming in an aquarium would be an understatement. I floated past hundreds of varieties of fish, trying desperately to remember the lecture that our marine biologist had given us the previous week on the subject of "One thousand and one things that can kill in the water". With eyes peeled for barracuda, cone shells and fire coral, I marvelled at enormous, multi-coloured fish, giant clams, sea urchins, starfish and corals. If I had had a day like this earlier in my life I might be a marine biologist today rather than a medical student.'

The ship's departure from Cocos Keeling was delayed for a day when American YE Greg DeFrancis unfortunately went down with suspected appendicitis and had to be flown out to Perth for treatment. Then it was on to the Seychelles. Here the YEs divided into groups and went off to carry out wildlife surveys on the various islands.

Zoologist Dr Ian Swingland – who has a specialist interest in giant tortoises and had previously worked with the expedition in the Galapagos Islands – rejoined us in the Seychelles, where these huge, lumbering creatures have fairly recently been introduced from Aldabra, and supervised a count of the current population. Deirdre Macleod was one of the party that went to investigate the situation on Frigate Island. 'We took the inflatable to the island, where, because of the rough surf, we had to slide into the water some two hundred yards from the glaring white beach and swim in one-armed, holding our water canteens and our cameras above our heads. Frigate is the epitome of the idyllic island on which it would be a pleasure to be ship-wrecked. From the beach we walked down a winding, gently sloping path that meandered through groves of tangerine and orange trees. We also passed coffee trees, lemons, star apples, custard apples, pumpkins, cinnamon, bananas, avocados and rubber trees whose husks exploded with the reverberation of a gun shot. Banyan trees rose like cathedrals in the forest and there were coconuts and melons and sangdragon trees with shaggy red-brown bark which, when cut, oozes sap as red as blood. And everywhere the fairy terns circled, looking like Walt Disney creations with their pure white feathers and round black eyes that seem too large for their heads.

'We found the tortoises resting in the late-morning shade of a strip of forest near the beach. In the dappled light it took a moment or two to distinguish them from the grey humps of rocks. Our job was to count them, which is done by counting the number of rings on the shell, just as one can count growth rings on a tree to find out how old it is. On the as one can count growth rings on a tree to find out how old it it. On the tortoises these rings also provide a clue to the date of their arrival from Aldabra, since their nature is determined by the level of nutrition in any year. Thus, the growth rings from Aldabra, a flat and shadeless island where the tortoises lumber slowly at midday to the few trees giving protection from the sun and lie there in great piles of dumb relief, are narrow and high-ridged, whereas since their arrival on Frigate − where space, food and shade is ample − they are broad and more smooth.'

On the island of Curieuse, nineteen-year-old Sue Llewelyn from Glastonbury in Somerset found that the main problem was persuading the tortoises to stand still while their rings were measured. 'When a tortoise weighing in the region of five hundred pounds takes it into his head to move, he does so with the tenacity of a tank in full charge and nothing will stop him,' she wrote. 'You can sit on him, even drive him into a brick wall, but to no avail. So guerilla tactics come into play. You lie in wait until some unsuspecting tortoise lumbers by and then quickly crawl up behind him, measure him, count the rings and then beat a hasty retreat.'

It was also on Curieuse that a hunt for the rare vine *Toxocarpus schimperianus* met with spectacular success. Only thirteen of these plants were known to exist in the world before the YEs subjected the island to a methodical, yard-by-yard dragnet search and discovered seventeen more in a matter of hours. Roger Wilson, an expert from the Botanical Gardens on the main island of Mahé, came back a very happy man. Another plant species that is now slightly less rare thanks to Operation Drake is the jellyfish tree, so called because its fruit look rather like tiny jellyfish. Only six remaining examples of this were known until the YEs started combing the hillsides of Mahé and, although they were not quite able to match their *Toxocarpus* triumph, they did manage to add one more to this total.

One group spent three days on North Island, where, among other things, they had to try and catch as many geckoes as possible for use in a comparative study of the genetic differences among species from the various islands. The little green lizards proved extremely elusive and even when caught they often managed to escape from the clutches of their captors by the simple expedient of shedding their tails before shooting off and seeking refuge at the top of the nearest tree.

[222]

Despite such minor frustrations, Joan Dank found her stay there enchanting. 'It was, to put it mildly, idyllic,' she recorded in her diary. 'With only twenty-five inhabitants, all of whom lived in picturesque palm- and banana-leaf huts, it lived up to all our expectations of what the Seychelles should be like. We woke each morning at seven, when the village bell rang, to the sight of a bull turning a copra press, squeezing the coconut meat for cooking oil. The Seychellois watched us with amused tolerance as we went about our projects – searching for the parasitic Bruchid beetles which can destroy the coconut crop, collecting the geckoes, looking for the large fruit bats which are known as flying foxes, and conducting a survey of the vegetation.

'We would set off every morning, clad in bathing suits, army boots and webbing belts complete with water bottles, and we returned at the end of the day, exhausted, having fallen down cliff faces, having been bitten by skinks and devoured by mosquitoes, but with new specimens and information and a greater appreciation of the natural history of tropical islands. I went swimming in the surf off deserted beaches and feasted in the evenings on presents of bananas and paw-paws given by the local villagers.'

Not quite so pleasant, but equally unforgettable, was Joan's experience on the sandflats of St Joseph. She, along with Chris Sainsbury and some other YEs, were returning from yet another gecko safari when they decided to take a short cut across the flats which had been uncovered by the receding tide. 'We started wading in about six inches of water and our mistake soon became evident as dozens of sting rays slowly flapped away at our approach. Then an unmistakably shaped dorsal fin sliced through the water. As this was only six inches deep, it wasn't difficult to see the three-foot sand shark to which the fin was attached! As the torpedo headed right towards us, our worry grew and rapidly turned to terror as the shark didn't veer from its course. It was only two feet away when Chris began flailing at it with his camera tripod and managed to drive it off.'

Chris Sainsbury was, in fact, almost more worried by the rays than he was by the sharks. In Fiji he had seen a child attacked by one and so was well aware of the terrible wounds that can be inflicted by the spiny tail, which simultaneously rips the flesh and injects a powerful poison. The child was in such agony that he had to be forcibly held down as hot towels were wrapped around his gashed leg. The poison of the sting ray is such that, although the victim's pain goes after a couple of days, it often returns in a much worse form weeks later and goes on for a long time. And many people in Fiji had hideously deformed legs as a result of severe ray attacks.

The final scientific project in the Seychelles posed an interesting

[223]

problem – how to make an accurate count of somewhere between twenty-five thousand and thirty thousand sea birds as they roosted on and wheeled above one tiny island, less than five hundred yards long. The solution involved a combination of high technological sophistication and almost comical simplicity. Several photographers were first stationed at vantage points around the island and then, on hearing a blast from *Eye of the Wind*'s foghorn, Ian Swingland led the YEs in a mad, noisy charge aimed at scaring all the birds into the air. It was an amazing sight, as the unruly mob of 'beaters' hurled themselves across the island like dervishes, screaming and yelling at the tops of their voices in an effort to make themselves heard above the deafening din of the birds themselves. But it worked. The huge colony of sooty terns rose into the air like a vast cloud and the cameras clicked away. Later, the negatives would be fed into a special computer capable of picking out each individual bird and coming up with a very accurate head-count.

It was a week after leaving the Seychelles and setting sail on the last lap of the Indian Ocean crossing that *Eye of the Wind* came alongside at Liwo Tani wharf in Mombasa. The YEs stepped ashore and prepared themselves for adventures of a very different kind.

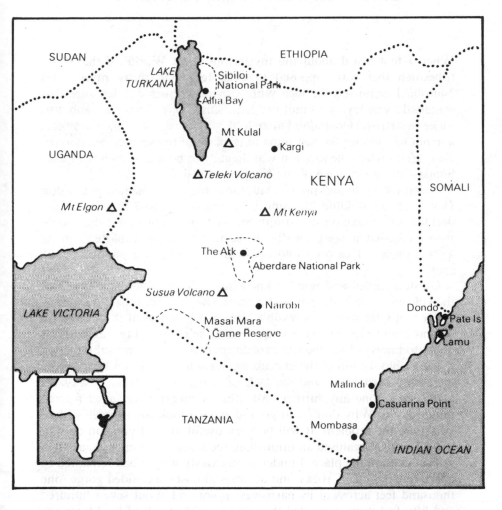

Chapter Twenty-Five

Dateline: Mount Susua, Kenya, September 1980

When I first heard about the mysterious 'Lost World' of the Masai tribesmen that was supposed to exist less than thirty miles from Nairobi, I dismissed the idea with a cynical chuckle. I felt sure that somebody was trying to pull my leg. Either way, I was not about to make myself and Operation Drake look silly by announcing a dramatic attempt to conquer the last remaining piece of unexplored territory in East Africa when the location was actually to be found within an easy Sunday afternoon drive of the Kenyan capital.

'I don't want to end up as a laughing stock,' I explained to Gordon Davies of the Wildlife Planning Unit when he asked me why I had decided not to take on the Mount Susua Volcano project. 'The people who suggested it were clearly using the word "unexplored" in its loosest sense – I've been told since that the area is a popular picnic spot!'

Gordon smiled and nodded knowingly. 'That's the outer crater of the volcano – anybody can get up there,' he said. 'But there's an inner crater that's far more inaccessible and in the middle of that there is a central island plateau that has quite definitely never been explored. I ought to know – I led the last expedition that tried it, and although we made it onto the top of the plateau we were forced to turn back by the incredibly hard going and the lack of water. There was no way we could have gone any further. All other attempts have failed for the same reason. Why don't you go and have a look for yourself – then you'll see the problem. It will be very useful to us if you can do it.'

So Tac HQ organised an immediate recce and, sure enough, as soon as I set eyes on the place, I understood exactly why it had remained so effectively cut off. A rocky and at times almost sheer-sided gorge, one thousand feet across at its narrowest point and about seven hundred and fifty feet deep, separated the central uplifted raft of land from the rim of the inner crater like a gigantic dry moat. To get down into it and up the other side would require mountaineering techniques. On top of that, the terrain was murderous – jumbled rocks and boulders the size of houses, with treacherous crevasses in between, wicked thorn bush that can tear you to shreds if you are not careful and spear cactus with its sharp, poison-bearing spikes that are like bayonets. And not a drop of surface water anywhere. A strange fact struck me − the central plateau and its surrounding moat was a mass of dark green vegetation, in stark contrast with the surrounding area, which was covered with thin yellow grass. Yet apart from the steam vents, the place was bone dry − or was it?

Our recce party, which included John Hines and his wife Dicky, plus experienced explorers like Richard Snailham, had quite a hectic two days examining this formidable region.

Whereas I had ignored Susua originally because I thought it was likely to be too easy, I now began to worry that it might prove too difficult, given the limited time and resources available to us. From the point of view of logistics alone, it promised to be a nightmare. It was necessary to establish some kind of supply line across the gorge and the only feasible method of doing this was to rig up an aerial ropeway of tensioned steel cable on which a sort of cable car could be suspended. But even if we could find a steel cable long enough for the job, there was still the considerable problem of how to get it up there when there was at least a mile of boulder-strewn lava field between the point which landrovers could reach and the edge of the crater. A one-thousand-foot steel cable, wound on a drum, would weigh nearly a ton and it would be impossible to carry or roll it over such rugged ground. Apart from that, I wondered how we were going to keep the advance party supplied with water once they started hacking their way across the plateau. In the kind of conditions and temperatures they would be encountering, each man would require at least one gallon per day, maybe more, and there was no chance of their carrying sufficient quantities with them as they went.

However after an air recce with John Sutton, we decided to go ahead. If it seemed like Mission Impossible − well, really tough challenges were just what we were supposed to be looking for. Also, we had had one or two strokes of luck that helped to reduce the odds against us. For a start, our QM, Lieutenant Colonel Stan Huggett, had found a company who said they were able to provide a cable of the right length. What was more, our friends in the Kenya Army could provide the explosives necessary to blast a path through the lava field along which we could roll the cable drum to the crater's edge, and to dig anchorages for the ropeway. Amongst our stores were six cargo parachutes which could be used for water drops on the plateau from the Beaver aircraft flown for us by veteran Army Air Corps pilots Colonel Mike Badger and Major Mike Sommerton-Rayner − the

[227]

Biggles Outfit as they were affectionately dubbed.

As the preparations went ahead, including the setting up of a base, excitement and enthusiasm mounted not only within Operation Drake but also in the local and international press.

John Sutton invited his committee and many local sponsors to visit us, and Julia Barnley, working with John's own boys from his safari company, organised a truly splendid camp. John's head boy, Julius, built such a luxurious base and our procurement lady, Jennifer Stephens, did such a fine job that I sensed a certain amount of resentment by Operation Drake members in less fortunate circumstances. However, the visiting sponsors certainly appreciated it, and as a result we got another sponsorship which enabled a young Kenyan to join *Eye of the Wind*.

There was a slight hiccup in our plans when the company who were to supply the cable suddenly confessed that they had made a mistake and that the longest section they had was actually only seven hundred and fifty feet. This seemed like a major set-back, until we discovered that Kenya Railways had experts working for them who could splice steel cables, whereupon we bought the seven-hundred-and-fifty-foot length and another of five hundred feet and had them joined. Splicing steel cable is a delicate and precise art, especially when the join has to be good enough to stand being put under high tension, and if it is not done exactly right, you can be in trouble. Kenya Railways did a marvellous job, but even so they were not prepared to guarantee it for more than one and half tons of strain. This was less than we required ideally and meant that we had to modify our ideas a little – for instance, we obviously dared not allow personnel to ride across in the cable car. However, as so often during the expedition, we were happy to accept the old cliché that beggars cannot be choosers and to fall back on our growing talent for improvisation.

Sapper Warrant Officer John Leach took charge of the project and dynamited a path through the lava field, but it still took a full ten-hour day of heaving, sweating and straining by the entire twenty-strong work force to manhandle the heavy cable drum up to the edge of the crater. At the end of it all, people hardly had the strength left to tear the ring-pulls off their beer cans!

If only we could have got hold of a Holdfast Apparatus Rocket Projector (HARP) – the next stage of the job would have been relatively easy. I had used this admirable piece of Royal Engineer equipment fifteen years before in Cyprus and it had proved most effective. Basically, it consisted of a large rocket which you fired off like a harpoon gun, with your cable attached to it, so that it embedded itself deeply in the rock on the other side of the gap you were trying to bridge. Unfortunately, inquiries revealed that the HARP had since become obsolete, and we were therefore obliged to do things the hard way.

This involved using special 'Beehive' explosive drilling charges to blast two narrow trenches, eight-foot long and five-foot deep, one on each side of the gorge. In these holes we buried the trunks of cedar trees, wrapped in corrugated iron, to act as anchors for the cable which had to be dragged by hand down into the moat and across to the opposite side before being tensioned.

A team of the toughest YEs available helped John Leach with this exhausting and potentially dangerous task. They had to climb down into the moat and up onto the central plateau with the explosives strapped to their backpacks.

'Basically I had to try and forget what was behind me as I hacked away at the vicious spear cactus that assaults one from every angle like giant hypodermic needles, and manoeuvred across multiple lava fissures,' wrote Bradbury Williams from Norwich. 'Under the careful direction of the Sapper, we laid the explosive "Beehives" in the lava plateau, fixed detonators and fuse wire, and waited anxiously two hundred yards away for the dramatic event. I wasn't disappointed by the spectacle of flying boulders closely followed by a large "Bang!".

'It took seven hours the following day to haul the steel rope across the gorge. I led the advance party of six YEs, heaving the massive wire to the anchorage we'd made on the edge of the inner raft. Communicating with a small Tannoy, we controlled the exercise which was like a giant tug-of-war and had to be halted every few minutes while we changed hands and caught our breath.'

It was when the cable got snagged on rocks at the bottom of the gorge as it was being tensioned that Zimbabwean Graham George and Scotsman Steve Ballantyne had a narrow squeak. 'I climbed down from one side, checking the cable as I went, and Graham met me in the middle of the gorge where the cable was jammed in the rocks,' recalls Steve. 'Some tension was released and we struggled and heaved to free it. Eventually it broke free and shot into the air under tension, knocking me for six and catapulting Graham into the air. It was very lucky that he managed to hold on to the cable as it bounced him around ten to fifteen feet above the massive lava rocks. Hell knows where he would have landed if he had let go! It is funny to think of it now, but it was pretty hairy at the time.'

Once the cable had been rigged and the first water cans and equipment were sent over on the little trolley suspended from it, the exploration of the tantalisingly mysterious plateau began. It took five days to blaze an eight-foot-wide trail the two miles from one side of it

[229]

to the other and up to its highest point at 6,850 feet. There the Kenyan flag was ceremonially raised to the accompaniment of a thunderflash salute. It then took three and a half hours to scramble back along the path that had been cleared – an indication of just how thick and impenetrable the virgin terrain had been. Our scientists spent the next two weeks carrying out a thorough survey of the flora and fauna on what zoologist Ian Redmond described as 'a unique ecological island'. The one fear that bothered me was that of a casualty on the plateau. 'How on earth can we get an injured man back to base?' I thought. Thus, when Gordon Davis' son, Ben, went down with violent stomach pains and diarrhoea I ordered up the strongest medicine we could get. The plateau was no place for an epidemic of 'the runs'.

Although I did see one strange antelope-like creature during an air recce, any hopes that the fiction of Conan Doyle's 'Lost World' might come true with the discovery of weird and wonderful creatures, marooned there since pre-historic times, were quickly dashed. But the fact that there was a considerable amount of wildlife up on the plateau was a mystery in itself since no source of fresh water could be found. The only water on the plateau came from steam vents which issued jets of hot vapour, giving the area the appearance of an old steam locomotive yard at dawn. Later in the day, as the temperature rose, the steam was less visible. Using plastic sheets, we managed to collect a few pints of the precious liquid, but were soon finding that it was too difficult to carry sufficient water forward from the head of the aerial ropeway. Luckily, the Beaver arrived and was able to parachute supplies to the advancing exploration team. But before this could be done, we had to make a 650-yard airstrip in the outer crater. This was accomplished by a team including Maria Szpak and Barbara Martinelli, who were on leave from the New York Pan Am office, plus Carolyn Longhurst, our PR lady from Tac HQ, my wife, Judith, and Kenyan YE Julia Barnley – almost an all-girl airstrip construction gang.

The groups of baboons that inhabit the plateau were quite concerned about the intrusion into their long-established privacy, as Trevor Moss was made uncomfortably aware. Trevor – one of two 22-year-old twin brothers from Wickford, near Southend, who both joined Operation Drake in Africa – was with fellow British YEs Hazel Preston and Liz Sutcliffe, and Jim Davis of the Wildlife Planning Unit, when they had an alarming encounter. 'We had scaled the moat and had just started to follow the main path across the plateau,' he reported. 'Within close proximity we could hear the barking of Olive Baboons and it was not long before we came face to face with a group of approximately forty of these animals sitting on and around the track. Initially they showed no fear of us, probably because we were the first humans they had ever

[230]

seen. They appeared inquisitive, and our yelling and shouting did nothing to make them move off the path. Suddenly they seemed to feel threatened and two large males rushed at us with teeth bared. Jim and I had machetes in hand, but the odds of getting away without injury were slim. Luckily, the two animals stopped short, and we decided not to push our chances and retreated back several hundred yards hoping that they would move along in their own time. But it was an hour before we felt it was safe to continue.' In fact many of the female baboons acted in a strangely carnal manner towards us. 'Perhaps they thought we were rather attractive apes,' commented one YE.

Kenyan YE Justin Bell had an alarming experience when he was moving back at last light to one of the temporary camps set up along the route across the plateau. Hearing a soft sound close by, he turned to find a fully grown leopard following him. Justin did not panic, although he admits he was scared stiff. 'It seemed to have no fear of me – obviously it wasn't hungry,' he said afterwards.

For me, personally, the most odd thing about the place was its distinctly eerie atmosphere. I am not normally worried about being by myself in remote areas, but whenever I was walking alone on the plateau I always had the feeling that I was being watched, and that is something I have never experienced anywhere else in the world. Several of the team told me that they had felt the same thing. I think it had something to do with the terrain, the huge rocks and boulders behind which it was easy to imagine all sorts of things lying in wait, and the many unexplained noises. It was quite common to hear a sudden crashing in the undergrowth without being able to see anything. The strangest sound of all was the ghostly whistling that seemed most noticeable at dusk and about which we had been warned. The acacia trees play host to a particular type of ant which nests in ball-like growths on the branches. These are full of holes made by the ants and when the wind blows through them it makes the whistling sound.

Equally creepy in their way were the lava caves and subterranean passages that are to be found on the eastern flank of the inner crater, where, when the volcano erupted, the red-hot lava spilled over and ran down the mountainside. As the outside surface of this molten tide cooled and solidified, the inner core continued to flow, thereby creating hollow underground tubes that opened at intervals into large caverns. The network of passages, ranging in diameter from ten feet to eighteen inches, is estimated to extend altogether to over five miles. They were once used as a hide-out by Mau Mau terrorists, but now there are plans to turn them into a tourist attraction, and it was with this in mind that some of the YEs helped cave experts John Arkle and Jim Simon to survey and map the tunnel system.

[231]

John, an ex-soldier who now runs the United Touring Company in Mombasa, had one hair-raising experience when he and Jim penetrated far into the network. They had just wriggled their way through a long section of tunnel that was only eighteen inches high when they burst through into a large chamber, the roof of which was open to the sky. A shaft of sunlight was pouring through this natural skylight and creating a pool of warmth on the floor of the cave in which was lying, fast asleep, an enormous fifteen-foot python. The two men tiptoed past it and continued on their way up the next section of tunnel. But when they came back, the snake was nowhere to be seen. There was only one way it could have gone – and that was down the eighteen-inch passage along which they had no option but to crawl. Their hearts were in their mouths as they inched forward, expecting to see at any moment the shadowy outline of the snake rear up out of the gloom into the light cast by their torches. In fact, they never did catch up with it, but John admits that the prospect of coming face to face with it in such nightmarishly claustrophobic circumstances still makes his flesh crawl whenever he thinks about it.

With the YEs to help him, Ian Redmond was able to make several transects across the plateau, noting the variety of animals and plants to be found there. The results were particularly interesting as the inner area of Susua has been effectively cut off from outside influences since it was created. The WCMD is particularly keen to see if Susua could be developed as a wilderness area for climbers and trekkers, so diversifying Kenya's attractions. With the information we gained, appropriate plans can now be made.

The Susua project turned out to be a tremendous success all round – one of the toughest and most adventurous assignments of the whole expedition – but it almost ended in disaster when a wildlife expert flew up from Nairobi to see us in his private light aircraft. He signalled his arrival by doing a few low-level circuits of the gorge. It was then that I realised with a chilling feeling that he was totally unaware of the steel cable that was stretched across it! If he hit that, it would slice through the plane like a giant cheese-cutter. I waited on tenterhooks, unable to see what was going on from where I was standing in the main camp, but following his progress by the sound of the engine and tensing myself, ready for the rending crash, each time he came round to the area of the cable. However, he managed to avoid the hazard and landed safely and he seemed utterly unconcerned when told about the death-trap he so easily could have flown into. Far from being chastened, his attitude was so cavalier that, when the time came to leave, he decided to buzz the camp. People threw themselves to the ground as he swooped in low, mowing through all our radio aerials and then chopping the top branches of a nearby tree with his tailplane. We could not believe our eyes. Inches lower and he would have been brought down by the tree. As it was, we were anxious that he might have damaged his undercarriage severely, but we were unable to contact his base to warn them to expect a possible emergency landing because our aerials had been destroyed. After John Bland, one of our Signallers, had joined up all the broken bits of copper wire we still could not get through to Nairobi – but, using the amazing Plessey PRC 320 radio, we did manage to raise the Signals Centre at Blandford in England! We asked them to put an urgent call through to John Sutton in Nairobi, but our fears proved to be unfounded. The would-be Red Baron clearly led a charmed life – his plane had suffered no serious damage and he was able to land normally. However, he was very apologetic when he learned what had happened and kindly paid for the damage to our aerials.

In complete contrast to the rush, bustle and high drama of Susua, but every bit as physically demanding in its way, was the measured plod of the camel trek led by Captain Charles Weston-Baker of the Queens Royal Irish Hussars, through the blistering, waterless desolation of the barren country up around Lake Turkana – formerly Lake Rudolph. Here, the purpose was to follow in the footsteps of Count Teleki Von Szek, the legendary hunter and explorer who discovered the lake in 1888 and named it after his patron, Crown Prince Rudolph of Austria. The Count took along his own personal biographer, Lieutenant Von Höhnel, who faithfully recorded every detail of the great trail-blazing safari, and the story gripped the imagination of Charles Weston-Baker. He tried hard to set up a regimental expedition to retrace the route pioneered by Teleki, but had been thwarted by the practical problem of how to get his men out to Kenya in the first place, except at great expense on scheduled air flights, and had been forced to postpone his project. He was therefore delighted with the opportunity to fulfil his ambition on behalf of Operation Drake, and also to do a recce for his own expedition at some later date.

His first requirement was a Swahili-speaking guide with experience of camel-trekking. Just as he was beginning to despair of finding anybody suitable, he had a stroke of luck when he made contact with a remarkable lady called Fiona Alexander. Fiona – a bush pilot who had been on several treks before and was familiar with the region and the local people – happened to be free at the time and was happy to join the expedition. Right from the start she proved to be worth her weight in gold, helping Charles to hire fifteen camels and seven Rendille camelmen, and also enabling him, through her local knowledge, to avert a possible crisis over rations. The staple diet of the Rendille is a particular

[233]

type of ground maize meal, called Posho, and powdered milk. Neither of these items was available in Nairobi because of a national shortage, but Fiona was quick to warn that without them there would be no trek since the Rendille were very particular about their food. In the end a supply of the maize was located, although it had to be specially ground, while the milk powder was flown out from Britain by Ruth.

Eventually everything was ready for the 380-mile round trip from Kargi to Allia Bay, on the shores of Lake Turkana, and then back to Kargi. The party that set out at dawn on 15 July included Hussein Adan, a zoologist from the National Museum in Nairobi, who was to direct the scientific survey work along the route, and four YEs – Kenyan 'Rusty' Knight and Britons Sue Llewelyn, Margaret Smart and Wesley Lowdon – who were to change over with four others at Allia Bay.

The camels were used throughout the trek purely as pack animals, as is customary in the area, and the complicated loading process was a daily ritual that took anything up to two hours. The Rendille handlers – tall, lean men with earlobes pierced and stretched in grotesque fashion – carried out the job with patient expertise. They would first tie on skins as a protection against chafing, then they would construct a wooden frame, and finally they would stack the high-piled load, making sure that the weight was evenly distributed. This has to be done exactly right because if anything is loose, flapping or in any way uncomfortable, then the camel will not budge, displaying a streak as stubborn as any mule. They are strange and remarkably unloveable creatures. They can smell terrible, their stomachs rumble continuously in the most disgusting manner, they emit an endless selection of belches, gurgling growls and bad-tempered roars and, most revolting of all, they spray spit, froth and regurgitated food in all directions and break wind without any thought for those lesser mortals who follow.

After a brief good-luck ceremony, which involved walking twice in an anti-clockwise circle and then through an arch of spears, the little caravan moved off. They soon fell into a fairly regular daily routine and a steady trudging pace. Each morning they would rise at five o'clock, so as to be ready to get on their way by seven, and they would then walk for six or seven hours before making camp at around 2.00 p.m. The first couple of hours, in the cool of the day, would be relatively comfortable, but as the sun climbed higher in the sky and the temperature soared relentlessly to 120° F in the shade, conversation would gradually die away, heads would go down and an effort of willpower would be needed to keep going in the sweltering heat. The short rest-breaks, when water would be sipped or an orange sucked, tended to become more and more of a blessed relief as the day wore on.

[234]

The camels needed to drink only once every four or five days, but dehydrated human bodies required twelve pints a day.

It took three weeks to reach Allia Bay. The party did not actually keep exactly to Count Teleki's route all the time, but when they did Charles read out the relevant passages from Von Höhnel's book and it was fascinating to find that neither the awe-inspiring scenery nor the irritating discomforts had changed much in the intervening century. Like Von Höhnel, they were struck particularly by their first sight of Lake Turkana – the remote expanse of water, one hundred and fifty miles long and thirty miles wide, which lay undiscovered for so long, and yet which now, in the light of the archaeological findings at Koobi Fora on its eastern shore, has come to be regarded as the very birthplace of mankind. Unlike Von Höhnel and the other members of the Teleki expedition, they did not make the mistake of rushing to slake their thirst in the cool, clear water of the lake, having been forewarned that one of its many interesting features is the very high soda content that not only makes it taste odd but also tends to have a distressing purgative effect if drunk untreated.

Lions were occasionally heard prowling near their camps at night, but the dangerous creatures that the camel trek party had to look out for were smaller and less obviously menacing. Hussein's nightly scorpion hunts – conducted with the aid of an ultra-violet lamp – proved alarmingly fruitful. On one occasion he 'bagged' no less than fifty-six, two of which were found under people's camp beds. On another evening Margaret Smart had an uncomfortably close encounter of the creepy-crawly kind with an even more unpleasant customer. Sue Llewelyn noted: 'As Margaret was writing her diary, I noticed a fast movement by her feet, and as I looked more closely I realised that it was a hunter spider. I clamped a film canister over it and called Hussein, who immediately made a search in the vicinity and found two more. He told us that he had once been bitten by one when he was a boy and they have a poison which affects the nervous system, paralysing you for three days!'

After the changeover at Allia Bay, the return to Kargi by a route that struck eastwards away from Lake Turkana and down around the other side of Mount Kulal, did not take as long as the outward journey. Lack of water was the main problem on this section of the trek, as the party trudged on through the loose, sugary sand of the luggas – the dried-up river beds – stumbled over boulders of the lava fields and pushed painfully through the wait-a-bit thorn – so-called because of the way people constantly have to request a brief pause while they unhook themselves from the vicious thorns. (The way the camels munched away happily on these razor-sharp spikes without apparent discomfort

[235]

was a source of continual amazement to one and all.) The camel men professed to know the area well, but even so they still managed to get lost, actually leading the party away from waterholes on several occasions. Whenever this happened, they would blame *Shauri a Mungo* – 'the will of God' – thereby shrugging off all responsibility for the mistake.

All the life of the surrounding area is drawn magnetically to the waterholes, and the bustle of noisy and colourful activity that is concentrated around these isolated places contrasts vividly with the profound peace and vast, brooding loneliness of the barren country in between. Donkeys and camels wait patiently to take their turn at the water, along with their owners, while chattering children help their mothers to fill the family bottles – gourds plugged with grass or capped with snug-fitting cups. There is a strict order and if you happen to turn up at the wrong time you may have to queue for hours. That was no great hardship to the trekkers who found plenty to fascinate them in a scene which, as Charles noted in his log, was Biblical in its timelessness.

The distinguishing features of the various different tribes were especially interesting – the magnificent high collars of beads that stretched the necks of the Rendille women, the intricate beadwork which the Samburu women wore hanging down their backs and the elaborate coiffures of the Turkana men, who plaster their hair in mud, sculpt it and set it, and have to carry special head-rests so that they can sleep without disturbing their crowning glories. The temptation to take photographs had to be resisted, however, since this was greatly resented by the locals – even when they themselves were not in the frame. They made sure that their possessions, too, were never within camera range, and Hussein once got told off severely for snapping a picture of the waterhole itself. When he pointed out that surely the waterhole was not owned by anyone, he was asked: 'Have you ever seen anything that is not owned by *somebody*?'

Shortly before reaching Gus, some members of the party climbed to the top of the peak Kino Sogo. At the summit they discovered a rusty cigarette tin marked 'Winchester Brand Cigarettes' in which was a decaying piece of paper with a note scribbled on it. This read: 'Anyone who finds this must sign it.' This first signature was dated 1907 and there were then three more, dated 1921, 1939 and 1951. Unfortunately, no one present had a pen or writing implement of any kind with them at the time, and so the fact that Operation Drake had passed that way was sadly not recorded for posterity.

Later, when Charles returned to regimental duty, my old friend Richard Snailham took over the camels and with YEs Fynn Davey and

[236]

Richard Hopkins they organised a most successful and highly enjoyable expedition to investigate the incredible El Kajarta Gorge that leads into the crater of an extinct volcano in the Kulal Mountains. I joined Richard's patrol for a truly welcome break, along with Margot, my hard-working PA and Chris Sainsbury, now our film maker (since Alan Bibby's team had been forced to withdraw through lack of funds).

Under the able command of Royal Marine Captain Ian Gardiner, Operation Drake ran a separate project on and around Lake Turkana. Our party used the Kenyan Fisheries Department vessel *Halcyon* to travel round conducting an ecological survey under the direction of two scientists from the National Museum – Alec MacKay, the Curator of Herpatology, and Cunningham van Someren, the Curator of Ornithology. No comprehensive survey of this kind had ever been made before and among the large collection of animals, insects and plants that was gathered were many previously unknown species.

The lake – which is also known as the Sea of Jade due to the algae which float to the surface on calm days, changing the colour of the water dramatically from the usual blue to a deep green – teems with wildlife. It is famous for its fantastic Nile Perch – which can weigh up to a staggering three hundred pounds – the aggressive tiger fish, lurking hippopotami, and some of the world's largest crocodiles. It is suspected that either the hippos or the crocs – of which there is a population estimated at nearly twenty-five thousand – were responsible for the mysterious disappearance of two members of the 1934 Fuchs expedition. They had been left to carry on with some research on the lake's South Island – and were never seen again. Some time later a pair of oars and a hat belonging to one of them were washed up on the shore seventy miles away, and as the weather was fine at the time the most likely theory seems to be that their boat was attacked and overturned as they rowed back. Maybe they were tipped into the water unintentionally. It is all too easy to be taken by surprise by a surfacing hippo, as Brad Williams and five other YEs on the project found out when one of these huge and terrifyingly ugly monsters suddenly materialised only inches from their assault boat. Had he stayed under for a few seconds more, he would have come up right underneath the craft and all those aboard would have been floundering in the water. And the crocs would have been on hand to take terrible advantage of such an accident.

The other part of Ian Gardiner's task was to mark the boundary of the new Sibiloi National Park. Ably assisted by veteran expeditioneer Sandy Evans, Ian set up his base camp in the shade of some flat-topped acacia trees standing on the side of a dry river bed and from here sallied forth daily to erect cairns of home-made concrete blocks at appropriate

[237]

points. In the baking heat this was taxing work, but nevertheless Ian's team persevered and by the end of the expedition they had laid eighty cairns along one hundred miles of the boundary – a remarkable achievement. Back at Tac HQ, it was no easy task to keep them supplied and the long haul north was frequently carried out by trucks and drivers kindly provided by the Kenyan Army and by John Sutton.

Chapter Twenty-Six

Dateline: Kitum Cave, Mount Elgon, Kenya, September 1980

It is sixty years now since a farmer called Renshaw Mitford-Barbeton first explored Kitum Cave, up near the Ugandan border ... and got a very nasty shock. Having edged cautiously through the wide, low, letterbox-shaped entrance, he then penetrated right to the back of the 250-yard-deep cavern, crawling over fallen boulders, inching past narrow crevasses and skirting dark pools into which water dripped with echoing plops. It was as he prepared to make his way back out again that he suddenly realised with a start that he had company. He heard them long before he saw them – heavy, shuffling footsteps, a strange flapping noise, and some terrifyingly loud huffing and puffing. There was also a sound that seemed to him like the rumbling of giant stomachs. His mind boggled. Whoever or whatever they were, they had him trapped in the dead-end cave. He strained his eyes into the darkness beyond the range of his lamp and then gasped in amazement as he eventually managed to make out a group of huge shadowy forms in the gloom. It was a herd of elephants.

Mr Mitford-Barbeton escaped unhurt when, after an hour that must have seemed to him like an eternity, the elephants left and allowed him to scramble to safety. It emerged later that his confrontation was no chance meeting, since the herds regularly visited the cave to the extent that they had beaten a well-worn path to the entrance. But the reason why they should want to go out of their way to squeeze themselves into this one particularly inaccessible cave remained for many years an even greater mystery than the legendary Elephants' Graveyard. Part of the problem was that it was impossible to see what they were doing in the darkness and lights would scare them off and possibly start a stampede. It was the tusk marks all over the walls and roof of the cavern that gave the vital clue to the fact that the elephants were going there to mine vital, health-giving mineral salts for themselves.

The Wildlife Planning Unit had heard this story and asked Operation Drake to investigate. If it was true they wanted to improve tourist viewing facilities at the cave by cutting a path up to the entrance and

[239]

constructing an observation platform. I offered a team of YEs to carry out a survey of the cave itself and hopefully to find out more about the frequency and duration of the elephants' visits.

This was an especially exciting prospect because, only a few weeks before we arrived in Kenya, Gordon Davis and a WPU team happened to visit Kitum when elephants were actually inside the cave and were able to record one of the closest and most rewarding observations that had ever been made. They were alerted to the presence of the elephants as soon as they arrived by the fresh droppings near the entrance, and sure enough, as they advanced warily into the darkness, they could hear rumblings coming from behind a pile of rocks at the back of the cave where Mitford-Barbeton had been cornered. They quickly decided to find a hiding place among the boulders in the mouth of the cave so that they could watch developments.

There were some moments of slight anxiety when a large bull elephant suddenly appeared round a bend in the path outside, clearly intending to join the rest of the herd inside, and then came to a halt, scenting danger. He backed off and returned to the top of the cliff, apparently waiting for the human intruders to move. Meanwhile, those inside had begun to leave, but had also sensed the presence of the observers. They paused for a moment and then, gaining confidence, moved forward to within a few feet of the hidden watchers.

'We had a very close-up view indeed,' said Gordon. 'There were between fifteen and twenty in the group and all of them appeared to be females. Some had very young calves. While they were obviously aware of our close situation they showed no sign of aggression and merely confined their activities to sniffing with raised trunks and a little ear-flapping. At a sign from the group matriarch, the party then moved out of the cave in single file, squeezing their bodies between the narrow confines of the wall and various rocks so that the friction made a rasping noise. Youngsters were given the odd nudge to help them on their way. As they went down the narrow defile, clouds of dust filled the air, lending even further to the unusual atmosphere.' One of the team said: 'The sight of these elephants leaving Kitum Cave will remain one of the most unique and enthralling experiences I have witnessed during many years spent in Kenya. It is to be hoped that others may also be so privileged.'

In fact, the five YEs who maintained a round-the-clock vigil outside the cave during the week-long project never had quite such a clear, daylight viewing, but what they missed in terms of spectacle they more than made up for by way of the drama that surrounded their sightings.

They took it in turns to man the hide for four-hour shifts, accompanied by an armed National Park ranger. Kenyan Charles

Langat took the first night shift and met with almost immediate success. A group of elephants entered the cave, but they seemed to know that he was watching them and they did not stay long. Barry Moss was in a state of tense expectation, therefore, when he arrived to take over the 4.00–8.00 a.m. shift. The camp was over a mile away and after driving in a Land Rover to the foot of Mount Elgon there was a walk of several hundred yards up the ill-defined path to the cave entrance. 'In the complete darkness this was an incredible and rather frightening experience,' wrote Barry in the report he compiled for his sponsor. 'There were known to be numerous wild animals in the area, including buffalo, giant forest hog, and leopard, and one had a sense of acute awareness of the least little noise. We had only just started clearing the path at this stage and it was quite easy to lose it, especially at night. The ranger led on cautiously through the thick vegetation and undergrowth, his rifle loaded and cocked – ready for action. I followed close behind him with my flashlight picking out large trees which we might be able to hide behind or climb in the event of attack by buffalo or elephant. I felt that the blood in my veins had been transformed to adrenaline. It was like walking down a narrow, darkened alley in the middle of gangland, expecting an ambush from every doorway and corner.

'We reached the hide fifteen minutes later and settled in as quietly as possible. The sky was clear and the moon and stars lit up the entrance with an adequate amount of light to see anything coming in or out of the subterranean hall. As dawn approached the only sound to be heard was of fruit bats returning to their roosts, at first in ones and twos, and then in hundreds, fluttering and squealing inches above our heads.'

The next evening more than made up for this slight anti-climax. Barry, Charles Langat and his accompanying ranger went up to Mount Elgon ready to start their stint, but there was no sign of the previous shift who should have been waiting at the bottom of the path for a lift back to camp. After waiting for half an hour, Barry and Charles decided that they both ought to go up and check that everything was all right. The ranger was not so keen since he was unarmed – his colleague who was already up there had the gun. 'It wasn't an easy job persuading him that he should come with us,' wrote Barry. 'But eventually he agreed and we set off into the darkness. We slowly picked our way through the dense undergrowth as quietly as possible, stopping and listening at every rustle and sound. Our only weapon was my drawn machete. As we approached the top of the path we heard a loud scream and much trumpeting followed by crashing trees as a herd of elephants came charging down the valley. We froze in our tracks, trying to pinpoint their position and whether they were heading

[241]

towards us. I looked at my machete, realised that it would be totally ineffective against the charging animals and started looking round for a large tree. There weren't any to be seen and, besides, trees would be no obstacles to maddened elephants. I had seen them push over full-grown trees quite effortlessly. I then thought about running, but the path was too steep and the mass of tangled undergrowth was nearly impenetrable so all we could do was go to ground.

'At last we heard the crashing and trumpeting heading into the distance and realised that the elephants had changed direction and gone down the other side of the valley. When we reached the cave entrance we found that the two girls who had been sharing the previous watch were in almost as much of a panic as the elephants. They explained that they had been delayed because they did not want to leave while the elephants were there. Then the sound of our approach had spooked the herd which immediately stampeded.'

For Barry the excitement still was not over. A couple of nights later when he went on the 8.00 p.m.–midnight shift he was met at the bottom of the path by English YE Barbara Jude and Linda Batt-Rawden, the phase three YE who had rejoined us as the official Capital Radio reporter, with the news that there were three elephants in the cave and more hanging around outside. He went up with extra care and tiptoed to the hide.

'For the first half-hour or so I heard absolutely nothing and then, all of a sudden, a terrifying roar came from the back of the cave followed by a sickening thud. I learned later that the thud was the sound of their tusks chipping the salt from the walls, while the roar was the sound of a stomach rumbling! I could also hear a distant whooshing as the jumbos hosed water from the rock pools into their mouths. For a while all went quiet again and my eyes and ears strained into the still darkness. Then I thought I heard an elephant approaching our position, heavy footsteps like some giant mechanical monster making its way towards us. I cowered back until I could retreat no further. Was there really something there or had my imagination been carried away? The sounds then stopped and I never did find out whether I was dreaming or not. But I felt somewhat stunned by the whole experience.'

Considering how few people have ever actually witnessed this strange elephantine ritual, Barry and his fellow YEs were obviously fortunate to have been on the spot at exactly the right time. As a result of their work, it is hoped that many others will now be able to enjoy a spectacle that must rank as one of the wonders of the animal world.

Wart hogs may not be as big as elephants, but they are a good deal more ferocious and can be extremely dangerous if you catch them in the wrong mood, as Barbara Martinelli found out when we were being shown round part of the Aberdare National Park – a 400-square-mile wildlife haven which, thanks to the abundance of water and lush vegetation, boasts a higher density of animals per acre than anywhere else in Africa. Barbara was a member of a group I took up to the Ark Lodge, where one of the main Operation Drake projects was based, and it was while we were being given a conducted tour by the Manager, Sam Weller, that the incident took place which was to instil in her a new respect for the humble hog.

We were driving along in a Land Cruiser when we came upon a baby pig that was squealing its head off, having just been abandoned by its parents. Sam decided he had better rescue it to save it from being eaten by the local leopard, but as he went to pick it up, the little fellow disappeared down what looked like a very large rabbit burrow. He tried to retrieve it, but as he suffers from a stiff leg, he was unable to get far enough down on his knees and he called for volunteers, whereupon Barbara immediately stepped forward. No sooner had she started groping in the hole than she shot backwards with a look of horror on her face as a full-grown tusker came charging out with three squealing piglets in tow, and ran between her and Sam. How it missed Barbara I will never know and I dread to think what would have happened had it decided to attack her. It must have weighed five hundred pounds or more and with its wicked tusks it could have caused terrible damage before we could have done anything to help her.

Our project at the Ark Lodge involved the repair of a three-hundred-foot wooden bridge which connected the Lodge with the hillside, enabling tourists to get a grandstand view of the animals that come to drink at the nearby salt lick. It collapsed in early 1980, injuring a number of people and although the job of reconstruction, which we took on at the Kenyan government's request, seemed to be fairly straightforward, it soon proved otherwise. In fact, it developed into a nightmare, and was the one instance during the whole expedition where we feared that we might have bitten off more than we could chew.

The basic unforeseen snag that complicated everything and threw out all our calculations was that the piers which supported the span were also unsound, and so, instead of a reasonably simple repair job to the decking, we suddenly found ourselves literally starting from the foundations and rebuilding the entire bridge from scratch. From then on, our problems escalated rapidly and we got involved in a desperate race against time. Getting hold of the huge amounts of properly seasoned timber that were necessary and transporting it to the site was a major headache – and that was only the start of our troubles. Everything we needed in the way of materials seemed hard to come by

[243]

– even such ordinary items as nuts and bolts – and we had to work with few proper tools and equipment. Huge sections of the walkway had to be hoisted into position by hand and Tirfor jacks. The YEs sweated and toiled under the direction of, first, Lieutenant Nick Ray and, later, Lieutenant Colonel Ernie Durey, who had come out to supervise the packing up of our stores. Ernie, who loves a challenge, drove everyone on relentlessly, twelve hours a day and more, and, miraculously, we just managed to get the work finished on time.

For the YEs who laboured so magnificently there were consolations. Thanks to the kindness of Sam Weller, they had a marvellous camp a mile from the walkway, where they feasted on delicious local food instead of the endless compo rations which everybody else had to put up with most of the time. And at the Ark – Kenya's best viewing lodge, built in the style made famous by Noah – they were able to observe at close quarters the most spectacular variety of wildlife to be found anywhere in Africa.

With so many animals about, it is all too easy to allow familiarity to breed contempt and forget that they can be dangerous. Two American YEs were given a sharp reminder of the need for constant alertness when they were out, alone and unarmed, working on a new culvert in one of the outlying areas of the Aberdare Park. A Park ranger happened to drive by and was disturbed to find that they had been dropped off and left with no transport. 'So, what are you planning to do if those two chaps decide to come down and take a closer look at you,' he said, pointing to a spot no more than a hundred yards away where two lions were watching them hungrily. He put five shots over their heads to scare them off, but they did not budge. However, he did manage to frighten the YEs by informing them that a lot of lions had been forced by drought to leave their normal hunting grounds and had started foraging nearer to centres of civilisation where cattle made easy prey. There was no reason to suppose that they would turn their noses up at a convenient human snack!

The only other slightly anxious moment came when Sam Weller and some of the YEs went to rescue a buffalo that had got itself stuck in the mud in one of the Park's wallows. The only way to get it out was to put a rope round it and give it a tow with a Land Cruiser. The difficult part of the operation was to get the rope off afterwards. The eighteen-hundred-pound animal showed no sign of being grateful for this helping hand, and immediately charged the vehicle, putting an extremely large dent in the back of it.

July sees the beginning of the largest animal migration in the world, when almost a million wildebeest move from the parched Serengeti Plain in Tanzania, across the Kenyan border into the grasslands of the

[244]

Masai Mara Game Reserve in a period of just three weeks, travelling in enormous herds up to 100,000-strong. Under the supervision of wildlife biologist Mworia Mugambe, YEs carried out a series of game surveys on behalf of the Kenya Rangeland Ecological Monitoring Unit. These were specially designed to discover what changes occurred in the distribution of resident animals in the Reserve as the migration took place.

The surveys were made from Land Rovers, driving through the bush for up to seven hours at a time, and also from light aircraft, and even using Alan Roots famous hot-air balloons. All the large herbivores – including topi, gazelle, giraffe, impala and zebra – were identified, counted and sexed. Their territorial inter-relations with other animals were noted as well as the type of habitat they were occupying.

The YEs made contact with the people as well as the animals of the Masai Mara when they took part in a community project that involved building cattle dips for the Masai, whose herds are decimated each year by East Coast Fever – a disease carried by ticks that cling to the animals' skins. The construction of the dips, which are the only effective way of tackling the problem, was bedevilled by the same frustrations that had attended the building of the Ark walkway. For one thing, the ground was so hard that the only way to excavate the basic pits was to use explosives and pneumatic drills, and this inevitably led to all sorts of difficulties. Explosives were hard to come by and the compressor which we borrowed to power the drills broke down at the most inconvenient moment. Then, just when we thought we had sorted everything out, we discovered that there was a national cement shortage and we could not attain sufficient supplies. Despite all this, the team led by Lieutenant Peter Cosgrove of the Royal New Zealand Engineers managed to complete one dip and excavated the pit for a second.

The Masai watched the progress of the work with interest. These striking-looking people – once the proudest warrior tribe in all of Africa, with a reputation even more fearsome than that of the Zulus – have opted for a more gentle, nomadic way of life which centres around their cattle. These sacred cows are very rarely slaughtered and yet they provide the Masai with their staple diet. Barry Moss explained how in his diary: 'They have become skilled at tapping blood from the animals. A tourniquet is tied around the cow's neck and then a specially shaped arrow is shot into the protruding jugular vein from a distance of about three feet. The blood is caught in a special receptical and when enough has been collected the tourniquet is released and the wound allowed to heal naturally. Not much different in effect from giving a pint of blood to the transfusion service! The blood is then

[245]

mixed with milk and drunk, preferably when still warm.'

The men are tall and lean with finely chiselled features, and the young boys are still initiated into manhood with a series of tests which they have to pass in order to prove their courage and endurance. Although the killing of a lion single-handed is no longer included, many of the warriors bear scars where they have branded themselves with hot irons to show that they have no fear of pain. The women shave their heads and were fascinated by the long hair of the girl YEs whom they prodded about the chest with great curiosity, as if unconvinced that they were actually of the same sex as themselves.

Nearby was 'Hippo Pool' the home of a large herd of hippos that wallowed in it all day. Nurse Liz Sutcliffe from London was amazed by the bold nonchalance of the local wildlife. 'The animals would come right into the camp,' she noted. 'The monkeys, especially, soon learned where the store tent was and, given the chance, would seize whatever they could. The buffalo were more menacing – huge, black, unpredictable beasts, they would lurk in the shadows behind the tents and occasionally stampede as a lion stalked up on them. At night we slept to the sound of the frogs down in the creek and the eerie laugh of the hyenas.'

Chapter Twenty-Seven

Dateline: Abandoned City of Shanga, near Lamu, Kenya,
July–September 1980

'Operation Drake – Up the Creek and Round the Bend' – so read the signpost erected by some wit to point the way to the isolated site of our archaeological project on the island of Pate, just off the northern coast of Kenya. Among those who found their way there were plenty who came to regard this as a plain statement of fact rather than a helpful direction. Until Mark Horton and his team descended on the place, the ruins of Shanga had lain only partially explored for nearly five hundred years – and it did not take too long to discover why. Not only was the spot extremely inaccessible – presenting, yet again, major logistical problems – but it was also less than totally inviting when one did eventually get there. Even the ever-enthusiastic Mark Horton was forced to admit in one of his reports: 'Just to begin to investigate such a site required fortitude and determination on the part of the workers. Unused to the daily temperatures of over one hundred degrees, we found physical work exhausting. Snakes lurked in the undergrowth, mosquito bites were a continual irritant, and members of the team were often laid up with high fevers due to obscure tropical viruses. Each day water had to be drawn from a distant well and brought to the site by donkey. Because we could not wash in this precious fresh water, bathing in the sea among stingrays and sharks became a necessary hazard of life.

Despite such severe hardships, Mark and his fellow archaeologists from Cambridge University and the National Museum of Kenya welcomed the opportunity to undertake the first thorough exploration of this unique twenty-acre site which only came to light again some thirty years ago, after remaining hidden in the undergrowth for so many centuries. It was originally rediscovered by James Kirkman in the late 1950s, but neither he nor the handful of other experts who followed him there had the facilities to attempt a full investigation of the fantastic and extensive ruins.

Richard Leakey, Director of Nairobi Museum, suggested we tackle the project and generously supported it with Museum funds. This enabled us to employ forty local labourers, greatly speeding the clearance of the site and its subsequent survey. In addition, a number of Museum staff assisted in the work, constantly advising us as the work progressed.

Simply to clear the dense undergrowth of creeper, baobab and scrub from the site was a mammoth task, but as the labour force of YEs gradually cut away the mantle of foliage, the former extent of Shanga became impressively apparent. The crumbling coral walls of one hundred and sixty houses, two palaces, three mosques and hundreds of tombs emerged as the green carpet of vegetation was steadily peeled back to reveal what was soon confirmed as one of the earliest, most extensive and best-preserved Swahili trading ports in the region.

Sometimes we were guilty of upsetting the local people quite unintentionally. On one occasion a splendid Zimbabwean YE, Henry Madyavanhu (who told me his name meant 'cannibal'), was cutting the vegetation down along a compass bearing. Henry, working with great zeal, was so enthusiastic that he had not asked how far he should clear and he had slashed through a small orchard belonging to a local farmer before an almost demented Mark Horton stopped him. Henry apologised, the farmer accepted his apology and we paid for the trees.

As each section of wall was surveyed and mapped, the pattern of the once-thriving city became increasingly clear and then, as hundreds of tons of soil from fifteen test pits was painstakingly sifted, finds of bone, pottery, glass, metal and even gold – all meticulously logged and labelled by Maria Mabee – yielded further important clues to its six-hundred year history. This evidence suggests that the first settlement on the site dated from A.D 850 and consisted of mud-and-thatch huts, and that it then grew in importance under the influence of Arab traders until, by the early fifteenth century, it was a city of considerable size with a population of between two and three thousand people. The discovery of decorated pottery from Arabia, porcelain from China, and beads from India gives an indication of the extent of their trading interests.

The one remaining mystery is why such a flourishing community should have vanished so suddenly some time around A.D. 1450. Kenyan YE Elizabeth Wangari Rugoiyo talked to the people of neighbouring Siu and Pate about the legends and oral histories of the area that have been passed down from generation to generation to see if they threw any light on the subject. The most interesting version of what happened came from a seventy-year-old resident of Siu, called Mmaka Mohamed, who told her that the people of Shanga came originally from Shanghai in China – hence the name. They were known as the Wa-Shanga and at one point they went to war with the

[248]

people of Siu and defeated them. The people of Siu then got together with the people of Pate and won back their territory, whereupon the Wa-Shanga fled back to China. Some of them only ran as far as Faza and, according to Mmaka Mohamed, 'you can still see people with eyes like those of the Wa-Shanga in Faza to this day.'

Even though Mark Horton drove his team on at a relentlessly furious pace – digging all day in the hot sun, analysing, cataloguing and writing up reports half the night – he had no chance, in the limited time available, of doing everything that he would have liked to have done. Some of his excavations had to be cut tantalisingly short – in particular, the detailed investigation of the so-called Friday Mosque, which was situated in the middle of the city and which was by far the most interesting and well-preserved of all the ruins. Nevertheless, the work accomplished was of tremendous value and has produced a fine new collection at the local museum in Lamu. Mr Athman Lali Omar, Curator of Lamu Museum, described it as 'possibly revealing critical new archaeological evidence of the obscure Swahili culture of the coast which is contained in the traditional chronicles of the area'.

Under the steadying hand of Ken Norman, the Group Leader and Administrator, the project ended on a high note.

Mark and the rest of the team – which included Mike Carter and Kate Clark from Cambridge, and Janet Brooke from Nairobi – were understandably delighted with the success of their labours both at Shanga and also at Dondo, on the mainland, where they uncovered the site of another little-known trading town. But there was an awful moment when it seemed as if the whole thing might end in the most terrible disappointment. Some weeks after the expedition had packed up and left Kenya, we got a panic call from Mark in Cambridge to say that the two large cardboard boxes containing all the maps, diagrams and other paperwork had failed to turn up with the rest of the archaeological gear and had apparently been lost in transit. As he pointed out, without the paperwork all the immense effort that had been put into the project would be rendered totally meaningless. There could be no published report and no survey for the National Museum of Kenya, who had invested a considerable amount of money in the expedition on the understanding that they would get just such a survey at the end of it. Mark's panic spread quickly through 5B and from there down the telex and telephone lines to Kenya, and there were a few anxious days before the missing boxes were eventually spotted in the corner of a Nairobi warehouse.

Down the coast from Shanga – at Casuarina Point, just south of Malindi – our diving team carried out a survey of marine plant and animal life on behalf of the Marine Park. Their main brief was to examine the effects on the ecology of the local reef of increasing tourism and also siltation from the Tana and Sabaki Rivers. The diving conditions were excellent and, as on land, the chief hazard was the wildlife. Six-foot moray eels with teeth like razors, giant stingrays with their barbed tails, and marauding sharks demanded constant wariness. Not so obviously frightening, but just as dangerous, were the poisonous sea urchins, one of which put Zimbabwean YE Tony Bridger into hospital after he stepped on it.

A night dive provided a highlight which thrilled young Barry Moss. 'The sea was calm and settled and the moon looked as bright as a new penny and cast a silver glaze over the surface of the water,' he wrote. 'Strange electric blue neon flashes were produced as the propellor blades of our boat disturbed the phosphorescence in the water. Under the surface everything was peaceful and calm, but it was easy to become disorientated in the womb-like environment. All that we could see were the objects picked out by our torches as we swam down the side of the colourless reef. The fish that were so active and inquisitive during the day were now in trance-like suspension. We saw a giant turtle swim past and gave chase. Then we swam under a massive coral shelf and came face to face with a grouper so large that it dwarfed both of us, and we quickly went into reverse and headed back towards the submerged light that was suspended under the boat.'

It was on a Sunday evening in July that I picked up the phone and heard the words I had been dreading for two years – 'There's been an accident and one of the Young Explorers is dead.' Then I was given the full, grim story. Four Kenyan YEs, who were taking part in the Masai Mara Game Reserve project, had driven up to the nearby Keekorok Lodge Hotel to post some letters, and on the way back to camp their Land Rover had careered off the road near the Lodge gates, rolling over twice and finally coming to rest in a ditch. All four occupants were injured and one, Andrew Maara, died on his way to hospital after a desperate roadside battle to save his life led by nurse Clare Darrah – a YE sponsored by Capital Radio.

It was shattering news. At the back of my mind there had always been the nagging awareness that we must be prepared for at least one serious injury or illness, and maybe even a fatality, at some time during Operation Drake. With so many people involved in adventures that were often demanding, occasionally dangerous and nearly always conducted in a strange and hostile environment, it would have been extraordinary if we had escaped totally unscathed. But to lose someone in such a commonplace way seemed somehow tragically ironic.

We had already had a scare which had demonstrated how the

[250]

greatest disasters can so often be the least predictable. As *Eye of the Wind* sailed up from Sulawesi to Kenya we got an SOS from the ship's doctor alerting us to the fact that American YE Cindy James had developed an abscess of the retina of her eyes and was in urgent need of specialist hospital treatment. As soon as the ship arrived in Mombasa, she was transferred to hospital in Nairobi where it emerged that there was a real risk that if the abscess burst Cindy's sight would be seriously affected. There were some very tense moments before it subsided without causing any damage. It was a close thing. Cindy was lucky. Poor Andrew Maara was not.

I attended his funeral in the field beside his home and was greatly moved by the simple dignity of the occasion. I had steeled myself for scenes of hysterical grief and even understandable resentment, instead of which I was met with calm solemnity. Even his mother managed somehow to keep her feelings under tight control and when Andrew's brother started to weep by the graveside she stepped forward angrily and reprimanded him, whereupon the little chap bravely blinked back the tears. Shows of emotion were strictly forbidden.

We hardly had time to recover from the shock of Andrew's death before tragedy struck again in horribly similar circumstances. Six YEs were being driven back to camp from the Ark walkway site when their Land Rover, being driven by one of the most careful drivers I have ever met, swerved off the road, possibly to avoid a buffalo which quite unexpectedly appeared out of the bush. Although the vehicle was not travelling very fast at the time, it hit a shallow depression which started it somersaulting end over end. The people in the back were able to jump clear, but those in front were thrown out. Richard Hopkins landed on his head and was killed instantly.

As the terrible news spread, a deep depression settled over the whole expedition. Richard, a twenty-year-old student from North Humberside, had made his mark as one of the most outstanding and popular YEs. I, personally, had got to know him well on the camel patrol to the El Kajarta gorge. I had been particularly impressed with a young man who seemed to have an abundance of exactly those qualities we were looking for in our YEs − courage, initiative and common sense, allied with a questing spirit of adventure. His death was like a hammer blow that crushed us all, but whenever I think of it I try to recall the words of his father, David Hopkins, who said in tribute to his son: 'If ever you went with Richard and there was a mountain to climb, he always had to get to the top and had to get there first. I think he was always looking for the best outdoor life he could, and I think in Kenya he had found it.'

Chapter Twenty-Eight

Dateline: Red Sea, 8 September 1980

The unmistakable sound of an approaching helicopter brought everybody running up onto the deck of *Eye of the Wind* as she lay at anchor in the remote bay where she had been stranded for four days, after being forced to take shelter from stormy weather. Within seconds of the distinctive clatter first becoming audible in the distance, the chopper was hovering just above the ship, its rotor blades whirling only a few feet from the mainmast. Then the door slid open and a note, weighted with a large nut and bolt, was lowered down on the end of a length of wire. The message advised the YEs to stand by to be transferred to a motor launch which would be arriving shortly to take them to shore. This was the dramatic climax to a very tricky situation which had arisen when *Eye of the Wind* developed engine trouble while battling through some of the worst conditions of the entire round-the-world voyage.

From the moment that she set sail from Mombasa on the last lap of her two-year odyssey, the ship had found herself at the mercy of weather that changed from one extreme to another with bewildering rapidity. No sooner had she left port than she ran into a succession of fierce squalls and such rough seas that even the seasoned sailors of the permanent crew were seasick – let alone the totally inexperienced YEs. For them it was a terrible introduction to the delights of life on the ocean wave. They mostly crawled into the scuppers and lay there helpless, too ill to move, while Trish Holdway and Leslie Reiter – two of the very few people still on their feet – went round dressing pathetically limp, near-unconscious bodies in oil skins as they began to turn blue with cold.

The Equator was crossed two days out of Mombasa, but nobody was in a fit state to enjoy the wild frolics that traditionally mark this occasion, and so the sitting of King Neptune's Court had to be postponed until the wind shifted slightly, the mountainous seas subsided and suddenly the ship was creaming through the water at over ten knots in absolutely perfect sailing conditions. Such perfection was short-lived, however. The very day after the fair winds had hurried the vessel along to her record twenty-four-hour run of 251 miles, they were sucked from her sails in an instant and she was left wallowing in a flat calm. People who had been shivering with cold before, now found themselves sweltering in steam-bath humidity. Everybody started suffering with sweat rashes and other skin complaints, and collapses from heat exhaustion became frequent.

But there was still worse discomfort to come. After a three-day refuelling stop at Port Sudan there was a brief respite when skipper Mike Kichenside hove to for a day's snorkelling on Sanganeb Reef – where the variety of marine life was almost as spectacular as on Vesuvius Reef – and then *Eye of the Wind* started pitching and rolling violently as she motored into strong headwinds and a heavy swell towards Port Suez. The combination of this heaving motion and the stifling tropical heat was already causing considerable misery, when intermittent engine failure added a further dimension of unpleasantness. Every few hours Royal Navy Engineer Brian Holmes had to sweat in the unbearable 130°F sauna-bath atmosphere of the engine room to change the filters, which were becoming blocked repeatedly by dirt in the poor quality fuel taken on at Port Sudan. Every time he had to do it, the ship would be blown back the way she had come and, as she drifted at the mercy of the wind, she would occasionally turn beam-on to the waves, lurching alarmingly in the troughs. When the wind rose to force 8, Mike Kichenside finally decided to seek refuge in the safe anchorage of Merser Zeituna, one hundred and fifty nautical miles south of Port Suez.

Meanwhile, Colonel John Hines, who was coordinating our visit to Egypt, was growing increasingly anxious as he waited in Cairo for news of the ship's arrival. Not only were all his carefully laid plans for the expedition's visit under threat – in particular a major welcoming reception to be attended by a host of local VIPs including the Governor of Suez – but as time dragged on and there was still no definite ETA, he began to worry for the safety of *Eye of the Wind*. Matters were further complicated by a breakdown in communications – there were problems with both telephone and telex links in Egypt at the time – as a result of which, there was some confusion at his end as to exactly where *Eye of the Wind* was and what was wrong with her. Egyptian naval officers that he spoke to thought that she was probably at Shadwan rather than Merser Zeituna and were firmly of the opinion that even if she was not in immediate danger she was likely to be in need of assistance. At this point he started to mount his relief mission.

He borrowed a MIG fighter from the Egyptian Air Force and, jammed into the observer's seat, bade the pilot find the brigantine. As

[253]

the jet roared past our flagship a few minutes later no one aboard dreamed that 'our man in Cairo' was in it.

Having located the ship, he set off overland with a bus and a three-ton truck, hoping to reach the point on the coast near enough to *Eye of the Wind* to make contact, but this plan had to be dropped when it was discovered that the local road maps and the naval charts of the coast did not coincide. It was then that he went to Hurghada, where Mobil very kindly made available the helicopter from which he lowered his message. The oil rig supply and maintenance boat *Alex Tide*, on which the YEs were taken off at dawn on 9 September, was provided by Aramco.

The conditions were so bad by that time that it took *Alex Tide* two hours to manoeuvre safely alongside *Eye of the Wind*, and on the journey to Ras Shuakir – from where the YEs were taken to Port Suez by bus – everybody on board suffered from seasickness, including the regular crew. The winds continued to get stronger during the next few days, rising to force 10 as *Eye of the Wind* – resupplied with fresh water, food and fuel by *Alex Tide*, and manned by a skeleton crew – battled on to Port Ibrahim. She arrived there a week later, having taken a terrific battering. The engine had continued to give trouble, her jolly boat was badly damaged in one particularly strong gale, and the rigging was severely strained. It had been a tough trip.

During their two-week stay in Egypt, the main project in which the YEs were involved was the planting of 1,500 trees at a communal area in Ishmalia. It was no easy task since only the most primitive tools were available and it was necessary to work eight hours a day in sizzling temperatures in order to make up the time lost by their late arrival. Despite this, they also managed to visit the Sinai and to go on a camel trek to the pyramids before rejoining *Eye of the Wind* at Port Said to start the next stage of their journey.

This took them the 1,400 miles to Alassio, on Italy's Mediterranean coast, where *Eye of the Wind* was to rendezvous with the Goodyear airship *Europa* and the Army Air Corps Beaver for the last – and visually most spectacular – of Operation Drake's scientific projects. This was a unique experiment that involved taking simultaneous pollution samples from the sea and the air in and above the Gulf of Genoa, where the build-up of toxic trace metals in particular has been causing concern. The experiment, for which a sailing ship was perfectly suited since it would not itself add to the pollution, was to be carried out in co-operation with the United Nations Environment Programme (UNEP) as part of the Mediterranean Pollution Monitoring and Research Programme (MEDPOL).

British Caledonian Airways kindly flew Andrew Mitchell and

[254]

myself from London, and we arrived at Alassio in time to co-ordinate the experiment. At first, however, there was no sign of airship, Beaver or brigantine. The weather was appalling, but in the late afternoon the sky began to clear and I saw *Europa* approaching from the sea like an attacking Zeppelin. The tubby silver cigar looked really menacing as she flew low under the rain clouds and I felt that we were going back in time. The appearance of the high-winged Beaver, piloted by the two Mikes, added to this impression, and when dawn came, there, to complete the picture, was *Eye of the Wind* resting at anchor on a mirror-like sea two hundred yards off the beach.

I felt slightly out of place as I stood on Alassio Beach in desert uniform with a radio, whilst bikini-clad holiday-makers strolled by.

For once, everything went like clockwork – even the weather turned out just the way we needed it for the four-day exercise – and it developed into a marvellously colourful and exciting international occasion. It was also highly successful.

Professor Wolfgang Nurnberg, Director of the Institute of Applied Physical Chemistry at the Nuclear Research Centre in Julich, West Germany, supervised the collection of atmospheric samples from the *Europa*, while aboard *Eye of the Wind* Professor Aristeo Renzoni, Director of the Institute of Comparative Anatomy at the University of Sienna, and a principal investigator in UNEP's MEDPOL projects, took charge of the collection of neuston samples. At the same time, Dr Brian Wanamaker, an oceanographer from the Saclant Research Centre at La Spezia in Italy, studied temperature profiles across the Gulf using expendable bathythermographs, which relayed information from below the surface of the water to instruments aboard the ship.

The air samples showed levels of atmospheric mercury contamination to be two hundred and eighty times higher over Genoa than other non-industrial areas of the coastline. The airship proved a perfect craft for collecting them, being able to float over potential pollution hot spots whilst special instruments 'sniffed' the air.

In many ways this brief Mediterranean episode was one of the highlights of Operation Drake. Everyone was struck by the great spirit of international co-operation, the tremendous energy which was put into co-ordinating a complex operation, and the feeling that something really worth while had been achieved. And there was a bonus in that the dramatic newspaper and television pictures that flashed round the world showing *Europa* hovering above *Eye of the Wind* gripped the public imagination and did much to boost our image. The airship and the brigantine even featured on the set of special stamps issued by Jersey to commemorate Operation Drake.

As she left the Mediterranean, the ship put in to Gibraltar to have her rigging checked and to have her engine overhauled, and while this was happening the YEs went by hydrofoil to Morocco, where, having taken a train to the romantic city of Marrakesh, they went climbing in the snows of the Atlas Mountains with Hamish Brown.

And then it was time to set sail on what was truly the last leg of the voyage – Gibraltar to the Channel Islands, and then Plymouth, finally arriving in London on 13 December 1980, four hundred and three years to the day after Drake had set out.

Chapter Twenty-Nine

Dateline: Tower Bridge, London, 13 December 1980

Shortly before noon on a blustery Saturday morning, *Eye of the Wind* passed under Tower Bridge, with Kenyan YE Mwingi Japan at the helm, to mark the end of the great adventure. It was a wonderfully colourful and exciting occasion for the huge crowd of ten thousand who lined the banks of the river and packed into St Katharine's Dock to witness the homecoming, and a very moving moment for the many YEs from earlier phases who had made the pilgrimage from as far away as New Zealand to be in at the finish and to be reunited with the friends they had made during their time with the expedition. As the ship covered the last few hundred yards of the thirty-six-thousand miles she had logged altogether during her two years away, Capital Radio's David Briggs broadcast a live commentary from a vantage point in the lubberhole, half-way up the mainmast, while all around him the crew lined the yardarms. A flotilla of small boats and a flypast by the Army Air Corps Beaver and an RAF Hercules added an extra bit of theatre and helped to ensure that the enterprise closed on a dramatic note. At precisely 12.25 p.m. *Eye of the Wind* docked at St Katharine's pier to be greeted by the Lord Mayor, and it was all over.

For the YEs who brought her home, the excitement was high to the very end. After stopping off at Guernsey and Jersey – where, thanks to Adrian Troy's committee they were given a fantastic welcome – they then encountered some of the worst weather of all, as a force 11 gale blew up, and for six hours continuously the anemometer was off the clock as the winds topped seventy miles per hour. The result was that the ship's arrival in Plymouth was delayed until the early hours of the morning, by which time the reception committee of VIPs had long since gone home! However as our Australian Chairman Denis Cordner, who had made a special flight to the Channel Islands to join the ship for the final leg, said, 'I wouldn't have missed it for the world.'

Things quietened down a bit after that, although the winds were still fresh, and *Eye of the Wind*'s crew sailed up the Channel in fine style. On the eve of their triumphant arrival at Tower Bridge, they stayed at

Greenwich, where some of the more exuberant YEs had a brush with the law when they decided to demonstrate their prowess at going aloft by climbing the mast of the Cutty Sark at three o'clock in the morning!

The following week was filled with one endless round of parties, functions and VIP visits. Each of the four main land phases – Panama, PNG, Sulawesi and Africa – held their own special reunion parties, where the adventures were relived, the good times recalled, and even the hardships remembered fondly as being not nearly so bad as they had seemed at the time. Thousands of people came to look round the ship and also to visit the exhibition that was mounted to tell the story of the expedition and for the musically minded there was even a concert of nautical themes that included the first public performance of the 'Eye of the Wind Rhapsody' which had been specially commissioned by Capital Radio from composer Gordon Giltrap.

The highpoint of that memorable week was when our Patron, Prince Charles, visited the ship and the exhibition. Among the many YEs he met and chatted to was Cathy Davies, whom he had personally sponsored and who had written to him during the expedition to let him know how she was getting on and to describe in detail some of her adventures – including her harrowing experiences on the Balboa Trail in Panama. She had been thrilled to receive a charming handwritten reply from the Prince, who, among other things, expressed the hope that the insects were not biting too hard!

A few weeks earlier he had given a special interview to Press Association reporter Martin White (who had visited us in PNG, Sulawesi and Kenya) in which he reflected at length on the expedition which he had done so much to get off the ground in the first place, and which he had followed with close interest from start to finish. He agreed that in some ways he would have welcomed the opportunity to take part himself – preferably in Kenya. 'I operate better in dry, hot climates rather than sticky ones,' he explained. But he added, with characteristic humour: 'I would probably have got lost – navigation was never my strong point!' The hardships would not have bothered him, he said. 'I am a great believer in the banging-your-head-against-a-brick-wall syndrome because it is marvellous when it stops. I think the great thing about putting up with difficult conditions, hardship, mosquitoes and swamps is that it is wonderful when it is over and you have this terrific sense of achievement. You really appreciate the things in life you normally take for granted, like a hot bath or a bed with sheets.'

Operation Drake, he said, was the sort of 'crazy expedition' that the British were particularly good at organising, and went on: 'We have it somehow in our national make-up, the ability to withstand, with an

[258]

amazing degree of good humour, the most appalling conditions. The fact that on this occasion it was combined with scientific research and social projects showed the host countries that the British were keen on helping generally throughout the world. It can have done nothing but produce more good will and favourable reactions.'

Six months after the ship came home, we were still busy tying up the loose ends of the expedition, but as things gradually began to wind down I had time at last for my own reflections on the whole extraordinary adventure.

In general terms, one of the most pleasing aspects was the fantastic response that the project generated all over the world and the warm welcome that we received from so many overseas governments. Indeed, it seemed to create international good will wherever we went. Proof of this was that all the host governments invited us to return. A special tribute must also be paid to the Armed Forces of all the nations involved. It is perhaps natural that such organisations should be interested in the training of young people in an adventurous way, but still it must be emphasised that without their co-operation and without the whole-hearted support of our own Royal Navy, Army and Royal Air Force, Operation Drake could never have succeeded as it did. Their enthusiasm for our cause was undoubtedly boosted by the fact that many of today's senior officers fought in the Second World War and so understand very well the need to fulfil Prince Charles' requirement of providing young people with a chance to face the challenges of war in a peacetime situation.

The response of the young people to the venture was also overwhelming. I never dreamed, when we first started planning the project, that we would end up by attracting very nearly sixty thousand applicants from twenty-eight countries – but it was powerful proof of the need for just the kind of inspiring opportunities we were offering. It was frustrating to have to turn down so many people but, as far as those we eventually selected were concerned, I think it is fair to say that we got it right 90 per cent of the time. We had only one boy who gave up through what I suspect was homesickness, and although a small number found things tougher than they had anticipated, it was to their credit that they kept going.

On the other hand, there were those who felt that they were not stretched far enough. In most cases this complaint arose because, having undergone a very rigorous selection process, they imagined that the whole expedition would be along exactly the same lines. They did not realise that the Selection Weekends were designed to present them with a concentration of the very worst they were likely to encounter in order to sort out the sheep from the goats. There were times during the

[259]

expedition when the going did get very hard indeed – but clearly it would have been impractical, and also unfair on the slightly less-aggressively daring souls, to turn every activity into a make-or-break challenge. Our YEs ranged from hard-bitten Zimbabweans, who had been fighting in the guerrilla war immediately prior to joining up with us, right through to teenage secretaries who had never been away from home before, and so, in terms of setting tests of physical stamina and endurance, it would have been difficult, clearly, to please all of the people all of the time. However, it is true that the maturity and capabilities of many of the YEs did take us by surprise, and, with the wisdom of hindsight, I regret that we were not able to give them more responsibility. The older ones, certainly, could have coped very happily with it.

From the point of view of communications, I can say without any doubt that as the overall leader of this vast enterprise I owed a great deal to the Royal Signals and the magnificent radios kindly loaned by Drake, MEL, Racal, Plessey and Marconi, plus the back-up telecommunication facilities generously provided by Unilever. I do not believe that any expedition has ever had such widespread communications that worked so well under such adverse circumstances. To carry a briefcase-size radio, operating on a rechargable dry battery with an aerial that you simply threw into a tree, and to know that wherever I was in the world I could usually speak to Room 5B was very comforting.

I feel that we have every reason to be enormously proud of the success of the scientific achievements that we helped to make possible. We were fortunate in having a marvellous bunch of scientists and Andrew Mitchell did an outstanding job as co-ordinator – a difficult task that was not made any easier by the fact that he was younger than most of the experts with whom he had to deal. Scientists will always fight for their own particular field of study and this was no different on Operation Drake. However, I was delighted that they were so pleased with the results of their research and impressed by the dedication with which they worked, in circumstances that were often less than perfect, to produce studies that have greatly enhanced the reputation of the Scientific Exploration Society. We should not forget the help of the Society's officers, especially the Honorary Secretary, Philip Harrison, and the Treasurer, Dan Graham, who did so much to assist us.

I was also pleasantly astonished by the number of discoveries that were made. Even in my most wildly optimistic moments I had never anticipated that there would be so many important breakthroughs in zoology, biology and archaeology. It just goes to show what you can do when you have a lot of highly motivated young people with good eyes and strong legs.

[260]

As for the command and control organisation – no praise is high enough for the staff who battled on in the dingy Central HQ, under the pavements of Whitehall, where daylight never penetrated and where the air was often foul. The gloomy atmosphere of 5B was not exactly conducive to inspired and efficient work, and yet George Thurstan, Jim Masters, Val Roberts, Ruth Mindel, Nigel Lang and everybody else who led a mole-like existence in the cellar soldiered on superbly. They were the ones who had to deal with the crises, absorb the bad news and fight the endless, desperate battle for funds without seeing very much of the fun at the front end of the expedition. Inevitably, the strain sometimes showed and I often noticed, when I was in the field and we were on top of the world because things were going well, how glum the voices sounded that came over the radio or the telephone from that Whitehall dungeon. Their only consolation was the satisfaction of knowing that without them none of it could have happened. There were also the kind friends in the Gestetner offices in London and throughout the world who had done so much to back us up.

Our Executive Committee, under the leadership of General Sir John Mogg, was absolutely first class, but there is no doubt that we could have done with a few more expert sailors among the members. With the best will in the world, I do not think that those of us on land really understood all the problems faced by the Skipper of *Eye of the Wind* and, equally, I suspect that Mike Kichenside did not really appreciate just how difficult things were when viewed from our dungeon HQ. This lack of liaison is a common fault in situations where a large sailing ship is being directed by a land-based committee, and were I to repeat this sort of operation I would try my best to have several first-rate sailors working hand-in-glove with us at all times.

Our biggest headaches were, without question, financial ones. We had to raise a great deal of money along the way and, with inflation soaring up to 22 per cent when we had budgeted for only 17 per cent, we found that we were constantly struggling to make ends meet. There were times when we were convinced that we would have to call the whole thing off, but in the end we were saved by the superhuman efforts of our fund-raisers and the wise counselling of our Treasurer, Frank Taylor, and his staff at Esso.

Prince Charles quite rightly sums up expeditions as being like banging one's head against a brick wall – and that is as true for the organisers as it is for those taking part. Despite that, we were already planning our next venture before Operation Drake was over. More significantly, however, we were so overwhelmed by the response to the whole concept of Operation Drake and so encouraged by its overall success that we felt we had to do something to keep alive that spirit of

[261]

adventure which we had instilled in so many youngsters round the world. The result is the Operation Drake Fellowship – a permanent organisation based at St Katharine's Dock through which former YEs and other youngsters will be able to launch projects of their own, and from which we hope to be able to help many less fortunate young people.

The full extent to which the experience of Operation Drake changed the attitudes, broadened the outlooks and affected the lives of the YEs taking part will be better known when Mr Kitson Smith of Bristol University's Careers Advisory Service completes a detailed analysis of three hundred before-and-after questionnaires. But already the indications are that it has given many of them a taste for further adventure and in some cases it has undoubtedly led to a complete reappraisal of values and priorities and thereby opened up an exciting new approach to life. Philip Beale is arranging an expedition to PNG in search of further challenges, while American YE Terry Linehan is now planning an epic canoe journey in the South Pacific. New Zealander Erwin Van Asbeck sailed a forty-five-foot sloop across the Pacific, Miles Clark, now an officer in the Royal Green Jackets, went off to study sea cows in the Aleutian Islands, and Chris Willis from Jersey travelled through Oman, Ceylon and Nepal. Scotsman Robert Hunter took off for Alaska, Australians Alan Keller and Alan Poole organised a sailing expedition for young people round the coast of Australia, and Philip Oakes trained for work in the Pacific Islands. Margaret McKee travelled through central Australia, Indonesia and Asia, before moving on to Europe, and Tony Roberts, from London, went on a photographic expedition in the Sudan and Eritrean refugee camps.

Of course, not everyone's life will have altered dramatically – many will have gone back happily to their jobs, resumed their studies or picked up the threads of their careers. But I hope nobody will ever forget the experience, and for some, maybe, it will prove to have been the greatest thing that ever happened to them. As David Briggs told Capital Radio listeners when *Eye of the Wind* passed under Tower Bridge: 'And so, Operation Drake has now finally come to an end, but for those who took part the memory will live on forever.' Indeed, as Margot types this last chapter, Jim Masters is renovating a Thames barge for the HQ of the Operation Drake Fellowship, George Thurstan, John Whitney, John Hines, Edward Thorneycroft and Anthony Joliffe are raising money, and Simon Ames of British Caledonian Airways has just fixed a flight for me to Central America to recce a site for a new expedition. The wheels are turning again – but in truth they have never stopped. Thankfully, there is no shortage of people who will follow the example of Sir Francis Drake and keep the pioneer spirit alive.

Appendix A

Operation Drake's International Organisation

Patron
HRH The Prince of Wales KG, KT, GCB.

Honorary President
Walter H Annenberg KBE

Executive Committee
General Sir John Mogg GCB, CBE, DSO, DL (Chairman)
Lt Col. JN Blashford-Snell MBE, RE (Director of Operations and Deputy Chairman)
Col. AJ Hines MC, TD (Special Projects)
Mr GW Baker CBE, VRD (Foreign Affairs)
Sir Reginald Bennett Kt. VRD, MA, BCh
Sir David Checketts KCVO (Chairman Publicity Committee)
Mr M Drummond DL, JP (Chairman Ship Sub-Committee)
Maj. PJ Marett RE (Secretary)
Capt. J Masters (Director Logistics and Personnel)
Miss Ruth Mindel (Director Commercial Sponsorship)
Mr LM Price MA
Mr FC Rodger MD, MCh., FRCS, DOMS (Chairman Scientific Sub-Committee)
Mr FA Taylor CA (Treasurer)
Capt. GEF Thurstan (Director of Administration)

Area Organisers in Great Britain
Mr GR Snailham MA (Berkshire and Hampshire), Maj. JA Cuthill (Cornwall), Mr JW Kendall (Devon), Mrs JG Groves (Dorset), Mr HR Pratt-Boorman CBE, MA (Kent), Mr P Edgson-Wright (Kent), Mrs L Dawson (Scotland), Maj. MG Gambier (Somerset), Miss A Olley (Surrey), Col. R Weare (Yorkshire), Maj. WHG Kingston (Yorkshire), Mr J Edwards (Yorkshire and the North East)

Other major supporters in Great Britain
Dr J Alexander MA, PhD, FSA, Mr J Austin, Mr CCP Barnes, Mr AE Bartholomew, Baron Rolf Beck, Lt Col. JA Benham Crosswell RE, Mrs JN Blashford-Snell, Capt. P Blundell RE, Miss P Boydell TD, Capt. D Bromley-Martin RN retd, Miss N Brydon, Mr Wally Buchanan, Mr M Cable, Maj. Gen. and Mrs FG Caldwell, Dr AC Campbell BSc, DPhil, Commodore JH Carlill OBE and the Staff of *HMS Drake*, Maj. and Mrs JR Chapman, Sqn Ldr and Mrs D Chidell, Mr D Chipp, Capt. CPR Collis RN retd, Mr E Cornes MC, Mr and Mrs A Davis, Lt Col. EAE Durey MBE, RE, Mr JR Elms, Mr G Exelby, Sqn Ldr J Fox RAF, Mrs M Gambier, Capt. A George RN, Mr D Gestetner, Lt Col. DHC Gordon-Lennox, Grenadier Guards, Maj. P Gough REME, Capt. JG Graham RAPC, Mr and Mrs PD Harrison, Prof. and Mrs GAD Haslewood, Mrs AJ Hines, Mr D

Horobin, Maj. Gen. and Mrs AGC Jones, Mrs P King, Mr Kitson Smith MA, DEOC, Brig. CA Landale ADC, Maj. PA Lenthall, Capt. L Lodge RAMC, Sgt N Long R Signals, Mr D Lowry, Mr J Mallinson, Dr KS McLachlan BA, PhD, Mr and Mrs M Mindel, Lady Mogg, Mr K Monck, Mr N Munn, Mr N Neilson DC, Air Commodore BH Newton OBE, Ft Lt J Oldring RAF, Col. KH Osborne DSO, OBE, MC, TD, Mr EG Pratt, Mr R Raison, Gp Capt. WSO Randle CBE, AFC, DFM, Miss J Reid, Dr CH Roads, Mrs B Rogers, Mr D Russell, Mr K Shard, Cmdr GJ Shaw OBE, RN, Miss B Snell, Mrs B Starling, Mr HM Stephen, Dr S Sutton, MA, DPhil, Mrs GEF Thurstan, Maj. PTJ Tidman MBE, Mr A Tillotson, Mr M Tindall, Mr W Tute,Miss L Van Gruisen, Miss S Welsey-Smith, Prof. ER Whatley PhD, FRS, Mr M White, Mr J Whitney, Maj. AR Westcob DWR

Australasian Organisation

a. *Australian Headquarters*
Mr GD Cordner (National Co-ordinator), Mr RD Malcolmson (Victorian Chairman), Mr AG Cheetham, Mr LA Gursansky, Mr DLC Gibbs, Mrs C Consett (Secretary), Miss BG Park (Honorary Secretary), Maj. Gen. TF Cape (Canberra)

b. *Victorian Selection Committee*
Mr RD Malcolmson (Chairman), Mr JB Gough, Dr P Law, Mr S McGregor, Mr HAL Moran, Miss D Pizzey, Miss E Raut, Mrs J Searby, Mr J Shone, Commodore DHD Smyth, Mr KC Stone, Miss L O'Donoghue (Honorary Secretary)

c. *New South Wales – State Committee*
Sir William Pettingell (Chairman), Col. AR Glanvill (Publicity and Chief Liaison Officer), Mr PT Cabban (Selection), Maj. WMM Deacock, Mr W Manning, Mr E J Neal, Maj. Gen. JW Norrie, Commander TR Vasey (Training and Logistics), Mr DR Murphy (Secretary)

d. *New South Wales – Selection Committee*
Mr P Cabban (Chairman), Mr H Burman, Mr B Callaghan, Mr D Clarke, Mr J Cruickshank, Lt Col. D Gillies, Mr W Manning, Mr S Milgate, Australian Sail Training Association (Barquentine 'New Endeavour')

e. *Western Australia*
Mr D Lawe-Davies (Chairman), Miss J Bone, Mr C Sambell, Maj. KJ Wolfe, Mr R Jenkin, Mr J Zommers, Mr J Nicholson, Mr A Allen, Mr N Steel, Mr J Graham, Maj. P Drake-Brockman, Dr RG Chittleborough, Mr C B Paul, Dr PA Morton – President, Australian Sports Medicine Federation – Western Australian Branch

f. *Queensland*
Mr R Douglass (Chairman), Miss V Stafford

g. *South Australia*
Mr R Calversbert (Chairman)

h. *Tasmania*
Alderman DR Plaister

i. *New Zealand Committee*
Dr JS Chapman-Smith (Chairman), Mr G Wiles, Mr P Grayburn, Mr P Rose, Mrs I Wilson, Brig. J Aitken, Mr O Cook, Col. F Rennie

Helpers
Mrs A Gluckman, Mr H Thomas, Maj. G Shattky, Mr F Sweeney

Operation Drake (Canada)
Honorary President – Gen. Jacques A Dextraze CC, CBE, CMM, DSO, CD, LLD
Executive Committee – Mr Douglas H Murray (Chairman), Mr Stanley Burke, Prof. Robert JS Gray BA, LLB, LLM, Mr Peter AW Green FCA, ACMA, Mr William B Harris BA, MA, Col. Frank F McEachren CM, CVO, ED, CD, Mrs Mary J Murray, Mr Hugh L Smith BA, BLS
Vancouver Rep – Mrs J Henderson
International Education Consultants – Reford-McCandless, International Consultants Corporation

Communications & Printing Consultants – Gestetner (Canada) Ltd

Operation Drake (Channel Islands)
Mr AEO'D Troy (Chairman) and Mrs Troy, Mr REN Bellows (Treasurer), Mr TF Green, Mrs M Tucker (Guernsey rep)

Operation Drake (Costa Rica)
HE Mr K Hamylton-Jones CMG, Mr SE Warder OBE

Operation Drake (Fiji)
Mr JH Ah Koy OBE

Operation Drake (Iceland)
Prof. Sturia Fridriksson (Co-ord Director/Scientific Director), Mr AVJ Edwards, Mr Tutihalldorsson

Operation Drake (Indonesia)
HE Mr Adam Malik – President
Committee – Prof. Dr Didin S Sastrapradja, Indonesian Institute of Sciences; Dr Julius Tahija, Chairman PT Caltex Pacific Indonesia (Chairman); Mr Robin Leonard, President Director BAT Indonesia; Mr Frank Morgan, Mochtar, Karuwin and Komar; Mr Jeffrey McNeely, World Wildlife Fund; Mr Rudy Schouten, Hilton International Hotels; Mr Louis Fuller, PT International Nickel Indonesia; Mr John Blower, Project Director FAO/UNDP; Dr Aprilani Soegiarto, Director Nat. Inst. of Oceanography (Lon)
Other Supporters – HE Mr Terence O'Brien CMG, MC, British Ambassador to Indonesia; Col. Denis Whatmore, Military Attache; Lt Col. Prasanto, Liaison Officer; Mr Gordon Benson OBE, Adviser; Mrs Isobel Hughes; Mr Michael Sumner, Hon British Consul Surabaya

Operation Drake (Federal Republic of Germany)
Capt. RA Festorazzi RE, Frau K Wilms

Operation Drake (Hong Kong)
Maj. Gen. CWB Purdon CBE, MC, Maj. J Pickard (PR), Mr M Stevenson (Sponsor Coord), Mr D Pettigrew (Selection), Mr T Bedford

Operation Drake – Kenya Steering Committee
Mr JC Sutton (Chairman), Lt Col. CO Mkunguzi (Army), Mr Richard Leakey (Museums), Mr Daniel Sindiyo (WCMD), Mr D Andere (KREMU), Mr J Onyango (Forestry), *Public Relations* – Mrs Nola Bearcroft, Miss Jan Hemsing

Operation Drake (Nepal)
Mr AVJ Edwards

Operation Drake (Panama)
Col. F Flores, Maj. E Aguillera, Maj. AL Purcell, Archbishop Marcos G McGrath, Dr Reina Torres De Arauz, Mr Jack Davis, Mr G De St Malo (Chairman), Mr and Mrs M Kourany, Mr R Novey, Mr EA Blennerhassett, Lic C Patterson

Operation Drake (Papua New Guinea)
Col. K Noga, OBE PNGDF (Chairman), HE Mr DK Middleton CBE, Mr IR Andersen, Mr BT Blick, Mr EM Carter, Capt. JWH Cornish, Mr D Franklin, Maj. JH Girling, Mr R Grimmer, Lt Col. TM Hillier RAAMC, Miss S Jogo, Mr K Kisokau, Mrs J MacKeague, Maj. Sio Miasa, PNGDF, Mr and Mrs A Musicka, Capt. NJStC Porteous, Mr RC Sandbach, Mr R Thurecht, Mr L Varo

Operation Drake (USA)
Joint Honorary Chairmen – HE Kingman Brewster, HE Peter Jay
Executive Committee – Sir Gordon White KBE (Chairman), Mr Geoffrey S Barnett, Sir Gordon Booth KCMG, CVO, Hon. Henry E Catto Jr, Mr Russell H Gurnee, Maj. Derek T Jackson, Hon. Mrs Juanita M Kreps Jr, Hon. Emil Mosbacher Jr, Mr William T Seawell, Mr Peter Stanford, Mr Henry W Taft, Mr Barclay H Warburton III
Major helpers – Capt. Yaacov Adam, Mr Richard Barkle, Mr and Mrs Ralph Barnett, Miss Eileen Freidman, Mr Tom Goodman, Mr William Gowen, Maj.

Kelvin Kent, Mr Lee Laino, Mr Bob Lewis, Mr John Linehan, Mr and Mrs Vincent Martinelli, Mr A O'Brien, Dr Dan Osman, Mr Otto Roethenmund, Mr Robert Roethenmund, Mr Robert Silver, Prof. Norman Thrower, Mr John Wilcox, Mr John Noble Wilford

Operation Drake (Zimbabwe)
Capt. PB Fairgrieve RGJ, Mr G Handover, Col. CLS Henshaw, Mr SD O'Donnell

Directing Staff Operation Drake (1978–80)

Many of the staff carried out general duties, specialities where appropriate are shown in brackets. All scientists (except archaeologists) are indicated thus: (Sci). The expedition was divided into 10 phases, numbered 1 to 9, but including a phase 8a.

Eye of the Wind
Mr P Anderson (Watch Leader throughout) – Australia, Miss P Armstrong (Capital Radio rep ph 3–4) – GB, Mr B Arnvidavson (Watch Leader ph 8) – Iceland, Miss L Batt-Rawden (Capital Radio rep ph 5–8) – GB, Mr K Cameron (Engineer ph 2) – GB, Capt. CPR Collis RN Retd (Master ph 1–2) – GB, Mr G Clarkson (Bosun ph 1–3) – Canada, CMEMN (P) B Coupland RN (Engineer – ph 6) – GB, Mr U Danielsson (Watch Leader ph 8–9) – Iceland, Maj. F Esson AAC (Chief Instructor ph 3–5) – GB, Dr W Foster (MO ph 5–6) – GB, Mr S Glenn, CRO R Grass BEM, RN (Signals Officer ph 9), Mr R Grey (Watch Leader ph 5–6) – GB, Dr J Haigh (MO ph 8–8a) – GB, Capt. J Heck R Signals (Signals Officer ph 4) – GB, Dr P Holdway (Marine Biologist, throughout) – GB, CMEN (P) B Holmes RN (Engineer ph 8–9) – GB, Capt. M Kichenside (Master ph 3–9) – GB, Miss M Kichenside (ph 3–9) – GB, Capt. K Jolley RE (Chief Instructor ph 6) – GB, Cpl B Martin R Signals (Signals Officer ph 6) – GB, Cpl R Merritt RAF (Engineer ph 1) – GB, Dr D Nixon (MO ph 9) – GB, Dr N Pearce (MO ph 1) – GB, Mr B Phillips (Bosun ph 4–9) – Australia, Miss L Reiter (Purser throughout) – Australia, Mr G Robson (Watch Leader ph 1), Mr CJ Sainsbury (Watch Leader, Chief Photographer, throughout) – GB, Dr H Savill (MO ph 4–6) – GB, Cpl R Secker R Signals (Signals Officer ph 1–2) – GB, Cpl R Shortis R Signals (Signals Officer ph 8–9) – GB, CPO R Shrimpton RN (Engineer ph 4), Dr I Swingland (Sci/Project Leader Seychelles) – GB, Mr A Timbs (Mate throughout) – GB, Miss E Tonnison (A/Purser ph 5–6) – Australia, WOI G Widdowson R Signals (Signals Officer ph 8–8a) – GB, Capt. A Wildgoose RAEC (Chief Instructor ph 8) – GB
NB – Ship's crew also operated on land.

Panama
Maj. E Aguillera and the men of the Guardia Nacional, Miss C Ash (Sci) – GB, Maj. and Mrs L Batty – GB, Miss C Bertschinger (Nurse) – GB, Lt Col JN Blashford-Snell MBE, RE (Director of Operations) – GB, Mr D Briggs (Capital Radio) – GB, Cpl J Brown RE (Diver) – GB, Ft Lt and Mrs M Cameron (Diver/

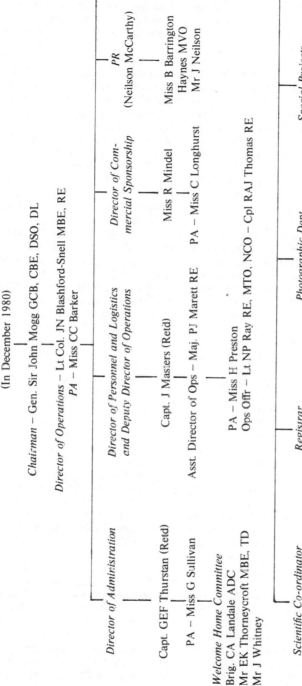

OPERATION DRAKE

Central HQ Organisation
(In December 1980)

Chairman – Gen. Sir John Mogg GCB, CBE, DSO, DL

Director of Operations – Lt Col. JN Blashford-Snell MBE, RE
PA – Miss CC Barker

Director of Personnel and Logistics and Deputy Director of Operations

Capt. J Masters (Retd)

Asst. Director of Ops – Maj. PJ Marett RE

PA – Miss H Preston
Ops Offr – Lt NP Ray RE, MTO, NCO – Cpl RAJ Thomas RE

Director of Com-mercial Sponsorship

Miss R Mindel

PA – Miss C Longhurst

PR
(Neilson McCarthy)

Miss B Barrington
Haynes MVO
Mr J Neilson

Special Projects
Col. AJ Hines MC, PD

Director of Administration

Capt. GEF Thurstan (Retd)

PA – Miss G Sullivan

Welcome Home Committee
Brig. CA Landale ADC
Mr EK Thorneycroft MBE, TD
Mr J Whitney

Registrar
Mrs V Roberts
Asst Miss P. Windsor Brown

Photographic Dept
Mr CJ Sainsbury
Mr N Lang

TV Film Team (phases 1–5)
Mr A Bibby
Mr R Gustavsen
Mr S Kennedy

Scientific Co-ordinator
Mr AW Mitchell
Asst Miss M Mabee

Admin Staff) – GB, Sgt DA Cartwright REME (Chief Fitter) – GB, Sgt M Christie RE (Aerial walkway) – GB, Mrs L Dawson (Admin Staff) – GB, Dr D Duggan (Forester) – GB, Miss S Everett (PA) – GB, Sgt H Elliott RE (Stores NCO) – GB, S/Sgt S Gair R Signals (Signals NCO) – GB, Sig D Gamble R Signals (Signaller) – GB, Mr A Garside (Admin Staff) – GB, L/Sgt A Gill SG (Signals NCO) – GB, L/Cpl J Gilluly US Army – USA, Ft Lt A Grey RAF (Diver) – GB, Maj. JG Groves 17/21 L (Field Leader ph 1) – GB, Mr P Hanson – GB, Police Cdt J Hockley – GB, Mr M Horton (Chief Archaeologist) – GB, L/Cpl D Hubbard US Army – USA, Mr P Hudson (Sci) – GB, Mr A Johnstone Coldstream Guards – GB, Mr J Kendall – GB, Cpl G Kirby 1WFR (Signals NCO) – GB, Capt. C Lawrence SG – GB, Dvr D Limbu, Gurkha Tpt Regt – Nepal, Spr M Limbu QGE – Nepal, Mr N Linsay (Sci) – GB, Piper R Little SG (Piper) – GB, Mr A Lonsdale (Magnetometer expert) – GB, Cpl C Lothian RAF (Diver) – GB, Dr D Mabberley (Sci) – GB, Miss M Mabee (Archaeologist) – USA, Miss C Mackenzie (Sci) – GB, Mr AW Mitchell (Sci Coord) – GB, WOI M Moody RAOC (Diver) – GB, Cpl B Ranner RAF (Diver) – GB, Cfn G Pengelly REME (Fitter) – GB, Sgt R Pringle-Scott RAF (Underwater Photographer) – GB, Miss M Sasson (Archaeologist) – GB, Sgt R Skene RAF (Diver) – GB, Capt. R Stafford-Curtis RAOC (Diver) – GB, Mr A Sugden (Sci) – GB, Cpl RAJ Thomas RE (Fitter/Boatman) – GB, Capt. (retd) GEF Thurstan (Deputy Field Leader) – GB, Mr R Williamson (Diver) – GB, Maj. A Westcob (Field Leader) – GB, Capt. J Winter RE (QM) – GB, Dr W Wint (Sci) – GB

Papua New Guinea

Capt. R Bampfylde 15/19 H – GB, Miss CC Barker (PA) – GB, Mr I Bennett (Diver) – Panama, Miss C Bertschinger SRN (Nurse) – GB, Lt Col. JN Blashford-Snell MBE, RE (Comd) – GB, Dr D Bowdler (MO) – GB, Mr J Bourne-May, Coldstream Guards – GB, Cpl M Boxall R Signals (Signals NCO) – GB, L/Cpl C Butfoy REME (Fitter) – GB, Maj. (retd) JR Chapman MBE – GB, WOI L Chandler RE (QM) – GB, Cpl D Clamp RAF (Diver) – GB, Dr L Cook (Sci) – GB, Miss C Davies – GB, Dr R Domrow (Sci) – Australia, Third Offr C Downham WRNS (Adjutant) – GB, Dr P Driscoll (Sci) – Australia, Miss M Dunn WRAC, TA – GB, Pte P Durey TA (Diver) – GB, Mr C Enzer (Diarist) – GB, Capt. A Evans, Coldstream Guards – GB, Dr I Fanning (Sci) – Australia, Lt The Hon T Fitzherbert SG – GB, Sgt L Gallagher BEM, RE (Aerial walkway) – GB, Maj. (retd) M Gambier – GB, Mr B Gaskell (Sci) – GB, Mrs J Girling (Nursing Sister) – Australia, Viscount Gough – GB, Dr S Goosem (Sci) – Australia, L/Cpl C Grant SG (Piper) – GB, Mr R Grey – GB, Miss E Guardia – Panama, Cpl M Gurung QGE – Nepal, Sgt J Hill – GB, Dr D Holdsworth (Sci) – PNG/GB, Lt J Horlick, Coldstream Guards – GB, Cpl R Jackson R Signals (Signals NCO) – GB, Dr D Johns (MO) – USA, Miss S Jogo (Liaison Officer) – PNG, Lt Col. R Jordan RE – GB, Cpl M Kerr RE – GB, Sister S Kerr (Nurse) – GB, Cpl G. Kirby 1WFR – GB, Capt. M Knox RHF (Ops Offr) – GB, Dr D Lamb (Sci) – Australia, Sgt P Lavers R Signals (Signals NCO) – GB, Dr Y Lubin (Sci) – PNG/USA, Sig M Luckes R Signals (Signaller) – GB, Mr and Mrs V Martinelli – USA, Dr J Martin (Sci) – GB, Capt (retd) J Masters – GB, Cpl B McGuiness RE – GB, Mr AW Mitchell (Sci co-ord) – GB, Capt. A Molony RE (Diving Officer) – GB, Dr J Montague (Sci) – PNG/USA, Lt D Monteith, Coldsteam Guards – GB, Mr P Morrissey – GB, Dr M Needell (MO) – USA, Mr W Neumiester – USA, Dr T Pratt (Sci) – PNG/USA, Dr DA Osman (MO) – USA, L/Cpl A Rai 7GR – Nepal, Lt N Ray RE, TA – GB, Mr I Redmond (Sci) – GB, Dr D Roberts (MO) – GB, Dr V Robson (MO) – GB, Mr R Roethenmund – USA, Dr H Savill (MO) – GB, Miss S Spicer-

Few (PRO) – GB, Cpl N Stevens, Coldstream Guards – GB, Dr R Stobbart (Sci) – GB, Dr M Swain (Sci) – GB, Miss M Szpak – USA, Mr Y Thami – Nepal, Cpl RAJ Thomas RE – GB, Mr M Tindall – GB, Miss E Van der Watt (Sci) – GB, Gdsm A Walker, Coldstream Guards – GB, Cpl D Watret RE – GB, SSgt. D Weaver RE – GB, Chief Tech D Whitehall RAF (Diver) – GB, Dr A Wilkins (Sci) – GB, Mr R Williamson (Diver) – GB, Dr W Wint (Sci) – GB, WOI L Winterburn REME (Chief Fitter) – GB, Mr R Woods (PNG Govt) – PNG/ Australia, Dr D Yates (MO) – GB, Dr M Zequiera (MO) – USA

Many officers and soldiers of the PNG Defence Force were also attached to Operation Drake as DS.

Indonesia (Sulawesi)
Lt R Bacon RCT (Diving Officer) – GB, Mr C Bailey – GB, Maj. A Bedford-Russell Int Corps (Sci) – GB, Miss C Bertschinger SRN (Nurse) – GB, Mrs D Bovey (Artist) – GB, L/Cpl A Bretherton RE (Surveyor) – GB, Mr M Brendle (Sci) – GB, LAC M Brindle RAF (Diver) – GB, Mr A Budiman (Sci) – Indonesia, Maj. E Carradus RE (QM) – GB, Sgt DA Cartwright REME (Chief Fitter) – GB, Mr C Chute – GB, Sgt J Cornish 15/19 H – GB, WOII K Crawford D & D (A/QM) – GB, Cpl K Cunningham R Signals (Signals NCO) – GB, Mr D Darnaedi (Sci) – Indonesia, Mr P Darsono (Sci) – Indonesia, Pte P Durey TA – GB, Ir L Effendi – Indonesia, Mr B Gaskell (Sci) – GB, Miss M Garner SRN (Nurse) – GB, Dr I Gauntlett (MO) – GB, Mr G Grimes (Sci) – GB, Sgt N Gurung, Gurkha Signals – Nepal, Ir M Halin (Sci) – Indonesia, Miss B Holmes – GB, Sgt B Hooper R Signals (Signals NCO) – GB, Miss I Hughes – GB, Maj. (retd) DT Jackson (Field Leader) – GB, Dr Kastoro (Sci) – Indonesia, Dr P Kevan (Sci) – GB, Dr A Lack (Sci) – GB, Dr A Laurie (Sci) – GB, Capt. R Lloyd-Jones R Signals (Signals Officer) – GB, Sgt P Maye RE (Surveyor) – GB, Miss F Maut SEN

(Nurse) – GB, Mr E McGee – GB, Mr AW Mitchell (Sci coord) – GB, Mr J Morton – GB, Mr C Owen (Treasurer) – GB, Capt. (retd) B Powell – GB, Lt Kol. J Prasanto (Senior Liaison Officer) – Indonesia, Cpl M Prior RE – GB, Mr R Ridgeway (Photographer) – GB, Dr C Rees (Sci) – GB, Miss P Regent (PRO) – GB, Cpl J Rimmer RE (Aerial walkway) – GB, Mr D Smith (Cook) – GB, Capt. A Stasuik WRAC – GB, Mr R Sumner QOH – GB, Dr S Sutton (Sci) – GB, Maj. W Swales (Deputy Field Leader) – GB, Ir A Swarno Budi (Sci) – Indonesia, Mr B Timmis (Sci) – GB, Mr R Warwick-Smith (Sci) – GB, Dr R Watling (Sci) – GB, Dr C Watts (Sci) – Australia, Mr R Williamson (Diver) – GB

Kenya
Mr H Adan (Sci) – Kenya, Mrs F Alexander – Kenya, Col. M Badger DFC, AAC (Comd Beaver) – GB, Mr C Bailey – GB, Miss CC Barker (PA) – GB, Dr G Bates (MO) – GB, Sig J Bland R. Signals (Signaller) – GB, Lt Col. JN Blashford-Snell MBE, RE (Comd) – GB, Mrs JN Blashford-Snell, Miss I Brooke – GB, Lt H Brown RCT (MTO) – GB, Mr M Carter (Surveyor) – GB, Miss K Clark (Archaeologist) – GB, Lt P Cosgrove RNZE – New Zealand, Dr J Dalgleish (MO) – GB, Cpl N Davie R Australian Signals (Signaller) – Australia, Mr R Davis (Photographer) – GB, WOII T Doherty IG (RQMS) – GB, Mr J Dumont (Sci) – GB, Lt Col. EAE Durey MBE, RE (QM in Chief) – GB, Pte P Durey TA (Boats) – GB, Mr S Evans – GB, SSgt D Felton RE – GB, Capt. I Gardiner RM – GB, Viscount Gough – GB, Cpl R Gravett RE – GB, Cfn A Gupwell REME – GB, Col. AJ Hines MC, TD – GB, Mr M Horton (Archaeologist) – GB, Lt Col. S Huggett RE (QM) – GB, Cpl B Jenkins RE – GB, Capt. A Johnston 15/19 H – GB, Mr J Kendall – GB, Sister S Kerr SRN (Nurse) – GB, Mr A Laidlaw (Treasurer) – GB, Mr A Lali – Kenya, Cpl J Lathbury R Signals (Signals NCO) – GB, WOII J Leach RE – GB, Cpl J

Lebeter RE – GB, Miss C Longhurst (PRO) – GB, Miss M Mabee (Archaeologist) – USA, Sgt I McDonald RM (Diving Officer) – GB, Mr A MacKay (Sci) – Kenya, Capt. M Mans RE (Operations Officer) – GB, Maj. PJ Marett RE (Operations Officer) – GB, Mr C Mason – Zimbabwe, Cfn M McGuiness REME – GB, Mr AW Mitchell (Sci coord) – GB, Mrs V Martinelli – USA, Mr M Mugambe (Sci) – Kenya, Mr and Mrs KLT Norman – GB, Dr D Osman (MO) – USA, Cfn G Pengelly REME – GB, Miss H Preston – GB, Lt N Ray RE – GB, Mr I Redmond (Sci) – GB, L/Cpl M Richardson D & D – GB, Mr T Roberts – GB, Cpl A Sampson R Signals (Signals NCO) – GB, Mr GR Snailham – GB, Maj. M Sommerton-Rayner AAC, TA (Beaver Pilot) – GB, Mr E Soutter – GB, Sig P Spilling R Signals (Signaller) – GB, Miss J Stevens – GB, Miss M Szpak – USA, Sgt J Topping R Signals (Signals NCO) – GB, Cpl RAJ Thomas RE (MT, NCO) – GB,

Mr N Tremlett (Vet) – GB, Mr C Van Someren (Sci) – Kenya, Capt. C Weston-Baker QRIH – GB, Miss S Wilkinson SEN (Nurse) – GB

Egypt
Rfmn F Day RGJ – GB, Col. AJ Hines MC, TD – GB

Italy
Lt Col. JN Blashford-Snell MBE, RE – GB, Mr R Breder (Sci) – Fed Republic of Germany, Mr H Flucht (Sci) – Fed Republic of Germany, Mrs V Martinelli – USA, Mr AW Mitchell (Sci Coord) – GB, Prof H Nurnberg (Sci) – Fed Republic of Germany, Prof A Renzoni (Sci) – Italy, Dr B Wannamaker (Sci) – USA
The crew of the Goodyear Airship *Europa* was involved in operations in Italy.

Morocco
Mr H Brown – GB

Young Explorers

PHASE 1. (GB–Panama) G Arngrimsson (Iceland), E Van Asbeck (NZ), A Bonnick (UK), M Browne (UK), R Burke (Canada), S Campbell (UK), S Chadwick (UK), J Denny (UK), K Henderson (UK), M Henrys (UK), N Hopkins (UK), R Jackleman (UK), N Kean-Hammerson (UK), N Lang (UK), D Limbu (Nepal), M Limbu (Nepal), C McHugh (UK), M Newman (UK), D Newton (NZ), R O'Connor (UK), P Shea (UK), B Shopland (Canada), J Wright (UK).

PHASE 2. (Panama) S Arthur (UK), S Barrow (UK), I Bennett (Panama), R Bennett (Panama), T Burns (Canal Zone), J Bracewell (UK), J Calland (UK), M

Clark (UK), A Courtney (UK), C Davies (UK), K Drinkwater (UK), M Fong (Panama), D French (UK), T Grey (Canada), E Guardia (Panama), I Hillier (UK), H Mallinson (UK), D McAlpine (Canada), S McCallum (UK), J McGregor (UK), E McMillan (Panama), D Meechan (UK), R Murray (Canada), C Ong (UK), R Pascoe (Panama), N Peberdy (UK), H Preston (UK), A Richards (Canada), N Simpson (Canada), A Smith (Canada), F Welstead (UK), P Whitehouse (UK), J Wiggins (UK), C Willis (UK), M Wright (UK).

PHASE 3. (Panama–Fiji) R Adrian (Canada), J Barlow (Australia), L Batt-Rawden (UK), A Beresford Foster

(Australia), S Brown (Australia), B Buckley (UK), G Combes (Canada), M Creer (Canada), C Downes (USA), J Flavell (NZ), C Goy (Australia), W Hargroves (USA), A Houiellebecq (UK), J Howard (USA), C Lawrence (Canada), D Mills (UK), D Patterson (NZ), N Person (USA), G Rice (UK), D Rickleen (USA), T Spence (UK), S Turton (UK), J Wall (USA), I Murray White (UK), G Whitelaw (S Africa).

PHASE 4. (Fiji–PNG) P Beale (UK), S Budibent (UK), J Catt (UK), R Chandler (Australia), P Cosgrove-McGuirk (UK), S Davis (NZ), K Ditges (Germany), S Gambier (UK), A Gay (UK), L Gibbons (UK), W Goodwin (USA), C Hale (UK), G Harch (Australia), P Harrison (Australia), D Huber (UK), R Hunter (UK), A Keller (Australia), T Linehan (USA), M McKee (NZ), P Oakes (Australia), R Paterson (NZ), A Penney (UK), A Poole (Australia), C Richardson (UK), M Stockdale (Australia), J Suchy (Canada), N Waghorn (USA), G Watson (UK), P Wesley (UK).

PHASE 5. (PNG) T Akivi (Papua New Guinea), B Bathe (NZ), B Boloti (Papua New Guinea), D Brough (UK), C Buxton (UK), C Chapon (UK), R Charette (USA), M Clough (UK), S Collins (Australia), P Daur (Papua New Guinea), S Elisha (Papua New Guinea), F Elly (Papua New Guinea), A Fila (USA), K Foellmer (Canada), E Francis (Papua New Guinea), S Gibson (NZ), S Glass (USA), C Greham (Australia), G Griffiths (Australia), M Grosze (USA), C Hall (UK), M Heinrich (USA), J Henderson (Australia), C Hignell (UK), C Hobden (Australia), M Holt (Australia), J Hulo (Papua New Guinea), R Jacques (USA), J Johns (Papua New Guinea), S Jupuc (Papua New Guinea), S Kamia (Papua New Guinea), D Keeley (Australia), W Kepelei (Papua New Guinea), B Koiti (Papua New Guinea), G Kunlong (Papua New Guinea), J Kupul (Papua New Guinea), A Lakamanga (Papua New Guinea), B Laker (Papua New Guinea), F Lewis (Australia), H Lufa (Papua New Guinea), S Lulupa (Papua New Guinea), P Mann (Australia), D Mansell (UK), B McDonald (Canada), F Mingen (Papua New Guinea), K Morobe (Papua New Guinea), S Mountford (NZ), T Mouvaira (Papua New Guinea), C Munagun (Papua New Guinea), I Munei (Papua New Guinea), Q Narampan (Papua New Guinea), O Nimita (Papua New Guinea), P Om (Korea), B Pilokos (Papua New Guinea), B Rhind (Australia), P Sharpen (Papua New Guinea), H Sigurdardottir (Iceland), S Sinsick (Papua New Guinea), T Sipo (Papua New Guinea), M Steven (Papua New Guinea), D Tarnas (USA), L Thompson (UK), F Tomangana (Papua New Guinea), M Turnbull (UK), J Varagi (Papua New Guinea), P Vakaloloma (Fiji), J Violaris (Papua New Guinea), B Wamoi (Papua New Guinea), T Wanzing (Papua New Guinea), J Wemin (Papua New Guinea), A Wilcox (UK), V Wohinga (Papua New Guinea), W Yamuna (Papua New Guinea).

PHASE 6. (PNG–Sulawesi) R Baldock (Australia), A Beavis (Australia), M Brookes (Australia), W Bygrave (UK), D Coleman (Australia), H Erf (USA), T Du-Feu (UK), L Fogarty (Australia), K Gurung (Nepal), B Jackson (Canada), N Johnson (UK), C Kaczmarek (Australia), S Mattson (Australia), A McPherson (UK), C Merryweather (UK), A Miller (Australia), S Rice (Australia), S Rigley (UK), A Roberts (Australia), T Roberts (UK), A Savage (UK), A Short (Australia), R Tarlov (USA), L Wakefield (Australia), J Warne (UK), I Westlake (Australia), P Wright, (Australia), S Young (UK).

PHASE 7. (Sulawesi) N. Adwin (Indonesia), I Ain (Indonesia), T Alamsyah (Indonesia), B Atkinson (Australia), Atmaji (Indonesia), A Cannon (UK), L Carter (USA), E Cecil (USA), C Cheung (Hong Kong), C Cotton (USA), P Ellison (UK), N English (UK), D Etter (USA), C Flather (USA), R Hakim (Indonesia), J Hardjono (Indonesia), B Harris (USA), D Hudson

[271]

(Australia), E Jones (USA), A Latief (Indonesia), P Lau (Hong Kong), C Leung (Hong Kong), J Levens (USA), Puspa Liman (Indonesia), L Lumingas (Indonesia), A Lyall (Australia), M Mahamit (Indonesia), S Manning (UK), A Melville (USA), J Milbank (USA), D Moffat (Australia), B Om (Indonesia), T Parenghuam (Indonesia), E Reppie (Indonesia), S Richardson (UK), Z Ridayah (Indonesia), A Sabarung (Indonesia), E Setiawan (Indonesia), F Siu (Hong Kong), J Southey (Australia), Sularto (Indonesia), R Tantu (Indonesia), E Wardhana (Indonesia), M Wibisono (Indonesia), C Wong (Hong Kong).

PHASE 8. (Indonesia–Kenya) B Arnvioarson (Iceland), W Bird (UK), D Burroughs (Canada), J Byrne (UK), J Dank (USA), C Darrah (UK), E Dolan (USA), G De Francis (USA), T Hood (UK), C James (USA), S Llewelyn (UK), W Lowdon (UK), D Macleod (USA), E Marquis (UK), P Morris (USA), H Nisenbaum (Canada), H Pettigrew (UK), R Poskus (UK), M Schnitger (USA), M Smart (UK), R Titmarsh (UK), P Ward (UK).

PHASE 8a. (Kenya) R Araujo (Panama), C Avila (Panama), O Ayim (Kenya), S Ballantyne (UK), J Barnley (Kenya), J Bell (Kenya), F Brancato (Gibraltar), A Bridger (Zimbabwe), A Campbell (UK), T Catton (UK), D Chong (Hong Kong), F Davey (Kenya), P Dobbs (UK), D Elliot (UK), I Ellman-Brown (Zimbabwe), N Galma (Kenya), G George (Zimbabwe), A Gibson (UK), R Hopkins (UK), B Ingolfsdottir (Iceland), G Johnstone (UK), B Jude (UK), P Kamau (Kenya), K Kassam (Kenya), D King (Zimbabwe), B Kisilu (Kenya), R Knight (Kenya), K Kuck (Kenya), C Langat (Kenya), P Lawton (UK), A Maara (Kenya), H Madyavanhu (Zimbabwe), P Mangla (Kenya), R Mangoka (Kenya), A Mar (Fiji), A Marshall (Zimbabwe), C Mason (Zimbabwe), A Mazvidzo (Zimbabwe), S Mbuguah (Kenya), C Moscrop (Hong Kong), B Moss (UK), T Moss (UK), G Moyo (Zimbabwe), A Musiiwa (Zimbabwe), V Mutasa (Zimbabwe), S Ndegwa (Kenya), W Ndongi (Kenya), M Ngundo (Kenya), A Niemandt (Zimbabwe), K Njururi (Kenya), S Odonga (Kenya), W Oduor (Kenya), B Okatch (Kenya), P Onyando (Kenya), D Osu (UK), R Rioga (Zimbabwe), E Rugoiyo (Kenya), M Shah (Kenya), V Sikuku (Kenya), A Smithdorf (Zimbabwe), E Sutcliffe (UK), I Tapiwa (Zimbabwe), P Todd (UK), S Vincent (Zimbabwe), S Walton (UK), N Watson (Zimbabwe), B Williams (UK), T Williams (UK), W Yamuna (Papua New Guinea).

PHASE 9. (Kenya–GB) S Abbot (USA), R Boalch (UK), B Burns (USA), M Cohen (USA), S Crockett (UK), G Dade (UK), C Evans (UK), B Finnie (Canada), D Hackett (USA), J Hood (UK), C Jackman (UK), M Japan (Kenya), R Johnson (USA), K Jones (UK), A McBrine (UK), C Mead (UK), G Morgan (UK), A Pearson (USA), A Rawson (USA), P Ryan (Australia), S Thomas (UK), M Totton (UK), B Wasuna (Kenya), A Wotton (UK), D Yates (UK).

In addition, a total of 38 cadets from BP Tanker Co. Ltd joined the expedition during Phases 2 and 5.

Appendix B

Operation Drake Sponsors And Supporters

Australia

ACI
Advertiser Newspapers Ltd
The Age, Melbourne
ALCOA of Australia Ltd
AMCO Wrangler Pty Ltd
ANL
ANZ Banking Group Ltd
Arnotts
Australian Army
Australian Consolidated Ind. Ltd
Australian Gas Light Co.
Australian Paper Manufacturers Ltd
Bailleau Bowring Pty Ltd
BHP
BNSW
BP
Brisbane Gas Co.
Brisbane Water (NSW) Legacy
The Broken Hill Pty Co. Ltd
Channel 7 TVW Perth
Channel 9 TVW Perth
GJ Coles & Coy Ltd
Colman Foods Ltd
Csiro
Dalgety Australia Ltd
Charles Davis
Mr PV Driscoll
Dulux New Guinea
Dunlop Australia Ltd
S Duzenman
Dr C Elliott
Esso Australia Ltd
Ford Motor Co. of Australia Ltd
Mr Lindsay Fox
J Gadsden Australia Ltd
Gail Park ICI Melbourne

Gas Supply Franchises (Queensland)
George Weston Foods Ltd
Gibbs Bright & Co. Pty Ltd
Gretel II Fund
H Haiford Pty Ltd
Hanimex Corp. Ltd
Howard Smith Ind. Pty Ltd
HSV 7 Radio
ICI Australia Ltd
Sir Asher Joel
John Holland (Constructions) Pty Ltd
Mayne Nickless Ltd
Monahan Dayman Adams (Vic) Pty Ltd
National Bank of Australasia Ltd
Sir William Pettingell CBE
Potter Partners
Quantas Airways Ltd
Queen's Jubilee Foundation
Queensland Alumina Ltd
Queensland Institute of Medical Research
RAAF
Radio 6 KY
Radio ZUE Sydney Pty Ltd
Sir Thomas Ramsay
RAN
REPCO Ltd
Roach Ward Guest & Co.
Santos Ltd
Science & Industry Endowment Fund
The Sidney Myer Charity Trust
South Australia Gas Co.
Sydney Legacy
David Syme & Co.
TAA
Tasmanian Government
Unilever Australia Pty Ltd
Victoria State Government
JB Weir & Son

[273]

Canada

Alan Bibby Film Group
Canadian National Sportsmen's Funds
Sir Arthur Chetwynd
Gestetner (Canada) Ltd
Mr RA Gustavason
Imperial Order of the Daughters of the
  Empire
Maclaren Advertising Ltd
Mr H Newby
Mr R Orieux
Outward Bound Canada
Mr A Patterson
Queens University, Ontario
Dr E Sinton
Toronto Dominion Bank
University of New Brunswick

Costa Rica

Mr K Hamylton-Jones CBE
Mr J Warder

Europe

Outboard Marine Belgium NV

Kriesparkasse Bank Villich, Germany
Stadt Villich, Germany

Fortress Headquarters, Gibraltar

Col. AA Julius, Italy
Goodyear Blimp Europa Inc. Italy

Egypt

Barclays Bank International Sae, Cairo
BP
Cairo Sheraton
Cementation International Ltd
Chloride Egypt Sae
ICI
ICL
John Laing Overseas Ltd
Lloyds Bank Ltd
Midland Bank
Morgan Grenfell
Rothmans
Lt Col. WLH Smith

Staff of the British Embassy, Cairo
Suez Canal Authority
Tarmac Ltd
Thomas Cook

Fiji

Boral Ltd
Burns Philp
Carpenters Ltd
Carpenters Shipping
Mr J Cavalevu
Mr P Corbett
Mr D Diment
Lord Dun-Russell
Fiji Navy
Fiji Sugar Corp.
Fiji Times
Mr & Mrs H Holdsworth
Mr M Joy
Mr J Ah Koy
Mr G Moody-Stewart
Pan American World Airways
Radio Fiji
Mr A Rappun
Mr W Tagilala

Hong Kong

Mr T Bedford
Cathay Pacific (Hong Kong) Ltd
Cheung-Kong (Holdings) Ltd
Golden Peak Maritime Agencies
Maj. I Gunn RCT
Gurkha Transport Regiment
Hang Seng Bank Ltd
Hang Tai Finance Co.
Hong Kong & Shanghai Bank
Hong Kong Brigade of Gurkhas
Mr E Hotung
Eric Hotung Trust Fund
Mr MD Kadoorie
Sir Elly Kadoorie Continuation Ltd
Li Ka-Shing
Mr Kwan Chung
Mr SS Leong JP
Nirlon Synthetic Fibre & Chemicals
Oriental Daily News, Seoul
Maj. RJ Pickard
Royal Hong Kong Jockey Club
Royal Hong Kong Police Force

Shun Tak Shipping Co. Ltd
Westminster Travel Ltd
Winglung Bank Ltd

Iceland

Mr J Edwards
Fiskidjusamlag Husavikur
Flugleidir-Icelandair
Fridrik Jorgensen Import/Export
Gurvik Ltd
Toti Halldorsson
Hans Petersen Ltd
Icelandic Aluminum Co.
Johns Manville Ltd
Kaupfelag Thingeyinga (Coop)
Kiwanis Club of Husavik
Labour Union of Husavik
Morgunbladid, Daily Newspaper,
  Reykjavik
Polaris Ltd
Rotary Club of Vestman Islands
Thorarinn Stefansson Bookstore
Three Lions Club
The Town of Akureyri
The Town of Husavik
The Town of Vestman Islands
Vifilfell Ltd
Visir, Daily Newspaper, Reykjavik

Indonesia

PT Aseam
Asuransi Inda Tamporok
Balfour Beatty Indonesia
Bali Age Shipping
Bank Negara Indonesia 1946
Binnie & Partners
Mr John Blower
PT Branusa
PT Bripindo Utama
British Airways
PT British American Tobacco Indonesia
Ben Ocean Line
PT Caltex Pacific Airways
Cathay Pacific Airways
Citibank
PT Coates Rejo Indonesia
Columbia Tours
Daerah Tni Angkatan Laut-3
PT Daya Pioneer International

Directorate General of Water Resources
  Development
PT Dumex Indonesia
PT Essex Indonesia
Fao National Parks Development Project
Garuda Indonesian Airways
PT Goodyear Indonesia
PT Guinness Indonesia
Hankam
Hasanuddin University Ujung Pandang
Hoechst Pharmaceuticals Indonesia
The Hong Kong Land Co.
Huffco Jakarta
Roy M Huffington Inc.
Mr & Mrs R Hughes
Mr P Huling
Hunting Technical Services Ltd
Indonesian Institute of Sciences
PT International Nickel Industries
Jakarta Hilton International
PT Kalba Farma
PT Manning Development
Mochtar Karuwin & Komar
PT Monier Indonesia
Mr WH Montgomery
PT Neptune Electronic
New Zealand Insurance
PT Perusahaan Bir Indonesia
Perusahaan Sepatu Bata
PPA – Directorate of Nature
  Conservation
PT San Miguel Brewery Indonesia
PT Setiawan Sedjati
Shell International Petroleum Co Ltd
PT Star Motors Indonesia
Surabaya International School
Tesoso Petroleum Co.
PT Timur Laut
PT Trakindo Utama
PT Trebor Indonesia
TVRI
Unilever Indonesia
PT United Can Co. Ltd
PT Wheelcock Marden Indonesia
Wisma Kosgoro
World Wildlife Fund
PT Zaskya

Kenya

Abercrombie & Kent

[275]

African Marine & General Engineering
 Co. Ltd
Alibhai Shariff & Sons
Mr AL Archer
The Ark Ltd
Arrow Express Ltd
Associated Battery Manufacturers (East
 Africa) Ltd
Avon Marketing Services (Kenya) Ltd
Bamburi Portland Cement Co. Ltd
Barclays Bank Kenya Ltd
Beechams of Kenya Ltd
Block Hotels Ltd
Brian Bell & Co. Ltd
British American Tobacco Kenya Ltd
British Army Training & Liaison Staff
 Kenya
British Leyland (UK) Ltd
Cadbury Schweppes Kenya Ltd
Coates Brothers East Africa Ltd
Mr Winston Costa Correa
Mr P Davey
Mr G Davis
Diners Club Africa
Doughty Ltd
East African Acceptances Ltd
Engineering Power Developments
 Consultants Ltd
Fourways Clearing & Forwarding
 Express Kenya Ltd
Gestetner Duplicators Ltd
Mr H Gill
Grindlays Bank (Kenya) Ltd
Maj. JL Harvey
Hamilton Harrison & Matthews
The Islands Shipping Co. Ltd
Ker, Downey & Selby Safaris Ltd
KENCEM
Kenya Airways
Kenya Breweries
Kenya Stationers Ltd
Kisima Farm Ltd
Mr RD Knight
Leyland Kenya Ltd
Lion of Kenya Insurance Co. Ltd
Lonrho East Africa Ltd
Malindi Air Services
Marshall East Africa Ltd
Mr R Meredith
Mr J Milland
Minet ICDC Ltd

Ministry of Defence
Mowlems Construction Co. Ltd
National Museums of Kenya Ltd
Mr MD Prettejohn
Price Waterhouse & Co.
Philips Harrison & Crossfield Ltd
Plessey (Eastern & Central Africa) Ltd
Robbialac Paints Kenya Ltd
Royal Insurance Company of East
 Africa Ltd
Mr AMD Seth-Smith
Shiwa Estates Ltd
SP Breweries Ltd
Standard Chartered Bank Ltd
Sunbird Aviation Ltd
Mr John Sutton
Securicor (Kenya) Ltd
Shell & BP Services Ltd
Mr & Mrs P Tilbury
Tradewinds Airways
TWIGA Chemical Industries Ltd
United Transport Overseas Services
Walibhai Karim & Co. Ltd
Wellcome Kenya Ltd
Wigglesworth & Co. Kenya Ltd

Miscellaneous and all other places

Firestone Ghana Ltd

Whitelaw Trust, Johannesburg

The Dong A Ilbo, Korea

Shell Co. Seychelles
Mr D Weston, Seychelles

New Zealand

Air New Zealand
Auckland Rotary
Dalgety New Zealand Ltd
Fletcher Holdings Ltd
Mr R Grono
Guthrey's Travel
Kerridge Odeon
New Zealand Government
New Zealand Red Cross
PDL Industries
South British Insurance Co.
Springhill Charitable Trust

[276]

Panama

Agencias de Viajes Panamundo S
Mr Mario Alfaro
Maj. Eric Aquillera
Mr Irving Bennett
Mr Horace T Castillo
Mr James Davidson
Mr & Mrs Jack Davies
Mr Rene Diaz
Mr Fernando Eleta
Mr Rolando Gonzalez
Mr Mario Guardia
The Guardia Nacionale
Mr George Novey III
Mr Roberto Novey
The Novey Family
The Panama Canal Co.
The Patrimonio Historico
Lic. Carlos Patterson
Mr Andres Lopez Pineiro
Mr Alexander Psychollos
Mr Mario Rognoni
Mr Guillermo St Malo
Mr Raul De St Malo Arias
Mr Jose A Perez Salamero
Mr Steven Samos
Amanda Savarain
Dr Reina Torres De Arauz
Brig. Gen. Omar Torrijos

Papua New Guinea

Air Niugini
AMEX
Andersons (PNG) Pty Ltd
ANGCO
Arthurs Bakery
Bali Merchants Pty Ltd
Bank Line
Mr T Beirne
Brian Bell & Co. Pty Ltd
British Petroleum (PNG) Pty Ltd
Buntings Stevedores Pty Ltd
Burns Philp (New Guinea) Ltd
Burns Philp Shipping
Cig New Guinea Pty Ltd
Co-Air
Mr D Copeland
Corals Restaurant
Capt. J Cornish

Dept of Civil Aviation
Dept of Customs & Immigration
Dept of Decentralisation
Dept of Education
Dept of Health, Office Environment &
    Conservation
Dept of Minerals & Energy
Dept of Primary Education
Dept of Tourism
Dept of Works & Supply
Douglas Air
Dulux New Guinea Pty Ltd
Dunlop (PNG) Pty Ltd
Mr & Mrs I Fraser
George Page Pty Ltd
GNE Insurance
Mr & Mrs R Grimmer
Guinea Gas Supply
Harrisons & Crossfield (PNG) Ltd
Mr Harry Heath
Miss Robin Horley
ICI PNG Pty Ltd
Karlander (New Guinea) Line Ltd
Lae Aero Club
Lae Battery Services
Lae Lodge Pty Ltd
Lae Plumbing Pty Ltd
Lae Squash Club
Lae Tyre Service
Lae Yacht Club
Mr & Mrs WJ McKeague
Melanesian Matches Pty Ltd
Mobil Oil New Guinea Ltd
Morehead Shipping Pty Ltd
Morobe Bakery
Morobe Dept (National Government)
Morobe Pharmacies
Morobe Sports Centre
Mr & Mrs A Musika
National Census HQ
National Council of YMCAs of PNG
National Government Reps & Agencies
    of each Province
National Mapping Office
New Guinea Industries Pty Ltd
NGI Trading
Niugini Builders
Niugini Nius (PNG Printing)
Niugini Pacific Pty Ltd
Pagini Brambles Transport Pty Ltd
Panguna Corp. Foundation

[277]

Pelgen Pty Ltd
PNG Banking Corp.
PNG Defence Force
PNG Government
PNG Harbours Board
PNG Motors
PNG Printing Co. Pty Ltd
Capt. & Mrs NG St C Porteous
Reckitt & Colman (PNG) Ltd
Rice Industries Pty Ltd
Mr T Richards
Rotary Club of Boroko
Rotary Club of Port Moresby
Lt Col. R Rowe MBE
San Miguel
Seeto Kui Pty Ltd
Serafini Soft Drinks
South Pacific Breweries
Steamships Trading Co. Ltd
Sun Aqua Club
Talair Pty Ltd
Dr R Terry
UNDP (Crocodile Project)
UNITECH, Lae
University of PNG
Victoria League for Commonwealth
    Interests
Wau Ecology Institute
West New Britain – Siaggi Fisheries Dept
WD & HO Wills
Zorba Constructions

United Kingdom

Abbotts Packaging Ltd
ABC TV
ABS Insurance Agency Ltd
A to B Freight Ltd
Action Secretaries Ltd
Mrs K Adam
Adwest Group
Agent General for New South Wales
Mr & Mrs J Ainslie
Airborne Industries Ltd
Mr AM Albury
Aldwickbury School Trust
Alfred Preedy & Sons Ltd
WH Allen & Co. Ltd
Allinsons Ltd
Alpha Laboratories Ltd

Viscount Amory KG, PC, GCMG, TD,
    DL
CF Anderson & Son Ltd
Mr R Anderson
Animal Finders
Anglo-Dansk
Anglo Italian Engines Ltd
Ansul Fire Protection
Apex (Pressure Cleaners)
Aqua Hydraulics Ltd
Mr RN Archer
The Archery Centre
Archery International
The Arco Group
Mr WJ Armstrong
Army Apprentice's College, Chepstow
Arthritic & Rheumatic Council
Mr & Mrs DJ Ashton
Ash & District Ladies Circle
Ashford & District Chamber of
    Commerce
Ashford Junior Chamber of Commerce
Mr & Mrs Assinder
Associated Biscuits Manufacturers Ltd
Associated Newspapers Group Ltd
Associated Octel Co. Ltd
Associated Speakers
Association for Conservation of Wildlife
Athenaeum Hotel
Mr D Atkinson
Atlas Pencils
Augustine Courtauld Trust
Mr J Austin
Australian High Commission
Avon & Somerset Police Authority
Avon Industrial Polymers (Bradford-on-
    Avon) Ltd
Avon Inflatables
Avon Rubber Co. Ltd
Avo Ltd
Azlon Products Ltd
Mr W Bahen
Bain & Dawes
Baird & Tatlock (London) Ltd
Balmoral Hotel, Essex
The Bank Line
Bank of Ireland
Bank of New Zealand
Bank of Scotland
The Barbados High Commission
Barclaycard Recro 80

[278]

Barclays Bank
Barclays Bank Bristol
Barclays Bank International
Baring Bros
Mr RJ Barker
EP Barrus Ltd
Mr AE Bartholomew
John Bartholomew & Son Ltd
Batchelors Foods Ltd
Bateman Catering Ltd
EW Barney (Bristol) Ltd
Basildon District Council
Mr M Baum
Michael Baum Holdings Ltd
BBC Publications Ltd
BDH Chemicals Ltd
Beachcombers Association
Beacon Educational Trust
Mr EME Beale
Beamglow Ltd
Baron R Beck
Sir Jacob Behrens & Sons Ltd
Belfast Rotary Club
Mr CD Bell
Bell & Howell AV Ltd
Mr R Bellows
Bellshill Academy
Sir George Beresford Stooke
Berger Paints Ltd
Berghams Ltd
Berol Ltd
Mrs P Berton
Bervey Black Fund
Betteshanger School
Mr A Bibby
J Bibby & Sons Ltd
GW Biggs (Butchers) Ltd
Bigwood & Staple Ltd
Bishopsalt School
Black & Decker (Professional Division)
Blue Circle Industries Ltd
Boehringer Corp. (London) Ltd
Boness A/V Services Ltd
Bonhote Foster
Bordier & Co.
Borodin Communications Group
Mr W Borosa
Borough of Thamesdown
Botany School Oxford
Boulton & Paul Ltd
Bournes

Bournville Works Charitable Co. Ltd
Bowater Scott Corp. Ltd
Michael Bowen & Co. Ltd
Bowens of London
Mr PEG Bowkett
Bowman Gilfillan & Blacklock Inc.
Mr M Bowman Vaughan
CT Bowring Ltd
Mr MC Boyes
BP Tanker Co. Ltd
BP Trading Co. Ltd
Bridgewater Marks & Spencer
Bridgewater Society of Friends
Bridport International Ltd
British Aerospace, Chester
British Airways
British American Tobacco Co. Ltd
The British Army
British Broadcasting Corp.
British Caledonian Airways
British Cellophane Ltd
British Gas Corp.
British Museum (Natural History)
British Ornithological Union
The British Petroleum Co. Ltd
British Red Cross Society
British Seagull Co. Ltd
British Steel Corp.
British Van Heusen Co. Ltd
British Youth Council
Bristol United Press
Brixton Estate Charitable Trust
Brocks Fireworks Ltd
Mr JM Bronson
John Brown of La Fontaine Hotel, Jersey
Capt. RM Bullen
TA Bulmer Ltd
Bulova (UK) Ltd
Burns Philp
Mr DH Burrell
Mrs F Burroughes
Trustees of SH Burton
Burton McCall Ltd
Lady Sheila Butlin
The Butlin Second Family Trust
Cable & Wireless Ltd
Cabriolet Enterprises
WA Cadbury Charitable Trust
Caesarsean Investments Ltd
Mr EI Calland
Mr HE Calland

Calor Group Ltd
Camberwell School of Art & Crafts
Cameron Markby
Camlab Ltd
The Canadian High Commission
Canford School, Hampshire
Mr AE Cannon
Mr S Cant
Cantrell & Cochrane Ltd
Capital Radio Ltd
Caravan Club Ltd
Cargo Fleet Chemical Co. Ltd
Carleton Perry Co. Ltd
Sir Andrew Carnwath Charitable Trust
Mr RLB Carritt
Mr JL Carter
Mr E Cartwright
Cathay Pacific Airways (London) Ltd
Mr JB Catton
Cawthorne Women's Institute
CBS Automotive & Industrial
DO Celt-Trevilian
Chalfont Fine Arts Society
The Chamberlain of London
Chance Proper Ltd
Channel TV
MB Charities Ltd
Charringtons (Brewers) Ltd
Cheam School
Cheltenham & Gloucester Building
    Society
Mrs D Chidell
Chilton Trinity Parents Association
Chilton Trinity School
WM Christie & Sons Ltd
Christies Ltd
Chubb Security Services
Mr YK Chung
Claremont Cash & Carry Group Ltd
Clark Foundation
Mr HWS Clarke
Clarks Ltd
The Clarkson Jersey Charitable Trust
Clean Factory & Office Cleaning Services
Mr FE Cleary
Trustees of Cleary Foundation
Cleveland Education Authority
Clogwyn Climbing Ltd
Club 21 Blackheath
Coates Bros (East Africa) Ltd
Coates Patons Ltd

Cockade Services Ltd
The John S Cohen Foundation
Mr LD Colam
Colgroves Ltd
Mr DJ Collins
Mr & Mrs G Collins
Mr R Collins
W Collins & Son Ltd
Mr JL Cook
Dr L Cook
Mr GV Cooper
Mr MNC Cooper
Concord Engineering Co
Connectors & Couplings Ltd
Constable Hart & Co. Ltd
Control & Readout Ltd
Controlled Packaging Services Ltd
Convent of The Sacred Heart
The Coral Leisure Group
Costa Rican Embassy
Courage (Eastern) Ltd
Cowdray Trust
CPC (UK) Ltd
The Craigmyle Charitable Trust
Viscount Cranbourne MP
Mr WKB Crawford
Crawford Heard Ltd
EW Creaser & Co Ltd
Credit Bank Sweden
Mr DJ Crenwell
Mr RE Crenwell
Croda International Ltd
Mr JJE Cronin
Crown Agents for Overseas
    Governments & Administrations
Crowthorne Trust
Curtis Brown Ltd
N Curnick & Sons Ltd
Mr A Cusworth
Maj. JA Cuthill
Cutty Sark Society
CYB Fats Ltd
C Z Scientific Instruments Ltd
Dacorprint Ltd
Daily Record, Glasgow
The Daily Telegraph
Dalgety Ltd
Dalgety UK Ltd
Dashwood Brewer & Phipps Ltd
Mr J Davidson
Davidson Radcliffe Ltd

Mr H Davis
Maj. T Davis
Mr & Mrs A Davis
Mr DY Davy
Mr WL Dawes
Mrs Lily Dawson
ChW Deacon
Delta Metal
Denim Den Ltd
Denley Laboratory Equipment
Denman's Insurance
Dept of Postal Administration Channel
  Islands
Devenish Brewery
Devon & Cornwall Police Authority
Devon County Council
Mr J Dewar
John Dewar & Sons Ltd
Mr WL Dewar
Dewhurst (Master Butcher) Ltd
Dexion Comino International Ltd
CH Dexter Ltd
Stanley D Dickenson Ltd
Mr G Dickinson
The Dickinson Robinson Group
Mr EA Dinham
Mr VH Ditgas
W Dixon & Sons (Car Spares) Ltd
D J Contracts (Weymouth) Ltd
HM Dockyard, Devonport
26th Doncaster (West Bessacarr) Scout
  Group
Dorchester Dramatic Society
Dorchester Ladies Circle
IAM Dorset Group
Downside Abbey Trustees
Drake Commission   .
HMS Drake
DRG Sellotape
Mr Frank Driscoll
DEL Du Cann
Alexander Duckham & Co. Ltd
Mrs Duffus
Dulverton Trust
P Dumenil & Co. Ltd
Dunkelman & Son Ltd
Dunlop Ltd
Du Pont (UK) Ltd
John Dupuis
Dylon International Ltd
Eastern Liner Services

ECC Quarries Ltd
Edge Grove School, Aldenham
Mr & Mrs P Edgson-Wright
Edinburgh District Council
Mr AVJ Edwards
Mr J Edwards
Mr WD Edwards
The Egyptian Embassy of the Arab
  Republic
ELA Motors
Electronic Laboratories Ltd
Electrothermal Engineering Ltd
Elf Oil Exploration & Production (UK)
  Ltd
Ellesmere College Sailing Club
Elliott Bros (London) Ltd
Dr PAH Ellison
Elmgrant Trust
Mr JRH Elms
Embassy of Panama
Employment Publications Ltd
Empress Products Ltd
Engineering & Power Development
  Consultants Ltd
Peter England Ltd
Peter England Shirt Co.
Capt. & Mrs P Enzer
Ecuadorean Embassy
Equity Law & Assurance Society Ltd
Ernex Ltd
Esso Petroleum Co. Ltd
Europower Hydraulics Ltd
Evans of Leeds Ltd
Everready Co. Ltd
Mr G Exelby
Explorers Club (British Chapter)
Mrs A Fairbarn
P Fairfax Ltd
Fairhaven Hotel, Essex
Far East Bank
Farleys Ltd
Faulks Pipeline Supplies Ltd
Felreaton Ltd
Mr A Fennel
Ferrant Computer Systems Ltd
Ferris & Co. Ltd
Capt. R Festorazzi
Fibre Makers Ltd
Fife Regional Council
Fiji High Commission
Mr P Fisher

[281]

First National Securities Ltd
Flexible Form Ltd
Fodeco (UK) Ltd
Foreign & Commonwealth Office
Foremost Catering Disposables Ltd
Derek Forsyth Partnership
Fortech Services Ltd
Fourway Marketing Ltd
Fowey Harbour Communications
Mr F Fox
Sqn Leader J Fox RAF
The Hugh Fraser Foundation
Miss S Fraser
Miss FL Frost
Fryer Travel Ltd
G & M Power Plant Co Ltd
Gallen Kamp & Co. Ltd
Galt Glass Ltd
Maj. & Mrs M Gambier
J Gardiner
Gardner Engines Ltd
Fay Garnett Appeal Fund
Garth Hill School
Gelman Hawksley Ltd
Gemstat Ltd
Gerrans Primary School, Cornwall
Gerrans Women's Institute, Cornwall
Mr Steven George
Gestetner Ltd
Gestetner (Holdings) Ltd
GA Gibbons
Hon. Clive Gibson's Charity Trust
Mr S Gileen
Gillette Industries Ltd
Mid Glamorgan Scouts
Glasgow University Women's Club
   (London)
Mr S Glenn
Gloucestershire Silver Jubilee Trust
Godfrey Davies Car Hire
EJ Godwin (Peat Industries)
Godwin Fire Pumps Ltd
Golden Wonder Foods Ltd
MEH Goldsmith Charitable Trust
E Gomme Ltd
Gordon Tools Ltd
Lord & Lady Gough Charitable Trust
Viscount Gough
Maj. P Gough REME
SF Gouldsmith
Lord & Lady Grade

William Grant & Sons (Steadfast) Ltd
F Graham & Partners
Capt. JG Graham RAPC
Gravesend Ladies Circle
Gravesend Townswomen's Guild
Great St Helens Educational Trust
Mr T Green
SIA Greenway
Mrs MJ Grey
Griffin & George Co.
Maj. JD Griffiths-Eyton WG
Grocers Trust
Group Photo Products
Grove Charity Management
Mrs Jeremy Groves
A De Gruchy & Co. Ltd, Channel Islands
Arthur Guiness (Park Royal) & Son Co.
   Ltd
BV Guild of Graduates
Guildford Travel Club
J Gunning
Halifax Building Society
Majorie Hall
Halls Barton Ropery Ltd
Hamble Rotary Club
Mr J Hamilton
Hamilton Harrison & Matthews
Hamish Publications
George Hammond (Shipping) Ltd
Hampshire & Isle of Wight Army Cadet
   Forces
Ham's Pencils Ltd
PD Hanson
Hanson Trust
Mrs J Hardie
RE Hardinge-Francis
JM Hargreave (Holdings) Ltd
Harper Lee Ltd
Mr BVC Harpur MC
Harrison & Crossfield
Harrison & Jones (Flexible Form) Ltd
Mr & Mrs P Harrison
T & J Harrison Ltd
Hartnell Taylor & Cook
NB Harvey
Haslemere Estates Charitable Trust
Lt Col. CC Hastings MBE, RE
Hattersley Newman Hender Ltd
HS Haughton & Partners
CCW Havell
DM Hay

[282]

KMM Henderson
Henri-Lloyd Ltd
DJ Herd
Herdmans Ltd
Herne Bay Round Table
Mr C Hewniker-Major
Mrs Susan Hicks
High Commission for New Zealand
Hills of Swindon Ltd
Col. AJ Hines MC, TD
ACM Hingley
Jane Hodge Foundation
Holiday Inn, Plymouth
Holland & Holland Ltd
Holyhead Boatyard Ltd
Honda (UK) Ltd
Hoo Hing Ltd
Col. Sir John Hood Trust
TJ Hood
Hookah Shellfish Diving Co.
Mr D Hopkins
Horlicks Farms – Dairies Ltd
EF Horne
Mrs J Horne
Robert Hounsome Associates
House of Toomer Ltd
Howells of Bristol Ltd
Arthur Howeson
GEJ Hoyland Trust
HRH Prince Richard Duke of Gloucester
 GCVO
HRH The Prince of Wales KG, KT,
 GCVO
Hudson Thomas Ltd
Hulls (UK) Ltd
Humberside County Council
Sir John Hunter CBE, DI, BSc
Hunting Technical Services
Hurstpierpont College
Husbands Shipyards Ltd
Hutcheram Grammar School
AD Hutchison
Hyett Adams Ltd
The Iam Camelot Group
ICL
The Idlewild Trust
Imi Kynoch Ltd
Imperial Tobacco Ltd
Inchcape & Co. Ltd
Ind Coope East Anglia Ltd
Indonesian Embassy

Initial Services Ltd
Inner London Education Authority
Inner Wheel Club of Weymouth
Institute of Advanced Motorists Camelot
 Group (Ilminster)
Institute of Marine Environmental
 Research
Interflow Ltd
International Military Services Ltd
International Stores Ltd
Italian Embassy
ITT Components Group Industries Ltd
Ivers Lee Ltd
Irving Trust Co
Irvin (GB) Ltd
Irish Society
JT Group Ltd
Mrs P James
James Clark & Eaton
Jarrold's
John Jarrold Trust Ltd
Jersey Canners
Jersey Philatelic Bureau
Jersey Zoological Society Ltd
Mr & Mrs DV Jessema
The Jocey Trust
Mr AK Johnson
Johnson & Johnson Ltd
Mr JWG Johnston
Mr R Jonas
Maj. Gen. AGC Jones CB, MC
Karrimor International Ltd
Kay & Co. Ltd
Keeler Instruments Ltd
Kelvin Hughes Ltd
RC Kelly (Packing) Ltd
KEM Electronic Mechanisms Ltd
Mr J Kendall
Kenneth Wilson Holdings Ltd
Kent County Council
Kent Messenger & Evening Post
MP Kent Property Development
The Kenya Coffee Board
Kenya High Commission
Khera Trading Co. Ltd
KH Publicity Ltd
Mr I Kidd
Kilmarnock Round Table
CR King & Partners
Mrs P King
The King George Jubilee Trust

Kingsley Carritt & Co. Ltd
Maj. WHG Kingston
Kingswood School
Capt. EJ Kirton MBE
Kleinwort Benson Trust
The Sir Cyril Kleinwort Charitable
  Settlement
Koch Light Laboratories Ltd
Kodak Ltd
KP Foods
Ladies Circle – Weymouth Charity
Mr N Labovitch MBE
Laird (Anglesey) ltd
Brig. CA Landale
Land Rover Ltd
Langtons Jewellers
PA Larard & Son
Latymer Foundation School
Laurence Prust & Co.
F A Lavard & Son
Laws & Co.
Mr DH Lawton
S Leffman Ltd
Lennards of London Ltd
Leon's Ltd
Leslie & Godwin (DH) Ltd
Harry Lester Ltd
Lighting Systems International Ltd
Lillywhites Ltd
Mr H Lindsey
Link House Publications Ltd
Lion Brush Works Ltd
Lions Club of Maidstone
Lions Club of Wareham
Lip Services Ltd
The WG Little Scholarship & Band
  Concert Fund
Mr TC Littler-Jones
Liverpool Queen's Jubilee Trusts
Mr S Livesey
Mr ME Llewelyn
Mr JS Lloyd
Lloyds Bank
Lloyds Charities Trust
Lloyd's Log
Lloyd's of London
Capt. L Lodge
London Street School
Mr M Long
John Longstaff (Rec) Ltd
Look & Learn

Maj. C Lowe
Loughborough University
Lucas Group Services Ltd
Lucas Industries
Lucas Marine Ltd
Lullingstone Golf Course
Mr AL Lutgendorf
Mr LM MacDonald
MacDonald-Buchanan Trustees Ltd
Mrs MacEachern
Mr DM McClure Warren
Mrs R McMurchie
Maidstone Tarpaulin Co. Ltd
Magdalene College Oxford
Maghera Round Table
Mr J Major
Malvern College
Mr ME Mansell
The Map Shop, Worcestershire
GEC Marconi Electronics Ltd
Marconi Space & Developments
Marconi Space & Defence Systems Ltd
Marconi International Marine Co. Ltd
Mariners International
Market Harborough Rotary Club
Marsh Publications
Mr PJD Marshall
Marshall Cavendish Partworks Ltd
Marshall of Cambridge (Engineering) Ltd
Sir George Martin Trust Co. Ltd
Mr K Mason
Maj. P Matthews
Col. BAE Maude MBE
Mr LR Mauleverer
May & Baker Ltd
Maylon Contracts Ltd
Meakers Charities Trust
Medfor Products
Megefoam Ltd
Mr JR Mein
Mel Defence & Avionics Systems
Melplash Agricultural Society
Mrs B Mercer
Merck Sharp & Dohme Ltd
Mr R Meredith
Merrydown Wine Co. Ltd
Merseyside Silver Jubilee Trust
Messenger Print Ltd
Metal Box Ltd
Metropolitan Police
Metrow Foods (Grays) Ltd

[284]

Michelin Tyre Co. Ltd
Midland Bank Ltd
Midland Educational Co. Ltd
Mr HJC Miles
Sir James Miller Edinburgh Trust
Mr AE Milward
Mr & Mrs Michael Mindel
Peter Minet Trust
Ministry of Defence
Mirror Group Newspapers
Maj. GR Mitchell MBE, BEM
Mitsui Machinery Sales (UK) Ltd
Molyneux Offset Ltd
Molyslip Holdings Ltd
Montebello Hall Ltd
George A Moore Charitable Ltd
Moorgate Trust Fund
Moss Bros Ltd
Mr JL Mouat
The Mount School, York
Mr RC Muirhead-Thompson
Mullard Ltd
Mr N Munn
Capt. A Murray
NAAFI
The Captain John Vivien Nascarrow
    Fund
National Association of Round Tables
National Federation of Young Farmers
National Magazine Co.
National Westminster Bank
Nationwide Building Society
Mr ME Needham
James Neill (Sheffield) Ltd
Neilson McCarthy Ltd
Thomas Ness Ltd
New Cheshire Salt Works Ltd
Louis Newmark Ltd
Air Com. BH Newton OBE
Nicholas Laboratories Ltd
Nikon
Northcott Devon Trust
North Dorset Fete Committee
North Eastern Gas Board
North Staffordshire & District Outward
    Bound
North West Education & Library Board
Northern National Bank
Northfleet Rotary Club
Norwest Holst Soil Engineering Ltd
Norwich Brewery

Norwich Union Insurance Group
The Nuffield Trust for the Forces of The
    Crown
Oakham School
Oakmount School
Mr & Mrs PJS O'Connor
Mr RRR O'Connor
Oldfield Music Ltd
Ft Lt J Oldring RAF
Olivestone Hanson & Peltz
Olympus Optical Co. Ltd
Operation Drake Young Explorers
AB Optimus Ltd
Orion Ins Co. Ltd
Col. KH Osborne DSO, OBE, MC, TD
Osborne Publishing Ltd
Ottery St Mary Round Table
Oughtred & Harrison Ltd
Outboard Marine (UK) Ltd
Outward Bound Mountain School
Ozalid & Co. Ltd
The Pacific Steam Navigation Co. Ltd
Package Control Ltd
Paines Wessex Ltd
P & O Group – Air Travel
P & O Lines Ltd
Mr AG Parker
Parks of Bromley Ltd
Mr N Parry Jennings
Mr M Parx
Paterson Products Ltd
Mr H Patterson
Payne Ltd
George Payne & Co. Ltd
The PE Charitable Trust
Miss Geralyn Peacock
Pentax (UK) Ltd
Percy Stone Garden Centre
Petergate Gifts, Yorkshire
Peterhouse College Cambridge
Capt. Petty
Philips Electronic & Associated
    Industries Ltd
Phillips Printing Co. Ltd
Phonogram Ltd
Piccadilly Radio, Manchester
Mr A Pickard
Mr DR Pillington
Pindisports
KS Pipeline Supplies Ltd
Mr DW Pittard

[285]

Plessey Avionics & Communications
The Plessey Co. Ltd
Plymouth City Council
Plymouth Health Studios
Plymouth Hotels & Catering Association
Plymouth Marketing Bureau
The PNG High Commission
Pocklington District Lions Club
Pocklington Round Table
The PH Pointer Charitable Trust
Poldark Mining Co. Ltd
Mr & Mrs G Pollitzer
Polytechnic Marine Ltd
Mr THR Poole
Port of London Authority
Portacel Ltd
Portland Rotary Club
Port Regis School
Portscatho Village
Port Sudan & East African Conference
    Lines
Potter & Clarke Ltd
FW Potter & Soar Ltd
Mr HR Pratt-Boorman CBE
Mrs M Prax
The Press Association Ltd
Press Paper Ltd
Price & Buckland Ltd
Price, Waterhouse & Co.
The Princes Trust
LE Pritchitt & Co. Ltd
Product Resources International
Provincial Grand Lodge of Yorkshire
Puritab Co. Ltd
Putney High School
Putney Round Table
WJ Pyke
Quart Pot Public House, Wickford
Queen's Silver Jubilee Trust
Racal-Decca Ltd
Racal Group Services Ltd
Racal Tacticom Ltd
Radio Clyde
Radio Shack Ltd
Rain Dawes & Partners
Mr R Raison
Group Capt. WSO Randle CBE, AFC,
    DFM
Rank Audio Visual Ltd
Rank Pullin Control Ltd
Mr M Reay

Reas Creamy Ices Ltd
Sir Phillip Reckitt Educational Trust
Recreation & Amenities Dept, Cleveland
Regent Trust Co.
Reproduction Services
Mr GRR Resker
RFD Inflatables Ltd
W Ribbons & Co. Ltd
Richard Huish College
Mr HJ Richards
Mr ML Richardson
Dr C Roads
Roando Holdings Ltd
Charles Robertson (Developments) Ltd
The CJ Robertson Charity Trust
Mr DC Rodger
Rohan & Haas UK Ltd
The Rolex Watch Co. Ltd
Rolls Royce Ltd
Roseland Rugby Club, Cornwall
Mr C Ross
Rotary Club of Wokingham
Roundel Productions
Round Table of Great Britain
Rousel Laboratories Ltd
Rowan Bentall Trust
Rowntree Mackintosh
The Royal Air Force
Royal Air Force Sailing Association
Royal Automobile Club
Royal Botanic Gardens, Kew
Royal Dorset Yacht Club
Royal Engineers Corps Funds
Royal Engineers Sports and Games Fund
Royal Insurance
Royal Marines
Royal Marines Reserve
Royal Naval Engineering College
The Royal Navy
Royal Oak Developments
Royal Scottish Geographical Society
Royal Society for the Prevention of
    Cruelty to Animals
The Royal Society of St George
RTZ Services Ltd
Runswick Bay Sailing Club
Runwell Garages Ltd, Wickford
Mr CPB Rurner
Mr D Russell
RYA Seamanship Foundation
Rymans (Reading) Ltd

SSAFA
Sail Training Association
St Austell Brewery
St Austell VI Form College
St David's College, Llandudno
St Faith's School
St George's Day Club
St John's School, Leatherhead
St Mary's School, Calne
St Michael's College
Marquess of Salisbury
Salisbury Trusts
Sanderson, Townend & Gilbert
Saunders-Roe Development Ltd
Mr M Savage
Save & Prosper Group Ltd
The Savoy Hotel Ltd
SCENE
Mr WRP Schmitt
Schroder Charity Trust
Schwartz Spices Ltd
Scientific Survey & Location Ltd
Capt. & Mrs P Scoble
Mr TR Scorer
Scotsman Publications Ltd
Sir S Scott of Yews Trust
Scottish & Newcastle Breweries Ltd
Scottish International Education Trust
DRG Sellotape Products Ltd
Seafarers Education Services
Seaforth Maritime Ltd
Sealed Motor Construction Co.
Sedgemoor District Council
Miss A Semenink
Services Kinema Corp.
Servier Laboratories Ltd
Seychelles Embassy
Shackle, Hamner & Partners Ltd
HW Sharp & Sons (Wickford) Ltd
Com. G Shaw OBE, RN
Mr L Shaw
Mrs M Shaw
Shaw Saville & Albion Line
Shell UK Ltd
Showex Scaffolding (Great Britain) Ltd
Sidcot School
JJ Silber Ltd
Silva Compasses (London) Ltd
Silver Springs Hotel Jersey
Henry Simon
Simpsons Restaurant, Wickford

Sinclair 1964 Charitable Trust
Sinclair Radionics Ltd
The Skinner Co.
Slough Social Fund
Smedley HP Food Ltd
Smith Corona Ltd
Smith Williamson Securities
Mr GR Snailham
Miss Barbara Snell
Soil Mechanics Ltd
Somerset County Council
DL Somervell
Soroptimist Club of Bridgewater
South Western Farmers Ltd
South Western Marine Factors Ltd
Specialist Outboard Services Ltd
Speechly Bircham
Mr JB Spencer
Sperry Gyroscope Division, Sperry Rand
    Ltd
Sports Council for Northern Ireland
Spread Eagle
Staedtler (UK) Ltd
Staffordshire Army Benevolent Fund
Staminade
Standard Telephone Cables Ltd
Stanley Press Ltd
Stanley Tools Ltd
Mrs Betty Starling
Staveley Taylor & Co.
J Stead & Co. Ltd
Steel Breaking & Dismantling Co.
Mr AR Stevens
Mr HJ Stevens
Mr HM Stephen
Mr JM Stevens
J & MA Stewart
Miss Jean Stewart
Stewart Wrightson (Marine) Ltd
Stewart Wrightson (UK) Ltd
Stockport Grammar School
Stonefield Vehicles Ltd
Stowe School
Strathclyde Regional Council
Streatham Engineering Ltd
Strides Ahead, Essex
Peter Strom Ltd
Submarine Products, Northumberland
Sudan Airways Ltd
Summer Fields School
Bernard Sunley Charitable Foundation

The Supper Club
Supreme Plastics Ltd
Survival International
Sutton Harbour Improvement Co.
Sutton Young Conservatives
Swan Hunter Group Ltd
Mr J Swire CBE
The Swire Group
Sword Ship's Chandlers
Sir Fitzroy Talbot
Tandberg (UK) Ltd
Tanganyika Holdings Ltd
Tannoy Ltd
Mr P Tappenden
Mr A Tate
Tate & Lyle Ltd
Tatler & Bystander
Mr FA Taylor
Mrs N Taylor
Taylor Woodrow
Tees Towing Co.
Teeside Imprest Account
Texas Instruments Ltd
TGWU Middlesborough
Thames Division Girl Guides
Thames TV
Mr A Theobald
Mr E Thomas
Mr R Thomas
M Thomas Motors Ltd
Mrs MP Thurstan
Maj. PTJ Tidman MBE
Tiger Tops Jungle Lodge, Nepal
Tilhill Forestry Ltd
Mr A Tillotson
Time Jewellers Ltd, Jersey
E Timm & Son Ltd
Tower Hotel
Town Centre Security
Tradewinds Airways Ltd
Trago Mills, Cornwall
Transatlantic Plastics Ltd
Maj. R Tregarthen RAOC
Trent Park
Tri-wall Containers Ltd
Mr AEO'D Troy
Mrs MO'D Troy
Truro School Old Boys Association
True Temper (USA)
Try Hire (Transport) Ltd
TT Containers Ltd

Mr MJW Tucker
Tupperware Ltd
Turnbull Garage Ltd
Turner & Newall Ltd
Tynedale District Council
UK Offshore Boating Association
Sqn Leader W Underwood MBE, RAF
Unigate Charitable Trust
Unigate Foods Ltd
Unilever Ltd
United Biscuits (UK) Ltd
United Grand Lodge of England
United Nations Environment
    Programme
United Transport Overseas Services Ltd
University Chest, Oxford
University of East Anglia
University of Leeds
University of Nottingham
USA Embassy
Van Leer (UK) Ltd
Van Neste Foundation
Col. J Vaughan-Williams DSO, OBE, TD
Vestric Ltd
Vickers Ltd
Mr T Villeboit
Viners Ltd
The Vintners Co.
Visnews
Volans Shipping Ltd
Mr JE Voule
Waddington Playing Card Co. Ltd
Mr MH Walden
Mr J Walker
Mr PN Walker
Mr JL Wallace
Walter Lawrence Tools Ltd
JD Walter, Partners & Randall
Wander Ltd
EB Ward & J Eddis Trustees
Mr MR Warneford-Thompson
Mr SE Warrer
Waterhouse & Co.
Watford Grammar School for Girls
Watney Mann (West) Ltd
Col. R Weare
Wellcome Research Laboratories
Wellingborough School
The Wells Organisation
Mr AG Welstead
Mr GE West

West Buckland School CCF
Mr JTR Westell
Westham Fisheries
Westminster City Council
Westpark Hotel, Essex
West Surrey Cheshire Home
West Sussex Institute for Higher
  Education
Westward TV
WEXAS
Weymouth & Portland Borough Council
Weymouth Bakeries
Weymouth Business & Professional
  Women's Club
Weymouth Hydro
Weymouth Round Table
Weymouth Sailing Club
Whitbread East Pennines Ltd
Whitby Yacht Club
The White Horse Public House, Essex
Whiteways Cider Co. Ltd
MH Whittaker & Sons Ltd
1474 (Wickford) Squadron ATC
Wiggins Teape Ltd
Wildfowl Trust
Wild Heerbrugg (UK) Ltd
Mr MD Wilkinson
Wilkinson Match Ltd
Wilkinson Sword Ltd
Wilkinson Warburton Ltd
Wildlife Preservation Trust International
Mr BR Williams
Mr CR Williams
Williams & Glyns Bank
Mr R Williamson
Mr D Williamson
E Williamson & Son Ltd
The HDH Wills Charitable Trust
Lt Col. JFW Wilsey
Mr CR Wilson
Mr E Wilson
Wiltshire County Council
Mr A Windham Green
Winstons Bar
Wokingham Lions Club
Wokingham Round Table
Woldhurst Ltd
The Wolfson Foundation
Woodhall Wednesday Club
Woodham & Wickford Chronicle
Mr TR Woodman

Miss N Woods
Woolbridge Motor Club
World Wildlife Fund
The Worshipful Company of Grocers
Mr PAM Worthington
The Wrigley Co. Ltd
Wycliffe College
Wyke Regis Social Club
Wyke Regis Working Men's Club
Yardley International Ltd
Yewstock School
York College for Girls
Yorkshire Post Newspapers Ltd
Yorkshire TV Ltd
Young Farmers Clubs
Youth Hostel Association Shop
The Arnold Ziff Trust
The Zimbabwe High Commission

United States of America

ABC TV
Alan Press Inc.
Allied Chemical Corp.
Allied Printing Co.
All State Manufacturing Co.
American Bakeries
American Enka
Andersen's Equipment Service Inc.
Mr Walter H Annenberg KBE
Arrow Office Supply Co.
Austin Biscuit
Automatic Products Inc.
Bay Bank Middlesex
Berry Bros General Contractors
Bonewitz Chemical Services
Brance-Krachy Co. Inc.
Broussard Brothers
Burton Shipyard
Peter Paul Cadbury Inc.
Cameron Construction Co. Inc.
Carisbrook Industries Inc.
Carl Byoir Associates Inc.
H Catto (The Catto Foundation)
CFS Continental
Champion International Corp.
Christie, Manson & Woods
Chromalloy American Corp.
John E Cichelli
The DL Clark Co.
Mr David H Clarke

[289]

Coca Cola USA
Coffee Mate
Jack B Cohen Enterprises
Compact Industries
Mr & Mrs Cotton
Joseph F Cullman III
Cutrone Building Systems Inc.
Delta Engineering & Conditioning Co.
Mr John T Durrance
Charles Dyson
Eberstadt Foundation
George Engine Co. Inc.
English Speaking Union
Ernst & Whitney
Explorers Club
Farmer Bros Coffee
Garber Bros Inc.
Pierce-Gardner, University of Chicago
Gelb Printing & Litho
Gersony-Strauss Co. Inc.
Gestetner Corp.
Goodyear International Corp.
Goodyear Tyre & Rubber Co.
Guildford Industries
Frank B Hall & Co.
Hanson Industries Inc.
Mr William Hargrove
Miss Mallory Hathaway
HJ Heinz Co. Foundation
Hess-Stephenson & Co.
Hygrade Food Products Corp.
Imperial Cup Corp.
Indian Head Foundation
International Matex
International Paint Co. Inc.
International Paper Co.
Interstate United Corp.
Intracoastal City Drydock & Shipbuilding
    Inc.
Jackson & Co.
Fred S James & Co.
Jersey Wildlife Preservation Trust
    (International)
AM Juge & Co.
Kramer, Lowenstein, Nessen, Kamin &
    Soll
Mr Lee Laino
Lehman Bros Kuhn Loeb
Liberty Mutual Insurance Co.
Mr John J Linehan
Francis & John L Loeb Foundation

Mr Mike McDonnell
Mrs NJ McIntire
Mar Jon Contractors
Mars Money System Division
Marsh & Mclennan
Marshall, Bratter, Greene, Allison &
    Tucker
Mr & Mrs V Martinelli
Mr PV Mazzaruli
Michigan Microwave Inc.
Donald H Miller Inc.
NABISCO Inc.
Mr George Nammack
National Maritime Historical Society
The Nestle Co.
Newton Glekel
Nol Wood Chemical Corp.
Northwestern National Life
Mr Michael E O'Dell
ORR Foundation USA
Dr DA Osman
Owens-Illinois
Pan American World Airways
Pentax Corp.
Dr Pepper Co.
Pepsi Cola
Plantation Confection Co. Inc.
David L Pransky & Sons
Price Waterhouse & Co.
Mr & Mrs S Roberts
James E Robison Foundation
Mr R Roethenmund
Mr O Roethenmund
Mr & Mrs James A Rost
Sabine Propeller & Marine Service Co.
Salem Label Co.
Sampson Electric
Scheppe, Doolittle, Krug, Tausend &
    Beezer
Schiff Terhune Inc.
Science Digest Magazine
Seacoat Products Inc.
Service Engineering Co.
John Sexton & Co.
SICOCCO
Daniel Silberberg
Mr RI Silver
Skadden, Arps, Slate Meagher & Flom
Standard Brands Inc.
Stan Pak Inc.
John E Staren Co.

Starmill Inc.
Superior Hydraulics Inc.
Superior Label Systems
Superior Service Co.
Superior Tea & Coffee
Sweetheart Cup Corp.
Taylor Apron Co.
TEEPAK
Thompson-Hayward Chemical Co.
Thomas Tilling Inc.
La Touraine Coffee Co.
Triangle Foundation
UMC Industries Foundation Inc.
Union Carbide Corp.
The US Army
US Sales Marketing Corp.
Voorhies Supply Company Inc.
The Waif Foundation
Mr & Mrs H Weinberger
WESTVACO
Weyerhaeuser Co.
Sir Gordon White KBE

Willkie, Farr & Gallagher

Zimbabwe

Barclays Bank International
British Airways
British American Tobacco Ltd
Dunlop
Guardian Royal Exchange Zimbabwe
  Ltd
The Jubilee Trust
Leyland
Metal Box Co. Ltd
Rio Tinto Mining (Zimbabwe) Ltd
Royal Insurance
Shell BP Marketing Services Ltd,
  Zimbabwe
Standard & Chartered Bank
Turner & Newall
Unilever
Williams & Glyns Bank

Index

[293]

[295]